# KELLY MORAN

Arai
STP
STP
STP
STP

# KELLY MORAN

## *'A Hell of a Life'*

BRIAN BURFORD

The History Press

Naturally, this book is dedicated to the memory, the talent and the personality that was Kelly Moran.

'No love, no friendship can cross the path of our destiny without leaving some mark on it forever.'

François Mauriac

First published 2014

The History Press
The Mill, Brimscombe Port
Stroud, Gloucestershire, GL5 2QG
www.thehistorypress.co.uk



British Library Cataloguing in Publication Data.
A catalogue record for this book is available from the British Library.

ISBN 978 0 7509 5388 7

Typesetting and origination by The History Press
Printed in Great Britain

# CONTENTS

# KUDOS

A book like this doesn't come together without a lot of help and input from many people from around the world. I'd like to express my gratitude to everyone who spared the time to share their thoughts and memories of Kelly.

A special thank you to Ron Preston, who was a true friend to Kelly – anyone would feel blessed to have a friend like Rapid Ron. Many thanks to Susan Murray-Bridges for the photographs from his early days and also to Lorna Brindley-Moran for her insight and invaluable assistance. Pete Rovazzini also went out of his way to open a few doors and I'm very grateful to Jojo Guerin for her help with speaking to Danny Becker. An important thank you must also go to 'The Picture Man', John Somerville, for turning up some absolute gems from his extensive photographic archive featuring some of the sport's best photographers. Also much gratitude to John Chaplin, Alan and Julie Clark, Richard Clark, Dave Curtis, Scott Daliosio, Mike Donaldson, Phil Handel (RIP mate), Shawn Moran, Eric Richardson, Anne Richmond, Carol Stock and, for those in the know, an honourable acknowledgement for Blackie Lawless.

Finally, a special and very important mention for my best friend, Sylvester, for keeping me company and entertained during long days of scribbling and sometimes long nights of deliberating – you showed me what's important.

# CREDITS

The drawing on the title page is courtesy of Greg Humphreys.
You can view and purchase his artwork at:

www.greghumphreysartist.jimbo.com;
www.facebook.com/GregHumphreysART;
email: greghumphreysart@gmail.com.

*Chapter 2:*
The opening quote is from 'No Man's Land', recorded and written by Bob Seger, which appeared on his 1981 album, 'Against the Wind'. It's published by Gear Music Publishing and administered by Minder Music Ltd and is reproduced, under licence, with their permission.

*Chapter 12:*
The opening quote is from *Three Little Tracks* by Robert Pfetzing, which appeared in the launch issue of *Speedway Magazine*. It's published with the author's permission.

*Chapter 21:*
The opening quote is from 'That Holy Touch', recorded by Magnum and written by Tony Clarkin. It appeared on their 2002 album, 'Breath of Life', and is published with the author's permission. Special thanks to Annie Minion of www.magnumonline.co.uk.

*Chapter 23:*
*Fides Non Timet* means 'The Faithful Fear Not' and is the motto from the Irish Moran family coat of arms created for Patrick O'Rourke Moran of Ballinamore, County Leitrim in 1856.

# INTRODUCTION

'The role of the writer is not to say what we all can say, but what we are unable to say.'

Anais Nin, French-Cuban author (1903–77)

If you grew up in the 1970s, the chances are that you've heard of Deep Purple's temperamental guitarist Ritchie Blackmore, the insanely talented player who gave us the now classic riff to their smash hit, 'Smoke on the Water'. The band's bass player Roger Glover described Blackmore's talents in the guitarist's unofficial biography by Jerry Bloom as 'One of those odd people that God pointed a finger at and said, "You're going to have something that nobody else has got."'

I believe, when it came to handing out natural talent for racing a brake-less 500cc speedway machine, God pointed a finger at Kelly Moran and presented him with a similar gift of awe-inspiring ability. However, unlike Blackmore, whose moody character often overrode his brilliant playing, Moran possessed an engaging and charismatic persona that endeared him to everyone he met.

At first glance music and speedway racing don't really go together, but I mention this because it was often a topic of our conversations and produced a giggle during the last time I spoke with Kelly – who counted AC/DC and Led Zeppelin among his favourite hard rock acts. I had been to see Motorhead and was recounting my amazement at the ageing audience queued up outside, the majority of which were seemingly well past that 'life begins at forty' stage and had swapped their suits in favour of ill-fitting jeans and the obligatory Motorhead T-shirt that struggled to cover midriffs that had seen far too many pies and pints. No longer being in the first flush of youth myself I quipped, 'I almost went back for my bus pass!'

These were the types of conversations that we had over the years. Inevitably speedway and motor sport took centre stage, but you could, and did, talk about all manner of subjects from music to movies and to times past and present. However, that last conversation had more poignancy to it than it first appeared and as time passes little things that he said have become more meaningful.

It's said that you shouldn't meet your heroes, but Kelly Moran was a hero, a friend and an inspiration. While he wasn't perfect, his happy-go-lucky outlook on life, combined with his gentlemanly spirit always overrode his short-comings. I accepted him for what he was a long time before his international speedway career came to an end in 1992.

Some of you will already know that I penned *The Moran Brothers* in 2002 and may wonder why I have decided to write Kelly's story. Well, mainly because he wanted me to.

It first came up in conversation when I picked him up from Heathrow Airport to take him to Brighton to appear in the Brighton Bonanza in 2003. 'The real story of Jelly Man' he called it. I wasn't really sure if he was being serious and I said that we'd have to tell the whole truth this time. During the meeting, the announcer asked him if he would be producing his autobiography and he quipped: 'We could, but it would cause a few divorces!' Needless to say his response elicited a lot of laughter. I should have known then that this project wasn't going to go away that easily.

As time passed, and the more I talked to him, this subject came up frequently and I began to realise that he was becoming serious. In fact, when I did a two-part interview with him for *Speedway Star*, somehow it got out that I was planning a tell-all biography with him. The only thing was, no one had told us. Later he explained that someone had got the wrong idea.

When Malcolm Simmons released his book, which contained several passages that were not particularly complimentary, Kelly called me, cursing and questioning why he felt the need to put such things in print when as far as he knew they hadn't as much as had a crossed word between them – ever. We decided that some things are better left unsaid but it's all part of the rich tapestry of life. And clearly, it must have been something that left an impression on Simmo at that time, part of his experience. Those tales and others revealed some of the happenings behind the scenes that the public at large don't get to see or hear about.

Once more, he declared that he wanted to put his side across and would call me again after he'd given it more thought. At this time, though, his living arrangements didn't make communication easy and the number he'd given me just rang out most of the time. Once again, the project drifted away.

It was about eighteen months before he died that we spent about an hour talking about it. Everyone has their darker days, moments and experiences that shape what we become, but we don't necessarily want to make them public.

Kelly's lifestyle meant that he may have had more than most, but one or two of those moments had a profound effect on his life and really couldn't be left out.

Previously it had been agreed from the outset that we would just talk about the speedway. This time, however, to make it different, and a proper biography, some of the behind-the-scenes incidents would have to be included. Moreover, he'd probably only get one chance to do this and it would be a travesty if, later on, he had regrets because he left out some parts that he really should have included.

Eventually, we did agree to do it, but by now his health was deteriorating and I had issues at home as well. Later I heard that his good friend, Ron Preston, had told Billy Hamill that someone should collect all these stories together about him before it is too late and it seemed my name had come up in the conversation.

Sadly we all know what happened next.

There were times shortly after his death when it appeared that Kelly was becoming something of a caricature with people asking, 'What's your favourite Kelly Moran story?' There was more to this talented man than a brilliant speedway rider who led a madcap lifestyle and it's this aspect that was also a motivation for doing this, to reveal the man behind the happy-go-lucky persona.

Like many things in life, some of the stories are best left between friends and enjoyed with the aid of liquid refreshment because they just don't transfer too well in print, becoming embarrassing instead of entertaining. There are also the feelings of those still living to be considered because Kelly, like us all, was no angel and while some like to remember him as a saintly, gentleman figure, many were the times when he discarded his halo altogether when it got in the way of a good time. This part of his life has required much thought before committing to print. However, I've included as many of the tales that cemented his reputation both on and off the track as I can – some have been well-documented, others less so – in an attempt to bring you the real Kelly Moran, the one that his family and friends knew so well.

# 1

# THIS MUST BE HEAVEN

'There was only one Kelly Moran and I don't know whether or not it's a good thing, but there will never be another.'

Ian Thomas

## Wednesday, 29 March 1978
## The Boulevard Stadium, Hull, England

From the heavens looking down, the large cloud of smoke wafting into the cool evening air may have looked like the gateway to hell on earth had emerged. Perhaps, to the angels above, who were not familiar with the earthly pleasures that accompanied the grey swirl, they may have mistaken the noise and smoke as tortured souls howling in protest. The collective, rhythmic roar of 500cc, methanol-burning engines thrumming with each twist of the throttle made the ground shudder with a combination of anticipation and protest. Occasionally an engine would pop and bang as the spent fuel would burn and explode in the exhaust. When fourteen or more speedway bikes were all being warmed up at once in preparation for the racing ahead, the pits were loud enough to please even the biggest Motorhead devotee. If Beelzebub needed somewhere to feel at home, then the pits shortly before race time may have provided him with some familiar comforts.

Into this busy, loud and smoky environment Kelly Moran entered from the dressing room and strode over to his pit. He nodded an acknowledgement to his mechanic, Peter Rovazzini, and placed his bag on the bench, while noting his bike was shaking and shuddering from the power vibrating within its steel frame. Calmly he reached into his toolbox and withdrew a cigarette from the packet and placed it between his lips, lit it with a lighter and tossed them back into the box. He looked around; settings like this would be his office for the next fifteen years.

At approximately 7.45 p.m., wearing white leathers and a matching full-face Bell crash helmet, Kelly rolled out onto the track for his first race in the British speedway league. At just seventeen years of age, little was known about him except that he possessed a cheeky grin and a wild glint in his eye. He was making his debut for the Hull Vikings in a Frank Varey Northern Trophy match against Yorkshire rivals Halifax.

Unsurprisingly, given the fact that he had just one professional season under his belt in the USA, combined with his lack of experience and his alien surroundings, he scored just 1 point from reserve but was afforded his full quota of three rides. In fact, it would take the likeable American a few matches before he began to show the brilliance that had persuaded the Hull management to move heaven and earth to bring him over to race in the world's toughest speedway league.

Press and practice day illustrated that he was destined to be something more than just a superstar of the speedway tracks, as his team mate, Graham Drury, recalled: 'During the winter months, Ian Thomas [Hull team manager and co-promoter] had said to me that he signed a young American lad called Kelly Moran, and in them days that didn't mean anything to me at all. At the beginning of the season we had our press and practice day and I was introduced to Kelly. To say that he was a character was a bit of an understatement. I wondered: what have we got here? When I saw him going around the track for the first time I could see that the lad had a lot of ability, not ordinary ability but natural ability. His balance and everything was superb.

'Afterwards, Ian had arranged for us all to go to a hotel, have a meal and just chill out and get to know everybody. As we were going down the corridor, Kelly said: "Oh, let's liven this up lads," pulled a fire extinguisher off the wall, smacked the top of it, and covered all of us in foam!'

Sponsor and close friend, Pete Rovazzini accompanied Kelly to England for his first season and helped him out in the pits. Rovo, as he's known, also sponsored fellow American Bruce Penhall and his company, Rovazzini Electric, was a regular fixture on Moran's race suit for many years.

'We got picked up in a Rolls Royce and I go, "Oh this isn't so bad," and eventually we were taken to a beautiful house in Beverley, and from that point on everything went downhill. But it was a beautiful village and there were loads of pretty girls there,' he remembered.

Speaking to the author in 2001, Thomas said: 'I had a contact in America in the '70s and they, a man and a woman, provided me with a lot of tips on all the

American riders. I had a lot of them over the years and that's basically how I got to hear about Kelly.'

Prior to Kelly's arrival, the Hull side had previously included US riders Mike Curoso and, for a short period, Steve Gresham. However, for 1978, Thomas had pulled off a major coup by signing multiple World Champion and superstar, Ivan Mauger, which virtually transformed this unfashionable Yorkshire team from also-rans to league title contenders overnight.

'I saw Kelly when he was fifteen at Costa Mesa and on other Californian tracks. When he was seventeen or so I recommended him to Ian Thomas as I was riding for them,' recalled Mauger.

In truth he shouldn't have been able to race in Britain at that point because he wasn't yet eighteen years old and the rules said that a foreign rider had to be eighteen before he could hold an international licence. His tender age was certainly known by the authorities because it prevented him from racing for his country in the UK qualifying round of the World Team Cup, leaving the side short-handed, and they had to draft in Steve Gresham's brother, Jim, to complete the team at reserve.

Convinced he had a special talent on his hands, the wily Hull boss had somehow managed to exploit a loop-hole in the regulations in order to bring the exciting Californian over to race for the ambitious Vikings team. Rovazzini revealed how they managed to get around the rules in order for the talented Californian to race in Britain.

'I became Kelly's legal guardian; that was the only way, at seventeen, they were going to allow him to go over there in case something happened. I figured that if he went to Europe he'd have a better opportunity. Ivan kept calling me about getting him to sign for Hull. We discussed it and I thought it was in his best interests considering the lifestyle that he led. I knew that if he stayed in California it would be too easy for him to get into trouble. And you know how much trouble we could get into over there; well, amplify that by ten-times!

'We did the deal, and I had another arrangement going with Bruce Penhall when he was going to ride with Bruce. It was a two-bike team. The Penhall Company was going to put up the money for Kelly's bikes and then I was going to run Bruce and Kelly. That was a very attractive offer because, when I look back, they would have dominated between the two of them. It could have been a really great opportunity for Kelly but his lifestyle wasn't conducive to stay in California. So we made the decision, signed the agreement, and I became his legal guardian.'

However, Moran revealed that the presence of Mauger was all the inspiration he needed to become a Vikings rider. 'I could have stayed home for another season, but all I thought about was racing with the great Ivan Mauger. We were always hearing about how good Ivan was, it was always Ivan this and Ivan that. So when Ian Thomas offered me a chance to go and ride with Ivan at Hull, I couldn't wait. It was a chance to ride with Ivan Mauger! Bruce Penhall thought that I should stay at home for another year, he was going to sponsor me with a van and such, but all I could think about was riding with Ivan.'

Despite his obvious ability, Penhall had yet to race in the British League although he did ride in the Inter-continental Final at London's White City in 1977. However, Rovazzini – who's also a close friend of Bruce's – believed that it was Kelly's decision to head to Britain that inspired him to follow.

'A few weeks later, Bruce called me up and said, "I've been meaning to go to Europe and if a seventeen-year-old kid can go, then I'm going too." So he went to Cradley and Kelly went to Hull. You can thank Kelly indirectly for the onslaught of American talent into Europe because when two of the most popular riders left, then everyone followed suit. If Kelly didn't go to Europe, you wouldn't have had the onslaught – I truly believe that. There was big money to be made in America at that time, but everyone followed because it became the trendy thing to do, but it took the two most popular riders to start it off.'

Kelly wasn't the only one influenced by Mauger signing for them. Joe Owen had completed one year riding for the Vikings but didn't like the track. He was keen to move away but once he heard that Ivan was coming, any thoughts he had about moving on were put aside.

'I had full respect for Ivan, he was my hero, and that was the only reason I stayed on at Hull. I'd have been well gone if they hadn't signed him. I'll put my hand up and say that I love the guy, I think he's terrific. A lot of riders are jealous of him,' said Joe.

When Mauger arrived at Hull he was the reigning World Champion and the previous season he'd equalled Ove Fundin's record of five World titles. More importantly, from a Vikings' fan's perspective, with the exception of his first club, Wimbledon in 1958, the Kiwi's influence had brought major honours to all the clubs he'd raced for. No more so was this noted than by the team he'd been signed from, Exeter.

The Falcons raced at one of the most intimidating circuits in the world and although that provided the team with a big home advantage, on their travels they often struggled. Furthermore, being located out on a limb in Devon, this meant that journey times to home meetings were long so star names avoided Exeter Speedway as much as they could.

That all changed when Mauger joined them in 1973 and he brought with him a new level of professionalism, new riders and, more importantly, pride and determination. By the following year the Falcons had won the league championship and transformed themselves into a competitive side on any track. Therefore, the Hull management, fans and the man himself hoped and planned to do the same for the Vikings.

However, as a relative newcomer to the British League, Hull were not so much a Cinderella club as more like the ugly sister, having been to the ball once already and returned with the Inter-League Knockout Cup in that memorable summer of '76. The ambitious management wanted more though, much more. And American Kelly Moran was very much a part of that plan. Just as Ivan had recommended Scott Autrey to Exeter in '73, so tiny Kelly replicated that formula for success and the supporters had every reason to feel optimistic.

Other members of the team during that opening night against Halifax were Frank Auffret, Scotsman Bobby Beaton, the very promising Owen and Phil Kynman. Unfortunately, they made an inauspicious start and lost to the Dukes 36–42, and were beaten at Halifax 45–33, where Kelly failed to score.

That match did, however, afford him with an early opportunity to experience Britain's notoriously unpredictable climate, as Pete Rovazzini recalled:

'Our first meeting was at Halifax, and Halifax was scary on its own and they kept playing that song, "I Can't Stand the Rain (Against My Window)" [the Eruption version]. It started snowing and he looked at me and said, "Pete, they don't expect me to race in this do they, because I can't tell the crash wall [the wall was white] from where the track ends? I can't tell where the racetrack stops and it begins." "I don't think so dude," I replied. But we rode. That's where we met Chris Pusey and Kenny Carter's father.'

The Frank Varey trophy was a regional competition that also featured Sheffield and Belle Vue – clubs that Moran would later ride for – and was meant as a warm-up before the serious business of league racing began. Those opening weeks were tough for the Californian; there was so much to learn and get used to with bigger, faster tracks, passionate and enthusiastic supporters, the dialect, different machinery and, of course, Britain's infamous weather where it would often be 'siling down' – a local phrase to mean raining heavily.

Although universally known as Hull, the city's full name is Kingston upon Hull and it's located in east Yorkshire and sits on the River Hull where its junction meets the Humber estuary – approximately twenty-five miles inland from the North Sea. At this stage the Humber Bridge was also under construction, a single span suspension bridge that joined the East Riding of Yorkshire with north Lincolnshire.

Its construction had begun in 1972 and while Kelly was a Hull rider he wouldn't see it completed – it was eventually opened for vehicles in June 1981. Locals became dismayed by the length of time it took to build as it was delayed by poor weather, strikes, and difficulties with the bank's foundations, and it became such a political issue long before work commenced that Christopher Rowe wrote and recorded a protest song with Ian Clarke entitled 'The Humber Bridge'.

Therefore, the bridge would serve as something of a metaphor for the building of Kelly's own career because by the time he left the Vikings, like the bridge, he had built himself a very promising profession, but wasn't quite the complete rider. Richard Harrison, whose father Bernard would be Kelly's full-time mechanic in 1979 and would himself twirl the spanners for Shawn Moran and help out the elder Moran on occasion, used to travel with his dad to Hull when the club first joined the top division in 1974. Bernard used to prepare the bikes for Bobby Beaton and, subsequently, other Vikings riders.

However, Richard doesn't exactly have romantic recollections of the Boulevard, although he reveals that they did witness the slow construction of the bridge during his regular journeys to the stadium: 'It was a bit of a dump really, not the best of places. We watched them build the Humber Bridge, it started with like stumps in the ground and then over the years we watched them towers climb up. We used go down the M62 and then take the dual carriageway straight in – quite an easy place to get to. It was on the outskirts of Hull, at the end of the M62, but there were houses built around it. The houses were quite close by.'

The Vikings team shared the Boulevard Stadium with Hull Rugby League Club. Therefore, the track was built around the rugby pitch and its 415-yard (379-metre) circumference was significantly larger than anything that Kelly had raced on in California – America's leading track at the time, Costa Mesa, was only 180 yards (165 metres) but very wide. The turns were quite tight, the straights narrow and it didn't have the natural arc in the corners that other circuits of that size had, something that esteemed sports journalist, Richard Bott, amusingly noted when he wrote, 'The track was so narrow even the mice went round in single file.' Naturally, they utilised the stadium's floodlights but they were not angled specifically for the speedway and this meant that the corners were relatively dark.

Bott covered Hull's fortunes for the local and national speedway press in those days and recalled in a correspondence with the author: 'Kelly once described it as being like "walking down a narrow hallway and turning left into the dining room. It had long straights and tight corners and not many visiting riders liked it. But I loved it."'

Nonetheless, the fact that Moran adapted to the awkward track was an illustration of his natural talent and his positive attitude. In the last interview he gave to *Backtrack* magazine, he revealed Hull's bizarre and unbelievable method of track preparation that certainly wouldn't appear in the track curator's handbook – should one exist.

'Bryan Larner and the fella who prepared the track used to throw 4x2-inch bits of wood onto it and then set it alight with petrol. The away riders would arrive and see our track in flames and wonder what the heck they were letting themselves in for. But Bryan would just tell them that it wasn't a problem – he was just drying out the surface!'

Perhaps that approach was meant more for the psychological impact on their visitors, but Joe Owen didn't recall the surface getting a great deal of attention between meetings. 'Bryan did the track and after the meeting he'd just go round with the tractor and that was it until next week.'

Furthermore, the Harrisons may have been thankful to have been plying their mechanical skills for the home side because the pits area wouldn't be described as state of the art. 'I think this was an Ian Thomas thing,' Richard believed. 'The home side was a concrete floor, but the away side was just soil. It wasn't very clean. It was quite small, especially on the away side and they were set well back from the track, at the back of the first turn and down like a tunnel. From the pit area you wouldn't be able to see the track, very narrow and would bank-up to where the terracing was. Ivan had the best place, he had like a corner spot. The changing rooms were really old, with the old big bath type changing rooms.'

Many years after the Boulevard had closed, Thomas admitted that the pits weren't the best by any means. 'Half the pits leaked water when it rained and half the pits were proper and that was where Hull used to go.'

Therefore, the opposition wasn't afforded many comforts when they came to race against the Vikings. A fact that didn't go unnoticed by the American Test team when they turned up at the Boulevard early for an international against England in 1980 and stole the home side and refused to move. All these little things combined to make the Hull Vikings' base an intimidating place for a visiting teams and riders.

Unsurprisingly, for a seventeen-year-old used to blue skies, smaller race tracks and different equipment, Kelly Moran took a little while to acclimatise to his new surroundings and became homesick. It took the prospect of failure and possible ridicule from seven-times US National Champion Mike Bast to convince him to stick it out.

'I think it was a minimum of four to six times that he wanted to go home,' recalled Rovazzini. 'I remember Mike Bast came up to us before we left and said, "Well, okay, I'll see you guys in three months." Every time Kelly would want to give up I would remind him that Mike Bast is waiting for us to come home with our tails between our legs. "That ain't gonna happen, there isn't any way that's going to happen, Kelly," I'd say. Every time I would make a deal with him, if he stayed we would do this, this and this, you know what I mean? Like I'll let him have an extra £20 a week or an extra beer, and I always tried to monitor everything … but how do you get rationality out of an irrational person?'

Kelly's mood wasn't helped during these early months when they struggled with their machinery. Disappointingly, the advice that they expected from superstar Mauger wasn't forthcoming.

'We were really struggling with engine issues and Ivan wasn't as much help as we thought he was going to be,' said Rovo. 'He'd sell us sprockets and it was cheaper for us to go to Taffy Owen and everyone knows how Taffy was. I used to say to Ivan, "Ivan, these sprockets cost us more than if we buy them new." "Yeah, but I've drilled them out for you!" He was a good influence for us, though – I have the utmost respect for him.'

Their innocence when dealing with Britain's wily promoters had a massive effect during Kelly's first year, in particular his payment structure. For all his natural ability, he was still an unproven talent in the British League and his wage reflected that uncertainty. Needless to say, Moran's inexperience combined with his enthusiasm stretched their meagre resources very thinly indeed.

'He'd [Mauger] have a new tyre edge for every heat, we'd have a new tyre every two meetings!' laughed Rovazzini. 'We never had the money then to have new edges for every heat. It just wasn't in the budget. It's a big difference from factory Jawa rider to burned-up Weslake motors. We went through six motorcycles in the first six weeks.

'One time he crashed so hard that he ripped the engine head off and it went over the fence into the terracing area in the pits. Another time a bike seized on the stand and we had to borrow whoever the reserve rider was, his back-up bike, it had a tyre like baloney on it, and it was the first time we had a motorcycle that actually lasted for four laps! It took us a while to get things figured out and we had a junk car. We only had two rolling chassis, so it wasn't the big time.'

Thomas, who would go on to be England's national manager, was eager to get his teenage star settled into British life and set about doing all he could to enable the young American to concentrate fully on his racing.

Transport is vital for a professional racer, especially when you're expected to travel the length and breadth of the country to represent your team. Therefore, Thomas wanted to arrange a car for his teenage star to travel in to the team's away matches. He asked him to produce his drivers' licence so that he could organise the insurance but, despite assuring Ian that he had passed his test in California, for one excuse or another, he couldn't produce it.

Taking matters into his own hands, Thomas eventually contacted the relevant department in California to discover that he hadn't passed his test after all, even though he could drive in such a way that many speedway riders do – flat out, all the time! Indeed, for more than half of his career, Moran never had a drivers' licence.

'I had a rider who could race but couldn't drive and, for the rest of the season, I had to provide him with a driver, which probably made him speedway's only chauffeur-driven star,' said Thomas.

However, he was behind the wheel long enough for the press to hear of his driving exploits. *Speedway Star* magazine ran a short story that revealed that he was finding Britain's road network confusing, especially the roundabouts. It reported that during a trip to Newcastle he somehow found himself in Liverpool – on the west coast of England instead of the north-east. Even an eight-mile trip from his home to the Boulevard for a practice session took him over an hour.

'It's the roundabouts that throw me,' Kelly said. 'I had never seen one until I went to England. There were all sorts of arrows pointing this way and that, but we ended up going straight over the top of it and nearly taking off. It was like something out of National Lampoon. Ian would give me a map and point at an area on it and say, "You're here and that's where the speedway track is." And that was it. I used to get some funny reactions when I asked for directions, with me being a real Yank and everything.'

Rovazzini was mostly the 'chauffeur' that Thomas referred to and stressed how naïve and inexperienced they both were, plus their transport was hardly a kitted out van or motorhome that today's stars have.

'Kelly and I had no clue. Heck we didn't even know where anything was. We'd set off, and this was before there were mobile phones, GPS, and we'd get to London and then ask for directions to get to the race track,' he laughed. 'I was amazed how some people had never left their village. You'd ask them for directions and they didn't even know any further than a five-mile radius around their neighbourhood! Everywhere we went we'd pass McDonald's on the North Circular and this was before there was a McDonald's in every town. We made sure that where we were going we went by a McDonald's. The only reason I did that was to try and keep Kelly happy because he was so homesick.

'I can't remember the make,' Pete pondered of the car, 'but it was something tiny and awful [Kelly said it was a Morris Marina] – when a Lada is step-up you know that thing was a shit box! I was so lost all the time. No radio or anything like that, all we had was this motorcycle sticking out of the boot. We didn't have a motorcycle rack until a few weeks into the season, so then we got to take the front wheel off, take the trunk lid off and stick it in the trunk. We didn't know we had vans over here. We never even knew there was an under-21 World Championship, not even the World Pairs, we just went over there to race. He was too young to do anything with the FIM.'

Later in the season, their travelling mishaps once again filled a column in the press during a trip to Ipswich. This time the vehicle he was in had broken down.

Determined to reach his destination and compete, and showing scant regard for the cost involved, he engaged a taxi to transport him the forty-mile journey from Newmarket to Foxhall Heath Stadium – only to arrive just as the match had finished!

Another essential for the racer abroad is accommodation. To begin with he stayed with Thomas' secretary, Lesley Sharp, until they provided him with a flat in the nearby bustling market town, Beverley, which was around ten miles north of Hull.

No longer under the watchful eye of club management, Kelly soon set about making the most of his new-found freedom and Britain's relaxed drinking laws. His happy-go-lucky nature and his charming disposition soon made him a popular figure on and off the track. Furthermore, his southern Californian twang brought some Hollywood glamour to the East Riding region and, of course, made him particularly popular with the young ladies in the area.

Inevitably, being so young, far from home and full of excitement, the Californian got into several scrapes off the track, which meant that Thomas' relaxing evenings were often interrupted by a telephone call informing him that his rider was in need of a ride home at the very least. Ian recalled one such occasion in his biography.

'He'd been partying one night in a local pub and I got a message that he wasn't in too good a state. I went along, collected him and took him back to the flat. It had a retractable bed that went up into the wall when it wasn't being used. He started jumping off the sideboard onto the bed. It suddenly retracted into its wall space, jamming Kelly in the recess where the bed wanted to go. I couldn't pull it down and Kelly was up there spread-eagled and squealing away for me to get him out. But it just wouldn't move and, in the long run, I had to call out the fire brigade to release him.'

And Beverley had other attractions as well, one of which in particular appealed to the young Californians as Rovazzini explained.

'We were right near Beverley racecourse, and they had the hospital there and all the nurses slept in this one area. We got hooked-up with one of those nurses and I remember leaving there with a bottle of champagne at 8 o'clock in the morning just as all the nurses were waking up. I think it was Kelly who said, "Doctor Rovazzini, Doctor Rovazzini, one moment please." It was a great time, we were going to a party if we weren't racing. Between the racing the people were great, we fell in love with them all, they were so, so nice.'

Nice they may have been, but none compared with the girl he left behind, Marice Supry. 'The first year he was over there, he would always send me flowers and cards, postcards, just to make me feel better because I was so sad that he wasn't with me here,' she said.

Clearly Moran had bundles of natural, raw talent, but as Owen recalled, they soon realised he liked the wild side of life too. 'The first year he came over he was only a kid then. He was quite a handful, a bloody handful. He used to drink a lot, which was a shame really because he had a lot of talent that he wasted.'

However, according to Owen, Kelly fitted in well with a side that were personalities in their own right, sportsmen that enjoyed their racing and had fun doing so.

'Hull was made up of people like that, a team of characters really because we also had Frankie Auffret there, Mitch Graham and Bobby Beaton, who were such characters, and then Kelly came along and I had never seen so many lively characters. And Ivan was totally different. He was the true professional and then you've got Kelly the clown at the other end, but a clown with a lot of talent. Ivan would have given a lot for that talent – two totally different people. Kelly fitted in without a problem. He slotted straight into Hull because it was that sort of team.'

In order to be able to race in Britain the following year, he had to reach a calculated match average of 6 points and over to be automatically granted a work permit. Such a figure during his first season was considered to be quite high to achieve and it was set at that level to ensure that only the best raced in the British League and to keep foreign imports at a minimum. Within a couple of years, however, the rule served as little more than a guideline as neither objective seemed to be met. For Kelly, though, this regulation was a potential barricade to his international future. With his youth and inexperience, he'd have to turn on the determination as well as his talent if he wanted to make a career in Britain.

On 26 April, in a Knockout Cup match against King's Lynn, he registered his first race win for the Vikings by defeating Ian Turner, David Gagen and Mauger. Just to prove that it was no fluke, he then won heat 8 as well, again defeating Gagen with Frank Auffret in third and Pete Smith at the back.

His eagerness to score points and his inexperience of the British League's bonus point system led to him hassling Auffret for the lead during one of his early races when he didn't have to, thus putting his team-mate under unnecessary pressure and potentially threatening his team's points.

'Kelly didn't realise he got paid the same for finishing behind Frank as beating him,' Thomas recalled. 'When Frank told him, he apologised and promised to form a strong team-riding partnership.'

There was also another piece of track etiquette in Britain that he also had to learn, something that would be reversed quite soon after Kelly's arrival in the UK. In fact, in 1986 he described this as his most embarrassing moment in the sport at that point:

'When I first came over to England, I always used to raise my arm on parade. Unfortunately Ivan told me to stop doing it because it wasn't the done thing in those days. It was quite embarrassing at the time because it was as though I was an alien doing something nobody else did! Nowadays it would be unheard of the other way round.'

In early May, it was clear that it would take more than a few race wins to convince the critics that the Californian could reach that all-important 6-point average. Initially it was reported that foreign riders had to reach that figure by the end of June or they'd lose their place – it's not clear any of them did though. However, in his analysis of the imported riders that were the subject of this regulation, journalist Eric Linden expressed his doubts over Moran's chances. 'He's down at the foot of their [Hull's] score sheet where averages are concerned, and yet they just know he's a talent. Just the same, he'll have to be twice the talent if he's to get above the barrier.'

It's doubtful that the Californian took much notice of what Linden wrote, but his performances improved rapidly. When he top-scored with 15 paid 16 points at Wimbledon on 22 June during an incident-packed match at Plough Lane, where Mauger scored only 2 on a difficult surface, he'd definitely turned the corner. Although he didn't follow that with a succession of double figure returns, no longer was he contributing the odd point here, or a race win there, he was now making strong and exciting contributions to the team that helped them creep up the table.

More importantly, his improved scoring meant that his average passed the all-important 6-point figure and he was rewarded further by moving out of the reserve berth to partner Mauger at No.2. However, he received no favours from the Kiwi.

'I was so inexperienced, I just used to go for it,' said Kelly. 'Ivan used to say – and fair play to him – "I'm taking the inside," and I was like, "Okay, take whatever you want." In America we used to have handicap races and the start wasn't as important because there was always some dirt down to get traction and pass people. In the British League it wasn't like that, but I didn't know any different. I didn't know the inside gate was the best gate. I didn't know that gate three was the worst because that's where the dirt would get really packed in. So Ivan was always gone, man! I never team rode with him much. It never really bothered me what gate I had, even later in my career.'

There were few Americans racing in Britain in 1978 and, apart from Moran, none in the far-flung reaches of East Yorkshire. Therefore, advice from fellow countrymen was rare, so help came mostly from his team-mates and from others he'd befriended along the way. Super professional Ivan Mauger, though, realised that this talented tearaway wasn't one for studying his profession in detail and dedicating himself to refining his ability in order to be the best.

Mauger recalled: 'Halfway through the 1978 season I took Kelly to my place for a couple of days to try and get him to be a bit more professional about his speedway and I told him he had more talent for speedway in his little finger than I had in my entire body. But it was a waste of time. Kelly was a party boy.'

Nonetheless, while racing a speedway machine was regarded as Kelly's greatest talent, this was rivalled by his ability to assimilate and endear himself to his surroundings and its inhabitants very quickly – a gift that stayed with him throughout his life. During his first year, he acquired a flatmate who, with hindsight, may not have been a good thing for a teenager in a foreign land, but observation does reveal two kindred spirits separated by a vast ocean and ten years.

'When I was living in Beverley, Chris Pusey came to stay one night and ended up staying for the rest of the season,' said Kelly.

'That's Chris, he would do that,' laughed Joe Owen. 'Chris was an English version of Kelly, he really was. He goes under the radar a bit, but he was a brilliant rider and he inspired a lot of us. He was a bit of a hero of mine but once the career was over, that was it, the booze came and he hit it heavy.'

Like Moran, Pusey was a talented rider, an international and had skippered his country – he also liked to enjoy himself. Importantly, he'd competed in the USA and had some idea of what his flatmate was facing from a racing perspective, so the Californian lapped up his advice.

'He was riding for Halifax then and he used to say: "You don't want to be locking up on these tracks." He taught me what to look for on the track and what to look out for, because I was pretty green back then and he had raced in the US,' said Kelly.

However, Rovazzini soon realised that having Pusey around wasn't such a good idea on an impressionable teenager who lived his life as fast as his flatmate.

'Chris was a very good man and he taught Kelly a lot in the way of mechanics. Basically, he was the captain at Halifax and he was at that point when his career was going down. We looked after him a bit, housed his bikes and he stayed with us for months and months. But you shouldn't have a rider going down with a rider going up.

'We used to keep our motorcycles outside of Hull at Beverley at a stud ranch and they had a hangar just for us. I would walk in and started finding these small bottles of vodka. It was Chris, he was like self-medicating himself. I loved Chris but it wasn't a good influence for Kelly at the time.'

Joe Owen was regarded at this point as one of Britain's brightest prospects; he was a former National League Riders' Champion and was enjoying a good season until he crashed heavily during a second-half race and almost lost his life. Although he did well round the Boulevard, he never adjusted to it in the same way as the kid from California did, and within such a short space of time too.

'Considering what tracks they [the Americans] were riding on, I was surprised, but the Yanks could do that couldn't they. But there again Kelly'd been riding a long time, he'd probably been riding longer than most of us because they had that junior programme out there for when they were kids. He had the skill, he only needed to adapt it,' Joe evaluated.

Hull wasn't the only venue in Britain that had its track laid around a football or rugby pitch and in doing so, with narrow straights and tight square corners, their safety was questionable. Bristol was another and before Moran came to the UK Newport's Somerton Park Stadium also had a scary reputation, so much so that Peter Collins, who was the 1976 World Champion, refused to ride there on one occasion – it closed after completing the '76 campaign.

Nevertheless, it was Mauger's former track, the Country Ground at Exeter, that scored the highest on the intimidation register. With a steel safety fence lining the fast 433-yard (396-metre) circuit, it was feared by some riders and many preferred not to race there. It was the fastest and biggest track in the country, and holding the track record there would ensure that you entered the *Guinness Book of Records* as the fastest speedway rider.

During his first year, Moran was invited to compete in their annual individual meeting, the Westernapolis. Given its reputation, the field wasn't as strong as it might have been and Phil Crump won the meeting from Exeter's American, Scott Autrey. Kelly scored 3 points which, considering it was his first appearance there, wasn't bad. The similarities between the Boulevard and the Country Ground weren't lost on him though as he recalled later: 'The Boulevard was a bit like Exeter in that we had that home track advantage, but those mad Czechs didn't seem to mind the place at all.'

When asked about Exeter, or any of the tracks that may or may not have given him cause for concern, he responded: 'All the tracks are the same.' Whether this bravado was inspired by the fact that he had been long retired at this stage, safe in the knowledge that he was never going to have to visit these circuits again in anger, or whether it was just an illustration of his seemingly unflappable character, it's hard to say. What can be said, though, is that Cradley Heath's Dudley Wood track was the only venue that he continued to struggle with.

'My worst track was Cradley, I could never get round there consistently for some reason. I would ride in the Golden Hammer and win prizes and stuff, but it was my unluckiest track. It was okay, it wasn't as if I hated it or anything, but I just didn't get good results there. I'd go there and do okay for my club, get 9 or 10 or something and then Cradley would ask me to guest and I'd get something like 2 or 3. The supporters used to think I did it deliberately, I didn't, it was just one of those places for me.'

However, he still lacked experience and not just in the different venues, sizes, equipment and so forth; also the standard of racing he faced in Britain was vastly different to that in the USA. Learning to read a race, or read an opponent, only comes from lots and lots of competition – no matter how talented or fast you are. Perhaps it was that appearance at Exeter that provoked this response from Kelly when questioned about reading your opponents:

'You don't go round the outside of Vaclav Verner, especially not at Exeter, you just don't do that!' he laughed.

Despite his improved scoring, his youthful zest and exciting approach to racing would lead to some spectacular falls. In America they have a saying: there are those who've hit the wall and those who are going too.

'He certainly had no fear,' Owen recalled. 'One day he was that high or whatever and there was a bit of a thing in the centre green, like a bit of a fountain or something, and he ended up in that!'

Rovazzini added: 'Once Kelly got it into his head that he could do it, there was no stopping him. He was out there riding inferior equipment and when you don't make the gate, you've got to ride that much harder.'

By now though, word had spread that Hull had unearthed a special talent, and he was immensely popular on and off the track with the Vikings supporters. His never-say-die style of racing combined with his cheeky charm and his wild exuberance not only made him well-liked, he was also a character and a media man's dream. Always ready with a smile and a humorous quip, it was only Mauger's consistency and his brilliance on the world's stage that prevented the teenage American from stealing the Kiwi's status as the club's biggest star.

This fame, within the Hull area at least, threatened to curtail the youngster's off-track fun. In Britain you had to be eighteen years old before you could legally drink alcohol in a pub – it was twenty-one in California – so when stories in the sports press emerged of the brilliant performances from this seventeen-year-old American, nervous landlords began to get worried about falling foul of Britain's licensing laws.

'I can remember going into a pub in Beverley,' Moran said, 'and the landlord had seen all this stuff in the paper about me being seventeen and, of course, I was too young to drink. But Pete Rovazzini said: "No, no, it's just publicity, he's really eighteen." And the landlord looked at me for a moment and then said, "What are you having, Kelly?" Phew! Thanks Pete.'

Indeed, Rovazzini remembered that such was the impact that they were having in the area from racing and partying, one of the locals tipped him off to be on their guard for potential problems.

'The owner of the pub, he used to be a police chief, walked up and said, "I need to talk to you. Pete, this is a small village, Beverley." "Yes it is." "So you've got a good chance that whenever you get in trouble you're going to get caught. You guys got your own police, your parties all night long that you throw, your flamboyant lifestyle, they're really looking to get after you, so you've got to be careful." "Okay, thank you." When we weren't racing we were having a good time.'

Two more individual meetings, the Northern Riders' Championship at Sheffield and the Yorkshire TV Trophy at Hull, illustrated Kelly's growing confidence and ability to mix it with world-class riders of the period – the latter included World Champions Peter Collins, Mauger, Penhall, Michael Lee and Ole Olsen. He scored 8 at Sheffield and 10 in the TV Trophy that was won by one of the 'mad Czechs', Vaclav Verner.

Great things were undoubtedly expected of him when he came within 0.01 of the Boulevard's newly set track record on 21 June at home to Coventry. Mauger had set the new mark of 70.4 seconds in the opening heat, but if Kelly hadn't been forced to slow-up to avoid the fallen Frank Smith it seemed certain that the track record would have gone to the American.

His exciting style and his inexperience contributed to a number of spectacular falls, which wasn't helping their strained financial situation. On 29 July, the Vikings travelled to Coventry, the reigning league champions, and Rovazzini was faced with a major equipment problem.

'We went through so many bikes that week, everything was broken, I just looked at the heap and I didn't know what I was going to put together, but I had to do something. I salvaged what I could and put together a "Frankenstein" bike from the parts we had.

'Ivan wasn't there, Jimmy McMillan was in his place and Ole Olsen came over and took one look at my cobbled together "Frankenstein" bike and said: "Look at this, you're an embarrassment! You're letting the sport down, you're not professional, you shouldn't be in the British League. How have you got the balls to turn up with this crap!" That motherf★★★★r actually pissed me off, he wouldn't have had the balls to say that if Ivan was there, it was only because McMillan was there. I told Kelly: "If you beat this f★★★★★g prick, we'll take every penny we make, get f★★★★d up and stay in Coventry."

'He went out and beat Olsen in the first race and pulled in and said, "I did my part!" That was the best gate that Kelly ever got in his life, probably the only one! Back then at Coventry, if you didn't trap, it didn't matter how quick you were you wasn't going to win that race. I went up to Olsen and said, "Even on a piece of crap he can still beat you!"

'If Kelly was a trapper there would have been no beating him. He would have streaked ahead of everyone. The second heat the clutch blew up and flew across the race track. Third heat we won, the fourth heat, bam, we pulled up again.'

By mid-August, his on-the-edge racing and his equally adventurous approach to life off the track were sounding loud warning bells for Rovazzini and he had what he called an 'inkling' that something was in the wind, as he explained:

'It was more like a wake-up call; we had a big falling out. I said, "You're going to kill yourself, you cannot live this lifestyle and be racing. I'm not doing it, you've got to stop." We got into a big argument, but I said, "I'm not going to stay around and watch you kill yourself – I'm over it." Even though Kelly and I were notorious for having good times, there was a time and a place when it became dangerous for him – I couldn't be a part of that. It was dangerous because he was up all night long and he was hanging out with Chris Pusey – a guy who was going down.'

Pete's concerns weren't without substance. Ian Thomas recalled an incident with the police that also illustrated that the teenage American was pushing the boundaries of what was good for his health, was lawful and threatened his liberty.

Following a meeting, Thomas' night was interrupted during the early hours of the next morning by a telephone call from the police. Kelly had been arrested and Thomas, who he sometimes referred to as the 'IT Man', had to go and bail him out. After he took him back to where he was living, Ian returned home to Leeds and back to bed. Evidently, the night was still young for Moran, though. At 6 a.m., Ian was woken again by the telephone, and once again it was the police informing him that they had arrested one of his American riders.

'No, no, you've got the story wrong, I've taken care of that,' he told the officer, 'I collected him from the station and took him home hours ago.'

But the cop responded: 'We've arrested him for the second time!' Kelly had sneaked out after Ian had dropped him off and proceeded to get into more trouble.

In a move designed to keep Kelly away from the strong arm of the law, Thomas asked team members to look after their wayward team-mate. *Speedway Star*'s editor, Richard Clark, related this tale: 'Ian asked "old hand" Frank Auffret to take the Californian under his wing. One night, after Kelly had refreshed himself in the Hull bar after the meeting, Frank was driving him home. Turning into one particular road, Frank spotted a parked police car and, understandably, had no wish to bother them at that time of night, so drove ultra-cautiously. That is until Kelly leaned over, yanked the steering wheel down and the car mounted the pavement right in front of said patrol vehicle! They were swiftly, and inevitably, flagged down and Frank expected the worst. Rolling down his window, he thought he'd try one last, desperate tactic. "Would it mean anything to you if

I said that I've got Kelly Moran in the car?" he asked the officer. "Kelly Moran? Oh, not again. Go on, just get out of our sight," said the exasperated custodian.'

That wouldn't be the last time that his cheeky charm would disarm a member of the law. Much later he rolled Billy Hamill's truck on the famous Route 66 and the Highway Patrol turned up. 'The cop asked him, "What happened?" And he said he was getting it sideways because that's what he did for a living! You should have seen the CHP officer's face!' Hamill laughed.

Meanwhile, Hull had climbed up the league table to fourth place and maintained an outside chance of winning the crown when they travelled to Hackney on 25 August for an Inter-League Knockout Cup match. The club was staging a double-header to keep pace with their fixtures and Wolverhampton raced before Hull, defeating the Midlands' club 43–35.

Mauger was absent from this meeting as well and Hackney were also missing their Danish star, Finn Thomsen, so both teams promoted their number eights. Kelly got his side off to the perfect start by winning the opening race with Frank Auffret in second to record an opening heat 5–1.

In what would appear to be a pre-cursor to what would follow, the American lifted on the pits bend during his second race, crashed and was excluded from the re-run. In heat 8, Moran lifted again on the pits turn, but this time he fell off the back of his motorcycle. Unfortunately, the chasing Bobby McNeil rammed into him and the following Robbie Gardner was unable to miss the fallen racer. It was a horrific crash.

'It happened coming out of the fourth bend,' recalled McNeil. 'Kelly did a great big wheelie and came off the back. I remember him sliding toward the fence, I was going towards the fence as part of my racing line, but I had nowhere to go and, unfortunately, I hit him. I went over the top of the handlebars and I was splattered across the track, but I didn't get injured myself.

'Kelly had some bad injuries ... it was the wrong place, the wrong time. He looped it coming out of the corner and Hackney was a bit famous for a bit of dirt coming out of the corner, you'd get that bit of grip and whoosh! And he was a bit on the limit at times.'

Graham Drury's recollection of the crash was slightly different, but he was shocked by what he saw. 'I thought he wouldn't walk away from it. It was a horrific crash – unbelievable. He was going down the back straight at Hackney and then he went ass-over-tit through the third and fourth corners.'

It's believed it was McNeil's engine case that struck Moran, and he was flung end over end like a rag doll – it was a sickening sight. Although blameless – and it was a type of racing incident that happens all too often – McNeil admitted that the crash affected him afterwards.

'When you can't avoid someone, they're right in front of you and you have nowhere to go, it's never a nice thought to not be able to avoid someone,' he said. 'There just wasn't enough room, nothing where you could lay it down, he just slid to the outside and there was nowhere for me to go. I don't think I ever saw Kelly after that incident because I retired in 1979. He was a special talent, a lovely person.'

Kelly was taken to Whipps Cross Hospital, on the outskirts of Leytonstone, east London with multiple injuries and Gardner joined him in the ambulance but was later released with just severe bruising. The East End in the 1970s, on a Friday night, could hardly be described as a friendly place. While seated in the waiting room to hear of his rider's condition, Ian Thomas recalled seeing a man enter the establishment with a bottle sticking out of his head.

Moran required quite a lot of surgery to his injuries, which consisted of a broken pelvis, two fractured lower vertebrae in his back, a broken shoulder, a broken left leg, hip injury, broken arm and a concussion. The original diagnosis was not good, as Kelly remembered in 2006:

'I was drifting in and out of consciousness. But at one point I woke up and there was this guy with a drill – he was plating my leg! It felt like a bee sting. The impact of the crash had forced my leg up into my hip joint.'

Unusually, Rovazzini wasn't present at Hackney and was spared the horror of the crash, but not its aftermath. 'Oh my God, when I got there it was like Humpty Dumpty and all his king's men, his arm was up, his leg was up, but he had that big smile when I walked in. The doctor told me, "Listen, he'll never race again and will be lucky if he walks again." Quote unquote, "he'll never ride again, lucky if he walks." Then, of course, Kelly was like my little brother. I didn't have to say anything or look at him, he was just happy to see me because I'd always been his safety net.

'I was actually on the continent, because I told Kelly a week or so before that I was done. I felt bad when I had the telephone call to come home because he had a bad accident. When I got that call it was like life and death. From what I heard from everyone he was sprawled out on that race track at Hackney, he was like a broken doll, leg one way and arm the other.'

'They told my father I would never walk again,' said Kelly. 'I can remember Dad calling me at the hospital and he said: "Don't worry about riding again," and they were all pretty worried. I was in traction for seven and a half weeks.'

His family in California were kept informed of his progress through the club and friends. Younger brother, Shawn, was also racing speedway on the west coast at this time, but, having yet to experience the higher speeds of racing in Europe and the bigger risks that came with it, he was shocked by the severity of the accident.

'When I heard it was like, he broke that AND he broke "that"! It was alarming. It was a terrible feeling because you can't do anything or see him. It was the fact of knowing what he'd broken because it sounded bad. We didn't do anything major like that at all in our early days of junior speedway – probably the same for our speedway in the States here, nothing major.

'I knew that Pete was over there with him so he had a nice little team to look out for him. One of the guys had a phone on that side to call us when he was better. It was the usual stuff, how are you feeling, that sort of thing.'

Understandably, Kelly regarded this crash as the worst of his career and after fellow American, Denny Pyeatt, was killed racing there in 1982 and then Shawn sustained a broken leg on the circuit the following year, Kelly described the Hackney track as 'the armpit of the speedway world'.

The effects from this big crash would stay with him for the rest of his life and it wasn't just the way he walked. Kelly claimed that he was left in traction too long, which meant that he had one leg shorter than the other, 'It makes me walk like John Wayne!' he'd joke.

Nevertheless, despite the severity of his injuries, he remained upbeat. He charmed the nurses with his politeness and humour and, of course, that Californian accent attracted him to the staff. Joe Owen visited him and recalled that he had all the nurses running after him. 'It was like a Carry On film,' he grinned.

'When he had that crash, it must have been about a week later when it was the World Final at Wembley,' said Drury. 'I went into the Hackney hospital to see him and he was in traction all over the place, in a dreadful state. He had the run of the place, he had all the nurses running everywhere for him. But he could charm the birds out of the trees, though, couldn't he?'

'I signed a photograph for all the nurses and I'm told that it's still there to this day,' Kelly revealed (it's still present at the time of writing).

The staff, nurses and patients all helped the teenager to enjoy his eighteenth birthday while he was an involuntary guest in Whipps Cross. Now, of course, he could legally drink in a pub, but he wasn't fit enough to venture into such an establishment. Ever resourceful, he discovered there were means and ways of getting hold of the liquid refreshment he desired.

A fortnight after the crash, Hull were scheduled to race at Wimbledon and Thomas took advantage of the opportunity to visit his young star. He was pleased to find him in good spirits but was disappointed to discover the probable cause for his buoyant attitude.

'He was quite perky. He'd got a big bottle of orange juice on his bedside table and, knowing Kelly, I was suspicious so I had a sip. It tasted more like gin to me!

Somebody had smuggled it in for him. I took it away with me but I knew full well he'd get another.'

It was during this unhappy episode that the Californian struck up a friendship with Carol Stock. In *Backtrack* magazine in 2010, Stock explained: 'I used to make the teas in the first-aid room at Hackney Speedway and for some reason I followed Kelly as he was carried through the pits on the stretcher to be put into the ambulance. He was clearly in pain, but he didn't make a murmur.

'Afterwards I visited him regularly over the seven weeks he spent in hospital and got to know him well. He was so nice to talk to. He was seventeen at the time and so was I – we just clicked and have remained friends ever since.'

Nonetheless, in typical Kelly Moran style, this serious accident did furnish journalist, Richard Bott, with one of his favourite and also most memorable quotes from the racer: 'I was thrown into a flower bed when I crashed and was completely knocked senseless. Suddenly, I opened my eyes and found myself surrounded by all these flowers. I thought I had died and gone to heaven!'

# 2

# THOUGHTS FOR A PILLOW, DARKNESS FOR COMPANY

'Between the ever restless crowds, and the silence of your room,
Spend an hour in no man's land, you'll be leaving soon.'

Bob Seger

Even though Kelly was medicated to combat the aches and pains to help him rest, with weights, pulleys and ropes drawing on his fractures to maintain their alignment, the nights were not made for sleep. And hospitals, despite their insulation to provide a peaceful environment for their patients to recuperate, don't really sleep either because life and death, illness and cure, don't respect the conventions of time.

It was during these hours, interrupted by the occasional chaos of hospital life that contributed to broken slumber, when he began to think of home and his early life that brought him to this point. England's climate was vastly different from the one he enjoyed in California, and outside the chill of autumn had already begun to cool the air as it prepared the path for the next phase in nature's cycle.

He closed his eyes and thought of the cliffs on Huntington Beach where he would sit and look out over the Pacific Ocean, the light from the sun dancing off the azure-coloured water and if he really concentrated he could feel its warmth soothing his broken bones. The sunsets were something to behold, mighty in their scale with deep warm colours – a natural spectacle that he would grow to appreciate more with the passing years.

Not that he needed a recap, but his girlfriend at the time, Marice, gave him a reminder of home when she called him at Whipps Cross. 'I used to call him from the payphone at the beach, so he could hear the sea. He was lying in the hospital bed while I was telling him how beautiful the beach was. I hoped it made him feel better, but it may not have now that I look back.'

Kelly didn't need to hold a seashell to his ear to hear the sea; the roar of the waves that provided some of the best surfing in the world was a private symphony in his head that he carried with him throughout his travels. And boy didn't people want to hear about life in the Golden State where he grew up, so much so that wherever he went they didn't seem to tire of his tales.

The state of California on America's west coast has always been a desirable destination. Explorers, pioneers and trailblazers all set their sights on the area as a Promised Land with its diverse geography and its predominately agreeable Mediterranean-like climate. The gold rush of 1849 sealed its reputation as a place of riches, while the sound of the Beach Boys in the 1960s established a tanned, laid-back, surfing utopian image. Add in the City of Angels, Los Angeles, home of Hollywood, the movie capital of the world, and California meant glamour of all kinds.

However, despite its alluring image, California wasn't immune from the less prosperous times that the Great Depression dished out to the developed world. In one of civilisation's great ironies, it was the Second World War that revived the economy. Aerospace manufacturers like Douglas, Lockheed and North American Aviation were based in the state. The Cold War and its arms race helped maintain its place at the forefront of modern defence technology with the establishment of research laboratories such as the Lawrence Livermore National Laboratory – where the Polaris missile was developed.

With so much military research and development in the area, this gave rise to a boom in housing and white-collar labour. Therefore, its economic advantages played a big role in the social and political movements and preserved its place on the map of desirable places to live.

Due to good rail and water links, Ford Motor Company had established a production plant at Long Beach before the war. They were able to ride the biggest waves of the Depression because of good luck mainly. The US Army Air Corps occupied the factory during the conflict and then it reverted to car production.

But a flood and its ageing facilities saw it close and its staff were moved to a modern site at Pico Rivera, near Los Angeles. This is where Kelly's father, Tom Moran, worked for nearly thirty years but, crucially, he was a couple of years short of that landmark number when the plant closed in 1980, as his youngest son, Shawn, explained:

'He'd worked there for twenty-eight years, but the plant closed down and he needed thirty years to be fully retired. He was on the assembly line and they had thousands of people that worked there. It was a good, steady job and you had all your benefits, a good thing to have and he seemed set. After he got laid off I think things went okay, but he didn't get his full pension shall we say. It wasn't for him to go back east to finish off his last two years – he had things going on in California.'

Unsurprisingly, defence giant Northrop Aircraft Co. bought the facility and used it to develop the B-2 Stealth Bomber. Ford, meanwhile, moved their operation back to Michigan.

Nonetheless, it was into this seemingly attractive area, which was thriving from potential conflict, that Kelly Michael Moran was born on 21 September 1960, in Lakewood (Lakewood General Hospital), not Huntington Beach like most profiles would state during his career. He believed this well-published mistake had been confused with his schooling, which was in Huntington. His brother, meanwhile, always had the correct place of birth beside his name when he followed his elder brother to Britain. Shawn was born the following year on 19 November.

Lakewood has been described as 'an instant city' because of its rapid development during the post-war years from a small village community in 1950 to more than 70,000 residents within three years and city status by 1954. Bordered by Long Beach on the west and the south, and Bellflower on the north, the city was considered to be an archetypal post-war American suburb, partly due to its combination of local and county services and also for its ground-breaking community. This reputation was enhanced by Lakewood's resident author D. J. Waldie's book, *Holy Land: A Suburban Memoir*, regarded as an American classic and one that's attracted interest from Hollywood.

Obviously, Kelly's parents, Tom and Sharon (née Game) were pretty worried about the extent of their son's injuries. They had married in 1959, but they divorced when the boys were quite young.

'We were the ages of five to six,' recalled Shawn. 'We were kids, it wasn't really a big deal with us – we just went with the flow. As far as the courts ruled, we were picked up at the weekend by my dad, we'd stay the weekend and we'd come back Sunday nights because we had school Monday to Friday.'

Although parental splits aren't a pleasant occurrence for any child, the brothers' closeness and their easy-going outlook helped them to take the experience in their stride. Nonetheless, Shawn recalled that Kelly soon used his natural charm to get out of the chores when they stayed with their father, especially when Tom remarried.

'Her real name was Charleene but we were always told to call her Beanie. We behaved but she sided with Kelly, put it that way. We were both fine but it had its times! If there was stuff to do I'd have to go with dad to do it while Kelly could kick back with Beanie. Not that it was real bad with that situation, but it was sided.'

Good manners and respect were instilled in them from an early age, characteristics that they'd carry with them throughout their lives. Such qualities, combined with their communication skills, added to their popularity with supporters when they raced around the world and were certainly a big asset to Kelly in Whipps Cross where, unsurprisingly, he made many friends during his enforced stay.

'We weren't rebels or anything like that, we were always taught to have good manners at an early age,' said Shawn. 'We were taught to say please and thank you and when we were told to sit there, we knew not to move. We never got slapped or anything like that, but you just knew, it was the stare … and that was enough! That was mainly from my dad.

'Dad was a hard-working man, all his life really. He'd be a bit on the strict side, like he'd want things done by the book. Don't step out of line. Like our manners, he'd like it proper, say please and thank you, be polite, he did it in his own way. I never saw my dad have a drink when I was a kid. He wasn't like that when we got older, he was a coffee man from morning 'til night.

'Our mom was more relaxed, she would let things slide a bit – and that's not a pun! She would do her work, get home at 5/6 o'clock and then relax and have a beer. She was always a worker, always had a job. She worked at a machine shop and she was working with a drill press and her fingers would get cut from the shavings from the metal. When we were starting our careers she had odd jobs here and there, but she was never fired or anything. And she'd always find something else.

'We were brought up decently, and our neighbourhood where we lived was always good. There was no major trouble and nothing bad happened. We had to be in by 10 o'clock. We wouldn't come in at 12, it would be closer to 10.30 for something to be said.'

As brothers they were different but still very close. They had a strong bond that lasted throughout their lives and even existed when they raced each other in competition. Their telepathic understanding as racers and their endearing charm and personality made the Morans two of the most popular speedway stars in the world at the time. Although they certainly weren't alone as brothers competing in the sport, their relationship was agreeable with speedway's family atmosphere. Their similar size, stature and style meant that they'd often get mistaken for each other. The sport's media certainly found it confusing when they both wore almost identical leathers when they were sponsored by STP.

'I enjoy it if it's the right people who get us mixed up,' Kelly would laugh, and added. 'Shooey's the one with the moustache.'

However, like any siblings, when they were youngsters they'd quarrel and test each other. Their father was keen that his sons grew up tough and learned to absorb and deal with any difficulties – if it ain't bleeding, it don't hurt.

'We were fine, like all brothers we'd get into our wrestling things, but no punching,' Shawn recalled. 'At that time it was a mind game, because he was a year older and he was the intimidator, let's say, when it came to wrestling matches. Also, he would watch me to see what trouble I would get into. He'd egg me on to do it and I'd do it, then I'd get busted by my dad. That was just being kids.'

Eric Boocock was the team manager at Sheffield when the Morans rode for the Tigers, and he recalled: 'If they started falling out, you didn't get in between them. If you tried to separate them, they would both turn on to you! I've seen that so many times, but they adored each other.'

Bobby Schwarz remembered following the brothers when they were travelling to a race meeting and laughed: 'They were arguing in the van, then they stopped, got out, had a little fight, then got back in and kept going! They'd just wrestle on the ground by the side of the motorway, settle their differences and then get back in the van and go.'

Although there was a little over a year between them, when they were kids that may as well have been a decade because the older you get, the closer you are to doing grown-up things. Kelly would often hang out with older boys and when little brother came along for some company, he could count on his big brother's support. 'He always stuck up for me with his older buddies, or anyone, he had a heart of gold,' Shawn said.

Like many racers, Kelly's education wasn't the most important part of his life when he was growing up. In a profile published in the sport's press in 1986, he said of his schooling: 'I had a great time, but didn't enjoy my lessons too much. Probably my best subjects were physical education and lunchtime! I always used to hang out with the "rough" kids while Shawn would be with all the sports people – which was better and something that I should have done.'

Unfortunately, he departed Huntington Beach High School without any formal qualifications. He left before taking his exams because he was set for a career on the speedway tracks. Nonetheless, while he may not have obtained as much knowledge from his schooling as he should have, he was surprisingly conversant about a great number of subjects. He said that he enjoyed English and history lessons and, as his future wife, Lorna, discovered, he liked to read.

'He loved Stephen King, every time a new novel came out I had to go and buy it,' she said. 'He was like an encyclopedia – he knew everything. He was very clever, very knowledgeable and knew stuff. He was very good with his history. He must have been smart at school because he knew loads. He knew about wars and what happened and I used to say, "Why has this happened?" and he'd know.'

He once declared that, should he ever participate in Britain's popular TV programme, *Mastermind*, his specialist subject would be spelling. Shawn recalled that, unlike himself, his brother did display an interest in reading and absorbing knowledge. Yet, although he enjoyed sport, he wasn't as keen as one might have expected.

'He was into the reading part, I was totally not! Pictures and captions – cool! I was way more into sports. Kelly was a little bit. He wasn't active in that area you could say. My friends liked to do sports, whatever it was, and Kelly got good. He was very knowledgeable, yes, and his memory was good too.

'We'd play chess, and I know a lot of people hate chess, but it was a good mind game. I got active in that area at a young age, whereas Kelly liked his kickback time with his buddies. He'd also play a bit of chess, though we didn't challenge each other too much. We were pretty decent at a young age.'

However, it was during his high school years that Kelly first met Marice Supry. At the time of his accident they had been in a relationship for over a year and although it was a fun relationship, they shared quite a connection and one that grew stronger with the passage of time.

'We met when we were sixteen and we were in high school, but not the same high schools. I first met him at Janice Peterson's house, we used to hang out there as kids. He was one of the kids there. He was funny, cute, and little!' she laughed. 'We were the same height, 5ft 4in – you see pictures of us and we're the exact same height. His birthday was in September and mine is in January, so he was a few months older than me. He was a really smart guy, always sweet and very, very friendly with everybody. When we were kids we used to ride our bikes around and do wheelies in the street. He taught me how to do a wheelie. If it wasn't for him I would never have learned how to pop a wheelie.

'He used to call me Murphy – that was my nickname. He said that if he ever had a kid he wanted to name it Murphy, but since he didn't have one he'd just call me Murphy! Everyone called me Murphy, Bruce (Penhall) and Dennis (Sigalos) still do.'

Kelly was certainly smitten, even resorting to some cheeky behaviour in order to circumnavigate parental controls and curfews. 'When we were teenagers he used to sneak in through my bedroom window and my dad used to kick him out! He'd throw him out of the front door. He'd be kicking and screaming all the way out of the door,' she smiled.

As the night wore on in hospital, he could ease his discomfort from being in the same position for long periods by adjusting himself with the aid of a handle that was suspended above him, which he did with his left hand. Kelly was left-handed, which was by no means rare, but he smiled at the memory of his and his brother's distinctive participation in baseball when they lived in Lakewood.

'We were in little league baseball, which we did for a couple of summers. Then we moved to a different team, while still in Lakewood. That team was kind of unique because Kelly and me are left-handed; our team, if everybody is out on the field, pitcher and catcher, plus first base, second base, third base, short stop and three out fielders, we had nine left-handers on our team. You weren't really the odd one out but most people are right-handed,' said Shawn.

Sports columnist, Jayson Stark, described baseball as 'a unique paragon of America's culture', but sport was more ingrained in the nation's psyche than it was in other parts of the world at that time – except maybe in the USSR where their success was used to promote the supposed superiority of the Communist system.

Therefore, as children, the Morans were exposed to a lot of sport. Some regard American football as the nation's number one sport – the Super Bowl regularly posts massive worldwide audience figures. However, with his height and a weight of around 8 stone (115lbs), Kelly would hardly fit the image that we'd normally associate with these athletes – who are like rugby players with helmets and body armour. Nonetheless, as part of his sporting education while growing up, he sampled the delights of America's version of rugby with all the rhythm taken out of it and it was once published that he preferred the running-back position – a role that can favour players of smaller stature for their shiftier and agile abilities.

The divorce of their parents eventually saw them move to Huntington Beach, Orange County – via Downey – in the early 1970s and a different culture. It's known as the Surfing Capital of the World, not for its high waves but for its consistent quality of surf, and consequently it's staged major national competitions there since 1959. In 2004, the city trademarked its nickname of 'Surf City USA'.

In the 1960s and '70s, the surfing culture in Huntington manifested itself in several clubs, but with its eight and a half miles of picturesque sandy beaches and agreeable warm climate, other pastimes were also practised to give the image of a perfect lifestyle – certainly one that appealed to Brits whose shores were lapped by predominately freezing cold waters and wild seas that made a dip a tortuous experience rather than a pleasurable one.

'We learned to swim at a very early age at my dad's parents', who we called grandma and pop; we were in their pool at two and three years old,' said Shawn. 'We tried surfing – I was average at it – but it was really about being at the beach and the surfing helped with the fun thing about it.'

Shawn enjoyed it more than Kelly, who was content to do other things. 'Kelly wasn't one to kick back and get a tan and all that. He'd go to the beach, sure, but we were teenagers and he had his buddies and we'd just hang out with our group of friends. I tried to get to the beach as much as I could, though. There was a band in our area called Kickfire, a three-piece band. Now and again he'd hang out with those guys – I did too. They had their group of friends that would go with them to where they'd play and we'd go along. Kelly would mainly hang out with that group of people.'

All youngsters want transport; its freedom, the opportunity to flee from the watchful eyes of your elders and have valuable time to be with your friends. The first form of transport is usually the bicycle.

'We learned to ride bicycles pretty early, like most kids did, that was our major fun,' Shawn said. 'We learned to do wheelies, all that stuff, not to the extreme like they do now, but we got to learn to slide and do wheelies. Then, where we lived, we ended up having a pack of guys who all had bicycles. When we moved to Huntington we still rode bikes and that, but I got into skateboarding. It was a good thing that everybody started doing. If you didn't have your bicycle to go to your friends, you'd ride your skateboard. It was transportation.'

Kelly, though, stuck to the two-wheeled variety. He wasn't that comfortable on a skateboard and preferred his bike. Of course, with hindsight, the bicycle holds more significance in the advancement of two future heroes of the track than it does for most of us because it helped develop their balance and control. In Europe, there is a bicycle version of speedway called Cycle Speedway that did provide a path for some riders to transfer their skills to the motorised version, but it has a very small existence in America.

However, as he gingerly shifted his position in his hospital bed, Kelly remembered that his penchant for pushing the boundaries ignited the spark that started his frightening record of shoulder injuries. He recalled his stuntman exploits:

'I did a jump over fourteen wagons; they were little carts kids used to pull along on your bicycle. We lined up the wagons side by side and started jumping over two, then three and so on. The record was twelve and, being Kelly, I put two more on the end of the line. We lined them up and made a wooden ramp, trying to be Evel Knievel. I hit the last one. I was only eight and that's when I broke my collarbone for the first time.'

'Kelly would take chances and he wanted to go further than anybody else, whatever it would be – let's take it up a notch!' said Shawn. 'We didn't use that wording then, but he wanted to do it a little bit better than anybody else. If we were doing jumps, he'd double the jumps, because he'd want to make a scene – be extreme.'

With the medications starting to lose their effect, the aches and pains were becoming more acute and he was looking forward to his next round of painkillers to ease his burden. Multiple injuries like he had sustained were not as common in the US where tracks, in the main, were smaller so speeds were not as great. And certainly not so at a junior level and, in particular mini-bikes, which was how he began his motorcycle education – but they weren't injury-free either.

As he glanced at his broken left leg, he remembered it was in mini-bikes that he sustained his first broken bone. 'I was on a mini-bike in 1968 when I was only seven. I fractured my left ankle in two spots,' he said.

Mini-bikes played an important role in the development and progression of budding US motorcycle racers. Not only did they provide the youngsters with a motorcycle to hone their skills on, they also furnished them with a contest to take part in and groom them for serious racing competition as they grew older – should they decide to pursue such an activity.

Having seen his sons display balance and control on their bikes, Tom Moran decided that their energy and enthusiasm may suit a mini-motorcycle. Although he wasn't a biker himself, according to an interview with Kelly that was conducted in 1984, Tom had been looking for a mini-bike when he was growing up but was unable to obtain one. When he separated from his wife, Tom acquired one for the boys without their mother's knowledge and they used to ride it behind a K-Mart store.

'He got us a Powell Challenger,' said Shawn, 'which is what we started on and he'd take us to a couple of places, not tracks, but like fields where no one was at. I think we were five and six, so we had a good year to ride the bike, practise, just to learn how to stop – that's always the primary, if in doubt, stop! It took us a little while, not a long time at all because of the bicycles I think – at least we knew how to balance that can confuse anybody.'

However, when the brothers were in their teens, Sharon got them a Honda XR75 motorcycle for them to ride. It wasn't a racing motorcycle, although it was a fierce contest to determine who was going to ride it that day.

'That was just for us, for me and Kelly to have at the house,' said Shawn. 'I guess it was like, "Well he [Tom] can do it," so it was one-up on dad in their deal in life. We didn't know that, it was just we were getting a bike! Mom said, "It's for both of you." Yeah, right! Deciding who would ride it, oh man … and we were at that age when anything would start a fight. Somehow it sort of handled itself, but there were a lot of pissed off times and a lot of bitchin' times!'

Naturally, the boys' competitive spirit soon out-grew the area behind the store. By now, Tom got to know some of the people involved in organising racing events for kids through the various motorcycle shops. Therefore, they moved out to the desert and the dry lake beds to motorcycle parks like the Indian Dunes and Saddleback Park where a new breed of American motorcycle racers were being born.

It was something of an American phenomenon that provided the training ground where racers would progress to the highest levels of their disciplines and race around the world. Among some of the biggest names were 500cc World Champions Eddie Lawson and Wayne Rainey, motocross stars Ricky Johnson and Jeff Ward as well as speedway stars.

Sport in America is often split between different sanctioning bodies and mini-bikes were run nationally by the National Mini Cycle Association (NMA), which operated independently from the American Motorcycle Association (AMA) – the national governing body for motorcycle racing. However, they arrived after the Southern California Mini Bike & Kart Association, which was a non-profit organisation while the NMA wasn't.

Nevertheless, it was the NMA who cemented the regulations as they sanctioned the National Championships. Riders were classed as novice and expert, with engine sizes that ranged from 0 to 61cc, 0 to 81cc, and 110cc. The 61 and 81cc were subject to further divisions through stock and modified machines. Furthermore, they defined a mini-bike as not more than 70 inches long overall on 16-inch wheels and a width of 32 inches with a standard muffler. But the 110cc class was wide open, you 'run what you brung' and those lax laws certainly provided scope for invention and tension.

Celebrated British TV journalist, Alan Whicker, who was famous for his often satirical travelogue documentaries entitled *Whicker's World* in the 1960s and '70s, was also fascinated by this spectacle of little kids racing miniaturised motorcycles. In one episode of the series, entitled *Whicker Way Out West*, which was broadcast in 1973, he visited Costa Mesa and the production filmed the youngsters in action. Shawn Moran is seen in close-up and his brother's name can be heard on the PA as he races. However, Whicker chose to concentrate on a three-year-old called Jason Hawk and in his own unique style observed, 'On his mother's knee, Jason learns to drink his milk, watch his revs and bring home that trophy.'

Whicker was anything but keenly observant and wondered about the wisdom of parents seemingly pushing their small son along a competitive path before he was ready. It was his scrutiny that suggested that it was the parents who were living their dream through their children. Eventually, it was the competition between the parents that damaged the junior speedway programme and while it seems unlikely that there wasn't some rivalry between the parents at this point, Shawn Moran didn't remember it affecting their fun too much.

'There was competition, probably more than we saw. But you don't really want your parents involved, if you understand. We were kids, we didn't know, we were having fun racing, but sometimes they would act our age – I think it's the same with any sport.'

However, there was one incident that Shawn recalled that really didn't go down well with his father. 'We had our nationals at the end of the year. Lance King had won that night. Well, whatever number he was racing with at that time, my dad saw Don King walk over to Lance and pull off that number from the back of his leathers which he had Velcroed on and underneath he already had

No. 1 on his back! My dad didn't like that, it was like: "Hey smart ass!" We didn't care though, it was no big deal for us.'

America's famous, photo-heavy *Life* magazine, which ran in various formats for over seventy years, carried a feature about the mini-bikes craze in their January 1971 edition, in which its author observed that competition between the parents was probably hotter than between the kids on the track, describing their collective attitude as, 'Little League syndrome all over again.'

The writer continued: 'They instruct their charges on such sneaky techniques as to how to inch up on the starting line without being caught. Sometimes they get carried away and tempers flare. "I've seen things you wouldn't believe," says one track official. "I saw one father run up to his son who had just lost a race, screaming, "Why didn't you do better?"'

From outside the track, parents' enthusiasm could be heard as they shouted their encouragement. The more excitable, or ambitious among them, called out advice, disguised as encouragement of course. 'I don't mind telling you, when the boys are out there I get wound up tighter than a kite,' said one keen dad.

Not so Tom Moran. He didn't pressurise his sons. Sure he wanted them to do well and he was extremely proud of them, but he took it all in his stride, every triumph was a celebration and for every disappointment there was something to learn and there was always tomorrow. He believed that they should enjoy their racing first and foremost; desire and ability would provide the rest.

For Sharon it was different. She saw racing through a mother's eyes; that protective arm may let go in a physical form as time passes, but the instinct to protect and keep your loved ones from harm never leaves – even when they've grown up. As they moved up the ladder and the competition became hotter and the inevitable crashes grew larger, watching became a fearful rather than a pleasurable experience. The severity of Kelly's injuries sustained at Waterden Road in 1978 was particularly shocking and this may well have changed her attitude toward the sport.

'I think Kelly's crash turned her off,' Shawn agreed. 'She used to watch us come out, but then she'd put her hands over her eyes when we were actually racing. She enjoyed the speedway until she got a little older, then she didn't like it as much because of the injuries – that was being a mom. When we started she'd go now and again, but not every week.

'After a few years that we rode and [then] went to England, it started to die off for her, after the injury to Kelly and watching me, it made her scared for us – as a mom, I would guess. The dads want to see you do it, but mothers see the fear factor more. I remember when I started, Costa Mesa was always on a Friday, I'd always had to get her some supplies, Chinese food, and then use her truck to go to the races and then come back again. Hopefully I was coming home in the truck and not in an ambulance.'

As Kelly surveyed his battered body in Whipps Cross, he couldn't have known how many times he would damage his collarbones during his career. Shoulder injuries are the curse of the motorcycle racer and later in life he would chuckle at the absurdity of the situation left by so many breaks, when he told the author that it had left him with one arm slightly shorter than the other!

All motorsports are dangerous, bike racing especially so. But in speedway, with all that power in a confined space and no run-off area, injuries are an occupational hazard. Air fences hadn't been introduced to the sport then – it was 2000 when the air fence was first brought into the World Championships – and technology, then like now, was progressing much quicker than the venues or the track surfaces.

Nonetheless, some riders are more prone to injuries than others, a few because of the way they race, some through a lack of skill and inexperience, and others are just plain unlucky. Kelly Moran didn't lack ability, in fact he possessed a rare natural talent for racing a brake-less 500cc motorcycle that was the envy of his rivals; he was a racer and an entertainer, yet he was often in the wrong place at the wrong time, as he once reflected.

'I'm one of these guys who, when he crashes, can't do a simple lay-down. I've got to do it in style or someone hits me. I have always got to do the spectacular ones. I have always got to break bones.'

Overall, since arriving in England, Kelly had been welcomed. However, he knew that politics was a no-go area when it came to making friends. He grew up under the cloud of his country's controversial participation in the Vietnam War, which led to many anti-war demonstrations. Actually one of the biggest protests was in Los Angeles in 1970 where two people lost their lives. Who knows, had America not withdrawn five years later he could have been in a very different place – his father had served in the armed forces.

Nonetheless, in Britain, he couldn't escape hearing about the troubles in Northern Ireland. Stories of bombings and other terrorist activity perpetrated by various groups made Londoners nervous after the bomb attacks by the IRA in Guildford and Woolwich in 1974. Staff at the hospital may not have spoken directly to him about it, but there was plenty of violence on the Emerald Isle in 1978 that fuelled their paranoia – when he celebrated his eighteenth birthday the IRA carried out a bomb attack in County Derry – although thankfully England was not targeted that year.

Kelly believed that the family hailed from the Dublin area in the Republic of Ireland, and while he made a mental note to find out more in the future, there is no evidence that he did. However, it's believed that the origins of the Moran name can be traced back to Connacht, which is a province in western Ireland and its meaning is 'descendent of the great one'. In a census of 1659 there are Moran families registered as present in Dublin County, thus bearing out his belief.

It's not clear whether he did visit Ireland, but he didn't compete in that country where, despite some efforts, the sport has never gained a permanent foothold. Brother Shawn, however, did ride at the Ballymena Showground in County Antrim, Northern Ireland in 1982, in a special meeting arranged by Peter Adams and Robert Mather. He was shocked by the high level of security when soldiers would check beneath vehicles for booby trap devices with special mirrors. Soldiers carried machine guns at checkpoints accompanied by armoured trucks and armed men would be concealed within hedgerows and at other strategic points. The Troubles would not be resolved in any form while the brothers raced in England.

As youngsters learning their racing, they reflected their Irish connections when they wore distinctive green and white shamrock leathers. The clover is a symbol of Ireland and of their patron saint St Patrick who, legend has it, used it as a metaphor for the Christian trinity. Those suits certainly made them stand out and also left a lasting impression.

'I was never really told that we had a strong Irish background,' said Shawn. 'The Team Shamrock suits, my dad came up with the idea, it was his plan and we stood out. He bought the leathers but, to begin with, we just had the tops – it was probably a money thing. So we each got a top first because, obviously, your upper body is important, cover that up first. Then we got the bottom half and it was great to have all that gear on as a kid. When you've got all the leather on you feel sort of invincible – it's a great feeling. You want to show off at that age, wear them when you're out. I think that was why people remembered us with the shamrock on the back. A lot of people who rode mini-bikes in the '70s would just wear Levi's, a long-sleeved sweater, T-shirt underneath and regular boots. Jeff Ward had leathers, and he was orange and white.'

Cool suits were one thing, but they had the ability to back it up. Wayne Rainey's father, Sandy, recalled their pace in his son's biography: 'On a long track we just couldn't run them down.'

Organised events were usually staged at the weekends, often starting at 9 a.m., and Kelly recalled that they could race in as many as ten races per day. 'We didn't know any better,' he once said. 'Being small and light gave us an advantage over some of the others, but thank God we were naturals.'

'Ours [mini-bikes] went by horsepower, we would buy horsepower and we had 3-horsepower with what we ran,' Shawn recalled. 'Then after a few years Kelly got bumped up to 6-horsepower. I know it doesn't sound like much but when you're a little guy it sure is! I believe we started racing around six or seven;

I was always in the six- to eight-year-old class while Kelly was in nine to eleven. We never raced each other much and I was kept down in that class for like five years! The thing was there was only one bike for a while and we had to share it so I couldn't race against him. And that was for a year or so. I stayed there until Kelly could move up. That's how it ran for us in mini-bikes, we were grouped by ages six to eight, nine to eleven, and twelve and over. I never got to race with Wayne Rainey; all those guys were Kelly's age and although it was only a one-year difference, it made all the difference in the class.

'The tracks we raced at were mainly Indian Dunes and Saddleback Park; those two were also our championship races. The other guys had other places they used to go, but we didn't hit all the places like the other fast kids – like we know now that some of the pro-motocross riders like Jeff Ward and Ricky Johnson used to go to Corona and Trojan.'

Those venues were motorcycle parks, or motorcycle playgrounds as some called them, and these days they're recalled more for their contribution to America's motocross stars rather than its equally effective influence in other disciplines. 'The Dunes', as they called it, was located near Valencia, past the Magic Mountain theme park on Highway 126. Approximately 600 acres, it included two motocross circuits – 'Shadow Glen', so called because of the trees lining it, and the 'International'– an oval for flat track and speedway, a cycle track, sand track and several other circuits for practice. It was also where the majority of Steve McQueen's scenes were filmed for the *On Any Sunday* movie and its vicinity to Hollywood made it an attractive location for film-makers.

Many riders dabbled in other disciplines before settling on the one that they felt best suited to. Kelly also tried motocross but later remarked, 'They do too many laps, four is enough for me!' That was a typical throwaway comment from him, but many believed that he had the talent to race any motorcycle. He chose speedway to refine his skills, yet there are plenty who believe that he could easily have adapted his talent to other disciplines. In 1986, when asked what he would have been doing if he hadn't become a speedway rider, he replied: 'Probably still riding motocross.'

The nurse on duty that night in Whipps Cross was enjoying a relatively peaceful shift. Despite his body needing its rest to help itself to recuperate, his fixed position and the occasional bumps of hospital life would jolt him awake again. With everyone else also attempting to sleep, there was little chance of striking up a conversation to help the hours of darkness slip by, so his thoughts drifted back to his mini-bike days.

The mini-bike scene was not only fun, but also competitive. Kelly and his brother both enjoyed success and had some silverware to take home. In their age group and class, they both won the Mini-Bike Grand Prix.

While their dad may not have urged his boys to win as some parents did, he wanted to make sure that they had a competitive chance of being successful. Stu Egli, who was a professional motocross rider at fifteen and would also go on to have a short career as a speedway rider in the US, was doing very well when Tom approached his shop to improve his sons' chances.

'He brought their engines to us because we were winning everything,' Egli said proudly. 'I was sponsored by Bay Mini Bike, a guy called Stan Gilbert ran it. Shawn had a Powell Challenger 3hp Tecumseh (lawnmower) engine and Kelly a 6hp Tecumseh. They called their modified Powells "Shadows".'

Some fathers took it a stage further, though, like Rainey's dad, Sandy. Eager to get his son at the front and ahead of Kelly Moran who was in Wayne's age group, he began tinkering with the fuel to get an advantage.

He recalled: 'The rule book says yes you must have fuel, but it didn't say what kind. In go-karting we always ran methanol with a bit of nitro. So I bought five gallons of each. I made new needles and jets, because everything has to be sixty per cent bigger. I took Wayne out of school one day and we went to Saddleback Park and I got her dialled in. And Wayne was pretty hard to beat from then on.'

So good was Wayne, that Steve McQueen sought out Sandy's expertise for his son, Chad. Kelly smirked to himself at how inadvertently the movie star's profile blew the whistle on Rainey senior's special brew when the authorities became suspicious of this aromatic concoction and doctored fuels were outlawed – consequently the NMA stipulated that only pump fuel was permitted. However, while lying in Whipps Cross, Kelly could still remember his own thrilling experience of using nitro in his machine during his first year as a pro-speedway rider.

Nonetheless, while some fathers may well have been living their Grand Prix ambitions through their boys, this was still racing and the youngsters' enthusiasm and excitement did sometimes make for a risky cocktail if not a dangerous one. Speaking in one magazine report, an unidentified father did admit to having some concerns over his boy's safety – especially when he disappeared from view.

'I don't mind too much when the boys fall where I can see them; as long as I can see them I'm alright. But sometimes if they go off over an embankment and I can't see them my heart goes right up in my throat.'

As with all youngsters, they seldom see the danger that a worried parent would. In the same article, one of the competitors gleefully told the reporter, 'I was thrown over the handlebars once and landed 30 feet away and all I did was worry about my bike instead of about me, which was pretty silly I guess, because the bike could be repaired and I couldn't.'

The small horsepower of a mini-bike became frustrating for the more talented riders because their ability and confidence outgrew their machines, so in order to continue with their progression they required something more conventional with more HP. Around 1971, Tom Moran acquired Indian mini-cycles for his sons. These were more like a conventional MX bike and were 50cc and capable of speeds of up to 60mph – in the right hands.

'Mini-bikes had no suspension and boy they could be hard to ride,' recalled Kelly. 'The Indian had a bit of suspension and it was like, why did we spend so long on mini-bikes?'

Kelly believed that his father had tied up some sponsorship arrangement with Cycle Town, which was a motorcycle shop run by Ted Moorhead. Along with some other brands, he sold Indian motorcycles and it was suggested that he also had a hand in supplying the shamrock leathers. Cycle Town remained on their race suits throughout their junior racing days.

Much later in his career, despite riding alongside and against some of the biggest names in the sport, he said that his father was his biggest influence in his career. 'He was the one who started us in mini-bikes and stuff like that. He never raced himself but he encouraged us and he was really proud of us when he came to watch us race in England. If it hadn't been for dad, we may not have been racers.'

Another former racer, who would also go on to play an important role in the careers of Kelly and Shawn, as well as World Champion Billy Hamill, was Ken McGoldrick and he recognised the significant part their father played during their early days.

'I knew Tom pretty well. He was a good guy and he tried hard to help the boys in any way he could. He was largely responsible for taking them out into the desert to ride, like the Indian Dunes and places like that when they were little kids, to teach them how to ride mini-bikes. He brought out their natural talent.'

Their father's support was recognised by many in California and Kenny Best believed that Kelly responded well to his dad. 'Kelly would have some spats with his dad. But he did seem to get along better with his dad than his mother, but Shawn was the opposite.'

However, these motorcycle parks were not solely for boy racers; all ages were able to utilise the facilities, plus the dry lake beds and other areas of the desert. Even professional racers would test and train there. The Dunes in particular, with its banks, humps and ridges, would be popular with weekend dirt bike riders and the area would echo to the sound of revving motorcycles.

'We never really got to get on our bikes, like guys do, and go ride through the sand beds for an hour – one way and come back. We were too young, we just went there to race,' said Shawn.

The Dunes, and others like them, gave many youngsters their first taste of riding and racing motorcycles in organised competition. Moreover, they were located in designated areas that were separated from busy highways and were also far enough away from urban sprawls so that the unique sound of their two-stroke engines wouldn't annoy the sensitive public. It was also a phenomenon that was spurred on by a youthful counterculture, popularised in the freewheeling motorcycle road movie, *Easy Rider.*

While the doctors and nurses in Whipps Cross were fascinated by the tales of life on the west coast of America and intrigued by Kelly's profession, there is little doubt that, among the females at least, it was his proximity to Hollywood and the movie stars therein that fascinated some of them. Steven Spielberg and his science fiction blockbusters, *Star Wars* and *Close Encounters of the Third Kind* were very popular and the now largely forgotten *Convoy*, with country music singer Kris Kristofferson in the lead role, was similarly trendy because it was issued at the height of the CB (Citizen Band) Radio craze – it was released the day before his crash at Hackney.

However, it wasn't the location of his home that brought him into contact with one or two of the Hollywood stars, it was a common interest in racing motorcycles. Steve McQueen, star of such movies as *Bullit, The Magnificent Seven* and *The Great Escape*, was inducted into the Off-Road Motorsports Hall of Fame in 1978 having already competed in the Baja 1000 and produced and starred in the cult classic motorcycle racing movie, *On Any Sunday.* Therefore, it was no surprise that the Moran family found themselves rubbing shoulders with McQueen while the boys raced against Steve's son, Chad and daughter Terry, in the desert. Kelly thought that the young nurses in particular would probably wet themselves with excitement if they knew that he and his brother had both stayed at the actor's home.

A grin crossed his face as he remembered how his mother would make a special effort to get dressed up just for the boys to be picked up and returned by the man himself. She was further delighted one Halloween, as he remembered:

'She got what we called "egged" by some kids. And Steve came out with hand towels and helped her to clean herself up. She was so thrilled, she would tell everyone that she knew Steve McQueen.'

'He was just like all the other parents,' recalled Shawn. 'When we were out racing, we were racing, but all the dads would talk to each other and stuff. It wasn't like everybody was staring because it was Steve McQueen … it was like, "woagh!" but it was all cool.'

It was especially exciting for Kelly. In an article published in 1986, answering a question about his first love, he revealed that it was Terry McQueen and future *Charlie's Angels* actress Cheryl Ladd that captured his interest. Many years later Kelly said, 'Steve's daughter had a crush on me – I was only twelve then – and it was through them that I met Cheryl Ladd.'

'Cheryl Ladd's maiden name was Stopplemore and there is a photo somewhere at home with Kelly standing there with her,' Shawn recollected. 'There were a few actors and actresses that came out. The actress who played the mother in *Bewitched*, Agnes Moorehead, she'd come out to the track a lot because one of her relatives rode. I don't remember his name. I'm sure there were a few others but those are the ones that I remember mostly.'

'We got along really well with Chad,' said Kelly. 'We had no idea who his father was, but when we found out it was real neat. Steve used to run on the "big track" as we used to call it and he was a good motorcyclist. We met and got to know a lot of the Hollywood stars. When we see these people on TV, it's nice to look back and remember that we knew them.'

There was Hollywood interest from Gene Hackman, whose son Christopher also dabbled with motorcycles and there is even a photograph of John Wayne riding a mini-bike. But it was McQueen who shone the movie light for riding motorcycles; his enthusiasm made it cool at a time when bikes and bikers were still associated with violent gangs like the Hells Angels – especially after they mishandled security at a free Rolling Stones' concert in Altamont, northern California in 1969, which became notorious for a fatal stabbing.

However, it was quite an experience visiting the home of a movie star for two boys from what some called the 'Slater Slums' district of Huntington Beach, as Shawn Moran remembered.

'We got to know Chad and Terry pretty good through riding mini-bikes. I guess the dads got talking and they invited us, Kelly and myself, to come over and stay with them at a time that was convenient. The first time we stayed there for two weeks. They lived in Beverly Hills. They had a big house, my God, for a little guy to see that, sheesh … I think they had forty to sixty rooms. His driveway, you'd come up his driveway, it would do a little snake, then you'd travel further on for fifty yards and then you'd get to his gate where you have an intercom to speak into. His gate was like medieval times, not a drawbridge, but it opened up sideways, the wood was that thick – you're not going to get through it! He had maybe a six-car garage and that was full of his Huskies (Husqvarna motorcycles) and he had about eight there. He had a couple of other bikes, but I can't remember their makes. But he did have a limo and a driver.

'We didn't go out much, not out on trips or stuff like that, we mainly stayed at their place. We'd go out to eat but mainly we'd eat there and they had a cook. As Kelly remembered, more so than me, he really enjoyed his meat loaf; I wouldn't say it was his favourite but I think it was the way that she made it. It's not like you were waited on hand and foot; if you wanted a drink or something you'd get your own, but meal time was meal time. Everybody would sit down together. Steve was there and he was married to a lady called Neile [Adams], who was a nice lady.'

McQueen might have enjoyed the trappings that success in Hollywood would bring, but special treatment wasn't extended beyond the grounds of the house, as Shooey recalled.

'We had gone out, Chad, Kelly and myself, to see a movie of Steve's – I don't think Terry came. I can't remember which one it was, but the limo guy took us and we went in the limo. When we got there, Chad said, "You guys have got to pay for yourself!" It was just a standard movie theatre, a walk-in one, and it was like, f★★k – we thought we'd all get in!'

There were times, as Kelly lay there listening to the commotion of hospital life, when he heard some strange noises – some of them body noises! But one, which he swore sounded like a saw (he shuddered to imagine what they could have been doing), reminded him of his junior speedway days.

Having been riding mini-motorcycles in competition, one day in 1972 Tom took them to their first speedway meeting at Costa Mesa. The sport had been through some dormant times, but it was revived to huge success in southern California by Harry Oxley and Jack Milne and this was US speedway's boom period. Tom couldn't have known what that one evening would start.

'We couldn't believe it,' Kelly said later. 'We were used to riding on bikes, but watching guys on 500cc machines with no brakes was something that really excited us. It was real neat and these guys were getting paid for it too. From that moment on, that's all we wanted to do.'

During the interval the pathway to participating in this oval track sport was illustrated to them when Gene Woods, who they had ridden against in mini-bike events, emerged to do a demonstration ride on board a prototype junior speedway machine that had been developed by his brother, Rick, and Ron Stewart. It was powered by a McCulloch engine – which provided that distinctive, chainsaw-like sound.

'It was a little bit scary, though, to watch it,' Shawn admitted. 'Gene was buzzing round there pretty quick. But it was just being there that night because there were so many people and it was so noisy. We didn't get that in mini-bikes. Everybody was spread out, but being in like a baby stadium with everybody – it's a bit loud in here, isn't it?! We thought it was pretty cool, but we were also watching the big guys afterwards and before. It just caught Dad's interest. He ended up getting us a couple of junior bikes and we went from there. We had an interest in it, but it didn't happen until Dad got us the bikes and then we did it. We did a little practice and we ran for four seasons.

'We had our own little association with about fifteen guys in it, so we had matches in between the races and the interval at Costa Mesa, San Berdoo [San Bernardino], and we went to all the tracks that the guys raced at and that was up to five times a week. They had big crowds then, I mean big crowds, 10,000 a night or more.'

Their father acquired junior speedway machines for them both and they became familiar figures racing in support events on California's thriving speedway circuit. They rode Hodaka 100cc powered engines and, as Shawn recalled, it was tough competition.

'Anybody could win. We had standard Hodaka 100s, Lance King had a 210cc and it was called a Triumph Cub – you couldn't go over 210ccs – but he had some horsepower. JJ [Jay] Gianetti, I think he had a McCulloch and this thing sounded like a chainsaw, which was a cool noise. We just had standard stock. We did okay, we weren't the big winners all the time.'

At this point, the Moran family separation was creating hassles for Tom, because when he remarried he became father to three daughters, Kelly-Shannon, Kasey and Kristy. Of course, this meant that he needed to spend time with his young family and trying to juggle that responsibility with those of his sons' became challenging and caused some tension – especially now that his boys were building a racing career. In order to maintain their progress he had to make alternative arrangements and approached Kenny Best, whom Kelly called 'KB'. Best was also a speedway rider and could be found in places like the Indian Dunes practising and just having fun on motorcycles.

'I always liked their dad, I thought he was a pretty nice guy,' said Best. 'He had strong values and he loved those boys. He told me that his new wife said that he was spending too much time with his old family. And back then speedway was five nights a week; junior speedway guys weren't racing five nights but they were racing quite a bit and then there was Saturday and Sunday at the practice tracks. He asked me if I minded taking them to a couple of the race tracks when he couldn't go. I said, sure, so I started loading their bikes with mine and taking them with me and Kelly became like my little brother.'

It's not surprising that junior speedway became so popular, or the mini-bikes, because a scaled-down miniaturised version of what adults were doing appealed to precocious kids who just wanted to grow up fast. Furthermore, when National Champions like Mike Bast and Rick Woods began taking an interest and offering encouragement during race nights, this not only added to the overall show but poured more fuel on their rivalry and, by choosing youngsters of the future to support, that in turn bridged the current era with the up-and-coming one.

'The crowds liked the rivalry between Bast and Woods,' agreed Shawn. 'At the track they would just talk and be around us, to show that they're trying to do something. They couldn't give us pointers because we were on the junior bikes and they were on the big bikes. So they couldn't say, "Hey you've gotta go wide here," it was a different thing, but they hung around us when we were on the track. Lance King was a protégé for Bast and me and Kelly was with Rick Woods. I think it was good for the crowd with Bast and Rick out there with us because they were their favourites.'

This programme gave rise to many of California's future track stars. In fact, Mike Bast sponsored Lance King and he wore identical leathers, albeit in a smaller form. This association method was carried on into the future with Bruce Penhall backing future World Champion Greg Hancock, and they became miniature versions following in the tyre tracks of their supposed tutors.

Kelly's engaging personality, his humour and charm meant that he slipped into California's speedway scene with ease and he was soon accepted by the older pro-riders as one of the guys. The sport in America wasn't taken as seriously as the competition was in Europe; there was no team racing, it was individual and the whole event had a fun atmosphere about it and that was reflected in the stands.

'I can remember being with my heroes like Mike Bast, Danny Becker, Sonny Nutter and Bruce Penhall and all these people, and as a young kid I remember someone offering me a beer because I was one of the boys,' he recalled. 'I looked over at my father and he nodded that it was okay to have one beer and there were all these girls too. I remember thinking, man I wanna be a speedway rider! It was the lifestyle and it was fun.'

Coming to race in Britain was a big step for teenager Kelly. It's doubtful even he anticipated how homesick he would feel and he was especially grateful for Pete Rovazzini's help and companionship, even more so as he lay in a hospital bed waiting for the night to pass over – at least there was someone in this strange land he could depend on. As serious as his injuries were, he couldn't help but think about the ones sustained earlier that year by Belle Vue's Alan Wilkinson, who would never walk again. He pondered that point and came to realise that what they talked about would probably not now come to pass.

Walking again? Now that was a question. He was pretty shocked to think that he may not do so, but as Pete said they weren't having any of it: 'That wasn't an option. Kelly wasn't going to spend his career in a wheelchair or be a flash-in-the-pan. We never entertained the possibility that we weren't coming back, it didn't matter what the doctors said. We had this philosophy, a long life, then you run into a wall, if you allow that problem to stop you then it's a wall, if you don't allow it to stop you it's just a hurdle and that was one of his hurdles. So we never entertained it, we gave it zero attention.'

However, since arriving in England he hadn't lacked attention. Even while lying in hospital supporters sent get well cards and also visited him – in droves; in fact, Pete Rovazzini was stunned by their numbers.

'It was the World Final at Wembley and there was nothing but coaches all lined up around the corner, some had come in cars, but mostly coaches. I remember wondering, what is it with all these people, I couldn't work out what was going on. They were waiting in the hallway to visit him! It was just an amazing experience, and from other teams, not just Hull. That's what got Kelly on the mend, all the cards from all the fans throughout the British League, they just supported him unbelievably.'

Kelly was particularly pleased to see a familiar face from back home – one of his heroes and friends, Danny Becker. However, given the extent of his injuries and the painkillers he needed while his fractures healed, it seems that he could have experienced a morphine moment because although he always insisted that Becker did visit him – and his memory was pretty sharp right to the end – Danny says he did not. A fellow racer, Becker also enjoyed himself off the track, so the foggy haze produced between them presented a moment of confusion where clarity never prevailed.

'He said I did visit him, but I don't remember,' laughed Becker. 'I say I didn't, he said that I did, so I'm glad that he thought that I did – that's all that mattered is that he thought I did – maybe I did! I didn't make it because I got so sick on the plane. We were all drinking and smoking and I got a really bad cold, so I know I didn't go. But he thought that I did; I was tickled pink he always thought that I went and saw him. He must have had too much morphine. My spirit may have floated over to the hospital!'

The 1978 World Final marked the sport's golden anniversary and Scott Autrey became the first American for forty years to finish on a World Championship rostrum when he was third. It was the beginning of a new era and Kelly had the opportunity to be a big part of it – a huge part in fact.

After all the effort and expense that his father had gone to, plus the help and encouragement from people like Rovazzini, KK and 'KB', there was no way he was going to let this setback prevent him from racing. Furthermore, now that he was eighteen, he would be able to compete in the World Championships and for his country.

Later in life, Kelly admitted that recovering from that crash was a 'big thing', but he was determined to prove the doctors wrong and he'd had enough of their hospitality. First of all, following the encouragement he received from his supporters, he felt compelled to pay them back. As the first rays of the morning sun lit up the ward his spirits lifted and his thoughts turned to attending one of the last meetings of the season at Hull – even though he couldn't walk.

# 3

# RIDE THE WHIRLWIND

'Racing's not all about winning, is it? It's about overcoming difficulties.'

John Caffrey, TT motorcycle racer

Once more the telephone rang and even before he answered Peter Rovazzini knew who it would be – an excited and impatient Kelly Moran.

'Pete?'

'Hi Kelly.'

'How long are you gonna be?'

'I've got to sign the paperwork, and I'll be down to pick you up. Don't worry about it.'

The doctor had agreed that Kelly could be discharged so that he could get to the Boulevard for that meeting and he was eager to leave Whipps Cross Hospital. A little while later, though, the phone rang again and Kelly was still fretting.

'Don't forget I need some clothes, I've just got this gown thing.'

'I know, I'll put some in the trunk. Kelly, don't I always make it? Don't I always come through?'

'Yeah.'

'Well, don't worry about it. I'll be there as soon as I can. You can't just walk out of those places, I have to sign these discharge papers, but I'll be there. And I'll bring you some clothes.'

'Thanks Pete.'

As well as he knew him, even Rovazzini didn't reckon on his friend's impulsiveness. After a few hours had passed, the phone rang again and he was staggered by what he heard.

'Pete, bring me some clothes.'

'I've got clothes in the trunk,' he answered wearily.

'No I mean at the race track. I checked myself out and I need some clothes.'

What his friend said didn't quite register at first, and Rovo said: 'Kelly, you've got to wait until I signed the papers before I come down.'

'Screw that, I got tired of waiting so I took a taxi from Hackney to Hull.'

'What?! You're not officially checked out yet!'

'Yeah I am.'

'What clothes do you have?'

'Well you need to bring me some.'

'So where are you now?'

'I told you, I'm at the track and I need some clothes.'

'How did you get to Hull?' Rovo queried, hardly believing what he was hearing.

'I took a cab.'

'Who paid for the cab?'

'I made Ian [Thomas] do it.'

'Did you negotiate it before you left?'

'No. I just told him I needed to get to Hull.'

It was a near-four-hour and 190-mile journey from Hackney to Hull and it's a measure of his willpower that he preferred to endure the aches and pains of being in a cramped car than spend another minute longer than he had to in Whipps Cross. Rovazzini continued: 'He pulled up, got out and it was like a £250 tab and £1 was $2.42 cents then, so it was a $500 cab ride! It was typical Kelly – "Pay the guy!" So I had to take him some clothes because all he was wearing was this robe!'

It must have been comical to see Kelly Moran emerge from the taxi into a wheelchair while wearing little more than a flimsy hospital gown – his racing leathers were cut off him when he arrived in the emergency room. Moreover, such garments were made for convenience rather than comfort, to cover up what was required for decency, and were hardly suitable to wear outside. That didn't bother the little Californian, who threw caution to the wind in his single-minded determination to leave the medical facility behind and be among friends. It was his first step on the comeback road.

Considering that he had been in traction for several weeks, his appearance at Hull was not only courageous but also surprising – in more ways than one. However, he had to take care because he was still in the very early stages of recovery. In particular his back and pelvic injuries were very weak. Nonetheless, in order to address the crowd, he defied doctor's orders.

'He wasn't supposed to get out of that wheelchair but he got up to a standing ovation and waved to everyone,' recalled Pete.

Initially, the sports press reported that he was disappointed that the extent of his injuries had ruled him out of the American round of the 1979 World Championship. His situation was not helped by the unusual date of the US qualifying round – 29 December 1978! This meant that he had a little over two months to recover, so it's not surprising that he felt that his World Championship hopes were dashed.

Only those close to him knew that he planned to take his place in the qualifier after all. Rovazzini revealed that even as he lay in Whipps Cross, with limited movement, that qualifier was a goal for him. 'We were already planning what we were going to do for Santa Ana,' he said. Therefore, with little or no information emerging in the press about his progress, it was surprising to say the least to see the little Californian roll up at the Santa Ana Bowl to take his place. While he was handicapped by his lack of fitness, with only the top two scorers qualifying for the next round, he faced a tough task on and off the track. Furthermore, he'd only been a professional for two seasons and joined far more experienced riders of international and national standard.

To describe the meeting as chaotic would be an understatement. Scott Autrey, who had finished third in the world, was so angered by the fact that the event didn't adhere to FIM standards (the World's governing body) that he sacrificed his own championship chances and walked out in protest over the organisation of the meeting. Although he did compete, Bruce Penhall was also reluctant to contest such an important meeting on a track that was less than world-class. 'I remember not wanting to go back for the qualifier because they didn't have a proper track,' he said.

Even though it was a World Championship round, FIM rules only partly governed the event. Steve Gresham and Bruce Penhall clashed in one race and the latter fell while Gresham went on to win the race. Later, Gresham was disqualified while Penhall was awarded a point when, under FIM rules, the race should have been re-run. Livid over the decision to remove his points, Gresham appealed to the AMA over the mishandling of the affair.

America's premier motorcycle paper, *Cycle News*, totally disregarded any controversy; the fact that the nation's leading rider refused to ride and others were dissatisfied completely passed by its journalist, Ken Kellogg, who enthused, 'The track was in outstanding condition … best racing of the 1978 season.'

Kelly, though, had other thoughts occupying his mind, not least managing the pain but also being competitive because he hadn't gone to these lengths merely to make up the numbers. World Championship rounds could be ruthless because they would bring the best and the worst out of the riders. Some competitors would look for any sign of weakness that they could exploit in order to gain an advantage over their rivals – both mechanically and psychologically. Mindful of this, Rovo was keen not to reveal the full extent of Moran's fragile state.

'I was standing close to him to make sure that no one knew what we were up to because he was hobbling around,' he recalled. 'We had our own people there. I prepped the motorcycles, but he couldn't do any practice because the week before we weren't sure whether he would make it, but he kept saying, "I'll make it." So we really went to the practice and just kinda put the bikes together and ran them there.'

By the time the action got underway he had to be lifted on and off his bike, which was pretty hard to conceal. For the people in the stands, though, there was little to suggest that this rider in white leathers was struggling with his fitness. The last thing he needed was a fall, so hearts missed a beat among his crew when he was forced to lay down his machine to avoid the fallen Penhall.

From the outset, Moran was in the leading pack; in fact, he was the lead scorer at one stage. After five heats and twenty races, Kelly had amassed 12 points and found himself in a run-off to decide first place, the two qualifiers and reserve for the next round. He lined up alongside Mike Bast, Gresham and Bobby Schwartz.

Tom Moran was also present and in one report it was stated that he was lifting his son on and off his machine. As the meeting continued, Kelly's strength was ebbing away, but somehow he had to draw on his last reserves of energy for one last blast for a World Championship place.

Initially, Gresham led, but his machine reared wildly and deposited him onto the track and he was out of the running. Meanwhile, Schwartz took the lead and never looked back and, briefly, Kelly held that all-important second place – one report said he led before falling – but Bast passed Moran and booked his place in the next round at London's White City with Kelly third.

Although obviously disappointed, third place and a reserve spot for the Intercontinental Final was quite an achievement when you consider that it was only a few months previously that he was told that he might not walk again, never mind race. Moreover, after competing in five races, perhaps that extra outing was a race too far and had he been fully fit it's debatable whether Bast would have passed him.

'He was exhausted,' said Rovazzini. 'It takes a lot out of you when you haven't been riding for so long, never mind being injured, so he was really tired by the end of the night.'

However, his World Championship dream wasn't over just yet …

As well as Rovazzini, Ian Thomas was also in attendance. He had some stern views on the whole scene in America, believing that its 'Mickey Mouse rules' would lead to its ruination. In the meantime, he was pleased to see Kelly perform so well. 'The way he picked riders off from the back without any fence scraping was colossal,' he praised. He also reported that his star wanted to return to

England right away but he advised him to remain in the sun on the west coast to aid his recovery.

What Thomas didn't know was that if fate had been kinder during the sport's Golden Jubilee year in the UK, things could have been very different and the exciting Moran wouldn't have been lining up at Hull at all in 1979.

'Kelly wasn't going to go back to Hull that next year,' said Rovo. 'Eric Boocock and Alan Wilkinson [Belle Vue Aces captain] would come and watch Kelly ride – Alan loved watching him. So us four had a meeting. Alan was an exemplary man – he was a man's man. I remember him at the bar and he looked across at Kelly and said, "You know what, you've got too much talent. You're going to live at my house, you're going to learn how to work on these bikes, you're going to get up in the morning, have your Wellingtons on, and we're going to take this talent and turn it into something." He looked at me and added, "Some days you're going to want to go home, but you're not going to go home." Wilkie had something that nobody else had. Kelly didn't really respect Ivan, but he respected Wilkie. That would have been the answer to our prayers.

'He was going to live at Wilkie's and he was going to teach him [Kelly] to work on his bikes and kick his ass! He thought he had the most talent he'd ever seen. If Wilkie hadn't ended up getting hurt, he would have ended up riding for Belle Vue and he would have kept his thumb on top of him. That's something that no one knows, only Eric, Wilkie, myself and Kelly. That all happened before Wilkie and Kelly got hurt – that was the deal. Just think what Kelly's career would have been like.'

It's debatable whether Wilkinson would have managed to get him to focus on the sport 100 per cent. After all, Wilkie would also have to concentrate on his own career because he was the Aces' captain at that time. Furthermore, having his wings clipped would only work for so long. Like any bird in a cage of some kind, Kelly would soon flap in frustration and he could get very belligerent and stubborn should his way to freedom be continually blocked. Granted, all the elements were there to turn the youngster into a dominant force to rival Mauger or Penhall because he was young, he was talented and he was still maturing. Although many more would try mentoring him and a few experienced some success, they all failed to turn him into the focussed racer that they perceived he should be. That wasn't Kelly; and to do it meant changing his personality and he was having too much fun to do that.

So it was back to Hull; but this time he had a new mechanic, Bernard Harrison, who had previously worked with Barry Briggs and other Vikings riders. Pete Rovazzini was still involved but he needed to concentrate on his business at home, so the day-to-day upkeep of his machines was handled by the very capable Harrison. 'I told Ian Thomas for that second year that Kelly needed a mechanic and Bernard was good,' said Rovazzini.

There were other changes too. Kelly had a new team-mate, fellow American Dennis Sigalos, who was having his first season in the British League; and he had new accommodation in a village called Easington, which was approximately forty-five minutes away from Hull's stadium. Located between the Humber estuary and the North Sea, Easington was around 6 miles from Spurn Point (or Spurn Head), which was a narrow three-and-a-half-mile sand spit on the tip of the coast. Its dangers to shipping were alerted by a distinctive black and white lighthouse, which provided inspiration for one of his quips, 'It's pretty bleak after California, but it does bring a regular spot of light into my life!'

He would be living with the Chapman family in a spacious house called Wheatcroft with grounds and accommodation for his machinery. Veronica Chapman recalled: 'My friend was the secretary for the Hull Vikings and her name was Lesley Sharp and she said that they had this young rider coming from California and we'd like him to stay with a family. I'd never been to speedway before in my life until Kelly and Dennis Sigalos came to live with us – I sometimes wonder if I was the lucky one or not! I'd always gone to see the bike racing at Oliver's Mount and Brands Hatch, people like Mick Grant and Barry Sheene.'

Perhaps the Hull bosses thought that locating Kelly in a rural part of East Riding would isolate him sufficiently to cut down on his wild antics. The chances are that was part of their idea, but placing him with a family provided him with a structured environment, a home from home, and he settled in right away.

'He fitted in well with village life, everybody liked him and anybody would help him out – he was well loved. You know what villages are like, it's quite hard to fit in sometimes,' said Veronica. 'He loved all that kind of food that I made on the range, stews, rice puddings, etc.; he had quite a good appetite. We had a big garden – you could put a JCB in there and not see it, it was that big. There were stables and they were made into sheds, and then there were these two out-sheds. They had seven racing bikes and I used to help clean their leathers – I was left to clean Kelly's leathers, make sure he got showered and had a meal before he went to the track. He was just a young, young boy at heart.'

On the eve of the season it was announced that Hull had clinched a sponsorship deal with car manufacturers, Lada. It was claimed that they were the first 'fully sponsored' team in the British League. The deal was arranged through Satra Motors of Bridlington and Thomas announced that should the team win the league title the championship would be worth 'thousands of pounds to the riders in bonuses'. Furthermore, it was also stated that their US duo, Moran and Sigalos, would receive Lada cars to drive during the season – a decision that the Vikings management would later regret!

Despite the constraints of the 50-point limit that governed the strength of British League sides, the Vikings team hadn't altered too much from the one that Kelly had signed for the year before. Clearly, not much needed to be changed because, despite the loss of their injured stars, Moran and Joe Owen, the Vikings still finished third in the league– their highest position up to that point. Therefore, the arrival of Sigalos was the only addition to the team that was still spearheaded by Mauger. Thomas was able to negate the effects of the points limit during the early part of the campaign by dropping one of his preferred team members on a rotation basis and replacing him with one of the club's No.8 riders, Robbie Blackadder or Rod Hunter. This meant that once the serious business of league competition began, the Vikings were at full strength, a cunning strategy that should have paid off.

The American invasion had really started in earnest in 1979 because as well as Sigalos at Hull, Bobby Schwartz had joined Cradley Heath and one of Kelly's closest friends, Ron Preston, had joined Poole on the south coast. Later in the year more Americans would appear, with Steve Columbo joining Birmingham and Tommy Morley appearing at Sheffield.

The arrival of Sigalos alongside Moran only enhanced the team spirit, as Owen explained: 'The Yanks had a different attitude to the rest of us. Before a race, he would wish us luck and all that and it was great, because we never got that team spirit before the Yanks came. He was a lovely guy, Kelly, he really was.'

And there was some fun too with Siggy in the team, as Moran remembered: 'We would wear a cod piece for protection but Siggy forgot to put his on when he got changed. When he realised he never had time to put it on under his leathers, so he taped it over the top instead. He went out to race and I was watching from the steps when I saw something fly off his bike. It was a wet meeting and I wondered what it could be, because it didn't look mechanical – it looked kinda weird. It turned out to be his protector. He came round again and ran over it!'

This was Sigalos' first trip to England and, like many, having Mauger as a teammate was one of the attractions, but so too was being in the same team as another Californian. If Dennis was hoping that he'd show him the ropes, he wasn't going to be disappointed. In fact, he got his first experience of Britain, Moran-style, during his first days in the country.

'We both had our cars and Kelly said that we were going to go to Taffy Owen's place to get our bikes,' said Sigalos. 'I forget which motorway it was, and Kelly was driving fast and I didn't know what the hell was happening at that time, so I was just following him. It was cold and snowy and I noticed in the motorway there were signs lit up that explained that it was going to go from three lanes down to one. So I was like, okay, and Kelly was still in the outside lane, or the fast lane, and he was just hauling butt, we must have been going 80–90 mph. Then all of a sudden,

I realised that those signs do mean that three lanes are going to go down to one. There was snow in two of the lanes and the third lane was snowy as well, but you had to filter on down into that single lane. Kelly had just passed another vehicle, got in front of him, but then span out! Then the guy he had just passed jammed on the brakes, so then I had nowhere to go and bashed right into the back of him. I span out and we ended up about five feet apart when we came to rest. I'd punched a hole in the radiator. So now it was snowing, Deborah [girlfriend and future wife] was covered up in a blanket, sitting in the front seat and she couldn't believe what was happening, we were cold and the car was leaking radiator fluid everywhere. So what are we gonna do? Well, let's get back into the car and continue on!

'We ended up getting to Taffy's by adding water every so often and we got the bikes and that was my first experience in England! Going along with Kelly I knew it was going to be an experience because I knew him from before, back home, so I knew he was a bit of a wild child. Everyone has a wild streak in them, but I found out the hard way that maybe I shouldn't listen to Kelly so much and do my own thing,' he laughed.

It was around this time that news started to cross the Atlantic that Mike Bast was a doubtful traveller to England for the World Championship round. However, it was pointed out that efforts were being made to provide him with the facilities he was seeking to practise and acclimatise in the UK before making his decision.

Despite his impressive performance at the Santa Ana Bowl there were still question marks over what effect Kelly's multiple injuries could have on him. Some riders never recover their spark following such a heavy crash and their confidence can take a massive hammering when they return to the heat of competition. Even though seven months had passed since the smash, so severe were his injuries that some wondered if he was yet fully recovered. Such concerns were heightened by the fact that he was absent from the USA team that raced a five-match series against the Rest of the World in California – brother Shawn did race and he top-scored with 15 at Ascot.

Britain's cool and damp spring was affecting Kelly and he was suffering from spinal arthritis. Veronica also witnessed him labouring with the legacy of his Hackney crash. 'I can remember him lying on the floor, in the lounge in front of the fire, and he used to ask Dennis to stand on his back. He did have problems with his back. He always had something going on with his body, but he was really broad, had a good physique and he must have been quite strong to be able to manoeuvre a bike like he did.'

There didn't seem to be much to worry about though. By April he was scoring double figures and on a few occasions he was within a point of his first maximum in the BL. That milestone score did come, first of all in the Inter-League Four Team Championship on 16 May, then he recorded a paid maximum in a cup match at Sheffield on 1 June before finally scoring his first 12-pointer in the league at home to Eastbourne on 11 July. Without doubt, he was no longer the promising young American; he was now producing spectacular performances that often outshone Mauger.

Several reasons contributed to his breakthrough to heat leader status: his renewed determination, a year's worth of experience behind him and, vitally, the mechanical expertise of Bernard Harrison.

Bernard's son, Richard, remembered a desperate phone call at the start of the season, which heralded the beginning of their relationship. 'I can remember my dad getting a phone call from Siggy when Kelly arrived. Hull had supplied him with two bikes but they wouldn't run and this was literally the evening before the Wednesday when they were going to race. I always remember driving with him to Veronica's late one night and we started these bikes up and neither one of them would run, they were just popping and banging. I know the guy who built them but it wasn't his fault that they didn't run. My dad took the engines out, worked on them, took them back and Kelly raced them. He used to do the whole lot. He had a full-time job – we both did. We used to come home, have our tea and [go] straight into the workshop. We'd wash the bikes, prepare them and Kelly just used to ride them. I don't believe he prepared any bikes. He was always lucky that someone did them for him – he'd ride anything.'

'I didn't really know much at that time about the gearing and what set-ups I needed,' Kelly said. 'If I came in and said that the bike's rear tyre was spinning too much in the middle of the corner, I wouldn't really know if I needed to reduce the tyre pressure, change the sprocket, or whatever. But Bernard knew and I learned a lot from him. I always had good, competitive bikes.'

Veronica noticed that Harrison's role was crucial to Kelly's success. 'My husband, Adrian, was an engineer and he used to help Kelly a bit with his machinery, but Bernard was a godsend. Kelly didn't want to do much; I'd say he didn't know a lot about bikes but he knew how to ride them.'

Bernard also tuned his machines as well. The age of the engine tuner that the sport lives with today hadn't yet arrived; although there were special parts and works sponsorship deals for people like Mauger and Olsen, the technical side wasn't as specialised as it is now. Kelly raced Weslake machines and although Harrison did the very best he could for him, it's unlikely that his engines were anything other than standard stock. What he may have lacked in technology, though, he was able to compensate for with his talent.

That raw talent was something to behold and, although his lack of technical feedback was frustrating, his ignorance of mechanical issues could also prove very costly for a racer who was still on a meagre budget, as Harrison revealed.

'The times he used to come in and the big end was knocked out and we used to say, "Kelly, can't you hear it rattling?" "No." When he'd blow up an engine he'd blow it to smithereens because he just kept running it. He just didn't have that technical know-how – it was just drop the clutch and go!'

For all his antics, Kelly was easy to get along with and enjoyable to work for and Bernard enjoyed his work. 'They had a good rapport and had some fun, although he didn't always agree with him because he thought he could have been better,' said Richard of his father's association with Moran. 'He knew how good he was and with just a little bit more dedication he would have been higher up the tree. We'd put a lot of hours in and it was like, hang on a minute, you're out partying and we're in the workshop until 10 to 12 o'clock at night! But my dad never actually had words with him. He just used to say to him, "Look you shouldn't be doing this and you shouldn't be doing the other." If anyone wanted to go out the night before then that's up to them. I've seen them both racing in a state, injured and still racing – they just had too much natural talent. Shawn has told me that he wouldn't turn the clock back and do anything different than what he has done and I think Kelly would have been the same.'

After juggling the line-up during the opening months of the season, Hull began to get into their stride when the league campaign started. With Sigalos as the new kid at reserve, Moran found himself in the main body of the team and would often ride with Joe Owen.

'He was a bugger to ride with because he was so light, and he had such speed coming out of the corners,' said Joe. 'I probably weighed twice as much as him. And on a 500cc bike, it's a big difference. He must have weighed no more than seven stone but he had a lot of strength – a lot of muscles. He had terrific balance and with him being so small he could hang off the bike. You wonder how a little guy like that could get any drive; with him being so light, there was no weight on the bike whatsoever and hanging off the bike as well … he was always riding on the outside in the dirt. He was amazing and probably the nearest we've seen to a Peter Craven.

'There were a lot of funny times with Kelly and there was one particular incident when he had finished a race. He was doing a lap of honour and Patsy, the tea girl, was bringing a cup of tea to Ian Thomas and Bryan Larner on a tray. Kelly was doing this almighty wheelie and she was walking across the track with this tray and they almost collided. He was coming around on his back wheel and at the last minute he flicked the engine off and laid it down. Tea, tray and cups went everywhere! He had pretty quick reactions, no matter what state he was in.'

Kelly's unique talent on board a speedway machine meant that he could push the limits more than most riders. His skill allowed him to run up close, almost touching his opponents which frightened them, especially as he wasn't quite the finished article himself and was testing the boundaries, which was illustrated by his number of falls. While his team-mates and some of his fellow countrymen were well aware of his ability, others were not, including vastly more experienced riders who viewed him as a bit of a danger.

'The thing was that everyone was afraid of him because he rode so close,' observed Rovazzini. 'Kelly would ride right up to your leathers, touch the lettering on your leathers, but never ride hard. He'd never ever deliberately knock anybody off. One time at Hull he went through a tiny gap, I looked at him and said, "What the heck was that? That was brilliant!" "Yeah I saw it, I had a choice, I was either going to shut off or go for it," he replied. "How did you not knock everyone off into a big ball?" "Oh, I got there and just lifted up my handlebars and went through the hole." He just went through the gap as he popped a wheelie, pulled up the handlebars and lifted them to squeeze through because he knew that he would get the drive. He did that so that he wouldn't hit the other rider's handlebars.'

In 2005, when asked who the hardest rider was he'd raced against, Kelly recalled an incident at Swindon that not only underlined the hostility that the team sometimes faced from the opposition but also marked the occasion when the top riders, at the very least, recognised that the Californian was a rare talent.

'I remember Phil Crump coming hard under me – hard, but fair. Then I returned the compliment, but I knocked his arm or something. This was before you looked back to acknowledge a rider after a race, so I just returned to the pits. My mechanic then was Pete, and when I came in he looked across at Crumpie and saw him take off his helmet and head toward us. Pete picked up a wrench and said, "Be ready." I looked at him and thought, what? Crumpie was a big guy, very strong, and he came over to where Pete was standing with this wrench and he just extended his hand to me and said, "Well done." And boy did he have a strong handshake! Crumpie was a tough rider but he was fair and totally cool.'

Having a couple of speedway riders stay – Dennis would move into a place of his own at Withernsea before the season ended – the Chapman family went along to the speedway to watch the Hull Vikings and support their adopted boys.

'Sometimes when I used to go to meetings my heart was beating, especially if there were races that Kelly was in that he had to win,' said Veronica. 'I used to put my hands over my eyes, I just dared not look. With Dennis, he was the solid one, but Kelly wasn't at all. Every time he rode he'd go on one wheel and to the outside – that was his style.'

Following a meeting at the Boulevard he would go home with the Chapmans unless he was too sparked-up from the night's action, or had a tempting offer elsewhere. However, after giving his all for the Vikings, he had an unconventional travelling arrangement that showed his sometimes off-the-wall approach to life.

'I went to a lot of the away meetings except right down south like Eastbourne,' said Veronica. 'Whenever he rode away we always used to come home and Kelly always slept all the way – in the boot! He would always get into the boot with a blanket and have a sleep because he was just exhausted. I remember one day I had to stop at my friend's place in Hull because I was desperate for the loo. I knocked on the door and I said, "June, I'm desperate for the loo," and there was this banging coming from inside the boot and June says, "Who the hell's in that boot?!" "Oh it's only Kelly." We opened it up and he popped his head out and I said: "It's okay, we've only stopped for the toilet!" You had to have that kind of whacky humour to understand him and I think he came to the right family with us. A normal family would never understand it and because I had always gone to sea with my husband – I was a senior hostess with the P&O Group, so I had always worked in a man's environment – I had that understanding.'

Veronica had taken to Kelly, 'mothered him' said Richard Harrison, but that was understandable. For all his fun-loving ways, he was still an eighteen-year-old teenager and he was charming, polite and helpful – and she enjoyed his sometimes zany humour.

'There was always a party going on where Kelly was,' she smiled. 'He lived for the day and I used to tell him to be careful with money, but you couldn't tell him. And he had so many hangers-on. He did like to enjoy himself and he was lovely. He was like a little boy at heart. He always used to call me Billie Jean King because of those spectacles she used to wear. He used to say, "Here comes Billie Jean," he always had names for people, didn't he? I really understood him and if I went to bed early he would come and sit on the edge of my bed, like children do, and talk about his home, his girlfriend at that time, Marice. He would open up his heart and he was very sincere. After half an hour he'd give me a hug and say, 'Goodnight Veron,' and then go to his own room.

'He had a nice home with us and my husband was really good and supportive. There were a couple of acres of land and we had a sit-on lawn mower and they [Kelly and Dennis] used to cut the lawns for us and were like one of the family. He wasn't brought up with money in the same way as Bruce Penhall or Dennis was. I think this is why everyone helped him a lot, because he was just a genius on a motorcycle – he could do anything with it.'

He also charmed the locals and they were used to seeing him around. His habit of making use of whatever was available for his own convenience provided them with a comical sight as he travelled the short distance to the local pub, the White Horse Inn. Often wearing his red Bell Helmet's jacket, he was sat astride a bicycle that was really too small for him, but it was accessible transportation and, like most two-wheeled machines, he adapted to it.

'The amount of people who said they had seen Kelly going to the pub riding my daughter, Renee's, bicycle!' Chapman giggled. 'One day she was looking all over for it and she came in crying and said, "Mummy, Mummy, I can't find my bicycle." I thought, I know where it would be. So I went down to the pub and it was stood outside the pub! I can just imagine him riding down to the pub on Renee's bicycle. Those bicycles were only for children of four or five years old. He used to do all sorts of tricks on it though. The children used to stand outside watching him. He used to go down the road on one wheel and things like that.'

One night, Moran had an unconventional lift home from the White Horse, as Sigalos related: 'I gave him a ride back on the hood of my car! He wouldn't get in, so he jumped on the hood, kissing the windshield, doing Kelly things, and I turned the wiper blades on to try and get him off, but no he was just going to hang on. It was only a quarter mile to Veronica's, very close, so I thought I would do something funny. I came into the driveway, made a hard right turn, grabbed the handbrake and so we'd slide sideways and Kelly went rolling off the hood, down into the little gully that was in front of her house. Then I thought, oh shit, maybe I shouldn't have done that, I could have hurt him. Then he just jumped right up and said, "Hey Siggy that was cool, that was the greatest!" He didn't get hurt at all and we're all laughing.'

The unwelcome sound of rain drops repeatedly tapping on a sea of umbrellas was not what anyone wanted to hear or see as four nations – the hosts England, Australia, New Zealand and the USA – gathered together at Reading's Smallmead Stadium for the first qualifying round of World Team Cup. Despite the inclement weather, a big crowd had assembled, which delayed Bobby Schwartz.

'It was pouring with rain and there was a whole queue of people trying to get into the stadium on that road; it was backed up all the way back to the motorway nearly. I was s******g myself thinking we're going to be late, or we're not even going to make it. I'd finally got in there and they're having a meeting in the dressing room with a Swedish referee, Christer Bergstrom, and he goes, "On the continent we ride in the rain, so today we ride in the rain." That's what he said, so I had to get my bike off the back of the car, get into the pit area, there was no parade, and that was the first time ever I saw the Reading track.'

Leading the Kiwis' challenge was Ivan Mauger, who was none too impressed with the authorities' stance. 'I was disgusted with the attitude of officials who told us to get changed at 2.45pm when it was pouring with rain. With an English referee it would have been called off; a league match would not be run in those conditions.

A one-off meeting abroad might have been run, but I don't think one of such importance would have been.'

Twelve months after he was prevented from riding because he was too young, Kelly Moran was set to make his debut for the USA. But the Americans were not at full strength because they were weakened by the absence of their number one rider, Scott Autrey, who the AMA had snubbed because of his walk-out in the American Final. Therefore, the side featured Bruce Penhall, Steve Gresham, Kelly and Schwartz, with the inexperienced Sigalos at reserve, and they were managed by Englishman John Scott.

The soaking conditions that turned the circuit into a slimy mudbath would be a great leveller. With only the two highest-scoring countries progressing to the semi-finals, it was sure to be a tight contest.

For Kelly, it was an opportunity to show the world what he was a capable of among such a strong field of international riders and, with the Stars and Stripes on his chest, he splashed his way past England's Peter Collins for a win in his first race. After four races, the Yanks held a 2-point lead over New Zealand, while the hosts were 6 points adrift of the leaders in third. Kelly's engine failure while lying second to Mitch Shirra stemmed America's charge and when Gresham fell in the next race the Kiwis edged into the lead.

New Zealand took control and it became a battle between England and America for the all-important runner's-up place, with the Australians also determined to get in on the act and spoil the party. When England's Peter Collins slid off in heat 14, Schwartz's second place meant that Moran had the opportunity to clinch his nation's place in the next round – all he had to do was finish ahead of England's Gordon Kennett.

Australia's Billy Sanders took the lead, but Moran turned inside to grab first place and a clear vision, while Kennett determinedly followed his rival onto the back straight. What followed was a titanic battle that illustrated the skill and determination of both riders. Kennett pressured the little American and on the third lap astonished the TV commentator, Dave Lanning when, in the middle of the first corner, he took his hand off the handlebar and pulled down his face mask to see where he was going. As they hit the third corner, for some reason Kelly removed his helmet colour, all within inches of each other on the slippery surface. The Englishman attacked the American on the inside but just received a face-full of slimy dirt for his trouble, which must have felt like suet pudding. Kennett's challenge was over while Kelly was welcomed back to the pits as a hero.

Penhall, who was suffering from flu that afternoon, viewed a returning Kennett to the pits. 'He was completely soaked from being behind him; he came in and he was completely mudded out. Kelly was the man that day. He was tremendous.

I'll never forget that. I remember I made a good start and headed into the first corner, and the handlebar came out of my hand because it was so muddy and wet, and down I went.'

History was made on that Sunday afternoon in May and a new era had commenced. It was the first time that the USA had qualified from that round; England's elimination in conditions that were seemingly better suited to them than the sunshine nations that formed their opposition, indicated that, although more success would follow, they'd slipped from the sport's highest peak; and the first spark of a rivalry was ignited with their transatlantic cousins. More importantly, Kelly Moran had announced his triumphant arrival on the international stage – thus strengthening his case for the World Championship spot should Bast withdraw.

He top-scored with 8 points in the next round in Sweden, but this time the USA finished third behind the winners New Zealand and Denmark and were eliminated. However, Kelly's international engagements were not over yet. He was paired with Penhall in the World Pairs Championship and they travelled to Ljubljana – then Communist Yugoslavia, now the capital of Slovenia – for their semi-final qualifier. New Zealand was also drawn in that meeting and Ivan Mauger recalled Kelly's laid-back approach during practice.

'He came into the pits and the engine was making a rough noise. Anyway, he's really laid-back, couldn't care less, as long as it was running and the piston was going up and down, he didn't seem to think anything of it. The others around said that the engine was bad and it should be changed. So they changed it the next day. It was a Weslake engine, and the engine they put in, the 'W' and Weslake was all written in red paint. Kelly rode in the meeting and afterwards we were all sitting around having a meal, me, Kelly, Bruce, Briggo (Barry Briggs) and a few other guys, when someone happened to say: "Wasn't it a good job we changed Kelly's engine." And Kelly said, "You know, I can't remember having any red paint on it, like Weslake being written in red." He hadn't even noticed they had changed it!'

That was one of the few occasions that Penhall and Moran raced together as a pair. Bruce found his buddy to be very accommodating when it came to agreeing on a strategy for the race.

'We both kind of liked riding the outside, but he didn't mind where he rode or what starting position. I'd go up to him and say, "Kelly, how about I go off of one or two?" and he'd go, "Take whatever you want." He didn't care what gate position he had, he cared because he wanted to do well, but you weren't going to have a problem with him on race day. The only other thing about him was, if he popped out in front of you a little bit, even though he was a great team rider, you had to keep your eye on him because he was all over the motorcycle. He was fluid, pretty much predictable, but at times he would get out into the dirt, lift the motorcycle and it was like, "Hang on Kelly, get it down, back it in," and he would every time. So, unlike Schwartz, who was so predictable, you knew exactly where he was going to be at all times, Kelly was a little bit different, but you knew he was going to perform.'

America scored 23 points (Penhall 14 and Moran 9) to finish third behind Poland and New Zealand and booked their place in their country's first World Pairs Final. Unfortunately, injury prevented him from competing with Penhall in the final. In fact, Bruce flew the US flag as the country's lone representative because a strike at Heathrow Airport prevented Steve Gresham from replacing him in the meeting.

Kelly's injury occurred while he was chasing Les Collins for the lead when he clipped his back wheel as he crossed the finish line. He was sent cartwheeling down the track for fifty yards at frightening speed and thumped into the fence. Many concerned faces greeted him as he was helped from the Boulevard track and whisked off to hospital for X-rays. In the main they were worried that he may have aggravated the extensive injuries he'd received the previous year, especially when he complained of pain from his hip. Happily it was nothing more than bruising and he was ordered to rest for two weeks – he was back a week later when he registered a paid maximum.

Unfortunately, not only did that injury rule him out of a World Pairs Final appearance, but he also missed Hull's victory in the Inter-league Four Team Championship at Sheffield. Moreover, the Vikings were third in the league table with matches in hand over leaders Coventry, and it was the American's performances that went a long way in making the Yorkshire side real contenders for the title.

He was running an 8.76 average at the time of his fall and his never-say-die style of racing and his poor starting meant that he was an inspiration to his team-mates and, of course, a big favourite with the supporters. Graham Drury believed he was an excellent team-mate.

'He was a team man and very safe on the track, you always knew where he was. I wish I had some of the ability to get into some of the positions that he had and be able to get out of them unscathed. He had such natural ability – he was unbelievable.'

Down time meant opportunities for fun for the happy-go-lucky Californian. And he'd involve his friends in these times as well, as Drury recalled.

'We had a meeting on a Wednesday and then Sheffield on the Thursday. So I stayed over that night and worked on my bikes at Hull on the Thursday morning. Kelly came round and says: "What are you doing for the rest of the day?"

"Not much really, it's not worth setting off for Sheffield until late afternoon.""Do you want to come Lada racing with me?" I said:"You what?""We go Lada racing when we've got some spare time." I didn't know what that meant, so he said, "Come with me and I'll show you."

'Lada wasn't the best make of cars in the world in those days, but they got us about. What they used to do was go to Beverley where there were these big sand dunes and he said,"Right, jump into the passenger seat." And he went careering around the sand dunes in this car. I said to him,"If Ian Thomas could see you now, he'd go mental.""Oh," he said,"it don't matter, he'll never know about it." So there was me and him going like the clappers, and you can imagine that the sand was going everywhere and getting into everything on the vehicle – he lived life to the full.'

The beach wasn't the only place where 'Lada racing' took place. Bobby Beaton told Richard Bott of another opportunity that came their way on the road.

'Dennis (Sigalos) said he had a millionaire uncle who had a big house near Cradley Heath and that we could borrow it for the weekend after the meeting at Dudley Wood. It was a massive eighteenth-century mansion with stained-glass windows and full of antique furniture. All three of us had sponsored Ladas by then and we had a stock car race in a field behind the house after taking a load of people back for a party on a Saturday night.'

Thomas may have got a clue as to what sort of treatment the Lada was receiving in the hands of the unruly Moran when he would joke among his team-mates, 'Them Lada cars rally quite well!' In fact, the Russian motors were put through a kind of road test that could be described as ahead of its time. It was just as well that they were built strongly even if their design was basic.

'There were plenty of winding roads around Withernsea and the Spurn Point area where we both lived with Veronica,' said Sigalos. 'When I moved out of Veronica's house from Easington into Withernsea there was a real nice stretch of road there, lots of lefts and rights, and it was like our built-in race track, from my house to hers, or my house to Kelly's house on the beach down there. We had a lot of fun and a lot of racing banging around in those cars and actually, they handled it pretty well, I must admit!' he laughed.

'I think Ian made the mistake of letting us go ahead and get some radial tyres and a leather steering wheel and then of course, there was a lot more speed involved because the car wouldn't slide as much, but we could make a good time out of anything.'

As well as living at Wheatcroft, Kelly had also managed to acquire a caravan to dwell in on the beach. It wasn't quite the blue seas and sandy white beaches of Huntington Beach, but the grey skies and choppy sea did provide a bleak romanticism.

Marice Supry recalled that the strong wind provided Kelly with plenty of updrafts to fly a kite.

Nevertheless, it wasn't all passion in the caravan facing the North Sea. Rick Kelly, who had known Moran since he was twelve, flew over to help him during the summer. He recalled an argument between the two young lovers, which resulted in the racer putting his hand through a glass partition. Rick had to rush him to hospital for stitches in a badly cut hand. During another disagreement with Marice, he managed to snap the steering wheel of the beleaguered Lada! Mostly, though, they were having fun and the short journey from Veronica's home to Spurn Point brought Moran's racing instinct into a competition with a bus.

'He decided to play chicken with a tour bus,' smiled Dennis. 'The roads around there were narrow and I don't know what came over him to do this, to split the lanes and go half and half, on one side to the other, but the bus didn't move and it ended up clipping him, or he clipped the bus or the bus clipped him, but he spun out, crashed and ended up driving the car down into the ditch and then walked into his trailer house from there. Then he called the police and said that his car was stolen. Well they came down to investigate and they followed his footprints from his car to his trailer! And they go, "Well oh my, look at this, there's footprints coming from your car back to your trailer, are you sure it was stolen?" I don't think he really got into trouble although I know that Ian was awfully upset with him, about wrecking the car and not manning up to what actually happened. Nevertheless, they got him another one and off he went.'

He would push the car to its limit and beyond, so much so that bits of the vehicle were flying off due to the vibration. Of course, it should be pointed out that Kelly still didn't have a drivers' licence, not that this seemed to prevent him from getting behind the wheel in order to get to his destination. There was, though, an incident that Veronica remembered that could have brought an end to the Lada's traumatic life.

'He drove a car like a tractor. During the early days, when he first arrived, he hadn't yet found his bearings. One night he came home, missed our gate, turned right and kept on going and finished up at Spurn Point. He said, "Veron, there was lots of water," and I said: "Yes, because it was the bloody North Sea, Kelly!" He was on the sand thinking, oh there's lots and lots of water.'

Long journeys to away meetings meant long stretches of time when idle minds proved a haven for the devil's work. Journalist Richard Bott shared this story from Bobby Beaton.

'Kelly, Dennis and me travelled down to London for a meeting in a sponsored Lada with our bikes in a trailer. I was driving and Dennis asked if I would mind going past Buckingham Palace because he had never seen it. I said, "No problem," but as we were driving past the palace, Kelly suddenly stuck his legs through the sunroof, farted and set fire to it with a cigarette lighter. The methane gas ignited and the flame set fire to the dashboard.'

Nevertheless, if anyone needed convincing that Kelly Moran had made the jump into international status, then that was confirmed when he finished third in Hull's big individual tournament, the Yorkshire TV Trophy. The field consisted of five World finalists, plus emerging talents like Penhall, Schwartz and Kenny Carter. The meeting was won by Mauger, who scored a maximum, with Michael Lee second, whom Kelly defeated during the event.

Mauger was setting the standard and, especially at Hull, he was the benchmark. But Moran and his crew hadn't forgotten how the help that was promised hadn't materialised. Furthermore, financially speaking, he wasn't getting the rewards his scores deserved. Therefore, when super-professional Ivan had a dig at the American's approach, he received a response that illustrated a side of his character that didn't come to the surface very often.

Rovazzini: 'Ivan came over and said to Kelly, "You need to start doing more practice here." Kelly turned around, looked at him, and replied: "Ivan, I'll go practice, you wanna give me a motorcycle and give me the money to do it, because right now we're starving, so f**k you! Everyone else might think the sun shines out of your ass, but give me your equipment and I'll beat you all!" That was great, I was glad Ivan did that because Kelly went out and scored a maximum. Little things like that would get him going.'

In mid-July, Mike Bast announced that he wasn't going to make the trip to England to compete in the Inter-continental Final of the World Championship. Of the small group of American riders from this period that could have crossed the water and had the ability to forge themselves an international career, Bast is probably the best rider not to have done so. Certainly outside of California, his achievements are eclipsed by the nation's World Champions and other stars that helped their country to gold medals, yet he was one of the dominant riders in the US. He won seven National titles and when the international stars came to compete on the Californian circuit, he was more than a match for them.

It wasn't that he was short of offers from the British League – far from it – but none were willing to match his financial demands. However, in 1977, he won the American qualifying round of the World Championship and, along with Penhall, journeyed to the UK to compete in the Inter-continental Final at White City. His lack of experience of racing outside his native country was there for all to see and he failed to score. He claimed that he and his fellow countryman were let down by British promoters who had promised them ample opportunities to practise before the ICF yet failed to keep their word.

Therefore, as soon as he stepped off the podium at Santa Ana, rumours spread like a forest fire that he wouldn't be heading across the Atlantic for another date at White City. This was made clear to Peter Rovazzini and his knowledge of Bast's character proved useful.

'He said to me, "Give me $8,000 to take the spot." "No, that's alright, you go ahead, I know how much you like flying." He just figured I'd write him a cheque, but I called his bluff and we got the spot for free. I knew Mike Bast was afraid of flying. That time when Bruce and Mike went over to England, he flipped out cold. Mike was a great National Champion, but I could read him. He was very easy to figure out.'

However, Kelly later disclosed that some of the authorities wanted the place to go to Scott Autrey, even though he was next in line by right.

'When Bast withdrew, the AMA weren't going to put me in; they wanted to put Scott Autrey in. But Ian Thomas got on the phone and made sure I got the place. When you get a break like that you don't throw it away. The dice rolled in my favour and in many ways I still can't believe it.'

Bast may have been highly rated in the US and also by people like Briggs and Mauger, but there was no doubt who the sport's press thought was the better prospect for the place. In his preview of the Inter-continental Final, Eric Linden wrote: 'Biffed, banged, buffeted, battered though he may have been, so much so it's a bit of a miracle he's riding at all and an even greater miracle that he scores as well as he does, this firecracker is a more formidable proposition over here than Bast would have been.'

The top nine scorers progressed through to the World Final, which was being staged at Katowice, Poland. Potentially, Kelly Moran was just five rides away from qualifying for his first World Final. He had never been this far in the World Championship chase before and the opposition he faced was tough; it was a meeting that was often regarded as harder than the final itself.

For this important meeting, sunshine and blue skies greeted him as he arrived at Wood Lane, White City. Resplendent in white leathers with patriotic stars set in a red and blue stripe running along the side of his arms and legs, he shone in the sunlight as he roared around the circuit.

Drawn at number three, he had three of his five races from the outside gates. By its definition, they're not as favourable as the inside, but on a dry, hot afternoon they proved less than advantageous and the track staff spent most of the meeting trying to dampen down clouds of dust.

With Bobby Schwartz also in the line-up, a contingent from America arrived at the meeting to lend their support for their fellow countrymen. Among their number were Dennis Sigalos and Ron Preston and two crates of beer for refreshment.

Kelly's afternoon began right at the beginning in heat 1. He'd barely got past the second corner when he clashed with Billy Sanders and they landed in an awkward heap on the track. Sensibly, for such a tense event, 'all four back' was the referee's verdict. In the re-run, characteristically, he made a poor start but grabbed third behind Sanders and winner, Ole Olsen, to score 1 point from his opening ride.

For his next outing he battled with fellow countryman, Schwartz, for second place, which resulted in a ruthless move that pushed his rival off-line and to the outside and Bobby was relegated to last. ITV Sport was covering the meeting and Kelly was asked for his explanation of the move by Gary Newbon, but they confused him by showing him a replay of the result of his actions instead of the manoeuvre that gave him second. Speaking in an adrenaline-charged tone, he explained:

'I knew Bobby had the line and I knew there was no dirt on the inside so I was just trying my hardest to go around him. I figured he'd know I would come around the outside, so that's when I just came underneath him and headed for glory.'

It was, though, another interview that fired him up for his last two rides. After a pointless third outing, Moran was outside the top nine in equal eleventh with 3 points at the interval stage, when another journalist put a microphone under his nose. Pete Rovazzini was in the pits with him that afternoon and described the scene that motivated the racer.

'Reporters started coming up to him and interviewing at the intermission, saying, "Do you think you will ever make it back to this level, do you think you have a chance?" And he turned, kind of hand-waved to me. "What?" I said.

'"The last time I checked this meeting wasn't over, right?"

'"Yeah."

'"They wanna know if I can make it back to this level. What do I need to make it?"

'"Well you're going to have to win the next one for sure, then maybe a second or third, depending on how the others go."

'"F★★k it, let's do it!"

'So I said to Martin Hignett: "Martin, we need all new edges. We're going to change edges every heat." So he went out to the Citroën and took Bruce's wheels off his bikes – he wasn't riding – and we got everybody around and we re-grouped. From then Kelly was on fire.'

He won heat 15 and then, despite holding the lead, narrowly missed out at the chequered flag in his final outing to Larry Ross in the penultimate race, but he had done enough to qualify for his first World Final on 8 points and joined his Vikings team-mate Mauger in Katowice.

'I felt I had the worse gates for my weight early on, but after my fourth outing with the inside gate to come I felt confident,' Kelly told *Speedway Star* afterwards.

'I'd like to know who that reporter was. I'd like to send him a thank you card because that pissed him off and he asked me what he needed to do. The first part of that meeting we were going downhill big time. That's what inspired Kelly at the Inter-continental Final when that reporter came up to him,' said Rovazzini.

Kelly may not have been enjoying the financial rewards that his performances should and would eventually give him, but he was riding on the crest of a wave. He was through to his first World Final as the youngest finalist, and he was valuable member of a team that was challenging for their first league championship and had qualified for the Knockout Cup final. Therefore, he had a good reason to celebrate, not that he needed one. However, on one occasion the good times overrode his commitments.

'Wednesday night was when the home meetings were at the Boulevard and I used to keep my eye on him all day so that he wouldn't go missing,' said Veronica Chapman. 'One night, he must have escaped me and everyone was ringing me asking me where was Kelly. It was almost an hour's drive from Easington to the Boulevard and I began searching for him. Eventually I found him in a caravan on the sea front, with a load of people having a party! There he was partying it up and I was amazed and I said to him, "Kelly, you're supposed to be at the speedway." "It's all right, Veron," he said. Of course he got into a party and completely forgot – that was Kelly! That was the only time he missed a meeting. I could hear all this noise from outside the caravan and I must have been crazy going along there because there were no lights or anything in those days.'

However, he did make it to the Boulevard but, unfortunately, he was too late to race and could only spectate.

'You never knew what he was going to do next,' Veronica laughed. 'It was a bit better when Marice, his girlfriend, came over. She stayed at my house for a while. Not having grown-up daughters at that stage, she seemed fine, a bit quiet, but you don't know what was going on. He was wild by nature and had to be for what he did. Some of them guys had this wild streak because, if you think about it, they'd take their lives into their hands when they go out on the track. We used to have parties and we all used to go to the Waterfront after speedway. The Waterfront was a hotel, disco and bar and Bryan Larner always used to come.'

It was Marice's first trip to Britain and while she preferred British speedway to America's version, adjusting to the UK took some getting used to.

'I hated it at first,' she laughed. 'I couldn't find anything to eat there. He used to laugh at me because all I would eat was Ritz crackers and cheese! I didn't like fish and I didn't like Chinese food. Veronica used to make us shepherd's pie and that was great – that was my favourite. I thought it was a little too cold over there, freezing. The heating was just a little radiator on the wall.

'When I went to Hull Speedway I loved it and I still have all the programmes that I kept score with. It was more fun over there because it was team racing, whereas here it was all individual stuff – just the one person you're rooting for. He showed me all over, took me to all the race tracks, we went to Scotland, and he lived on the beach there in this trailer. That was good, crazy times in there, partying, drinking and whatever … we didn't like being apart at all and I don't think Pete [Rovazzini] was too happy with some of that,' she laughed. 'Kelly always wanted to stay here with me, so I started going over there with him.'

Marice described herself as his 'biggest fan' but believed that racing in the UK was more intense than California.

'I was scared but excited. I was always worried that he was going to get hurt. It was crazier over there with the teams and the way they rode. He got hurt more over there than he did here. They used to have T-shirts at Hull that said, "I support Kelly Moran" on them. Well I had a shirt that said, "Kelly Moran supports me!"' she laughed. 'I thought that was funny, he reminded me of that when he was in the hospital.'

With a little under a month to go until the World Championship Final, Kelly's own observational quip after his triumph at White City, 'Now I've got to stay in one piece!' became almost prophetic when, just ten days before his big day, he crashed while attempting to pass Wimbledon's Eddie Jancarz and sustained a concussion.

Journalist Richard Tingle, who covered the Vikings for *Speedway Star* magazine, observed, 'That is the way Moran rides. If there's a gap he'll try to go through it and it is this never-say-die attitude which has turned him into a potential champion. He'll be no different in Katowice.'

Prior to the final Moran said, 'Obviously I am going there to win. If you don't go there with that attitude then there's little point in setting off, but that's probably expecting too much to be realistic and I feel I would have done extremely well to have finished in the top four – that's really my aim.

'Having never ridden the track I don't know what to expect, except what people have told me. Apart from anything else my only real fear is that the track is too slick. This would really kill what chances I have. If it is too slick it makes gating all that much more important and because of my weight I find it so difficult to pull away on these surfaces.'

Preparation for his big day started in earnest and they began by acquiring a special engine for the occasion from Weslake. One night at the Boulevard it was announced that this would be the engine that Kelly would ride in the World Final, but it wasn't what they expected, as Richard Harrison remembered.

'We took it to Hull and it was announced: "This is Kelly Moran's World Final bike," but it was as slow as hell! This was the Wednesday before the World Final and my dad had to work on it to get it ready.'

Moran had nothing but praise for Harrison, though, as he said shortly before departing for Poland: 'He's worked tremendously hard on my bikes throughout the season and I suppose I've not really given him a lot of help by these odd falls. But he has done a tremendous job in making sure that I have competitive machinery.'

Most pundits ruled him out because of his youth and inexperience. Interestingly, while he was the youngest rider in the field, his team-mate Mauger was the oldest. *Speedway Mail* assessed, 'He is an exciting and improving rider who would need all the luck in the world to take the title on this, his first attempt,' while Neil Evans footnoted his 'In the North' column: 'Kelly won't be overawed and wherever he finishes in the placing he will have enjoyed himself and probably shown a few more experienced riders a thing or two.'

'Whatever happens it will be far better than lying in a hospital bed as I was a year ago,' said Kelly. 'Nerves are going to play a big part in how I do, but at a meeting like this everybody's nervous. Even the greats like Ivan Mauger get wound up and I'll just be trying to convince myself it's another meeting.' Perhaps, though, he took the 'just another meeting' tactic a bit too far.

# 4

# TAKING ON THE WORLD

'What goes through your mind during a race? Your arse if you go fast enough.'

Barry Sheene (1950–2003), 500cc World Champion, 1976 and 1977

The People's Republic of Poland was the official name of Communist Poland in 1979. When the Cardinal of Krakow was elected Pope, taking the name John Paul II, having a Polish head of the Catholic Church had an inspirational effect on the people. Three months before Kelly Moran headed to Katowice for his first World Final appearance, half a million people had gathered to hear the Pope speak in Warsaw when he called for the creation of an 'alternative Poland'. Although the American would race before the biggest crowd of his entire career, Kelly's audience wasn't as appreciative or quite as big as that of his Holiness. Speedway has always been very popular in Poland and is one, if not the leading, speedway country in the world – indeed it had been reported that John Paul II was also a fan of the shale sport.

The stadium, called the Slaski Stadium, Katowice, was first opened in 1956. This was the third time that it held the Individual World Speedway Championships and it housed a 419-yard (384-metre) track. Its first staging in 1973 provided the competition's biggest upset and the country's first World Champion in Jerzy Szczakiel. This time the home challenge was expected to come from Zenon Plech.

Russia's president, Joseph Stalin, once said that imposing Communism on Poland would be like putting a saddle on a cow, but this didn't deter him from seizing power in the country at the end of the Second World War and foisting Communist principles on its people and its infrastructure.

While the roots of that socialist movement didn't run deep, it was still something of an eye-opener for an American who lived a free and easy life in comparison to his Polish counterparts. The social unrest and resistance to the regime simmered under the humid skies as the riders arrived for the 34th staging of the World Individual Final. They were greeted by a very different scenario to the ones that they were used to in the British League. But the hostile atmosphere meant that Rovazzini didn't feel that he should complain about the treatment of their machinery.

'We landed, all the riders were together, and all the motorbikes were being, basically, dumped out of the airplane. But there were guys stood around with sub-machine guns,' he said.

Practice was the day before the big meeting. Some riders take practice more seriously than others. Unlike other motor sports, even in today's GP series, there isn't a great deal to gain from the practice session. Nonetheless, some riders chose to use the time to test their equipment and make some last minute adjustments, others played psychological games by deliberately looking off the pace or struggling to make fast corners, while some just fooled around for the assembled media by pulling wheelies, etc.

The riders' draw had already been arranged before the meeting, so much so that tactician Mauger deliberately pulled up while leading a run-off for third in the previous round because he didn't want the No. 13 race jacket in Katowice – Kelly was drawn at No. 3.

Considering the nation's supposed opposition to Western excess, wild antics practised by the Californian had to be curbed – well that may have been the idea. Yet it wasn't long before Pete realised that Kelly wasn't going to take much notice of the Poles suppressed ways.

'We got to our hotel, it's a hot, clammy day and Kelly took a shower and then I took a shower. Then I walked out and go, "Okay Kelly, we're going to go down to dinner because we have to meet the American TV." I could hear him and I go, "Where are you?" And he's out there standing on the ledge because there's no balcony. "It's too freaking hot in there," he said. And all he's wearing is a towel standing on the ledge of a hotel. I said to him, "Get your butt in here, we're going to get arrested before we even go out."

'We were having dinner with Chris Economaki and Ken Squire, the two biggest sports announcers. They're legends in America now and this was the night before the World Final. Kelly had too many sons-of-bitches and Chris leans over to me and says, "Does this kid have any gum, does he have any chance of winning this thing?" I just said, "With Kelly you never know, depends what kind of mood he's in." Then he fell over the table and sat on the lady producer's lap and she goes, "All you athletes are the same!" Then he disappeared for the rest of the evening with a six-foot tall, blonde girl.'

With less than twelve hours to go before the biggest meeting of his short career, it wasn't early to bed for him to be fresh and ready to compete in the sport's biggest competition. Like any young man eager to experience what the world had to offer, he'd used his nationality in order to taste the forbidden fruits that lust provides, as he revealed in an interview with the author.

'She asked me if I would take her to America. I said, "Yeah, of course." Did I take her? You don't see her here now, do ya! I shouldn't have done that, but I was eighteen, what can you say … The night before I got drinking that Polish vodka and it went down like water, but to an eighteen-year-old it really hit home. They had two coaches to take us to the stadium, one was for the riders and one was for the mechanics. I didn't know about calling reception to get a wake-up call for the morning so when the coaches arrived to take the riders and everyone to the stadium, Pete and I were still in bed asleep and we missed it. Bernard Harrison got on the mechanics' coach and just thought we had got on the other one. But we were still in bed, we had to hitchhike to the World Final!'

It was panic stations, for Rovazzini anyway, and certainly not the best preparation for your first World Championship. Not only did he have to deal with getting Moran to the race track, somehow, he also had a young Polish girl who was eager not to abandon their company so she could leave behind the oppression of Communist Poland for the promise of the American dream.

'She said, "Kelly's taking me to America the next morning." "Er no, Kelly needs to go and race now, we'll talk to you later, honey." "Oh no," she insisted, "Kelly take me to America!" I turned to Kelly and said, "Don't you realise this is a day meeting and we've got about two hours before this race begins?" I finally got Kelly pulled together and we were on our way, but there were no cabs, everybody was down town, in church or going to this meeting.'

As they headed in the direction of the Slaski Stadium, the pair of them thumbed for a ride. By the side of the road Kelly held up his kit bag with his name on the end, "Kelly Moran USA", and pointed at it, which was then followed by frantic thumbing for a lift. Given the supposed tension between the United States and the USSR, that might not have been the greatest idea. However, it worked as he recalled:

'I remember pointing at it [the bag] and these two Polish supporters picked us up – "Yeah, yeah, Mo-ran," as they pronounced it, "get in, get in," they said. All the way there they were going, "Plech No. 1, Plech No. 1."'

Rovazzini remembered it differently: 'They had no idea who we were, no clue. So we were sat in the back seat and they said, "You go to the World Finals, we're going to go." And I said, "Who do you think is gonna win?" "Oh Ivan Mauger. Who do you think is going to win?" And I said, "I think Kelly Moran." "Oh no, too young, still a young boy." Then he looked and saw Kelly's leather bag with his name and the American flag on it, my gosh that guy lit up like a Christmas tree, he thought he had Prince Charles sitting in the back seat. Then when we pulled up,

Michael Lee was there and he had a bagful of decals. In those Communist Bloc countries they would do anything for decals. So Michael's stood above us and he poured a bag of decals over the top of us and the kids were crowding us and going crazy, we almost didn't make it into the pits.'

'I had to do the same thing by pointing at my name on my bag to get into the track,' added Kelly.

Luckily for them, Bernard Harrison had prepared everything with regard to his machinery and was calm and collected. While there was some urgency, Kelly certainly didn't have time to be nervous because as he strode into the dressing room, bag perched over his shoulder, the officials were beginning to gather the riders for the pre-meeting parade and the introductions. Rovazzini, meanwhile, was frantically trying to hurry up the little racer.

'They're getting ready to do the riders' introductions and he's getting dressed in the locker room and I'm on my knees cleaning his leathers because he didn't clean them from practice the day before! I said to him, "Kelly, this is the freaking World Final!"'

Impressive in his freshly scrubbed, patriotic white leathers, he took his place in the parade. Dwarfed by the Star Spangled Banner, he stood proudly before a massive crowd as his country's lone representative. He'd come a long way from that hospital bed in Whipps Cross.

By now Kelly knew not to expect any favours from Mauger, but it was another multiple World Champion, one whose record was about to beaten, Ove Fundin, who passed on some advice to the teenager. At some time between the dinner with American TV and meeting his blonde squeeze for the night, the Swede managed to corral him and give him a bit of advice that stuck with him right throughout his career, as he recalled in an interview with *Speedway Star* in 1991.

'The night before my first World Final, Ove came to speak to me. He told me that he had seen me ride and he said that he liked me a lot or something of that nature. He went on: "One thing I must tell you, the other riders are your friends off the track but, on the track, there are no friends, especially tomorrow." I have always stuck with that philosophy.'

If nerves could have been a problem for him, once more he didn't have time to manage them because he was out in the very first heat – it's only hindsight that enables us to wonder if this chaotic, mad dash to make it on time could have worked for him in his overall performance that day. Should he have needed any reminding that this was a prestigious event, he only had to look either side of him because alongside was former World Champion Peter Collins – who had won there in 1976 – the Soviet Union's only representative, Mikhail Starostin, and Billy Sanders. It was Aussie Sanders who made light work of winning the opening race from Collins, while Kelly opened his account with a third place and 1 point.

'We screwed up in Katowice because the plan was to follow PC [Peter Collins] around for that first heat, but they both missed the gate and we should have just let Kelly ride his own line,' reflected Rovazzini.

As well as Pete and Harrison, Kelly also had his Hull team manager, Ian Thomas, there and American promoter, Harry Oxley. Thomas, of course, was also keeping tabs on Ivan Mauger, who won his first race, and then the two Vikings riders clashed in heat 7 with Poland's Zenon Plech – who had also won his opening ride. Even at that early stage in the proceedings, it was obvious that this race with the home favourite would be an important one.

Having Kelly as his team-mate, Ivan had learned that the best way to get round his excitable, short attention span when it came to the business of racing was to pass on any instructions shortly before his race – preferably a close as possible before being pushed off.

'You had to tell Kelly just before he started his bike up. I learned that in 1978 and most of 1979 that you had to tell him something you wanted him to do, win a race or get second, third etc., just before he started his bike up. You could not tell him in the pits because he would forget about it.'

Therefore, Mauger approached Thomas. 'Ivan asked me before this particular heat to tell Kelly that he'd got to stop Plech, who was the biggest threat for the title.'

Moran was on the outside gate with Plech inside him, with Mauger starting from gate two – Zdenek Kudrna was on the inside. Kelly made a good start from the outside, but not as good as Mauger's and the Hull pairing dominated the first corner with the American dropping to the inside to block Kudrna while Plech was at the back. The Kiwi streaked away into the lead with Moran second as Plech passed Kudrna for third on the third corner – much to the delight of the crowd. Immediately the Pole set about Moran for second and as they exited the second corner and onto the back straight, Plech began his move and surged down the inside of his rival on the third corner as the audience roared their approval. Although it looked as though he'd passed the American as they slid through the bend – Zenon's challenge was robust to say the least, almost riding through his rival – somehow the teenager emerged from the corner and onto the home straight ahead of the Pole. Meanwhile, oblivious to what was going on behind, Mauger held a commanding and untroubled lead – just what he wanted. Zenon spent the next lap lining up his rival for another attempt to take second place and it came on the first turn of the final lap; again Plech tried to get through on the inside, only for Moran to close the door as he exited the corner and pulled away on the back straight. The expected challenge around the final turns never materialised and Kelly had taken the all-important second place.

'I just held my line,' Kelly stated matter-of-factly. 'Afterwards Plechy came up to me, shaking his head and said, "Oh my friend, oh my friend. You didn't move, even with my front wheel rubbing your arm, oh my friend!" "Sorry, Plechy, I want to win too," I replied.'

Veronica Chapman couldn't remember why she didn't go to the World Final, but noted the remnants of this epic race when she set about washing his gear. 'I remember looking at his leathers when he came back from Poland and there were tyre marks all up the back.'

Whether or not speedway is a contact sport is often called into question, but at such a high level of competition contact, of all kinds, is frequent and sometimes ruthless when challenging for the fastest line.

'I didn't want to push him too hard because if anything went wrong I would have been excluded,' said Zenon Plech. 'If I could have got just two inches in front I would have been okay, but I lost. One more point and I would have been in a run-off with Mauger for the title. We had a good race. He was a brilliant rider, he had excellent balance on the bike and when he was racing I used to like to watch him because he was so good. But that is speedway and everyone tries their best in the World Championship.'

'That was one of the best races I've ever seen in my life. There wasn't much more than a yard between them for the whole of the race,' enthused Thomas. 'They were touching at times while Kelly held him off. That race didn't give Ivan the title but it certainly helped him as well as Kelly's bid to get on the rostrum. But if ever one race showed me what a genius Kelly was on a bike, it was that one.'

Kelly won his next outing by the closest of margins at the finish line over John Titman and then fended off Michael Lee for second place behind Dave Jessup, before taking a tapes-to-flag victory in his last programmed race and finished his debut World Final on 11 points.

Once again, Mauger was instructing Kelly for his own benefit as much as for the American's: 'I told him, just before he started his bike up, to take a point off Michael or Ole as they had 8 points – the same as me – and they had a race in hand. In the event Dave Jessup made the start but Kelly took Ole all over the track. So Ole got 1 and Michael was last, so still on 8 after four rides.'

With his help, Mauger followed that race with two back-to-back wins that clinched a record-breaking sixth World title, while Zenon Plech had to settle for silver. But third was tied between Lee, Olsen, Sanders and Moran. Therefore, the American's final wasn't over yet and a bronze medal was the prize.

'That run-off was fun,' he said in 2006. 'I was never good from the start and I was that naïve that I didn't know that gate three was the worst gate to have. I was last coming out of turn two, but then I passed Olsen and then Sanders, but

I couldn't catch "The Champ" [Lee] – he was gone. If there had been another four laps I would never have caught him. When I got back to the pits, all the officials were around me and pulling me this way and that, and I'm like, "What did I do? I only got fourth." They wanted to put me on the rostrum, so I ended up on the rostrum with the top three.

'It was a hot day and a huge crowd – over 100,000 I think – but no one expected me to do anything and I felt no pressure at all, but I wanted to win,' he continued. 'It was sure different and everyone was going into the first turn really hard, but I would go in motocross style, feathering the clutch, let them go and then duck underneath them. The track was big, fast and quite slick, but once you got in front you could pick your line and they had to get around you.'

Mauger wasn't the type of racer who would give anyone much credit. However, in an email sent to the author he claimed that he brought Kelly out on the rostrum which, perhaps, was his way of acknowledging the role he played in enabling him to win a sixth crown. While it was undoubtedly the Kiwi's day, for many who were around at that time, the final was remembered as much for the exciting performance of the kid from California as it was for Ivan's victory.

ITV's *World of Sport* commentator, Dave Lanning, was at Katowice to cover the World Final and he believed that Moran's performance deserved more than equal billing.

'He was the star of that meeting. No disrespect to Ivan Mauger who won it, it was a downbeat World Final; Ivan was past his best, Penhall hadn't quite arrived, but Kelly was the star that day. He finished fourth and was in spectacular form and by far the biggest attraction and the most appealing aspect.'

An opinion endorsed by *Speedway Mail*, which described the American as a 'real revelation'. It continued: 'His spectacular style endeared him to the crowd as he finished in a highly creditable fourth place,' and added later, 'Moran battled hard for his points in his usual full throttle manner.' His performance also impressed *Speedway Star* and the magazine observed that he was 'one of the highlights of the final', and added: 'he rides in such a way that you cannot fail to be entertained.'

Arguably, given his young age, no rider matched Moran's sensational fourth place in the World title hunt again until Russia's Emil Sayfutdinov won his debut Grand Prix in 2009 when he was nineteen – he went on to finish third overall that year.

There is a further postscript to this remarkable performance. When his machine arrived back from Poland it was discovered that it had a broken valve spring. He remembered that his bike wasn't revving as much as it should do, and another said that his machine was also missing, so perhaps his lack of mechanical insight did cost him a bronze medal at least.

And everything didn't run smoothly in the pits either, as Rovazzini explained: 'We had a carburettor problem so Billy Sanders gave him his carburettor and Michael Lee helped us – everyone loved Kelly. We had a rider from Australia and England helping out with our motorcycle, your competition – pretty amazing, he'd bring the best out of everybody.'

While the riders arrived in Poland by plane, the British journalists travelled by train. The facilities on board were sparse and, on a hot, muggy day, they longed for the opportunity to freshen up. Unfortunately, the promised shower facilities were little more than a dribble of water, so Bob Radford welcomed some generosity from Moran when he arrived at the hotel.

'After the meeting I saw Kelly in the hotel and said, "Sorry if we're a bit less-than-fresh, but we've only had a trickle of cold water." Immediately he gave me his room key and said, "Go to my room and get a shower, get anything you want out of my bag, shampoo, deodorant ..." That was a very warm gesture and very welcome at the time. When I got back the others said that I'd smell them all the more now. That was very typical of Kelly, who was very warm-hearted and very generous.'

There was, of course, cause for celebration, and finishing fourth in the world in only his third professional season was more than a good reason. Mauger too was in high spirits and threw a champagne party at the Novotel Hotel for press and close friends, which ran well into the small hours. Communist Poland may have been used to Western-style celebration after staging so many world and international meetings, but they weren't familiar with the enthusiastic levels that Moran would indulge in. Indeed, when you consider that an Eastern Bloc country like Poland, which was preached to by the Communist Party and its followers that the West's ways were at best wrong, and at worst, evil, you can understand that on the surface at least, their attitude to such a public display of revelry would not be supportive.

'The trouble came when he realised that the hotel had smart, white plastic seats in the public rooms and he autographed the lot!' said Thomas. 'He might have got away with it in a bar at Hull, but not at a Polish hotel. I guess he did in a way because I had to reimburse the Poles for the damage.'

'He called me over to see what he had written,' recalled Ivan. 'He had written in detail how he took Ole for a ride on a white leather lounge chair! I had to pay the hotel for the damage because Kelly never (ever!) had any money on him.'

Such mutilation of the hotel's property is straight out of the rock star's handbook of misbehaviour and, without any sign of regret, Kelly confessed, 'I did sign all those chairs.'

Rumours and stories of Moran's off-track antics were already being embellished, usually a little bit of truth that was enhanced and often distorted by mischievous licence. After the final in Katowice, there was one doing the rounds that he had been seen dancing naked on a hotel balcony with a similarly bare blonde girl and a bottle of encouragement. Of course, this seems to be fragments of truth gleaned from tales that had emerged before and after the meeting, which were then tied together by vindictive minds. Nonetheless, many years later, Moran explained:

'It was practice day for the World Final, I took a shower and afterwards I pulled back the curtain and I was still naked, but there was no balcony, it was like a window ledge, and there was no girl.'

As the small hours ticked their way toward dawn, the festivities began to fade and eventually most of the revellers retired for some sleep before catching an early flight the same morning for England. Katowice was a big industrial town with one massive, main street. A coach was sent to pick up the British contingent to transport them to a military airfield where they would depart for the UK at 7.30 a.m. Commentator Dave Lanning was already on board the coach when it pulled up outside the Novotel to pick up, among others, Moran.

'We got everybody on the bus and then all of a sudden someone said, "Where the bloody hell is Kelly?" Barry Briggs, Ian Thomas and I decided that we'd better find him. We walked into the hotel, got to the first floor where the restaurant was, and Kelly was wandering around stark naked, apart from a baseball cap that he had on back to front. He was as high as a kite and it was, "Hey boys! How are you doin'!" He'd been partying all night and we found him wandering, wonderfully, in great form. We somehow managed to get him into jeans and a T-shirt – I don't know where the rest of his gear was. One of my enduring memories is of Kelly wandering around, as happy as the day was long, wearing just a baseball cap in the main hotel of Katowice,' laughed Lanning.

Due to his signing all the white leather chairs, the hotel management weren't prepared to let him have his passport back until the matter was cleared up to their satisfaction. It seems likely that Thomas had to foot the bill, but the party wasn't over yet, as Ian remembered: 'He even turned up at a military airfield for our charter flight home in a pair of shorts and with a bottle in his hand. The personnel who escorted us onto the plane couldn't believe their eyes, but he was entitled to let his hair down because he had turned in an immense performance the day before.'

Journalist John Chaplin was already on board the aircraft when Moran finally arrived, and he added: 'Kelly was last on the plane taking us back to sanity after the militarised mayhem that was austerity-ridden Poland in those days. He dashed onto the aircraft, obviously the worse for a night of celebration, wearing a grubby, torn T-shirt, and he handed his passport to someone to look after for him. He was telling the world that Kelly Moran didn't give a shit. And you had to love him for it.'

Kelly wasn't the only one whose departure from Poland was adventurous. In his innocence his mechanic, Bernard Harrison, almost plunged a local into a difficult situation with the feared apparatus of oppression the 'Bezpieka'. Bernard didn't feel comfortable leaving the bike with Ivan's mechanic, Gordon Stobbs, so stuffed it into a taxi. When they arrived at the hotel the driver drove off with his passport, ticket and everything in the boot. Stranded, with no immediate means of leaving the country, Kelly, armed with the knowledge that Poland was scheduled to hold the World Final again in 1982, opened the window on the coach and yelled, 'See ya in three years' time, Bernard!'

Fortunately, the hotel knew which firm they'd used and the driver came back. However, because Poland was Communist, the passport and ticket were worth a fortune, so the police wanted to arrest the driver and throw the book at him, but Harrison refused to press charges.

Thomas believed that Hull Speedway was looked upon by the rest of the sport 'as the team from a backstreet town'. Yet here they were parading a newly crowned record World Champion and the World No. 4 who was the hottest prospect in the sport. Therefore, commemoration and celebration were high on Thomas' promoting list for the team's first match since the Katowice final at the Boulevard against local rivals, Halifax.

He hired two-open top Rolls Royce cars to parade his world stars before the supporters and also acquired two seventy-two-piece gold cutlery sets worth in the region of £700 to present to his riders as a permanent reminder of their achievement and what it meant to the club and its management.

But it was a mixed night for their returning stars, mechanical gremlins restricted the Kiwi's scoring, while glitches of a different kind troubled Moran, who fell off twice in his two rides and then had to withdraw from the meeting. Joe Owen scored a maximum that night to help the team win 43–34 as they closed in on the league championship.

'He was that gone, I don't think he made it past the first bend. We had to lock him in the changing room because if the referee had seen him that would have been it,' recalled Owen. 'I think it was Ivan or one of them who said, "Just lock him in the changing room and let him sleep it off." This was while the meeting was going on.'

Thomas could understand that Kelly was still in high spirits from the weekend, he could even forgive him for his disturbed nights and the regular financial advances he required to sustain his fun. After all he was still a young man, and away from the excesses you couldn't wish to meet a nicer, friendlier person in the world. However, after the match, an incident came to light that did hurt Ian and may have tightened his resolve when it came to negotiating a new contract for 1980.

'I was coming out of the bar about an hour after the meeting and I saw a lady carrying a set of cutlery,' said Ian. 'It was the same as the ones we'd presented to the riders and I knew it wouldn't be Ivan's. I said, "Excuse me, madam, would you mind telling me where you got that cutlery?" She said: "I bought it off Kelly Moran for £30." I shook my head and explained to her the significance of the gift we had made to Kelly. I asked her to do me a favour and sell it back to me for £50. She understood where I was coming from and, in fact, she only took the £30 she'd paid. There was no point in giving it back to Kelly, so I had it parcelled up and posted it to his father, Tom, in California. I felt it was a special occasion for Hull and Kelly obviously didn't look at it from the same point of view as myself. I'm not saying what I did was right and what Kelly did was wrong. What was right in my book had no special significance or place in Kelly's lifestyle and his way of doing things.'

Graham Drury, who would go on to promote the Telford Indoor Ice Spectacular with Thomas, believed he was more upset by that incident than he let on. 'I know it did hurt Ian at the time – that was naughty. The following Saturday we were riding at Eastbourne and I said to Kelly: "Bloody hell – that was a nice thing that Ian and Bryan did." "Yeah," he said, "I took it to the bar and sold it for £30!" Even to sell it was a dreadful thing, but to go and sell it for that sort of money … it wasn't so much that, he lived life to the full and wouldn't have given it a second thought.'

It's pretty certain that he didn't intend to upset Thomas because he wouldn't knowingly hurt anyone. As much as he enjoyed his racing, the trophies, the medals and the plaudits were all welcome yet, beyond a few, they didn't maintain their value for him. John Chaplin got to know the Morans' father during his frequent trips to California as the editor of the in-flight newspaper, *Skytrain*, and was astonished to hear that he had few of their senior trophies.

'I remember Tom telling me that there was only one trophy on display in the house because Kelly had given away all the others he had won.'

However, he was soon back to his spectacular form. He finished second with Dennis Sigalos in the Inter-Nations Pairs at Birmingham and scored a maximum against Sheffield. His performances helped Hull through to the Knockout Cup Final and the club were at the top of the league when they travelled to Wolverhampton on 5 October and thrashed them 52–26, which meant they needed just a draw at defending champions Coventry a week later to win their first league championship. They barely had time to digest that prospect when Kelly crashed during the second half and sustained a broken collarbone. It was a tremendous blow.

In the audience that night was Marice and suddenly a realisation swept over the teenager that she was far from home, and the man she loved was sprawled out on the track. 'He was just laying there, no movement and I thought, oh my God he's dead! I remember thinking, now what am I going to do? I'm all alone in England – at Hull.'

While at home in Wheatcroft and recovering from his latest breakage, a disappointed Moran, who was obviously getting a bit tired of injuries, had a bright idea of acquiring Iron Man-style protection – and he knew the man for the job.

'In those days, my husband, Adrian, was a Chief Engineer for Esso Petroleum,' revealed Veronica Chapman. 'At one stage Kelly asked him, "Please could you make me a steel jacket so that I can ride my bike?' Being a typical Yorkshireman he gave him one look … and that was enough! He absolutely enjoyed having the boys stay, though, because it was his hobby and interest as well.'

Hull travelled to Brandon Stadium to take on Coventry in one of the sport's most famous winner-takes-all showdowns. It would be an uphill task without Moran and because the Bees were also missing Alan Molyneux, they could only promote their number eights. For the Vikings, their first choice, Tom Owen, was also injured so they drafted in Graeme Stapleton. Before an enormous crowd, Moran's loss was too much of a handicap to overcome and they lost the match, and the title, 42–36 and Coventry had retained their crown.

It's said that Ivan Mauger was livid with disappointment afterwards. Thomas recalls everything was flying in all directions, helmets, steel shoes, race jackets, etc., as he let loose his frustrations.

Joe Owen recalled: 'It was worse because Olsen was Coventry's top man and it was just like rubbing salt into the wound. Ivan came steaming in, he didn't even have a shower that night, took his leathers off, threw them in the bag, put his clothes on and went. He was so mad. If someone had said something he would have torn a strip out of us all. It was lost before Coventry and he knew that. We weren't going to win at Coventry.'

In his column in *Speedway Star*, Mauger wrote: 'I'm convinced that had Kelly Moran been fit to ride the Lada Vikings would today be champions.'

For all of Ian Thomas' brilliance with the rule book, he didn't manage to galvanise the rest of the team with the collective responsibility that was required to bring trophies to Hull. Wimbledon had been flying high near the top of the league, so when the Vikings visited Plough Lane for a match on 26 July, the last thing they needed was to take them on while under-strength. As the start-time approached, Hull took to the track missing Frank Auffret, Bobby Beaton and Graham Drury, who had failed to arrive, and they lost the fixture by 5 points.

Later, Joe Owen broke down in the West Midlands and missed their match at Swindon. On a wet night, the Vikings managed to grab a draw, thanks to the inspired riding of their Americans and Mauger, although had Owen been there it seemed a victory would have been a certainty.

A few excuses were thrown around at the time of the Wimbledon meeting, mainly a breakdown, but many years later Bobby Beaton admitted that they just didn't want to go because of their dislike of the Plough Lane circuit – Drury's absence was genuine, though, because he was involved in a road accident. Of course it was unacceptable for the management, but even more so for the supreme professional, Mauger, who blamed their absence on the team's failure to land the league championship.

Although he wasn't fully fit, Kelly returned for the second leg of the Knockout Cup final against Cradley Heath on 31 October. He scored 8 points but he couldn't prevent them losing the match and the cup to the Midlanders. In the end, an Inter-League Four Team Championship trophy was scant reward for the club after such an exciting campaign.

When Kelly had departed for home, Veronica received a phone call from Ian Thomas about collecting the Lada. While he spoke, she looked out of the window and grinned. The much used and abused Russian car wasn't as much parked as rolled to a stop into the bushes. She knew that Thomas wouldn't be happy.

'I told him what it was like and they sent a lorry for it,' she said. 'It was like crashed into the bushes! If the car could talk, can you imagine? It was left where it was, you could see what he had done. We were left with a massive phone bill as well. I had to speak to Ian about that and Hull Vikings paid it, which was really good of them. He said that I shouldn't have let him use the telephone but what can you say when he won a big race and he wanted to phone his friends and family.'

Charismatic and a super talent Kelly may have been, but Thomas wasn't pleased to discover what condition the vehicle was in. 'At the end of the season they [Lada] said that there was more oil in the boot than in the engines,' he said.

Drury said his misuse of the Lada also angered the Hull boss. 'That also upset him when Kelly sent the car back in an appalling state. I used to call him a loveable rogue and my wife used to think the world of him. He used to come here and have a meal with us, utterly charming, and then twenty-four hours later he was paralytic and you couldn't do anything with him. My view is, when he was in America he couldn't legally drink, then all of a sudden he came to England and he *could* legally drink – that's where the root of it was. He came from America as a young lad, he had no parents with him and he just went wild.'

What a year it had been. Approximately twelve months previously, he'd been getting around in a wheelchair and an assault on the World Championship seemed like a distant dream. Now he was no longer an unproven talent, he was one of the world's leading racers and also a much sought-after young man. He gazed out of his aeroplane window and saw the city of Los Angeles stretched out below him, its night lights sparkling like diamonds against dark velvet and he was home, back to where it all started.

# 5

# REBEL IN THE FDG

'Californian speedway is a party that's interrupted every few minutes by a motorcycle race.'

Author unknown

When Kelly Moran turned sixteen in September 1976, he was able to start alongside the senior riders and ride 500cc machines on the Californian circuit. But with only a few weeks left until the end of the season, it was agreed with his father that they'd put off buying a big bike until the New Year. He was disappointed, but understood that his dad had to juggle his finances between his boys and his other family.

At this stage he was well-known in the US scene as someone who had a lot of potential. It was as a fifteen-year-old that Mauger first took note of Kelly Moran as he roared around Costa Mesa Speedway on a junior bike. Of course he wasn't the only one who recognised that he had a lot of talent and many predicted that he could be destined for great things. Therefore, Kelly decided it was time to exploit some of the contacts he'd gathered while he raced in the juniors and also out in the desert; so he began to knock on some doors. First up, was Peter Rovazzini.

'Kelly was still a young boy in junior speedway and I once told him, because I used to watch him ride, once he got old enough to come and see me and I'd get him his first motorcycle. So he turned sixteen and knocked on my front door.'

Next on his list was ex-speedway rider Ken McGoldrick. But he recalls that not everyone was receptive to the cheeky lad from Huntington Beach.

'Kelly used to come around, like "Hey guys!", making a lot of racket and having a good time. He used to ask for cigarettes and we used to tell him to get lost.

I'd seen him ride mini-bikes and he was a really good mini-bike rider. He'd hang around and had a good pedigree as far as a mini rider. So, nobody was really interested in him and then one day he said: "Hey KK" – he named me "KK" by the way, there were so many initial names at that time like LJ, JJ, so Kelly started calling me KK and that's how it started. Anyway, he asked me: "Hey, when I get old enough to ride the big bikes, when I'm sixteen, would you look at me?" I told him sure I'd look at him and no one was really interested because he was just this whacky little kid.

'When he turned sixteen he came knocking on my door with a two-valve Jawa and said: "Hey, you promised you'd look at me." So I went out to the practice track with him and watched him, and he was a First Division standard rider the first time he got on that big bike. So I began to help him.'

Although KK got along well with Kelly's father, from the start he laid out some ground rules that he'd always stuck with. 'One of my things, always, when I was going to help a rider, be his guy, bat from his corner and have his back, the first rule was: no dads in the pits,' he said. 'That was the same with any of the riders I helped, Billy Hamill, Chris Manchester, any of them – no dads in the pits. So there was no conflict. We used to do a three-year programme, we'd help him with his bikes, bring him through the ranks and through the marks to be a First Division rider. Once you go through the learning process, how to ride, how to make changes and how to race against the big boys and gain a lot of First Division experience, then you can do whatever you want.'

KK and Rovazzini, plus Kenny Best, were wise choices to make when selecting people to get him started. All his clowning around masked an insightful intelligence that only those closest to him really knew. He certainly turned Bobby Schwartz's head.

'The first time I met him was at Irwindale and he showed up with Pete Rovazzini in this brand new, white van – probably from Pete's dad's electrical business. It wasn't sign-written or anything, but I couldn't believe it because I believe he also had a brand new bike, or what looked like a brand new bike.

'I was envious,' Bobby admitted, 'because he had this new sponsor and everything seemed new. I remember watching him and his brother racing at the Indian Dunes motocross park when I was riding motocross. I didn't know them as friends, I just knew them as two little guys with shamrock leathers on and I used to watch them ride their bikes around the mini-bikes course. They were pretty good, I thought. Next thing, like four or five years later, which was like a lifetime to me then, he showed up at Irwindale and he rode really good. I think he won something, maybe the Handicap Main, I can't remember for sure, but you could see right then that he was a great rider.'

While he had been good on mini-bikes and as a junior rider, he was something special on a full-blooded, brake-less, alcohol-burning 500cc machine. Riding a 500 came as naturally to Moran as breathing.

'I had no problems adjusting to a 500cc machine,' he said. 'In many ways it was easier to race than what I had been riding. And I loved to slide the bike and turn left. That's what I liked and I never really considered doing any other form of motorcycle racing.'

His brother agreed: 'You found it easier to slide and it was easier on the track to ride. You could hook up too quick on the little bikes, you couldn't slide through the dirt. The dirt to the big bikes was no problem in that sense because they could ride through it.'

Luckily they both caught the hurricane that revived American speedway, which wouldn't blow itself out until the 1990s. The sport had virtually died in the States during the '60s after their great hope for world glory, Ernie Roccio, was killed in 1956 while racing for Wimbledon. By 1968, Harry Oxley and America's first World Champion, Jack Milne, had begun staging racing at the Orange County Fairgrounds in Costa Mesa. And with little or no action for more than a decade, people were intrigued by this revived form of motorcycle racing and it started to gather momentum.

When the then reigning World Champion Ivan Mauger visited in late '68, his presence helped enthuse those who had shown an interest and helped further the cause by the media attention that his attendance attracted. 'I was shocked when I saw what had been called a new boom in American speedway. Riders were on old-fashioned, low-slung handle-barred machines and their styles were as outdated as their bikes,' said Mauger.

That situation didn't last long. Three years after making his initial visit to the west coast, an American team defeated a World Select that included Mauger and multiple World Champion, Barry Briggs, 2–1 in a Test series. Even though the sport was, and is, largely confined to southern California, they discovered their own stars like Mike and Steve Bast, Rick Woods, Bill Cody and Sonny Nutter. Others would rapidly follow and on their tiny circuits they proved more than a match for visiting sides from Europe.

By the mid-1970s the sport in California was thriving as Shawn Moran remembered. 'That was money time for the big guys because they used to get a percentage of the gate. If the crowd was over 8 or 9,000, say if they made 1,000 bucks that night, racing wise, you'd make $1,400 with the gate. When Mike Bast and Rick Woods and those guys were racing, we used to have both scratch and handicap racing then; in the scratch you had to get first or second out of four guys to get into the main event and the same again in the semi to get in the final, and that's where you made your money. In the handicaps I think it was three that transferred. If you won the scratch that night, that was about 700 bucks, but if you won the Handicap Main, and then the gate, you're talking almost two grand for that night – and this was in the late '60s and '70s. That was a lot of money for one night – it's still a lot of money now.'

Perhaps the affluent nature of California ensured that the speedway revival would have longevity as opposed to some of the other states in the nation. Furthermore, the predominately dry climate also meant that one of the sport's biggest enemies, rain, was also prevented from denting its reputation. There was also a motorcycle craze taking hold in America at the time, especially in the flat track and motocross disciplines, helped by celebrity endorsement from the King of Cool, Steve McQueen. So when Pat Hennen, Steve Baker and Kenny Roberts headed to Europe to race in the 500cc World Championships and experienced success, the nation's patriotic embracement of their triumphs helped propel all two-wheeled pursuits up the popularity ladder.

All these things combined together to ensure that speedway in the USA, or Californian speedway to be accurate, would be more than just a passing craze but would have a long-term future. A future that produced some of speedway's most exciting and charismatic racers, and it survived the inevitable fall that follows all boom periods of interest. It has also negotiated the choppy seas of speedway's recent turbulent history and managed to reach some islands of stability and hope, which means that American speedway still has roots from which to grow new talent for tomorrow.

The tracks in California were nearly all located in fairgrounds and the arenas were used for County Fair events, such as the rodeos. So this often dictated the size of the circuits and also meant that there wasn't much scope for banked surfaces. Kenny Best recalled that in between their races he and his fellow competitors would often sit on the shoots from which the bull and bronc riders were released.

The track at Irwindale was an exception, though, and it wasn't situated in a fairground but on the site of a drag racing strip. Therefore, it was a dedicated speedway track. Although its size had been influenced by the other venues by the time it opened in 1972, it was a little longer – around 200 yards (183 metres) – and had more banking. Costa Mesa was approximately 180 yards (165 metres) in length, while Ventura was around 1/5 of a mile. But when the Morans raced it had some banking and was the closest thing they had to what they would encounter in Europe – until Long Beach's Veterans' Memorial Stadium was opened in 1982. There was, though, a quirk to these circuits, which Ian Thomas noticed during a visit to Costa Mesa, that he thought reduced the credibility of the sport.

'A crazy idea … they have a portable white line. So if the track gets a bit too rough on the inside, they just move the white line!'

Moran once described Costa Mesa as his 'all-time favourite track', so it's not surprising that he didn't agree with his Hull boss' criticism. 'It made two tracks in one,' he defended. The white line was little more than a piece of plastic (PVC) piping that was laid out to form the inner kerb.

British journalist John Chaplin was flanked by Bruce Penhall and Bobby Schwartz at Costa Mesa in 1977 and he was mesmerised by the racing. Compared with what he'd observed in England and Europe, he found the experience more intimate and the Americans' penchant for showmanship and razzamatazz presented a unique atmosphere.

'It was a fabulous demonstration of very close, knee-to-knee, handlebar-to-handlebar skill,' he enthused. 'Everything about the place was exciting. Kelly was in the meeting and it became obvious that he was adored. Also that he had the personality that endeared him to not only the fans but to his fellow riders and officials too.'

Given the sheer number of talented riders that emerged from the Californian system and raced internationally, it's difficult to argue with Costa Mesa promoter, Harry Oxley, when he was asked about Kelly's success after his first World Final performance.

'Kelly Moran rode mini-bikes here and then after one year of speedway adapted to British tracks. They start young; we have a regular junior programme for nine-year-olds. They would be going too fast on a quarter-mile track but at Costa Mesa, for example, they are not going fast and quickly learn the fundamentals.'

Some of the surfaces were made up of what they called DG – decomposed granite. It's a granite rock that has been weathered to such a point that it can easily be mixed with sand and some clay. In Britain shale was used for the surface that contains a lot of little stones which, when they hit you at speed while chasing an opponent, is not a pleasant experience. Kelly would later complain, 'In America we race on dirt, not rocks!'

In keeping with America's individualism, the track at San Bernardino first operated as an 'outlaw' track when only second and third division riders could compete there. However, some First Division standard racers managed to get around that by competing under fake names!

Speedway in the USA wasn't taken as seriously as it was in Britain. An ex-rider once said that Americans go to speedway to 'drink beer and holler at the girls'. Bruce Flanders was one of the announcers at Costa Mesa and San Bernardino and he had a unique connection with the fans in the stands with his familiar phrase, 'More beer!' US supporters had their favourites but they didn't have the sort of devotion that they had in Britain, where they would know the history and all the stats. And very few American enthusiasts filled in their programmes to follow the action, whereas in the British League it was a ritual – you weren't a proper fan if you didn't fill in the scores.

In America's *Cycle News* publication in 1977, Rex Reece wrote a short humorous piece entitled 'How to Spectate at Speedway', and made the following observations: 'Although there may be rent-a-cops all around, when you seat yourself up in the grandstands, the basic structure of civilisation breaks down. You're on your own with only the law of the jungle to live by. Cheer for whoever your neighbour is cheering for, since to go against the grain will raise much ire amongst fellow fans. Have a good time like everybody else and do whatever the track announcer tells you to do – no matter how outrageous or illegal it may be. If you don't understand what's happening, or don't know any of the rules, don't worry since many riders are in the same fix.'

The party atmosphere at the tracks carried on long after the gates had closed, as Ron Preston recalled. 'I lived close to the track at Costa Mesa. They'd [the riders] come to my house every Friday night after the races during '77, '78 and '79 – there was always a party at my house. And there were some major parties. On any given night there was Steve Nutter, Steve Columbo, Dave Sims, Danny Becker, the whole bunch and half of them guys are dead now. They were like, well, what are we going to do to top last Friday night? There was drink, there was drugs and they would vandalise the house next door that was being renovated. They came over and told me that they had a karate contest of who could kick a hole in this dry wall of this brand new apartment next door. The cops showed up the next day and there were beer bottles everywhere, people were asleep all over the place and it was a den of inequity. I never drank, it was just a party and I was just like, okay there's a party at my house and the next thing you'd know there would be 100 people there.'

Having already met Kelly as a young guy making his way in the sport, Preston realised that he'd slipped easily into the lifestyle – and so began a life-long friendship, full of ups and downs, good times and bad, but through thick and thin they remained close.

'I'm not too sure how we met, but I told Kelly one night that I was heading for Ventura, which is a couple of hours north of Costa Mesa. And he said: "Oh I wanna go, I'm not riding, but I wanna go." So he gave me directions to his house in Huntington Beach and by the time I got there – he was about fifteen maybe, not sixteen – he was partying like a rock star already. I went up there and rode and he went to hang out in the stands. By the time I was done, they said, "Hey Kelly's over there drunk." He was just a little kid, but he was so drunk that I stuck him in my van and drove all the way back to Huntington Beach, but I couldn't remember how to get to his house and he wouldn't wake up! So I drove my van to my driveway, left it there with him inside asleep and went to bed. I opened the door the next morning and he was still asleep. He eventually woke up like a little puppy in the front foot well. That was the beginning and he'd hang out at our house in Costa Mesa. It wasn't his age, everybody was doing it – it was the lifestyle of speedway in southern California.'

Bob Dugard would be Kelly's promoter at Eastbourne for two years and he heard all about the American's attitude towards the whole scene.

'When Kelly went back for the American Final, my younger brother, Eric, travelled back with him to see if he could get him to win it. It was a big thing in them days. He was gob-smacked about the party life that Kelly, Pete [Rovazzini] and that all enjoyed out there. He thought how different it was to how the Scandinavians do it, how serious they take it and how laid back the Americans were – a completely different ball park. With that background, Kelly never knew the seriousness that was attached to league racing, or the responsibility. He did his job, a fantastic job, but he never got to grips with how serious it was – and he never would have done either.'

After they had provided World Champions and experienced team success, the revelry in Californian speedway continued. Therefore, it's not surprising that the dedicated professionals that were Denmark continued to defeat the USA and, crucially, gather the gold medals, even though the Yanks had just as much ability in their team. Regular losses didn't bring about a change in attitude until a new generation stamped their authority on the international scene.

When he wasn't riding motorcycles or finding a party somewhere, Kelly Moran found ways of making a few dollars, as he explained in an interview in 1986. 'I joined one of those Youth Employment programmes – where you have to work five days a week from 7 a.m. until 4 p.m. I used to have to go round all the schools and be the gardener. It only lasted a month because I hated getting up so early and all my buddies were all at the beach. In those times it was quite easy to get a job for a little while. We would work and get some money, then we would quit and enjoy spending it. When it was gone, we'd just get another job because they always needed brats somewhere!'

Although team racing was tried, it never caught the imagination in California in the same way as individual racing. In America the riders were graded by division; the best ones were in the First Division and the Third was for riders who were just starting out on 500s, while the Second provided the bridge between the elite and the rookies. You would climb up through the levels with the more success you had on the track and in 1977 there were plenty of opportunities to do just that. In one week, there was racing at Ventura on Tuesday (dubbed 'the commotion by the ocean' because of its proximity to the sea), Wednesday at San Bernardino ('inland motorcycle speedway'), Thursday at Irwindale, Friday at Costa Mesa (otherwise known as 'the Bullring' because it also staged rodeos) and Bakersfield on the Saturday, plus other meets were held at various venues in the state.

A typical night's racing in America would feature 23 or 24 races that would be a combination of scratch and handicap racing, as well as an occasional match race between two riders, some junior action and include other forms of entertainment.

'Scratch races were like what you have in England, four guys in a race starting from scratch over four laps,' Kelly explained. 'But then we'd have handicap races, with six riders over five laps and you were staggered by how good you were. The best riders would start fifty yards back from the start line (at some tracks the furthest line was sixty yards) and the ones that weren't as good started closer to the start line or at the start. You had to finish in the top three to transfer to the next heat. Sometimes, if you had a bad night and didn't make the qualifying places, you could only have two races, the handicap and the scratch, and your night was over – two races and you're on your way home and that was tough.'

The start of the '77 season was marred by a dispute between the riders, the Speedway Racing Association (SRA), and the promoters. Feelings were certainly running deep and at one stage the whole season was in doubt. In the 4 May issue of *Cycle News*, Costa Mesa promoter, Harry Oxley, refused to comment on the situation for fear of 'harassment' and left the board to run his track as he saw fit. The riders claimed that they had been on the same prize money for the past nine years and, no doubt inspired by its popularity, they wanted a bigger cut of the gate money. At the time the competitors were receiving a guaranteed $1,275 purse or 30 per cent cut of the gate, whichever was greater, but they were now asking for a guaranteed $1,575 and 40 per cent share of the gate receipts. The SRA said that the increase would go to second and third division riders, which would obviously improve the situation for riders like Kelly, who was starting out. None of this worried him too much, he was just eager to get out on the race track to compete and earn some money. Winning the Third Division Main would earn him around $75, while victory in the Second was worth approximately $200.

Unfortunately the dispute wasn't resolved as the season finally got underway, with some riders on strike – Sonny Nutter was one of them – even though US National Champion Mike Bast said that the current agreement was 'fair'. Only Bakersfield met the SRA's demands. Eventually, though, as the season wore on, the strike fizzled out.

Moran began his debut pro-season wearing number 131. With the exception of the much coveted number one plate – which was reserved for the reigning

US National Champion – riders could choose a number to compete under unless it had already been taken by another rider. What would become his regular number, 31, was still held that year by Guy Waterson. A triple National finalist, Waterson retired around this time so Moran was able to snap up 31 when the numeral was rested by its former owner. When the 1980 AMA Speedway Riders' List was published, Kelly was listed as number 31.

He made his debut as a professional at Ventura on 3 May and won every race to win the Third Division Main event; he was immediately promoted to the second division. The following week, though, his enthusiasm got the better of him and he fell while chasing eventual main event winner, Rick Jones.

When he won his first Second Division Main at San Bernardino on 1 June, the officials sent out two trophy girls to 'award' Moran. Announcer Bruce Flanders said that he had to choose which girl he would start with, but Kelly confidently replied, "I can handle both at once, Bruce!" His all-action style, which would thrill fans the world over, was making him one of the most popular riders on the circuit.

His fellow racers were intrigued, surprised and a little bit puzzled by this little rider's amazing balance and style. Quite soon his rivals would take time out when they could to check out his spectacular way of racing, a cloak-and-dagger method that seemingly defied belief and physics – the Wizard of Balance had been born.

'We were all pretty amazed that he had this incredible riding style; he wasn't big enough to have it fully sideways and go into the corner like normal,' assessed Ron Preston. 'I think he was one of the first guys that started riding like they do now because he used that to his advantage, to be able to sit way back and use his body English to lay himself out on the bike and compensate for being short. At Costa Mesa everyone else would be pitched sideways and scrub off speed, but he would be going in with a two-wheel drift – a totally different style. It was cool watching him because he was just raw talent.'

On 15 June at San Bernardino, Kelly qualified for his first ever Handicap Main event as a First Division rider when he finished third behind Bruce Penhall and Alan Christian. With fans' favourite Jim Fishback out of the running with mechanical issues, the crowd enthusiastically cheered on the daring Moran. Kelly also won three successive Handicap Mains at Irwindale, but his popularity and success didn't surprise Kenny Best.

'Irwindale had the most DG (dirt) and to me was the most fun to ride. The DG would get pushed out to the fence and the fence was probably only three feet high in the corners. They'd drag it back down to the pole by hand as much as they could between races and then used a grader during half time, but it ended back up at the wall in the corners. San Berdoo was at a fairgrounds but it was also a dedicated speedway track since there was lots of land at that facility. You would have liked the racing, I think, there was lots of DG, 22-inch rear wheels and nitro was legal. With all that there was lots of excitement and passing on the outside if you had the balls like Danny "Berzerko" Becker (that's how he got his name), Jim "The Animal" Fishback and of course Kelly Moran. Mike Bast was the master gater and pole rider but if he really needed a win, he'd ride the wall and was good at it, but he played the percentages.'

Although speedway needed new blood to ensure its survival, some of the established stars didn't welcome the young riders into the scene and in fact viewed them as a threat to their livelihood. McGoldrick remembered an incident at SRA-approved territory, Bakersfield, which not only illustrated that lack of support, but also demonstrated Kelly's quick wit that belied his tender years.

'When we first brought him out, there was a riders' strike at that time and not all the top riders were racing. Some of the top riders were but not all. So we travelled to all the tracks to give Kelly track time so he could get into the First Division. We went to Bakersfield, a hot, dry, dusty track and Sonny Nutter was there. Kelly had his shamrock leathers on and we rolled out onto the track, and Sonny was right beside us while we sat there and had our introductions. The other guys were there and Sonny looked over at Kelly and goes, "Hey Moran, this isn't a mini race," and chuckled with all the others. Kelly just kind of smiled at him and didn't really say anything. And then across the way they're announcing the riders, this is so and so and he'd wave, this is so and so and he'd wave. And when it came to Nutter, just at the perfect time, Kelly said, "Hey Sonny, your fly is down," just as they announced his name Nutter was looking down at his crotch with both hands on it to pull his fly up! Kelly never laughed, he never did nothing, he just turned his head and looked straight ahead. I was holding the push bar and I nearly fell on the back of the bike, it was so funny – I almost died. It was perfectly timed, he put Nutter down so bad, just a few little words, no celebration on Kelly's part, just very casually, "Hey Nutter, your zipper's down," and he fell for it big time.'

Not everyone viewed the emerging young stars as such a threat. Danny Becker isn't a rider who readily springs to mind when talking about the talented racers that ruled the Californian scene, yet he was one of those naturally gifted stars that unfortunately, for one reason or another, let it get away from him. Danny and Kelly hit it off right away.

'Danny Becker was the guy, my God he's still the guy!' laughed Shawn Moran. 'Kelly and Danny got on very good and Becker had that attitude. Whereas Mike Bast was serious, like Ivan Mauger, some of the other guys would have a beer after the races or smoke a bit, or whatever, which was the thing – some take it totally serious but some like to play hard afterwards. Becker rode hard and played hard, but he had a good brain on his shoulders.'

In keeping with his modus operandi at this point, Becker was older than Kelly but they shared the same passion for enjoying life and getting the most out of it.

'They had a real kindred bond,' believed Preston. 'They were both cut from the same Huntington Beach mould; they were extremely talented but wasteful in other ways. Both would party to the max, everything was sex, drugs, rock and roll and speedway. I'm serious; that was his whole, as they say, MO, just tear it up!'

'He lived by me in Huntington Beach when we were kids basically,' recalled Becker. 'He was racing mini-bikes and I was racing them too in places like Saddleback Park. I was about thirteen and I guess he wasn't more than seven – and he was just a little guy. I didn't really know him then but we met up later on in the early to mid-1970s. Then he broke into First Division and he started smoking me there and he used to smoke me when he was a little kid! We both partied a little bit, we were both into partying so that made us even closer. He used to come and watch me race a lot and I was probably only really good between '72 and '75. Then I started to fall off the pace and he sort of came through pretty quickly. I went downhill because I was drinking a little bit too much and taking the partying to the extreme. But he went way up.'

Before what was the biggest audience yet at San Bernardino, Kelly won his fourth Handicap Main in six nights which signalled that his Second Division days were over and reporter, David R. Daniel, wrote: 'Moran looks like a midget next to most trophy girls, but on the track he rode like a giant.' Afterwards Kelly thanked KK for his success. 'I just listen to my tuner. I know by now he knows what is best for me, so I listen to every word he says. I owe Ken a lot.'

His rapid rise through the ranks was slowed by a crash at Costa Mesa on 15 July when he strained his neck and back muscles. But then at Ventura on 26 July, he claimed his biggest victory to date, one that sent out a message that the Wizard of Balance wasn't all about style and dash. In the report it said that he negotiated 'heavy traffic' to beat National Champion Mike Bast on the line to win the Handicap Main.

'In those days you raced in a handicap programme, which was where all the young riders started out,' explained McGoldrick. 'And the further you go back the harder it was to win. Every time you'd win, they'd move you back another ten yards. I didn't give him any instruction, although I did try to slow him down when he was starting out because I wanted him to earn a little money for himself. Of course, he was so good he could beat anyone from the back at that time and I used to say to him: "Slow down man, don't go to the marks so fast." But he got mad at me and said: "Hey! Don't you want me to win?" "Yeah, yeah, I want you to win but I want you to pack your pockets on the way." But he wouldn't do it, he wanted to win if he could and that was it.'

His exciting style was popular in the stands, but racing so close to the edge, even on the smaller circuits, resulted in painful spills. As a result he missed the first weeks of August due to torn ligaments in his knee and a broken little finger. He was back in time for the first US National Championship qualifier at Ventura on 23 August and finished tenth.

But it was an event that attracted controversy. The act of adding nitro methane to the fuel had been outlawed for that season, but many of the competitors still used it. Suddenly, in the middle of the meeting, a fuel check was announced. Gene and Rick Woods refused to have their fuel analysed, which resulted in a scuffle and fines being handed out. According to Pete Rovazzini, although he wasn't using nitro at that point, Kelly did have it in his fuel during the season, if nothing else to be able to compete against the ones that were. Given his mechanical knowledge whether Moran really knew or not is questionable!

'At Costa Mesa Kelly would race with nitro and a 22-inch tyre, that's why those Americans were so damned good,' said Rovazzini. 'Can you imagine a long track tyre, on a tenth of a mile track, with 10 per cent nitro methane running in your motor? Give me break man, that thing was an evil, evil thing to ride. We ran straight pipes, nitro, 22-inch tyres and Kelly always rode round the outside. That thing was peppered full of nitro, it would be like a bronco, it would stand up and Kelly would just manhandle it. To this day it gives me chills thinking about him on that thing.'

However, Kenny Best believes that when they outlawed nitro and stopped using the expensive 'DG', that marked the turning point of the sport as it slipped from its highest peak of the mid-1970s. 'When they took away the dirt, 22-inch tyres and nitro, it was whoever got the gate and pretty much follow the leader, hence the dying of speedway in California,' he said.

Nevertheless, Kelly successfully qualified for his first US National Championship at Costa Mesa. This event was run using the traditional sixteen-rider, 20-heat format that was used in the World Individual Championship. In the press pack for the event, it reported that his favourite track was San Bernardino and that to stay in shape he liked to jog. It also stated that he hoped to travel overseas to race on the continent.

A week after winning his first main event at Costa Mesa, Kelly finished in a respectable seventh place with 8 points in the National – predictably the winner was Bast. Intriguingly, this was the first time that Kelly rode a four-valve machine and it was an interesting one at that.

'During that first year he qualified for the US Nationals, even though he didn't start the year in the First Division and he was only sixteen. He did that on a two-valve motor when everyone else had four valves; the first night he rode a four-valve was at the Nationals,' said Rovazzini.

'Ed Schaeffer was Scott Autrey's mechanic, he built motors for Scott and that speedway conversion was actually one valve out of an Offenhauser engine that they used for the Indy Cars. John Drake designed it and Ed was a brilliant mechanic and Kelly was riding his specially built two-valves, but the four-valve was the one with the Offy valve and the first time we used it was in the Nationals that year. We also ran it at Ascot and we tried running it over in England, originally, but we went from side port to centre port and that was the killer. We should have just kept it on the side and Kelly wouldn't have struggled and we spent the first few months trying to get that motor and carburettor working. I wasn't smart enough to figure it out, or the other mechanics, so it wasn't until Ed came over and worked on it that it worked. It made a lot of horsepower, it was a push-rod motor and we were riding on the shirt tails of Scott a bit.'

Kelly would get to pit his skills against the globe-trotting Autrey next. Scott was the nation's top international rider at the time and was just beginning to enter the best phase of his career when he arrived at Ascot for the US Long Track Championship at the end of October.

Located less than thirty minutes from downtown LA and within the shadow of three busy freeways, Ascot Park in Gardena became famous partly because of its heavy radio promotion. It also became equally notorious for staging America's then most popular motorcycle competition, the AMA Grand National Championship, during the sport's heyday in the 1970s. Yet it also staged other racing, including flat track, stock cars, motocross and sprint cars. Although it didn't hold conventional speedway races – that would come later – it staged a long track meeting at the end of the season, which had become the traditional season-closing event. Long track is a larger version of speedway and is held on bigger tracks of around 1,093 yards (1,000 metres) in length; while the bikes are similar, they have a longer wheelbase and also a gearbox. It was a sport that was particularly popular on the European continent and Kelly's brother, Shawn, would become America's only individual World Champion in the discipline in 1983.

Not only was Autrey in the line-up, but so too was Bruce Penhall, Mike Bast, Dennis Sigalos, Sonny Nutter and Gene Woods, to name a few. However, Moran took it all in his stride. Unsurprisingly, given his experience of the bigger circuits overseas, Autrey won an exciting Scratch Main event and was only troubled by Penhall. Many expected more of the same in the Handicap Main, but they didn't reckon on the tearaway teenager from Huntington Beach. He held the lead for two laps and was seemingly increasing it until his engine began to give up the ghost and he coasted to a stop on the first bend, which allowed Autrey to claim a double victory.

Moran had a stunning first season on a 500. He qualified for twenty-three main events and won fourteen, and with that sort of record there really were no other candidates for the title of Rookie of the Year.

While Autrey celebrated, Kelly's mechanics gathered around his machine like concerned medics to investigate the cause of the mechanical failure that had cost him a victory. He'd already removed his helmet and gloves, and was taking a swig of water as he surveyed his crew busily looking over his bike. He began to wipe away the sweat and grime from his night's work when he noticed that a crowd was gathering for his attention, all eager for an autograph and a photo of the youngster who had virtually stolen the show from the established stars. Keen observers would have noticed someone else hastily pushing his way through the throng to his busy pit, a man who possessed an unfamiliar accent when he urged, "Excuse me, excuse me please!" What this man had heard and been told about the Wizard of Balance was correct. He was excited by what he had seen and he was eager to introduce himself.

'He was a popular rider, had a good style and remarkable ability on a bike,' said KK. 'When we went to Ascot Park for the half-mile race, Ian Thomas was there and offered Kelly a ride in England. He was ready to go, so he took off and went to England.'

# 6

# THE QUERENCIA ZONE

'The present is already pregnant with the future.'

Voltaire (1694–1778)

At the conclusion of the 1979 season, Kelly had the world at his feet. Having finished fourth in the World Final at such a tender age, he was the hottest property in the sport; moreover, he was also one of the most exciting talents around. Yet renewing his contract with Hull for 1980 was looking less likely as each week passed by.

When the American arrived in England to race in the Indoor International at the Wembley Arena in December 1979, where Ian Thomas was one of the promoters, many felt that a face-to-face meeting would seal the deal. It didn't. What the Californian wanted as one of the world's top riders and what Hull were prepared to offer him were as wide apart as the Atlantic Ocean that separated the two countries. So the racer returned to California without a contract and his future in doubt. In fact, at the BSPA conference that followed a week later, Hull circulated his name as available for transfer.

Only two weeks had passed since his last match for Hull when he had to contest the American round for the 1980 World Championship at Anaheim. With only the top two scorers progressing to the next stage, he got off to the worst possible start when he suffered an engine failure in his first race. On a tricky surface, he scored one point in his next outing and then fell heavily on the back straight in his third ride, which forced his retirement from the meeting with a knee injury and, according to *Cycle News*, aggravated his back. The event was won by Bruce Penhall, with Scott Autrey second. Like many of his fellow countrymen, his failure to qualify for the World Championship may have turned his attentions to the big bucks and sunshine racing on offer in California and in turn strengthened his resolve to stick out for better terms from the Vikings. But he was certainly disappointed by his failure.

'I was really choked. It was such a big disappointment, especially after finishing fourth in last year's World Final,' he said.

It was believed that Thomas was interested in tracking both the Moran brothers. Younger sibling, Shawn, had made a trip to the UK at the tail-end of the '79 season and actually rode for a USA Select team at the Boulevard and scored 6 points. The Hull management were keen to see him in action but he didn't have the right permits. So Thomas got around this by tracking him under the alias of David East! However, riding his brother's equipment, someone discovered the ruse and Thomas and the rider were both fined by their respective federations.

'He's a bit taller than me and he rides with a different style,' Kelly said of his brother shortly after his World Final appearance. 'He's a different type of person too, but he should make it over here [Britain]. After two years here in England and fourth place in the World Final, neither of us would want people to draw comparisons because we are different – not carbon copies.'

As if to underline that potential, Shawn won the US Long Track Championship shortly before the American Final and scored 10 points in that qualifier. Those credentials, and those of his brother, didn't count for much when Ian Thomas announced in late January 1980 that neither would be included in his plans for the forthcoming season because he was unable to agree terms. *Speedway Star*'s Gary Briggs reported:

'It was common knowledge that Kelly became involved with a management agency at the end of 1979 and, although he was number four in the world, a figure of somewhere around £20,000 over the odds was being asked by the agency.'

The identity of this 'management agency' wasn't revealed in the report, possibly because it never existed! Unless the collective minds of Pete Rovazzini, Ken McGoldrick and Kenny Best were regarded as such, but none of them, and not even Kelly's brother, have any knowledge of such an organisation.

'That's not true,' Rovo said of the supposed agency. 'The thing is, Ian wanted Kelly to ride for next to nothing. What Kelly was getting was a pittance compared to what Bruce Penhall, Bobby Schwartz and everybody else was getting. Ivan got most of the money there, so there wasn't enough left.'

Rick Kelly also believed Hull woefully underpaid their Californian star. 'They ripped him off. I used to say to him, "Kelly why don't you get a guarantee like Bruce and Bobby?" Ian Thomas and Bryan Larner were not fair with him because he was the gate. They came to watch Kelly Moran.'

According to the Average Earnings Index, the average weekly wage in the UK during the 1978–80 period was around £18–20. Rovazzini can't remember the exact figure that Kelly was being paid per point but believes that it wasn't more than £3–5 which, on an off-night, was barely minimum wage and certainly didn't reflect a rider that was now ranked fourth in the world. Moran later said of the contract dispute: 'I was promised everything and got nothing.'

What seems more likely was a breakdown in relations between them. Explaining his decision to put the American on the transfer list, he revealed some of his frustrations: 'He went on the list because of his off-track antics and when this was revealed in Tenerife [British promoters' conference] only one track showed interest. It is amazing that a nineteen-year-old, placed fourth in last year's World Final, is almost unemployable in British speedway.

'He had a prosecution for driving a car without a licence, even though he had signed a document to say he would not,' Thomas claimed. 'I have checked with the American authorities and he has never taken a driving test – this has led to several serious problems.'

As we know, Moran was well-known to the local constabulary but, as these comments were published in January 1980, it suggested that the prosecution had taken place over the previous year. According to Veronica Chapman, who Kelly lived with in '79, this was highly unlikely. 'I can assure you that I never had any dos with the police while he was with me. I would have known because my niece was in the police at that point,' she said.

It's understandable that the Hull management had grown frustrated with their teenage star, Thomas in particular. Despite the fact that Britain was becoming used to hell-raising sportsmen like George Best, James Hunt and Barry Sheene, as a collective, British speedway, although not without its characters, was still relatively conservative and certainly not prepared for someone like Kelly who was capable of getting his name, and sport, on the front pages as well as the back of the national dailies.

'Kelly would always be subbing from Ian,' Joe Owen recalled. 'At first I think it was a bit of novelty for him, but then he started getting phone calls about him at 3 or 4 o'clock in the morning and he wouldn't put up with that. The Yanks were on the phone all the time and Ian didn't want that.'

At one point, the management made the mistake of giving him a cheque book, which he took full advantage of. 'He had one those cheque books that guaranteed the money to the sum of £50. He kept writing them out for £50 all the time,' Rick laughed. 'He said, "Well they gave me the cheques so I just write 'em! Why did they give them to me?" I think he ran up a debt of thousands and he gave me these cheques because he owed me for flying over Marice and I had to go all over town cashing them. Ian Thomas and Bryan Larner cleared up that debt but they stopped it out of his money.'

Moran's departure drew a line at Hull. They would never get as close to a senior league championship again. In fact, after some mediocre seasons, the club closed at the end of 1982 but would re-emerge at a different venue, Craven Park, in 1995. Off the record, Rovo wasn't very complimentary with his assessment of Messrs Thomas and Bryan Larner.

'It's better to be a promoter than a fan who is a promoter, that's really bad for the sport. Ian was smart enough to know how to put together a team, but Kelly was the heart and soul of the Vikings. Kelly was the gate; the worst thing he ever did was go against him because the fans were loyal to Kelly not Ian Thomas. You'd go to Hull and no one was there, when Kelly was riding the place was full. It was like going to watch Michael Jordan or David Beckham.'

Clearly Thomas had grown disenchanted with his off-track behaviour, yet he still held him in high regard. In 1996 he included him in his all-time team and said, 'What a talent he had. For all the mischief he got up to off the track, I could forgive him as soon as I saw him race.'

Originally Shawn was also ruled out because of his increased demands, but he did eventually agree terms and rode for Hull in 1980. As he made his way to East Yorkshire, he found himself on the platform at Victoria station with three suitcases and a pocketful of hopes and dreams. His brother had left quite an impression and, inevitably, comparisons would be made. 'Kelly stood out more because he was before me,' said Shawn. He adapted to racing at Hull but wouldn't see out the season with the Vikings and moved to Sheffield, where he would go on to establish himself as one of the world's top riders.

It's doubtful that Thomas believed his own words that Kelly was 'almost unemployable' because he certainly valued him highly, as he showed when he slapped a £12,000 transfer fee on the American – the same figure that the Vikings had paid to sign Mauger, which was a record at the time.

From a financial perspective, remaining in America was a good decision. The money on offer to race on the Californian circuit often eclipsed personal ambition for riders like Mike Bast and Alan Christian. Chasing the World Individual Championship wasn't a very lucrative endeavour. In fact it was reported that the American qualifiers from Anaheim, Penhall and Autrey, had earned substantially more that night than they would if they won the World title.

As the tapes went up on a new season, Kelly began to settle into racing on the west coast again. He made the Scratch Main Final at the Spring Classics season opener at Ascot and was looking to build on a domestic campaign that he had left on a high to head for England. Overall, it looked as though it was going to be something of a re-start season for him. Also making a return to action was his old buddy, Danny Becker.

'Kelly was that good that he'd block everybody and let me win a race now and again,' chuckled Danny. 'That's how good he was and he did that a couple of times. In the '80s it was probably the only way that I would win a race – I'm not kidding you. He used to wait for me, he'd sit there right next to me and block on the outside of the race track.'

On 30 April at San Bernardino, Kelly achieved his first double by winning both the Scratch and Handicap Main events. He passed Alan Christian who was the form rider at the time to grab his first Scratch Main victory; while the latter was achieved with a shoulder-to-shoulder battle with Mike Bast, so intense was their final lap struggle that leader Keith Chrisco bailed out to let them battle it out. Another Handicap Main triumph followed at Ascot, which illustrated that he was getting into the groove again.

Birmingham, England's 'Second City', deserved a speedway team that befitted a place regarded as the nation's most prosperous regional city. It was thriving from its regeneration after the Second World War through the booming motor and electronic industries, so much so that some called it 'the workshop of the world'. However, since the speedway club moved from the sport's second tier into the higher echelons they had not enjoyed much glory.

They entered the British League in 1976 after two back-to-back championship seasons in the National League where they raced in front of huge audiences. Unfortunately, success was harder to come by in the world's toughest league and, inevitably, supporters used to triumph began to drift away. The Brummies, as the team was called – taking their name from the nickname given to the people from that area – had lost fifteen out of their first twenty matches during the opening months of the 1980 campaign. Clearly something had to be done.

Boss, Joe Thurley, sought to strengthen the side and he cast an eye across the Atlantic to the west coast of America, where there was seemingly a plethora of talent waiting to conquer the world. However, the team was in no position to wait and nurture some young blood, they needed someone with a proven record and there was only one man over there who met those requirements, Kelly Moran.

From a high of finishing fourth in the world to being transfer-listed, Kelly was disillusioned and considered making his absence from British racing a permanent one. Having helped put the USA on the international map, he then viewed from afar as his brother helped his nation to a memorable Test series victory over England. Perhaps he felt that he was missing out? Or maybe he missed the cut-throat action of British League competition? Apparently, it was a chance of a new beginning, as he explained: 'I was so disillusioned at the time the last thing I wanted was to return to British League speedway. But then I heard that Birmingham were interested in me and after getting over that World Championship failure, the prospect of a new challenge with a new club soon began to appeal.'

Birmingham met Hull's asking price and seemingly had little trouble agreeing terms, as Rovazzini recalled: 'When Birmingham made him a proper offer, he went over. There is a big difference between £5 to £25–50 – that was ridiculous. Ivan was supposed to be looking after us, negotiating a good deal, but that was a load of rubbish – it wasn't good. I can't remember the exact figures but it was a pittance he was on at Hull. At Birmingham he was getting five times the money, which was in line with what the other riders were getting paid who were at his standard.'

There was some confusion over his debut. Thurley, having organised all the necessary paperwork and arranged accommodation, machinery and transport, had expected him to make his debut in the team on 31 May at Coventry. He didn't appear and it was said that he was holidaying in Mexico! The truth was somewhat different: he was having arguments with his girlfriend, Marice, and he didn't want to leave until he had resolved the disagreements. She didn't want him to leave. She'd got used to the idea of him competing at home and liked it very much. Although she understood that England was the place to go to further his career, she felt that the separation wasn't good for their relationship. Even though they lived in the same town, it was like conducting a long-distance love affair, but at the first opportunity Marice boarded a plane to join him in Birmingham.

So instead, he made his debut at home to Coventry on 9 June and scored 10 points. 'That'll do for starters,' he said afterwards. The Birmingham track was in the Ladbroke greyhound stadium in Perry Bar and was smaller than the one he raced on at Hull. It measured 349 yards (320 metres) and after making his debut he expressed some concerns he had about what he would be confronted with.

'I had a few problems with the state of the track because I wasn't sure of the traction I'd be getting. It takes time to get used to the conditions of a new track, but after five rides I was beginning to feel my way.'

Kenny Best flew over to England to be his mechanic/helper/bodyguard and his first engagement was at Coventry. He had no time to acclimatise and it was straight to work as soon as he landed. Given what he discovered when he arrived at Brandon, it was surprising that Kelly had done as well as he had up to that point.

'Someone picked me up from Gatwick and we went straight to the track at Coventry. I thought Kelly rode for Coventry at the time. We were late getting there and the bike that they had brought him to ride didn't even fit him! They hadn't adjusted anything, handlebars, the seat, anything like that, and I remember taking a bar bender in there to get the seat and the bars down. Kelly went out and had a good night! In the pits they had these urns of hot tea. They had these little tiny cups and I was used to America where they have big cups. I wasn't much of a drinker of coffee or tea either, but I was so cold that I drank all that tea and I didn't sleep for like a day and a half! I was so edgy and wired that I couldn't sleep at all – that was even after flying and driving all night to get there. And the next day, the sun came up, I was looking around and I was on this sheep farm in the middle of nowhere.'

He believed that the farm was owned by someone on the management team. Jet-lagged and a stranger in a strange land, Best then learned that speaking the same language didn't necessarily mean that there was a clear understanding. 'The farmer's wife asked me the very next day if I was going to have tea and I told her no. When it came to dinner time, everyone was sitting around the table and I came walking in and I asked Kelly, "Where do I sit?" She looked at me and she goes, "You said you didn't want tea." And I said, "No, I don't want tea, I want some of that roast beef!" She was talking about did I want dinner. That was my very first time in England. So not only did I not sleep for the first couple of days, I didn't eat!'

Kelly settled in quickly at Birmingham and his entertaining style meant that he soon became a firm favourite with the supporters. However, they didn't stay at the sheep farm long. 'I'm not sure if they really liked us [the farm owner and his wife], or maybe I just got that feeling because they were so quiet and we were so crazy,' pondered KB.

Following that short-lived experience they moved into an old manor house called Dove House, where Bobby Schwartz also lived. It was owned by Jeff May, who was a speedway promoter, sponsor and motor racing enthusiast, and it was a place that particularly impressed Best.

'It was out in the countryside of the Midlands, just beautiful. As you drove into the driveway, under an arch, you went off to the right on a circular drive where there were the mechanics/gardener's quarters – they had a couple of garages there. As you kept right, going forward there was a house, which was a guest house, where a lady and her two daughters lived – they stayed well clear of us! Then as you got to the back there was, gosh I don't know, six or seven garages across that made a circle – that's where we worked on the bikes and a mechanic looked after the owner's cars. And then as you came behind those garages there was like a maid's quarters, and as you kept coming back there was the main house. And that was a fancy place, suits of armour, old chastity belts hanging on the walls – it was very nice. Kelly and I stayed in the main house and Bobby was out the back, where he lived with his girlfriend, Pam. There was a caretaker that lived there. So we had that place to ourselves pretty much.'

There were other benefits to racing for a Midlands team. Hull was out on a limb in many ways, while the Midlands region was something of a hub for the sport at the time. Notwithstanding the teams in the area, Birmingham, Coventry, Cradley, Leicester and Wolves, there was also something of a motor sports industry there, probably helped by its proximity to so many automotive businesses and the motorway network, plus a number of businesses that served speedway such as Cov Comp and GTS.

Furthermore, with so many clubs in the area, this meant there were many riders located in the area, among them fellow countrymen Bruce Penhall and Schwartz, and some that Kelly knew well from when they'd visited the USA to race like New Zealander, Mitch Shirra.

As was his way, Kelly would drift between the various locations during the season, but sometimes he would wear out his welcome. Bruce Penhall lived in a house that he'd bought in Sutton Coldfield that was no more than five minutes away from Dove House, where he'd also stayed before moving. He'd been racing on the continent when he had to wait over an hour to be picked up from Birmingham airport and was somewhat irritated to find that Kelly was still there from when he left. More annoyingly, he had been partying hard and this was part of the reason why his mechanic, Mike Tzoganakis and Kelly were late picking up a tired Penhall from the airport, who also had to ride that evening at Reading.

'I was not in the mood for Kelly,' recalled Penhall. 'I could tell he was on a "good one" from the night before. Mikey was fine however, although tired from "baby-sitting" Kelly. We got back to my house and I was still pissed off that they were late collecting me. Kelly was in one of his moods that he used get into after a few days and nights of drinking. I told Mikey that we needed to get him over to Boogaloo's [Schwartz's] house – it wasn't the first time we had cause to do this. Bobby lived only five minutes from me, so we proceeded to put him in my car and the first thing he did was kick off my rear-view mirror. Then he started on my glove box, so we picked him up and shoved him in the boot of the car before driving him to Bob's. When we got there and I lifted the boot to let him out, he was just lying there laughing his ass off. He thought it was the funniest thing that had ever happened to him. He was fast asleep as soon as we got him inside.'

There were times when Schwartz also had to restrain a boisterous Moran, but he seemed to have a way of achieving this. 'We were going to Birmingham and Kelly wouldn't shut up,' said Bobby. 'Whatever it was, he was pissed off and getting crazy in the car. He was kicking stuff and was just crazy. He was like trying to get from the back seat to the front, like helping us to crash and it wasn't a good thing.

I had to do something to contain him, I can't remember what I did, I didn't hurt him, but I definitely stopped him,' he grinned.

Approximately six weeks after signing for the Brummies, Dan McCormick, who had transformed unfashionable neighbours Cradley Heath from also-rans to championship contenders, took over the promotional reins. He saw Birmingham as a sleeping giant and, having left Cradley, had ambitious plans to transform the club's fortunes.

Speedway likes to promote itself as a family sport and even in today's more professional era, a family atmosphere still exists. While other sports of this time had already begun to lock away their superstars from the public by their use of press officers, PR agencies and security staff, speedway stars were still accessible to their fans. Indeed it was and still is one of the sport's attractions that it has maintained its personal links with the people who ensure its survival. During Moran's era, it was not unusual to find a top rider mixing with the supporters in the bar after the meeting, especially before drink-driving laws became more stringent and when attitudes toward alcohol and its consumption were more tolerant.

Kelly would refer to Best as his minder, an unofficial role that many of his friends would take on, even though most of them lacked the stature of KB. Although he liked to do his own thing and to hell with anyone who wanted to stand in his way, he liked the security of knowing that someone was looking out for him. With so many people of all kinds calling on the racer's time after the meeting, it could be a very demanding and stressful part to play, but Kenny took it quite seriously in a bid to maintain his friend's image and reputation.

'Kelly had a mechanic for when he was riding different tracks for his club, but I helped out. Basically, it was keeping Kelly out of trouble. He was such a friendly guy, he wasn't egotistical at all and I would say he was a man of the people. They loved him and he loved being with them. So he would go to the pub after the races and start buying pints for all the fans. He was strange because he would get to a certain point where he was fine, then all of a sudden he'd have one more drink and then he'd become a Dr Jekyll and Mr Hyde. So I had to try to coerce, drag, whatever I could to get him away so that he wouldn't keep hitting the headlines as the bad boy of speedway – we were trying to prevent that.

'I was a site nurse and I worked with alcoholics, so I would try and figure it out. I would think, okay, what is he showing me, right before he has that one last drink that flips him over? I never could figure it out. I wanted to because I wanted to drag him out of the party, drag him out of the bar so that he wouldn't look bad. There was no warning sign, no sudden change in behaviour at all. It was like turning on a light switch, he'd go from happy-go-lucky and having fun to just plain mean.'

The business of speedway racing doesn't provide the best lifestyle in which to attempt to quell the revelry that can come with the territory. A racer's working hours are predominately the twilight period and while others are going to bed, the adrenalin from an evening's competition is often still pulsing through their veins. The excitement of competition and the adulation from supporters means that a rider doesn't wind down for the night in the same way as someone would with a regular 9–5 job.

The licensing laws in Britain then were more stringent than they are today. The selling of alcohol in public houses in the 1970s and '80s was generally restricted to the hours of 11.30 a.m. to 2.30 p.m. and 6.30 p.m. to 11 p.m. On Sundays some establishments exercised an earlier time of 10.30 p.m. for 'last orders'. Night clubs were subject to different licensing laws and usually operated over the weekends, with Thursdays for the younger, teenage clientele. Therefore, especially on a week day, when a rider had finished his work and people were heading home at around 11 p.m. in order to be fresh for work the next morning, riders like Kelly were still wide awake and eager to experience some fun and entertainment because their 'evening' was just getting started. But in those days most things were closed at that time of the night. Therefore, what was open were establishments you'd prefer not to frequent and it was mostly company that you'd rather not be keeping.

'When he was riding, was on top of the world and stuff, it was more of a having fun type of thing, but the only problem was that he would over-indulge himself and that mean side would come out. Later in life, I think, it was depression. He didn't want to be around anybody. I think he felt that he had let people down,' believed Best.

Best's task was made all the harder during this era because league racing on the continent wasn't open to foreign imports like it is today. A rider of Kelly's standard can race in at least three different leagues and in as many countries within a week, as well as his other personal commitments. This hectic schedule of fly in, race and leave for the next meeting didn't begin until the last years of Moran's career. Therefore he had more downtime than they do now.

Nevertheless, with no superstars in the side like they had at Hull with Mauger, Kelly formed a heat leader trio alongside Steve Bastable and the up-and-coming Andy Graheme. Unfortunately, support from the rest of the team was inconsistent due partly to Czechoslovakian Zdenek Kudrna missing half the fixtures because of commitments in his homeland, Ari Koponen's national service, the injury and early departure of Phil Herne, and Finn Jensen's unreliable scores. Their fortunes were not helped when Kelly chipped a bone in his right elbow during a meeting on 28 July when he was the innocent victim of a tangle between Jensen and

Cradley's Dave Perks in what was described as one of the most spectacular crashes ever seen at Perry Barr. This kept him out of the saddle for a few matches.

McCormick's arrival did instigate an improvement in the team's performances, but he had his sights set on 1981. 'When my colleague Jeff May and I came into Birmingham in July we knew it was too late to do much in the way of improving the side immediately,' said McCormick at the time. 'Next season has been our prime concern since we took over and it's still the case.'

Therefore, the club set about planting the seeds to grow better fortunes for the following year, and Kelly believed he was part of that plan. However, he did get to play an important role in the destiny of that year's championship when he guested for championship-chasing Reading at Halifax on 30 August.

Dave Lanning was the Speedway Executive at Reading and the club had attracted massive publicity by announcing a £40,000 bonus for the team should they win the league championship. He booked the American as a replacement for Jiri Stancl and he explained: 'Kenny Carter was approaching his prime then and the Shay was a bastard of a place to go to. Reading was running hard for the title. It was about August and we pulled a little flanker and told Jiri Stancl to stay home so we could use Kelly Moran as a guest. With all due respect to Stancl, Kelly was a much better proposition because we felt that we needed all the firepower we could muster. So we fiddled Kelly in. "Yeah, yeah, no problem boys, I'll come and defend your 40 grand," he said.'

Reading team manager Mick Bell was in his first season in the job and was far from sure about Moran's inclusion. 'That was a controversial one at the time because Bobby and Kelly didn't see eye-to-eye. I said to Dave, "Can't we get someone else?" and he was quite adamant, and said: "You don't realise how difficult it is to get guests. I've got Kelly and we're keeping him for that night." I was really upset and thought, why, surely there is someone else. But since I'd got involved, I soon learned that you can make twenty calls without speaking to a rider and when you get one in the end you think, thank God I got somebody. I didn't realise that at the time and Dave secured us a good man there. It didn't go down very well with Bobby. That does stick in my mind. I can't think what the problem was between them, but it wasn't my particular choice and Bobby didn't want him there.'

'He [Moran] had a fight with Schwartz in the dressing room before the start of the meeting, God knows what it was about, but Bobby was a bit of a character as well,' Lanning revealed. 'It was comical to watch, it was like something out of *The Keystone Cops*! We had to pull them apart and then they were riding together which made life very, very interesting! Anyway Kelly was absolutely brilliant [he top scored with paid 11, Schwartz had 7], and he'd go roaring up the banking and we got a point there, a 39–all draw. He helped us get that draw, which was critical to our chances in the league.

'He was a character, though,' Lanning continued. 'He was gloriously irresponsible. He always used to say that he would be World Champion if he lived that long. He always added, "If I live that long." He partied hard and everywhere he went you couldn't help but love the guy because he made you laugh. They're all faceless wonders now that are lacking in charisma.'

The disagreement between Kelly and Schwartz may have been inspired by an incident that occurred at Dove House, as Kenny Best related. 'Bobby Schwartz was very tight, very frugal with money. He's always been that way and still is to this day. He'd get all these sponsors and was able to work sponsors for a lot – that was a good thing, business-wise, but he had all this stuff. He was sponsored by Bell Helmets and he'd come over to England with cases of hats and T-shirts. He'd give a few away but mostly he would sell them. Kelly wasn't like that — he'd give stuff away that he got from his sponsors, he didn't want to be bothered with selling anything or do anything like that.

'Where Bobby lived at Dove House, there were some steps that went up to a little room on the top and he had all his stuff and parts locked up. He had so many parts I can remember Kelly laughing because speedway wasn't as big in America as it was in England, so there were only a couple of shops where you could buy parts for the bikes. But Bobby had as much stock as these guys did back in America and could have built two or three motorcycles from the parts he had.

'One time we were desperate for a new tyre because we were racing that night and Bobby wasn't there. We knew he had them stashed in his little room, so Kelly broke into the place and took one! He'd broken the lock and there was no way to fix it. Bobby got really mad and upset. There was nobody else there who could have done it – it was obvious who it was. They made up and everything but for a while there he was really, really mad. That was kind of funny. We all lived at this place but we had different schedules. There were times when none of us were there, or one or two of us would be – we were all going in different directions.'

Moran had another tyre-related issue with his friend later in his career. His van had broken down and he needed a lift to the track. He called Bobby and said: 'Hey Bobby, my van's broken down, can you let me ride to the races with you? I just need to put my bike in the back of your van.' 'Oh no, no, I'm already full up,' he replied. Disappointed, Kelly made alternative arrangements. When he arrived at the track he saw Schwartz and his van was indeed full up, but with tyres that the Second Division riders had discarded. 'Schwartz – you tight wad!' Kelly laughed, and continued to give Boogaloo a hard time over that for some time to come.

As a progressive city and one that was famous for its 'spaghetti junction', where the M6 and three other major roads sprawled above a railway line, a canal and two rivers at Gravelly Hill, Birmingham City Council sought to attract big events and big names. They even believed that its intricate inner city road system would be an ideal place to hold a street race – like a grey version of the Monaco Grand Prix. Patrick Neve drove a Brabham BT45 car around 'the Bullring' as an F1 demonstration in 1976, its powerful revs reverberating off the concrete walls and buildings like an alien being on a rampage.

However, the city's automotive industry made it an appropriate place to stage the British Motor Show at the NEC. As part of the publicity for the 1980 show, the speedway team was drafted in to take part in the action staged around the quarter-mile Bullring centre. In front of a big audience, a motor racing spectacular took place where Kelly Moran stole the show with an exhibition of wheelies.

'That was great fun,' he said. 'There were a lot of famous people there from car racing like James Hunt, Keke Rosberg, Dan Gurney and Barry Sheene. We were in a parade and the announcer said, "And here come the Brummies!" And it was like, well, what do we do now? So I just started pulling wheelies and they loved it. But, with our small fuel tanks, how we got our bikes to do that distance I just couldn't tell you.'

Having been instrumental in bringing Penhall and Schwartz to the UK, no doubt Moran felt that having McCormick in charge at Birmingham was a good omen and perhaps he may have expected some empathy. But as the weeks went by they noticed that he wasn't as forthcoming as they had hoped. 'I don't think he liked me,' Kelly later observed.

'He wasn't too friendly with us,' Kenny Best added. 'He didn't get along with Kelly very well. But the thing was, Kelly could get along with anybody, but he could rub people the wrong way only because he was always joking around and didn't take anything serious. That was just his personality. When I first went over to England, I know Ivan Mauger didn't take to it too well and the only one who was carefree and joking like that was Mike Lee.'

When Kelly was injured, he returned to America and while he was there he took the opportunity to fulfil one of his rider return engagements – an agreement between the British authorities and the US. He won a Scratch Main event at Costa Mesa which, according to some reports, didn't please the Brummies management, but greatly impressed *Cycle News* reporter, Ken Kellogg, who wrote:

'Kelly took the gate, but instead of easy riding, Moran gave it all he had. He had to as [Mike] Curoso was hot on his rear tyre. Moran again was everywhere on the track, outside, inside and almost upside down. He probably covered enough ground to make seven laps. It was a very impressive ride.'

Privately McCormick may not have approved of the American, but publically his comments didn't suggest that he planned to off-load him. He said that he found Kelly to be 'no problem' and admitted that he was a popular showman in a report in the sport's press. He ended 1980 with a respectable 8.24 average but later remarked of his spell in the Midlands, 'I couldn't seem to get my bikes going.'

However, when McCormick and May took over Wolverhampton that winter and planned to operate them in the National League, they inherited a number one in Hans Nielsen. The Danish racer soon signed a new contract with the Brummies and when it was revealed that they had also unsuccessfully approached Mike Bast, it was clear that wholesale changes were in the wind. Meanwhile, despite his insistence that he wanted to remain in the Midlands, Eastbourne was trying to contact the elusive Kelly Moran in the USA but, as was often the case during the off-season, he was difficult to track down.

Eventually though, Dugard did make contact with him. The agreement with Birmingham was in exchange for Moran – Kai Niemi would go in the opposite direction – but negotiations with the American seemingly delayed the transfer from being completed. The '81 season got underway and Dugard, mindful of the Californian's unpredictable reputation, insisted that Niemi couldn't join the Brummies until Moran had not only agreed terms, but had also put pen to paper whilst on British soil. He was due to make his debut at Hackney on Friday 3 April, but he couldn't get international clearance from the AMA in time. Therefore, Niemi rode for the Eagles in that encounter, while Kelly was due to make his debut the following Sunday at home to King's Lynn – when he would also sign his contract.

As Sunday dawned he was due to jet in to become an Eastbourne rider. Dugard was confident of his new signing's special ability and predicted, 'I certainly feel Moran is going to teach our riders some real flair.' As the supporters entered Arlington Stadium for their first meeting of the new season, the clicking of the turnstiles took on the sound of a clock counting down toward the 3.30 p.m. start time, because Moran had not arrived.

While the management were assured that he was on his way, Eagles supporters began to doubt those assurances when the four riders were pushed off to start heat 1 of the Eastbourne v. King's Lynn clash – and no Moran. Moreover, expecting the American to race that afternoon, Niemi was not in the team and had in fact made his debut for Birmingham the night before at Halifax, making the Sussex side short-handed. When he also missed his first programmed ride, some supporters exchanged anxious glances on the terraces, which then became tetchy when the opposition opened up a 5-point lead – and still no superstar from America.

Kelly and his passport were often parted, sometimes by careful design, frequently by careless misjudgement. This time he arrived at Los Angeles airport and realised that he hadn't got it. Fortunately he knew where it was – at home. He rushed back to get it, but as soon as he burst out the door and into the car to speed back to the airport, his plane was already climbing into the sky. He'd missed it, and he would have to wait for the next available flight. This meant that the original plan of landing at Gatwick airport, London, on Saturday morning – the day before his debut match – had to be scrapped.

Now he had to switch to a TWA flight and would land approximately forty-two miles further north at Heathrow – adding another forty-plus minutes to their journey time to the track at Arlington. He was due to land at 1 p.m. on Sunday morning (the day of his first match). Start time at Eastbourne was set for 3.30 p.m. and Kelly's first race was around 4 p.m., so the traffic would have to be kind, with no delays, for him to make it in time. He took his change of plan in his stride and left his arrival in the hands of St Christopher and if everything went according to schedule he would make his Eagles debut that afternoon. Unfortunately the re-arrangement didn't pan out as they'd hoped it would.

Danny Dunton was Eastbourne's co-promoter and his son, Lee, was dispatched to pick up their new signing at around 11 a.m. in the morning, allowing plenty of time to get there for Kelly's scheduled touchdown.

On arrival Dunton was a little concerned when the plane landed at 1.15 p.m., so closing up their journey time. Meanwhile, after eleven hours in the air, Kelly was hauled before customs and immigration officials because of problems with his work permit. With the clock ticking away, frantic phone calls were made. The Eastbourne management had to exercise great diplomacy with official Bernard McDowell, and had to make firm assurances so that Kelly finally emerged at 2.20 p.m. This meant that there were only eighty minutes until the start time and roughly an hour and three-quarters until his first programmed ride in heat 5. It was around seventy miles to the track from Heathrow and it took approximately ninety minutes on a good run.

Dugard wasn't surprised by his disorganised approach to travel, as he grinned: 'I gotta say, it was probably something that we half-expected because we had some dealings with him before he came to race for us. He always had a problem of some sort or another.'

Despite the hold-up, Kelly was excited about the prospect of making his first appearance for Eastbourne. As he jumped in the car for a hectic Le Mans-style dash to the track, they had just got outside of Heathrow when he asked Lee if he thought it would be a good idea to change into his leathers so that he was ready to race when they arrived. Luckily, in those days, Britain's roads weren't monitored 24/7 by speed cameras, so Dunton put the pedal to the metal while his passenger began stripping off. It's doubtful either of them noticed the astonished looks as they whizzed past slower vehicles.

Heat 8, his second programmed ride, was finishing as they pulled up at the stadium. The passenger door swung open and Kelly hastily stepped out, put on his crash helmet, slipped on his new team colours, pulled on his gloves and threw his leg over an unfamiliar motorcycle. There was no time for pleasantries because, 7 points down, team manager Arthur Nutley had put him in the next race as a tactical substitute.

He was bumped off, glanced over his shoulder and nodded a thank you to his pusher and then rolled out onto the track to an appreciative audience. Tired and jet-lagged he may have been, but he was full of enthusiasm and rode four times in the remaining eight races, amassing 3 points, which he scored in his last two rides and that represented immediate progress. And so began a spectacular era in his career, which was, arguably, his finest period of all.

# 7

# BEHIND THE PERSONA

'We all got pieces of crazy in us, some bigger pieces than others.'

Cowboy wisdom

The vehicle's lights searched ahead in the darkness. Hedgerows rushed past their peripheral vision and the front of the car swallowed up the broken white road markings, each one ticking off the feet and inches as they loomed ahead and then zipped past. The driver, Kenny Best, dropped a gear and the vehicle's engine revved in response as it speedily carried Kelly Moran and Best to their destination. Inside the occupants were on a marathon journey in order to make a race meeting, and they were desperately trying to stay awake. Wired up on coffee, windows down, you could hear them coming long before you saw them because the vehicle was rocking and rolling to the sound of Australian rock band AC/DC, in particular their 1979 'Highway to Hell' album.

'Kelly had committed to ride in a memorial meeting with the proceeds going to the fallen rider's family,' recalled KB. 'Some of those memories are foggy but as I recall we were in Gothenburg, Sweden for a meeting, maybe a World Cup, and the ferry that left the next day would not arrive in England in time for us to drive from the north to the south and arrive on time. So we drove all night and all day to make it from Sweden, Denmark, Germany, Belgium, France and then we took the ferry to southern England and made the meeting. If it wasn't for AC/DC we would have never made it. To this day AC/DC equals Kelly Moran to me. Kelly and I went to our first AC/DC concert in England. I can't tell you how many hours and hours of driving we did with AC/DC blasting to keep us awake.'

The Australian band was one of his favourites and their hard-rocking style of music would often serve as a form of inspiration to get him in the mood for racing.

He wasn't alone. Recently Travis McGowan has been known to turn up at a meeting loudly playing AC/DC's 'Back in Black'. It seems their particular brand of high-energy music provides some encouragement when racers are getting in the zone.

Kelly's musical tastes did stretch beyond that genre, though. However, in keeping with someone who did his growing up during an era that gave rise to the guitar heroes like Ritchie Blackmore, Jimi Hendrix, Jimmy Page and Keith Richards, he had a preference for artists of that ilk such as Led Zeppelin, Montrose, as well as less aggressive artists like INXS, the Police, Robert Palmer, T-Rex and Bruce Springsteen.

As a frequent flyer, he came into contact with musicians now and again and some of them were visitors to speedway, such as Greg Lake of Emerson, Lake & Palmer – it's believed that at one stage he was interested in getting involved with the sport on the management side – and Motley Crue's Vince Neil and Tommy Lee also attended meetings at Costa Mesa when Kelly was racing at home in 1983–85. However, the Punk movement of the mid-to-late 1970s that captured the British youth's imagination certainly didn't appeal to him, as he recalled.

'I was never into Punk rock, that whole scene didn't interest me. Johnny Rotten introduced himself to me once, though. It was on a TWA flight to Heathrow and there was this guy who was wearing this really expensive suit. I could tell it was expensive because of the way the cloth was cut – very nice. He had bright orange hair and was wearing white-rimmed sunglasses. I remember thinking, I recognise this guy. This was in the days when you could smoke on a plane, so I approached him and said, "Excuse me mate, do you have a fag?" And he said, "Mr Rotten at your service," and that was so cool. He had a place in North Hollywood, up in the hills, and he had a bright pink 1955 Cadillac. He was a great guy and he told me all those songs he wrote for the Sex Pistols were all about his dad, who was in prison in Northern Ireland.'

When the Rolling Stones' Brian Jones died in 1969, and was then followed in successive years by Jimi Hendrix, Janis Joplin and Jim Morrison (all aged twenty-seven, which has given rise to the so-called 'twenty-seven club') this crystallised the 'live fast die young' adage. Due to the lifestyle of the music industry the casualty rate didn't decline during the ensuing years and in Los Angeles in the early '80s the Sunset Strip – in particular the Whisky A-Go-Go club – was the location for a new wave of rock music that promoted a good time attitude. It's doubtful that Kelly, as a youngster, was influenced directly by their live fast, party hard message, but his comment to Dave Lanning that he would win the World Championship one day 'if I live that long' may well have been an unconscious acknowledgement of the consequences that can arise when you live such a crazy lifestyle.

The rock star comparison isn't lost on Ron Preston, who met AC/DC's legendary frontman Bon Scott in Australia a few months before he passed away at thirty-three years old. 'All of them young rock stars dying in their twenties and thirties, Kelly wasn't far off that. He should have died a lot earlier than he did considering the lifestyle he led.'

Away from a good time, Kelly kept abreast of what was going on in the world. Travelling around the globe racing a motorcycle probably gave him a greater appreciation of global affairs than some. Therefore, not only would he have an extensive understanding of a subject, he would also have an informed opinion that he wasn't afraid to voice. He wasn't, though, particularly political; his views are best summed up from this quote when asked what TV programmes he always switched off: 'Party political broadcasts. I find far more enjoyment watching all the politicians on *Spitting Image* [satirical puppet show]. They seem to make more sense on that too!'

Like most Americans he was very patriotic. During the late '80s and early '90s, the USA became concerned by the flood of cheap electrical goods and cars in their country by Japanese companies that were forcing many American brands into decline. 'Japan-bashing', as it became known, hit new heights when the Mitsubishi Estate bought the Rockefeller Center in 1989; thus US–Japan trade relations became a hot political issue, with some politicians likening Japan's approach to business as a Pearl Harbour-type of attack on their nation in the form of an economic war. Nonetheless, Kelly showed his support by carrying a sticker on the back window of his van that displayed the US flag fighting off a Japanese one with the slogan, 'Buy American'. Asking him about it, it was clear that his decision to exhibit his support was motivated by patriotism rather than a political stance.

Given his busy lifestyle he didn't get to watch much television, but did list *Cheers* and British soap opera *EastEnders* as 'top TV'. Both Clint Eastwood and Robert DeNiro were actors he admired and he once mentioned a Mel Gibson movie as his best film, *Mad Max – the Road Warrior*. 'I have watched it about twenty-eight times now and literally know the words off by heart. It's a brilliant film,' he said.

Furthermore, in view of his sometimes zany sense of humour, it's not surprising that he enjoyed cartoons, in particular *The Whacky Races*, describing individuals like Dick Dastardly and Muttley, and Penelope Pitstop as his favourite cartoon characters.

That humour – anecdotal, clever, wacky, wicked and sometimes satirical – he would demonstrate in his many ways. Most notably 'The Jelly Man Kiss'. The planting of a kiss on the cheek is a friendly gesture and in many cultures a form of greeting. Kelly would pucker up and smack a kiss on his male friends in a jokey manner, which provided humorous opposition to the macho environment that speedway racers operate in. In a man's world, such behaviour can be a bit awkward to take, even for fun, because its underlying truth can strike a nervous chord with some. Scott Autrey's father, Don, was a war veteran and a tough but fair character and he, like most of us, liked Kelly. Scott recounted his father's 'Jelly Man Kiss' experience.

'He's pretty old-school and he was down San Diego and Kelly recognised him and goes: "Hey Don, how's it going buddy!" He called everybody "buddy", and he went up and planted a kiss on my dad's cheek. My dad was telling me about it, and he said, "Not that there's anything wrong with it ..." but being old-school he was a little uneasy telling me, and added, "There wasn't anything wrong with it, it was just Kelly being Kelly – you know Kelly." And I said, "You don't have to defend yourself, dad!" Everyone got a Jelly Man kiss at least once. It was just his sign of affection and he genuinely loved people. He was always glad to see you and he was a sweet guy.'

Dennis Sigalos remembered that the Jelly Man Kiss could get a little more passionate when fuelled-up by a good time. 'He was the only guy whoever kissed me on the lips, that little leprechaun!' he laughed. 'He used to go, "Oh, Siggy, Siggy, come 'ere, f**k you," and then give me a kiss on the lips and it was like "Urgh! Kelly, Jesus!" He'd grab your ass or grab your balls or something – all that good, clean grab-ass fun!'

The 'Jelly Man' nickname became more widespread from the mid-1980s. Kelly explained its origins in an interview in 1986: 'It's mainly because of my reputation of getting into trouble! They say that if anyone can party like me they can end up like the "Jelly Man" or Kelly Moran – the two sound alike.'

After he retired, Kelly would often accompany his friend Ron Preston on long road trips. While he was always good for a story and a laugh, Preston found that his wide range of subjects meant that he was someone he was glad to have along to help the journey speed by.

'He was great company and a good road-trip buddy,' said Ron. 'We went on some long drives to Arizona, Nevada, all over California – everywhere. I'd call him and he'd go, "Well, I haven't got anything else to do – come get me." Sometimes they were eighteen-hour days. I would go and get him at five in the morning and wouldn't drop him off until 10 or 11 o'clock at night. We'd go and do some business in El Centro and I'd introduce him to all these guys I knew and they'd watched him race speedway in the Denny Pyeatt races – and they liked talking to Kelly. It was a breath of fresh air to meet someone like him, who was a world speedway guy, loaded with stories, and he was who he was and they loved him.'

During most of his career, the Cold War existed between the USA/NATO and the Soviet Union. Europe was divided and Poland, where the sport was very popular, was part of Communist Europe. When Western riders and teams raced behind the Iron Curtain there was much suspicion from the Communists and Western visitors displayed some apprehension, all of which was influenced by international politics. For example, no currency was allowed to leave the Soviet bloc and Western riders were often stopped and searched at the border checkpoints. Eastern riders that raced in Western Europe, and in Britain, were nearly always accompanied by a member of the Communist Party, usually under the guise of an 'interpreter' to prevent possible defection and stop state secrets from being smuggled into the West.

Due partly to the language barrier and their suppressed nature, relations between the western and eastern riders were, in the main, cool. None of this bothered Kelly, who displayed little prejudice toward anyone. Zenon Plech, who did ride in the British League, said of him:

'Not all the western riders were so open, but Kelly was different. Even someone like Colin Pratt, a respected rider and manager, he was not so open. I tried to be friends with everyone and help everyone, that's me, but a lot of them weren't very open towards me, or my countrymen. But Kelly was so friendly and would try and help anyone. We raced against each other many times. He liked to drink and have a joke. Not everyone liked it in Poland, not all of them were so open to that.'

His wife Lorna remembered: 'He was a very social person. He brought in everybody, he never left anybody out.'

Kelly wouldn't listen to what other people would say about a particular person, he would make up his own mind. He wasn't one to follow the crowd and if he got along with someone it didn't matter to him one way or the other what his friends or team-mates may have felt about that person or his friendship with him or her. If he liked you and you did right by him, that was good enough and he didn't care what others thought.

British rider Kenny Carter was a controversial and divisive figure. He was thought to dislike most of the American riders and at the height of the great rivalry between England and the USA, he is said to have had badges produced with 'I hate Americans' written on them! A tough opponent who was also an outspoken Yorkshireman, Carter first met Kelly at Halifax during Kelly's first season in Britain and struck up a good relationship.

'Kenny was my buddy. I never had a problem with him,' Moran said. 'If you could get along with him he was fine. I know he had a few issues with his team-mates and such, but Shawn and myself found him okay. He was a very fast and determined rider. I was very upset when he died.'

Despite the special relationship that's supposed to exist between Great Britain and the USA, the reserved British character doesn't always find its more gregarious cousins from across the Atlantic very agreeable. This was especially so among the people who were still around at this time from the Second World War. American forces arrived on these shores in late spring 1942 to find a nation in darkness from the anxieties of over three years of conflict with Germany. America's late entry into the war – which was likened to Hollywood's portrayal of the cavalry riding to the rescue of the beleaguered homesteaders – and their ways of gaining influence through gifts such as chocolate, cigarettes, gum and nylons, created resentment and hostility among some British citizens and servicemen. Therefore, when America's speedway invasion began in the late '70s and gathered pace in the early '80s, there were some who still harboured that antipathy from the '40s and in some cases passed it on to their children. When the Californians brought with them colour, flamboyance and big money to buy the latest equipment, it was happening all over again.

Carter may have been aggrieved by some of the Yanks' brash ways, but Kelly's generous spirit set him apart, as Rovazzini recalled: 'Kenny Carter was riding at Hull and was having trouble with his motorcycles. Kelly worked with Kenny after the meeting a lot, a hell of a lot because he used to go to Halifax when he wasn't riding with Chris Pusey. He really helped him and his first child was named Kelly.'

As a measure of how much Carter liked and respected him, Kelly was godfather to his second child, Malcolm.

'Kenny Carter hated the Americans, he hated all of us,' said Scott Autrey. 'But he and Kelly got on great. And Kenny had a lot of respect for his abilities and they genuinely got along. If there was ice that was particularly hard to break it was Carter's and I believe a lot of that was his respect for Kelly's natural ability.'

The rivalry that developed between Carter and Bruce Penhall was particularly intense and is arguably the sport's greatest ever rivalry. Moran, though, never let the friction between them interfere with his friendship with either of them.

'Kelly got along with everyone, I don't think he ever had a bad word to say about anyone,' said Bruce. 'I don't think Carter was threatened by Kelly. If Kenny was threatened by anyone, including guys like Peter Collins and Michael Lee, he'd have a problem, whether that was from an English standpoint or the Yanks, it didn't matter. And Kelly being the happy-go-lucky guy that he was, Kenny didn't worry about what he did, he loved him, and he knew he was going to go and party and he could beat him anyway. Plus he wasn't an Englishman he had to worry about, he's a Yank.'

That friendly attitude was just natural to him and it was a facet of his character that made him hugely popular. So long would he be talking to supporters, signing autographs and having photos taken with the fans, that quite often he'd be the last one in the stadium. He was in no hurry, so he could easily have been left with instructions to turn off the lights and lock up the stadium!

'He took his time and spoke to people. He made a lot of friends like that,' said Lorna. 'Even people that were there all the time and in your face, he made time for them and made a point of speaking to them. He never said, "Go away you're getting on my nerves." Wherever you go there are people like that, aren't there? He never did that and was always very patient. With kids, he loved kids, and they'd be thrilled to talk to him. He always made a bee line for kids. My cousin had two young children at the time, one was deaf and the other was partially sighted and Kelly took them to speedway. He took them on the back of his bike and they were thrilled. In those days you could do that, you're not allowed to now.'

Kelly always accommodated the supporters because, as he said, they paid his wages. But he particularly provided time for the younger fans because they were the future of the sport and, besides, it was them that brought their parents every week. Anne Richmond was a friend of Gordon May, who made the Comet frames that both the Moran brothers would ride. She liked to take photographs and would go with Gordon to the meetings to watch and snap away with her camera. She remembered an occasion at Sheffield that illustrated Kelly's empathy with the youngsters.

'At some stage Gordon went off into the pits to chat to someone and I was left there on my own to watch the racing when Kelly came over,' she said. 'He always gave you a hug and a kiss and asked how I was, etc., and we'd have a chat and a laugh. Out of the corner of my eye I could see this little boy with his father, he must have been only five or six. His father had his hand behind his son as if to say, go on then my son, go get Kelly's autograph. Finally, he came over and stood in front of us, quiet as a mouse, never said anything, just held up his programme for Kelly to sign. Straight away Kelly looked down at him and said something like, "Hiya, buddy!" and took the little boy's hat off, turned it around, took it off and ruffled his hair – just playing. Then he bent down and sat him on his knee. He was so caring towards that boy, he chatted away, even though he hardly said a word at first. He told him, "My little bro is riding," and was smiling away at him. It was really sweet and Kelly just loved children, didn't he? Anyway he got his autograph and talked a little but was very shy. Kelly asked him if he liked coming to speedway and was saying how he thought Shawn was a better speedway rider than him. The boy, who came across so slowly and unwilling at first, skipped back to his father as though he'd been given a brand new train set or whatever he'd have wished for the most. Kelly stood up and smiled. I must have looked like I was going to cry, maybe I had a tear in my eye, he asked what was wrong and I said, "Nothing, you just made that boy's night." Soon after, him and his dad came over to say what a genuine, lovely guy Kelly was.

'The next week I was there again and I saw them and they came over to say hello and that little boy never stopped talking … it was like he was a different person. He told me when he grew up he wanted to be a speedway rider, just like Kelly he said. His father said that he'd never stopped talking about speedway and how he had a friend called Kelly who was the best speedway rider in the world – he was so happy. And that was down to him, all he did was pay him some attention.'

He practised a live and let live philosophy, rarely wasting his time and energy on things he couldn't change. These days, possibly because they're on TV, riders run off to the telephone to protest to the referee so readily that it makes tennis player John McEnroe's infamous confrontations with umpires look sporadic. In comparison, Kelly hardly ever ran for the phone if he was excluded. There was, though, one occasion when he chose to use other ways of communicating with the official when he wasn't happy with some inconsistent decision-making from the ref's box.

In 1988, the USA faced Sweden at Swindon in a Diamond Jubilee international series match. On a dry, dusty afternoon, referee J.D. Homer had stopped heat 11 when Sweden's Henrik Gustafsson had crashed heavily into the turn three safety fence and it had to be re-run – replays showed that a ridge had appeared in turn three that Henka got caught in and it straightened him up. A carbon copy of the incident occurred in the very next race; this time it was America's Sam Ermolenko who crashed in the same place on the opening lap. Expecting that the race would be stopped, Kelly and Sweden's Peter Nahlin momentarily slowed up, while Per Jonsson, oblivious to what had happened behind him, continued to lead.

Realising that the race hadn't been stopped, Kelly twisted his throttle and took off after Jonsson. As he came over the start/finish line to complete lap two, he flicked two fingers at the referee's box in anger. He repeated the insult to Homer as he flashed by to complete the third lap. However, as he came round to finish the final circuit, he slowed as he approached the finish line, slightly twisted his body to face the ref's box and angrily gave Homer the one-fingered variety.

During the presentation ceremony, when the American team were being awarded their winners' medals, the members were introduced individually. When presenter Peter York read out Kelly's name, he stepped forward, collected his medal and off-mic he said to York, 'Did you see me signalling to the referee?' to which York retorted, 'Yeah we saw you waving, it was two pints wasn't it!'

There were times when he wasn't taken as seriously as he should have been, but he wasn't afraid to speak up. John Perrin was the promoter at Belle Vue when

Kelly and his brother raced for the Aces and he wasn't known for his compliance or diplomacy. Like many bosses, Perrin would get frustrated by Moran's behaviour and occasionally this would cause conflict between them. Nonetheless, if Kelly disagreed with Perrin, he wasn't afraid to say so, often speaking up when others preferred to look at their shoes – the younger ones in particular. Once the grievance was aired and dealt with, though, it was forgotten.

'He was bright, knowledgeable and he was no one's fool, he just chose to turn the cheek most of the time. He would never stay mad at anybody,' recalled Rovazzini. Dennis Sigalos agreed: 'Yes, he was very knowledgeable and he was a good mate to everyone – except Hans Nielsen!'

Free spirited, he wasn't always so accepting of people's criticism and got tired of people poking around for a madcap Kelly story. On one occasion, when a journalist brought up his off-track antics and questioned his professionalism, he didn't shrug it off with a smile or a characteristic wisecrack.

'As long as I'm getting the results, I don't think anyone should be interested in how I lead my life,' he responded defiantly. 'We all do things wrong when we're growing up, and who's to say I have or I haven't, or that I'm not a reformed character? I'm still going to party that's for sure!'

There was also a stubborn side to him. Especially later in life, he would accept advice, help and guidance, but only to a certain point. When it was becoming a bit of a drag and impeding on how he wanted to lead his life, he would dig his heels in, draw a line in the sand and wouldn't budge.

'He was a free-spirited guy and he never had any malintent [*sic*], he took the best of everybody and he didn't like being judged,' recalled Scott Autrey. 'I remember one time Ronnie [Preston] was getting onto him about something, trying to help him, and he had a drink first thing in the morning or something. He said: "You've got to do something about this, take care of it," or whatever. Kelly just looked at him and said: "Hey Ronnie, I am what I am." Anybody could find common ground with Kelly. Somehow he always managed to make my dad laugh. Even my son, Jet, he thought the world of him.'

Moran also had a sense of fair play and he didn't like to feel that the public were being cheated. Many times he would question the wisdom of excluding a rider from a race for a starting offence. He believed it was better to handicap the offender by making him start further back instead of denying the public the opportunity of seeing a rider in action that they'd paid to see.

No more so was his view of fairness evident than during an individual meeting in Amsterdam in May 1987. Some of the world's top stars were brought together to ride in the Dutch Golden Helmet at the Olympic Stadium where that season's two-day World Final was due to be staged. It was seen as an unofficial dress rehearsal for the sport's biggest showpiece. The winner was to be decided by a six-man Grand Final and in the race Sam Ermolenko slid off in the rain and was excluded. FIM representative, Jos Vaessen, was present and Kelly overlooked the referee and went straight to the official, arguing that Sam should be re-instated. 'The public came to see a six-man final, not a five-man one,' he said. Ermolenko and Moran were then involved in a titanic battle for first place with Sam getting the verdict on the line – his selfless gesture had cost him a victory, but not his principles.

He wanted to win as much as the next rider, yet he didn't feel that defeat was a crack of doom – far from it. He'd be the first to outstretch his hand to congratulate his opponent on a race well won and was also just as courteous to a conquered rival.

'I like to win but I don't think it's the end of the world if I don't. You see some guys who, if they get a second, a third or a last they come into the pits and they'll throw their helmet down, have a go at their mechanic or kick their bike. But it still doesn't change the result,' Kelly observed.

However, despite his sometimes wild ways, he could also be respectful. Kenny Best would have him stay at his house many times and there were few problems. 'When he'd be home during the off-season he'd spend time at my house and it was a place where he could get away. I think he enjoyed it. He would get quite boisterous sometimes but he knew that there were rules and that my daughters had to get up to go to school. There were a couple of times I'd have to tell him: "Kelly, not too loud, keep it down." He would always respect that, that's one thing he would do for me. So he would have to keep it down. He was quite a gentleman.

'He had a lot of insight on a lot of things and he was really, truly, a nice guy. He would have his bad moments, but he was so polite. I'm not sure if it was Tom or Sharon, but ever since those kids were little, they were so well behaved, had such good manners, they always treated people with respect. If they came to your house they would pick up after themselves. I can't tell you the amount of times that Kelly would come to stay at my house. Sometimes he didn't want to be with a lot of people, he would come over, have a few people over, we'd have a few drinks and stuff and finally the sun would come up and I'd go to bed. I'd wake up the next morning and Kelly's washed up all the dishes, emptied all the ashtrays and wiped down all the tables – that's just the way he was. He grew up with my two daughters and they felt like he was their big brother. Other places we would go he wouldn't be that way. I can remember dragging him out of a few pubs when people were angry with him, and when he had too many drinks he'd get angry back. But that wasn't the real Kelly. He had a big heart and he was always trying to help other people and stuff.'

His generosity and his caring side could also be his undoing – even detrimental to his own career, as Bob Dugard explained: 'He never actually wanted anything of value from anybody; if someone wanted something and he had it, he would give it to them. I had to stop him doing that several times when he wanted to give away engines when he wanted to help youngsters and I used to say to him, "Kelly, they're your best engines – don't!" That was Kelly all over – he was a nice lad like that.'

He also seemed to have little concept of money, indeed, some might say a scant disregard for it, as he would illustrate time and time again by regularly blowing a whole night's wage in one go in the bar after the meeting and then seek to borrow more! Billy Hamill, the 1996 World Champion, also said that he was generous to the point of self-poverty, 'He would give you his last dollar if he thought it would help you out.'

When you're racing at the top of your game, enjoying good times, sponsors and a decent income, you can fall into the trap of thinking that it will last forever. Unfortunately it doesn't. Kenny Best could see that unless he curbed his generous ways and realised that there would be a day when he couldn't race anymore, he wouldn't have the financial security that his rich talent deserved.

'Kelly made a lot of money for that time, I know, I was with him. In fact, I took part of his money at one time and put it in a bank account for him. I was trying to get him to save some money but he wanted it. Just because he would give you the shirt off his back, the last dollar in his wallet and that's why he ended up the way he did – it was such a sad, sad thing. We were good enough friends that I could do that for him, but I just got tired of him yelling at me and stuff, so I would just say, "Here, here's all the money." And he would give it to people.'

In a fan club newsletter published in 1982 he was quoted as saying that his ambition was 'to be well off in life'. That may have been how he was feeling at that point, or he may have been providing a different response instead of the stock answer of 'to be World Champion', because money wasn't a prime motivator for him. He sure missed it when he didn't have it, though, yet his smile stayed on and his personality ensured that there were doors open for him.

Four years later he told *Speedway Star* that the ultimate for him would be to 'try and win as many World titles as Ivan [Mauger] and to be a successful all-round rider', yet further on he revealed a little bit of his real beliefs, and some inner wisdom, when he was asked what he wished for in life. He replied: 'To be happy and healthy. As long as you are that, the rest doesn't really matter.'

Kelly wasn't one to complain and whinge. Even when he sustained multiple injuries at Hackney and there was a question mark over whether he'd walk again, his sunny disposition prevailed. He believed life was to be enjoyed because, as he said on many occasions, 'Life's not a dress rehearsal.' He didn't like his own company for long, mostly he preferred to be around family and friends, and he certainly wasn't short of company when he was a racer and in the public eye. He had a keen sense of humour and didn't take himself too seriously either, so his wit and his collection of stories from his experiences meant that he was never short of an audience. It was different after he retired from racing, of course, yet he was still able to make a favourable impression through his charm and humour.

It has been said many times that he didn't take speedway seriously. He once said himself that if he had one regret it was 'not taking myself seriously enough'.

'A lot of people have tried to persuade me to be more serious,' Kelly continued. 'It happens in whatever country we might be in, when we are having a drink after the meeting. Sometimes I think it's the alcohol talking because they'll say, "If I could ride like you … you just get on the bike and it's natural." They are rivals saying that!'

He once told the author that he couldn't be all-professional like Ivan Mauger or Ole Olsen because that just wasn't him, it wasn't in his make-up to be like that. Sure he had fun with his racing, but he also wanted to win races and do the best he could for his team. He may have treated it as a job, especially during the latter days of his career, but as he said, 'What a great job to have.' Besides, he wasn't regarded as one of the most exciting and entertaining racers of his era for no reason, and having spent most of his career racing against and alongside the best, his all-action style and the spectacle that he brought with it – an approach that produced plenty of injuries – aren't the actions of a man who didn't take it seriously. It seems it was only his critics and fellow frustrated racers, who would have given anything to have his ability, who threw that remark into any debate when talking about Kelly Moran. When it comes down to it, it's the people at the turnstiles that matter, the ones who pay the wages, and time and time again promoters have said that Kelly, and Shawn, brought in the public. They may have been impressed by the successes of the likes of Mauger, Gundersen and Nielsen, but it was the racers like Kelly that they came to see.

He was naturally relaxed and he'd give off this cavalier image throughout his career. After all the checks had been made, the adjustments to the bikes and the team talk before the match, the riders would head to the dressing room to get changed for racing, while the pits would reverberate to the sound of motorcycles being warmed up. Kelly was always among the last, if not the last, to emerge from the dressing room to make his final preparations. When it came to the racing itself, very rarely, if ever, was he the first to arrive at the start. The referee would have to sound the two-minute time allowance to hurry him up, and even as it counted down he would still be getting ready before he'd finally emerge from the pits, sometimes with just seconds to spare on the clock.

There were a few advantages to this approach: he wouldn't be subjected to the psychological games that racers play at the start line because they'd be waiting for him. Any nervousness they may be feeling could be amplified by having to wait for the American, and he took advantage of this, no matter how small it was. Furthermore, if he was feeling butterflies himself, cutting down that time between waiting and racing would only help. However, he rarely displayed any sort of nervous behaviour, even in the biggest of events.

'Kelly never got nervous at all, no matter what,' said mechanic, Craig Cummings. 'Nothing bothered him. It was like "it's in the history books, oh well, let's go and have a pint." That was his attitude. He had a routine. He'd leave everything for the last minute. He would always clean his leathers, his boots and helmet ten minutes before he would leave for the track. It was almost as if he wasn't bothered, but he was. He liked to portray that devil-may-care attitude.'

His ability was such that he could race well within himself and still turn in a succession of double figure scores. But in order to produce that jaw-dropping magic that mystified and thrilled us all in equal measure, it would sometimes require a different pre-meeting approach to get him all fired up.

'It depended what mood Kelly was in,' Pete Rovazzini assessed. 'With him, sometimes, you could flip a coin. He liked to argue with me before he got to the race track, it was his way of getting his aggression out and he'd get out of the car pissed off. And then he'd come up and apologise after the first heat in his own little way. But I knew what was going on – he was getting his race face on.'

Crashing is part of the game in motorcycle racing; crashing badly comes with the territory. This might be part of the business, but many racers don't like to think about it and prefer to avoid the whole scene when it happens to a rival during a meeting that they're competing in. Obviously they don't want to be reminded of the dangers when they've got to go out there and compete themselves. This didn't bother Kelly though; if a rider crashed, rival or team-mate, he'd certainly be among the first riders on the scene – sometimes the only one – to offer some sort of racer camaraderie for his fallen colleague. However, he once humorously admitted, 'I wish ketchup only came in a bottle and not on the track.'

Even after he had retired, he would pass on messages of support to riders he knew who had some big crashes. In 2005, Billy Hamill was involved in a nasty crash at Swindon, puncturing his lung, breaking his ribs and injuring his back. Kelly was friends with Hamill and heard of the accident and called the author to get the lowdown on his situation and to pass on a 'get well soon' message. It was a typical of him and was more caring than his hangers-on in the bar would ever appreciate.

Kelly would race hard, but fair. His skill meant that he was able to achieve things on the track that others wouldn't have managed, yet he didn't need to pinch riders off or shove his rivals around in order to get ahead. He'd close the gap, but always leave his rival with room to race. Even though he admitted that he was harder in World Championship meetings, he once said that he didn't like having to be tough on people who were his friends off the track.

'I wouldn't take anyone too far but I'll close the gap as much as I can, even if it means going up to him after the race and saying, "I'm sorry but this is World Championship racing." I don't like that side of it. On the track we are not exactly enemies, but we are rivals,' he said.

Of all the motorcycle sports, speedway is more of a head game than most. With the riders all racing similar machines and the duration of a race being just four laps and lasting a little over sixty-odd seconds, not only is it an explosive adrenalin rush for its participants, it's also a very short space of time in which to get it right. Therefore, the margin for error is small and success and failure often depends on confidence. Sometimes it doesn't matter how hard you race, how hard you train, or how much you spend on your equipment, for some reason it just doesn't work. It has been said that speedway riders are the most superstitious bunch of all motorcycle racers and Kelly was no different. He wasn't fond of the colour green, had reservations about the number 13, he didn't like to see women in the pits, nor, oddly, peanuts! The latter seems like a bit of a joke at the interviewer's expense.

It's interesting to note that in another profile, published in his fan club's newsletter, he also states that if he hadn't been a speedway rider he would have been a carpenter. 'My father is a carpenter, so I would have a very good teacher,' he said. This declaration is not mentioned in later interviews and Shawn Moran doesn't have any knowledge that his father worked with wood. However, Bob Dugard recalled that he once told him that he was training in carpentry at school.

Of course, Christians will know that Jesus was also a carpenter and later in life Kelly embraced the faith. However, this was in 1982 when he was twenty-one or twenty-two years old and, like many young people of that age, although he was curious about spiritual matters and a Bible was always available to thumb through, serious study didn't occupy his thoughts as much as other pursuits. That's not to say he was a non-believer, because he once said that the person he would most like to meet was the Pope. When he was married to Lorna, she observed that he practised his faith on special occasions, but not to the extent where he'd follow the Christian calendar. His racing schedule didn't allow for that degree of commitment and you don't have to attend church to believe in God, for as the scripture says, 'For where two or three have gathered in my name, there I am in the midst of them,' – Matthew 18:20.

'He was probably as religious as I was in those days; we got married in church and we had a christening,' Lorna recalled. 'What he did do, he'd go to church at Easter and so on. And since I was a girl I had been brought up to go to Midnight Mass (Christmas Eve), attend church on Easter Sunday and on Mothering Sunday, but not every week. He wasn't totally religious, no, I can't say he was. He didn't practise it when he was with me.'

Following four years as a professional speedway rider, Kelly had achieved more than most would in an entire career, yet he'd also experienced the darker side of racing while thoroughly enjoying the many benefits that his profession provided – and many it didn't. A charmer, a gentleman and a happy-go-lucky racer – Bob Dugard, the Eastbourne Eagles and their supporters were about to discover that the best was yet to come.

# 8

# WHEN YOU SOAR LIKE AN EAGLE, YOU ATTRACT HUNTERS

'My heart tells me Kelly Moran was the best. I never met anyone with more talent on a motorcycle.'

Bob Dugard

The Eastbourne Eagles Speedway Club was unlike any of Kelly's previous teams. For a start, it had a deep sense of tradition. The Dugard family had been synonymous with the venue dating back to the pre-war years when Bob's father, Charlie, first bought a share in the club in 1934. Bob had been a rider himself, most notably racing for Wimbledon and his promoting partner, Danny Dunton, had also raced. Having ex-riders on the management team was also an advantage for Moran.

The club's family atmosphere bred a solidarity that to opponents resembled a fortress-like mentality. While the team was very much at the heart of the club, so was the sport itself. Its track, measuring 330 yards (302 metres), was always prepared well and there were no compromises of the sort that Moran found at Hull. Kelly loved it at Eastbourne. He settled in right away. The weather on the south coast was generally kinder than it was in Hull or the Midlands and that helped him with his troublesome back. He would thrive on that circuit and excel within the club's unique atmosphere. If he was looking for a home from home in speedway, he had found it.

'I think Bob Dugard really helped him, kept him under control, he was a big draw down there,' said Sigalos. 'It was a smaller track, probably one of the smaller ones on the circuit, close to the beach, so I think it did suit Kelly – he found his place there, I believe.'

Arlington Stadium, where the Eagles raced their home matches, was situated around 3 miles south-west of Hailsham. Surrounded by woodland

and green fields, its exterior tranquillity masked the noisy excitement contained within the venue itself, and the whole atmosphere of Eastbourne was in direct contrast to the cosmopolitan experiences he'd had so far at Birmingham and Hull. Furthermore, they raced their home fixtures on a Sunday afternoon.

Following the meetings, many of the riders and staff would go to the Deanland Tavern, which was located in the 200-acre Deanland Wood Park at Golden Cross – just a ten-minute drive from the stadium. Its sumptuous setting was an ideal place for riders to relax after the high octane activities of the afternoon. Many people associated with the club during this period reported that they experienced some amazing nights there, especially when in the presence of the charismatic Kelly. The Eastbourne management soon realised that they would have to rein in their American's appetite for having a good time, as much for his own good as for the club's image.

'We used to all go down to a country club after a meeting at Eastbourne and you had to filter the money out to Kelly otherwise he'd buy the entire populace there a drink,' said Dugard. 'He could be a belligerent little bugger when he was drunk, but he would always be very sorry afterwards. I never really had too much of a problem when he had too much to drink, he could be made to see common sense for me, but if you showed him any sign of weakness he would latch onto that.'

Like Brum, the Eagles were also former giants of the National League, having experienced both league and cup success before entering the top flight in 1979. Despite including former World No. 2 Gordon Kennett, the team had struggled. But the management were hopeful that by signing the young Kelly Moran – who was still not twenty-one – his influence could provide a strong breeze for the bird of the broad wing to soar once more.

'I first saw him with Hull and I thought he was the most naturally gifted rider I had ever seen,' said Dugard. 'That's only rivalled by two or three other riders, the most recent being Darcy Ward. The only thing with Kelly was that he would never ever pump funds into his equipment like the stars do today. If he was up for doing things in a very professional way, he probably would have been in a class of his own.'

Eric Richardson became the American's new mechanic and, like Bernard Harrison before him, his experience would help Kelly slam in the big scores for his team. Richardson's son, Colin, had also raced for the Eagles, but they had a massive fall-out and they weren't working together. Therefore, team manager, Arthur Nutley, saw an opportunity for Richardson senior to wield the spanners for Moran.

'I believe Arthur spoke to Bob and they rung my wife and asked whether I'd be interested in mechanic-ing for Kelly,' recalled Eric. 'Well I didn't know anything about him, I didn't have a clue who he was really. I'd seen him ride, but he was just one of the Americans. I was asked if I wanted to do it and I thought I'd give it a go. You never know, you meet some stranger and you don't really know how it's going to work out. So I went down and I started mechanic-ing for him.'

It was, though, the perfect scenario for Moran. All he had to do was turn up at the track with his gear, get changed and throw his leg over the bike and perform.

'I did the deal for him to go to Eastbourne and the deal was all the motorcycles, all the motors, everything was done, all Kelly had to do was roll up and ride. Everything was taken care of,' said Rovazzini. 'The only thing I did was have custom-made fenders. That was perfect, because we knew that every time we showed up that the bikes were ready. He ran those Weslakes with the black tops, I can't remember who built the motors, it was a special black-headed motor and Kelly flew on that.'

'The bikes were supplied by Bob Dugard,' added Richardson. 'The trouble was that Kelly didn't know one end of a bike from another to be honest with you. You could put whatever gear on you wanted, he hadn't a clue. He had been around bikes for donkey's years, but he'd come in and say: "That bike's bloody spinning," or "this bike ain't driving or this ain't revving." But you could put whatever gear you wanted on and he could ride the damned thing. He just had great throttle control; it didn't matter what engine or what bike he was on he could ride it – he was excellent. He was a young lad at Eastbourne, twenty-one or twenty-two, and these days they talk about the youngsters today, but they aren't in the same league. He had his best years there without a shadow of doubt.

'I did the bikes and my daughter used to clean his leathers and do all his kit, pack it away. We used to turn up, and he'd come into the pits about ten minutes before it started, do a running jump at me, put his arms around us and go and get changed and I'd never see him until he arrived at the track! I was doing a full-time job as an engineer at Clifford's Dairies, so I was doing Kelly on a part-time basis. I was taking my holidays as half-days so that I could go to meetings.'

Julie helped her father prepare the machines and generally looked after the American's racing needs. Although Kelly stated that he had a superstitious aversion to women in the pits, he exempted Julie from that irrational belief.

'We did it together really. Dad did all the mechanical bits while I did the bits like cleaning the bikes and leathers,' she remembered. 'He was lovely, like a big brother. He was so caring, like every time he'd turn up for the meeting, it was almost as if I was his good luck charm, he would give me a little kiss and treated me like his little sister, which was lovely because I was only eleven or twelve – really young.'

His team-mates included the Kennett brothers, Gordon and Dave, Trevor Geer, Paul Woods, Olli Tryvainen, Robert Slabon and Eric Dugard. A week after his debut, Kelly was registering double-figure totals alongside Gordon but, unfortunately, the rest of the side didn't provide consistent backing. While they were more competitive than they had been and enjoyed some notable victories at home, silverware was a long way off.

However, the arrival of Moran provided the Arlington faithful with a charismatic talent and one that was world class. He became something of a sensation at Eastbourne, rivalling Gordon Kennett for the number one race jacket and settled in so well that he lifted his average by almost 2 points. Yet, more than that, he was providing the Eagles' congregation with a display of mesmerising skill on the Sabbath to such an extent that some wondered if he was indeed a gift from God.

'He was one of the most popular riders ever down there, he was a legend. Everybody loved Kelly, there was no ifs and buts about it,' recalled Richardson. 'I've seen him go down the straight – I can't remember who it was now – but they pinned him on the white line, and he just lifted his front wheel over the opposing riders back wheel and went round the outside of him!'

Broadcast journalist Tony Millard used to do the announcing at Arlington as well as carry out other media-related roles. He was also closely associated with nearby Brighton & Hove Albion football club, which allowed for some cross-marketing opportunities and benefits. It was Millard who arranged some of Kelly's sponsors, such as his sponsored car, and an agreement with British Caledonian airline that eventually appeared on his leathers as 'Travellers International'. Millard believed that the signing of Moran was the club's first bona fide international star.

'The fans loved him,' he said. 'Eastbourne were a low-profile team and they were lifted up a notch or two because, up until then, basically, they'd only really had local riders – the Kennetts, the Richardsons, they were all people who had graduated from the Eastbourne training school and they had grown up via the National League or Second Division, etc. So I think Kelly was probably the first overseas star they had, wasn't he? There was Kai Niemi, but he wasn't a star.

'We had all sorts of things in place, including a sponsored car that he drove for half the summer until we realised that he didn't have a driving licence!' laughed Millard. 'The car was from Arlington Motors, that's how we tied in the sponsorship. It was a magnificent car too, except for the fact that he never put any oil in it so he ended up seizing the engine.'

The vehicle was an Audi 80 GLS which, while not on a par with today's luxurious Audis, was still an attractive model. Although grateful, with his name emblazoned along the side and that of the club, he was conspicuous and he disliked that. He didn't like to draw attention to himself and every time he went out he did just that. Of course, he treated the car like he handled his motorcycle – raced it hard!

His decision to join Eastbourne was one that the American took very seriously – at least to start with. Although his form only got better and better, as the year progressed, due to outside influences, his priorities changed.

'Part of the deal when he came to Eastbourne was that he wanted to buy a house in this part of the world and settle down,' revealed Bob. 'That was really good news for us. We were all up for it and took total charge of his bank details. He was allowed to draw £100 in cash at a home meeting and that had to last him for a week. The other money would be paid into his bank account. We got to around June/July time and he should have had well over £20,000 in the bank and we checked it out and there was nothing at all! Although we set it up with a secure system, the bank had slipped up. They were allowing him to send money to America, he couldn't take money out, but he could transfer it to America. And so it had all gone and that was the end of any dream of a house. We're going back a long while now, but down south here you do pay a lot of money for houses, but he would have been well on the way to afford the deposit for a decent place. Unfortunately, the cupboard was bare when we went to open it. That's the sort of things you did with Kelly. When you used to say to him, "Look, this was the plan and the arrangement that we had," "Yeah I know," he'd say, "but someone needed the money more than I did." And that was it. He had no complaints about it, no sorrow really, it was just a little thing in life that was a bit of a slip-up but he'd get over it.'

Consequently, Kelly had no fixed abode when he raced for Eastbourne in 1981. He stayed with a variety of people within the region and also with some of his pals in the Midlands – the proverbial rolling stone that gathered no moss.

Following their popular Test series victory over England in 1980, a second England v. USA series was held in 1981 over five matches. But the English were not so much hungry for revenge, as ravenous. They won the first two encounters at Belle Vue and Poole, where Kelly made his first appearance in the competition at reserve. Prior to the vital third Test at Swindon, which the Americans simply had to win to keep the series alive, newly appointed captain Bruce Penhall told the audience before the match that, due to the win or bust nature of the international, the Yanks showmanship would be put aside that night in favour of serious dedication.

Serious wasn't really in Kelly's vocabulary but showmanship was. After two races the Americans had established a 4-point lead when Kelly arrived at the tapes for the third heat alongside Scott Autrey to face the English pairing of Michael Lee and Gordon Kennett. Moran leapt into the lead and didn't look back, with Autrey in second for a 5–1. However, as he came off the final corner to take victory – as was his style – he shifted his weight to the back of the bike and the front wheel began to float off the track. It kind of wavered slightly from side to side due to the power being transferred through the back wheel as it gripped the track. Instead of following his management's directive of seriousness by getting both wheels onto the circuit, he controlled the wheelie as it pawed the air and it climbed higher and higher as he crossed the finish line to a gasp of appreciation from the crowd. Meanwhile, his team-mates shook their heads and smiled wryly at his maverick skill.

He won his next race too, but an engine failure during his fifth outing saw him cut a forlorn and disappointed figure when he slowly walked back to the pits. England took command and Kelly finished with 9 points but America had lost the match and the series. Years later Moran said of the series: 'I didn't have a very good Test series for the USA against England in 1981, which I class as some of my worst meetings.'

Eastbourne may not have had the international profile that Belle Vue enjoyed at the time, but they were no less ambitious. In 1981 the Eagles carried out a short five-meeting tour of some of the Polish tracks. It was an arrangement that was made with the Polish authorities, the PZM, so that some of their riders could race in the British League for the Sussex club and Hackney. They began the trip without their top stars Kennett and Moran – the latter was on international duty. They had already lost heavily to Wroclaw and narrowly at Gdańsk, when their star duo joined the team in time for the third fixture – a pairs meeting also staged at Gdańsk.

Kelly and Kennett paired up and won the event ahead of Boguslaw Nowak and Marek Towalski, and Eugenius Blaszak and Piotr Podrzyki. Tony Millard accompanied the club to Poland and reported that a heavy fall for Kelly almost ruled him out of the meeting and the rest of the tour.

'He took a purler in his third race. A knee injury looked bad but he was twice helped on to his machine to earn vital points while Kennett dropped just 1 point in his five rides. For the pair's final race, Moran recovered and rode with great style to win the heat and earn themselves a handsome pair of crystal vases with a total of 25 points. At that particular time, security in Poland was tight and the Iron Curtain was well and truly down.'

The Western riders represented the forbidden side of life for the Communist Poles and they were seen as the adversaries by hardliners. It was one thing having a British side racing on Polish tracks, but to then have a flamboyant American, the enemy, in their midst, who was a bit naughty, well, that required some close observation. Therefore, they were accompanied everywhere by the official British liaison officer to the PZM, Richard Lubaczewski. Although there is no evidence to suggest he had any political links as such, given the Polish Communist Party's habit of sending along observers in the form of interpreters and liaison officers, it doesn't require too much of a stretch of the imagination to suspect that he was reporting back to the Party.

Fuelled by his success and other forms of excitement, Kelly decided to do his bit to improve relations between East and West. It's reported that Lubaczewski did his best to ensure all went smoothly. Needless to say, in his innocence, his best efforts to contain Kelly's unpredictable behaviour were insufficient.

'Food was very short in Poland at the time and the speedway club managed to spend whatever money they could to try and get us some absolutely amazing food for this banquet,' said Tony Millard. 'At the banquet, Kelly decided to stand on the table, remove his trousers and make a speech to the President of the Gdańsk Speedway Club to thank him for entertaining us! They had to end the banquet early because of his behaviour.

'We then went back to the Hevelius hotel, where Kelly met up with some ladies of the night and got arrested! He was totally drunk and disorderly. Bob Dugard had gone to bed. So I had to alert him that his star speedway rider had got himself arrested by the police, and he said, quite rightly, "Bollocks! He can stay there, and we'll sort it out in the morning." So he refused to get up. Kelly was in the local police station, we never saw him for the remainder of that night and he was just returned to the hotel the next day by the police without any sleep at all.'

Spending a cold, sleepless night in a Polish police cell had a quietening effect on him though, as Dugard recalled, 'He got slung in prison for a night and had to cool down. I think that rocked him a little bit because he certainly straightened up after that.'

It's not surprising that he was shaken from his experience when, on his return, he revealed to Marice the method employed by the 'SBeks' to sober him up. 'He said that they arrested him, stripped him naked and then they hosed him down with a fire hose.'

However, they then travelled to Gniezno where, despite using tyres that had already done four meetings, Kelly top-scored with 13 points but couldn't prevent his team from losing the encounter, 55–35. For the final fixture at Leszno, Eagles' manager Bob Dugard discovered that while their hosts were very accommodating and friendly in general, this kindness didn't extend to competition. The team arrived at Leszno to see their opponents practising hard for the visit of the Brits. Dave Kennett and Paul Woods decided to take advantage of this by suiting up to spin some laps of their own. However, their practice session was curtailed after just four laps! When Dugard enquired about the tyres that they had been promised for the trip he was told that they would only be provided at an extortionate cost – a fee reported to be more than if a rider had gained a maximum.

'Everywhere we went we were on our original tyres,' recalled Dugard. 'The Polish riders had brand new tyres. New tyres in Poland in those days were hard to get hold of. Apart from that, we were treated really well and in those days they were outstanding on their own tracks. Very few from outside Poland were able to crack it back then and it's only in recent years, in a regular way, that riders from outside have been able to crack Poland, isn't it? They're totally specialist tracks. Kelly was as lost on them as any other team member generally, wherever we went, because our bikes were nowhere near tuned up to do what the Polish riders were doing.'

'It was a lot different riding in Poland in those days,' added Kelly. 'I remember at the start line, we would dig in to try and get good traction out of the start, and the dirt was so deep it was like lining up in trenches. Sometimes I would pull away and my progress would be restricted because my exhaust pipe, or foot rest, would get caught up in the dirt.'

Using worn-out tyres, their equipment also began to break down. Kelly burnt out a clutch on his Weslake and was riding Roman Jankowski's bike. The situation got so bad for the team that only Robert Slabon's Jawa was still operational. Needless to say, Eastbourne were not competitive and lost the match by a staggeringly one-sided score line of 71–18. Frustrated by the tyre situation and also a little angered by the ludicrous situation created by their rivals, Kelly sought to redress the balance somewhat in his own humorous way, as Millard related.

'Young Paul Dugard was there and he had a tiny little motorbike (Honda 100cc), and Kelly decided that, as Eastbourne were so hopeless, he'd get hold of Paul's little mini-bike and rode that down to the start line instead of his speedway machine! He received the wrath from the referee for that and the Poles had a lot to say about it.'

Overall, their hosts were very hospitable and they took advantage of shopping expeditions to make some useful purchases. It made for an entertaining and interesting flight home.

'In Poland in those days, if you had dollars, because the exchange rates were so stupid, you could buy anything with them,' Millard explained. 'The most memorable thing about it was whether the plane would be able to take off because everybody had got so much glassware and things that they got cheap in Poland. We were all loaded up with this contraband to take home when we took off.'

It may not have been a great success results-wise, but Eastbourne's Polish trip was a triumph in many other areas. 'It was hugely different. It wasn't an easy task by any stretch of the imagination,' reflected Dugard. 'But we started a business in Poland shortly after that, we opened a machine shop out there, machine tools, and it's been immensely successful. So it was a fantastic trip in hindsight for us and that business is still going strong to this day.'

Unfortunately, Kelly's free-living lifestyle wasn't finding favour with Gordon Kennett. Their pairs' success masked a growing mood of antipathy that he was beginning to feel toward his Californian team-mate. Eric Richardson said that he 'hated him', which was maybe an exaggeration, but they were both vying for the number one spot in the side and there was competition for that coveted place.

'They weren't the best of friends, that's for sure!' Dugard grinned. 'I think it was more frustration with Gordon over Kelly because he could be so good and put so little into it. That's not said with any malice whatsoever, but I think it was bewildering for Gordon that he could be so good and still lead the lifestyle that he did.'

'He was jealous, it was impossible not to get along with Kelly,' believed Pete Rovazzini. 'Gordon was the captain and he wanted to be the number one for Eastbourne in all areas. As usual, everyone just fell in love with Kelly.'

If Moran felt that he needed to redeem himself in any way, he certainly did so the following weekend. Not only did he complete his first league maximum for the team, he also paired up with Paul Woods to win a last heat decider at Arlington and clinched victory over his old club, Birmingham – leaving Hans Nielsen in their dust.

There was another overseas trip that was also memorable for reasons other than the fact that it was the first meeting ever staged at Rijswijk, Holland. Kelly joined his US team-mates, Schwartz, Sigalos and John Cook, in a four-team tournament against Holland, England and Sweden. He scored 8 points as the Yanks easily won the meeting with 40 points – 14 ahead of their hosts. After the meeting, some of his rivals decided to have a joke at the expense of the diminutive American.

'We were in a hotel, most of the riders were there, but Kelly was at the pub. Someone moved Kelly's bed out of his room and they put a little cot, or baby crib, in his room for him to sleep in!' laughed Sigalos.

Schwartz believed it was the Swedish team that played this joke on Moran and he could hear the commotion coming from his buddy's room. 'When he got back from this bar, he tried to get in it! And as he was getting in, I remember him going, "It doesn't fit! It doesn't fit!" He almost did, but he had to curl up so he started kicking it at the bottom to fit in and he finally knocked the side off, and I guess he proceeded to break it up. I was in my room and I heard him coming down the hallway, he was swinging one of the posts, a splintered piece of wood, then he came into my room and jumped on me! He ended up taking this piece of wood into the bathroom, he was hitting the mirror with it and he's going, "It won't break, it won't break!" So I got hold of him and took him back to his room and that's when I discovered all the splintered wood.'

An ill-fitting bed and an inebriated racer wasn't a good combination. Sigalos said that he took some calming down. 'He was slinging all this stuff around and broke a few lamps. For some reason that rubbed him the wrong way – maybe he had a few too many cocktails. We were like, "Easy Kelly, easy, easy!" That was a wild evening.'

Schwartz added: 'Finally we got him on the mattress that was in the crib, we put it on the floor, piled up all the wood next to him and he passed out, like he was done, that was great, sleeping like a baby.

'The next morning we're trying our hardest but he just won't wake up! Finally I just threw a British Airways ticket on top of him and left. I said to Bob de Jong [promoter] – this was my biggest mistake – "He won't come." "No, no, he must go, he must go, special cheap ticket. He has to go today with everybody." "Well you go and get him." So he went into the room and there's Kelly still laid out there, and he managed to wake him up. He started to move a little bit, then Bob sees all the splintered wood and is not happy. We got to the car and it only had enough room for one in the front and three in the back. Kelly had to get in and it's a small car, so we had to put Kelly across us, sitting on our laps, with him breathing on the driver from the headrest in the back. And he's calling him all these names for waking him up and breathing vodka at him. He's cursing harshly at him, really bad. They got fined for that and threatened with bans and stuff.'

With American speedway's fortunes on the rise, the World Championship qualifiers were altered to accommodate the growing number of talented riders from California. Therefore, they introduced a new qualifier for American, Australian, British and New Zealand riders called the Overseas Final which, crucially, meant that there were four qualifying places available at the US round instead of two.

Moreover, it was announced that the 1982 World Final would be staged at the LA Coliseum in Los Angeles – the first time that a World Final had been held in the USA. The organisers, World Class Inc., a quartet that consisted of Barry Briggs, Ivan Mauger, Harry Oxley and Jack Milne, were required to hold an international event in order to demonstrate to the world's governing body, the FIM, that they had the wherewithal to stage such a special competition. The fact that three former World Champions, two of them multiple times, were involved held no sway with the faceless suits in Geneva. Therefore, the LA Coliseum was the scene for the 1981 American Final on 30 May.

Four places were obviously better than two, but the margin for error was still very small. Penhall won it with a perfect score while Kelly also transferred in third after losing a run-off to Sigalos for second when they tied on 13 points. Brother, Shawn, meanwhile, was a run-off victim and his title hopes were dashed by the experienced Autrey, who stole the last qualifying spot. After the meeting, *Cycle News*' reporter Dale Brown asked Kelly what was the hardest part of the meeting and he replied with a typical one-liner, 'The fifteen other riders, that's always the hardest.'

At this point he'd hit a rich vein of form and had already scored two maximums for the Eagles including a 15-pointer. His confidence and that of those around him at the Eagles' nest was high as he prepared for the Overseas round at London's White City on 12 July. He stayed at the Richardson's house that weekend and a little gesture from Moran went a long way to impressing a receptive youngster.

'In those days they didn't have tear-offs did they, you literally had to sit there and cut up pieces of Perspex,' said Julie Richardson. 'He came to stay with us before the Overseas Final for a couple of days and I sat there for hours getting sore fingers cutting all his Perspex for his tear-offs. And then he left £6 in change for me on the side and that was a lot of money in '81. That meant a lot and I was so young and impressionable. I remember once he came in and said: "I'm colour-blind, you can have these," and they were a couple of T-shirts – one was pink and yellow. I don't know whether he bought them or whether they were given to him, but he said: "You can have these." He was so generous and gave everything away. My dad never got a penny at all, just expenses, whereas today they earn a fortune as mechanics. Dad had a job as well and I went to school, so it was our hobby if you like.'

The omens were good, but he was slightly worried when he arrived at the track and was handed the No. 13 race jacket. However, Bob Dugard grabbed it, turned it over and wrote inside, 'Lucky for some', which went some way to laying his superstitions to rest.

Julie was more capable than just a little girl running around the pits helping her father. No more was this illustrated than during this meeting when the importance of the event was not lost on her, as she eagerly put her mechanical skills to work while the superstar racer left his crew to do what they do.

'I wanted to alter the timing and my daughter was changing the gearing!' laughed Eric. 'Bob Dugard was standing there with Martin [son] and he says, "Shall I do it?" "No, leave it, she can do it!" When she'd changed the back sprocket, she'd wipe the bike down, while Kelly was just talking to the rest of the Americans!'

On this occasion the ten highest scorers progressed to the next round and from the moment he defeated Bruce Penhall in heat 5, it seemed that qualification was certain. He did so comfortably on 10 points. In a meeting that stood out for Richardson as one of the most memorable, in the midst of all that serious competition, Moran astounded him when he still found time for some fun.

'He came past the pits. Penhall, Sigalos, all the Yanks were standing on the side of the pits watching, and he came round the corner, lifted his right leg and was waving to them and the crowd! He was amazing on a bike, utterly amazing.'

Julie remembered watching Kelly race in that meeting and recalled his spectacular style, 'He was virtually not on the bike and it was so easy for him.'

Just how easy it could be was illustrated to his mechanic again the next night. 'He was racing at Reading the next day,' he began. 'He went out in his first race, but for some reason the race was stopped and he'd got a puncture. When he came in, I pulled the back wheel out of the spare bike and stuck it straight in. Now the sprocket on the back was set for White City, which was a much bigger track than Reading. Anyway, he went out, gated last, picked them off one at a time and won the race by a mile. That's the sort of guy he was. He could suit his throttle control to the sprocket he had on the back of the bike.'

While Kelly was displaying some of the best form of his career, his brother Shawn was also making a similar impact at Sheffield. He had taken over as their number one rider and won the European Junior Championship (the forerunner to today's World U21 competition). Therefore, with their stars very much on the rise, the prospect of seeing both of them competing against each other at Arlington on 2 August attracted quite a bit of interest. Moreover, neither of the teams were high fliers in the league so they were evenly matched.

The Eagles won the encounter, 46–32, and the Morans met twice in the meeting with Kelly emerging as the victor on both occasions. It was reported that their races lived up to expectations. A month later, Eastbourne travelled to Sheffield for the return fixture and anticipation in Yorkshire was just as great. This time, though, Shawn came out on top defeating his big brother three times, but Sheffield thumped their rivals, 56–22, even though Kelly was the team's top-scorer with 9.

Sibling rivalry wasn't as intense as it was when they were kids, but as much as they liked to race each other, they also liked to beat each other. Kelly later mischievously said that he'd make his brother work for it.

'I could beat him around Eastbourne and he used to get pissed off, which was kinda funny,' Kelly laughed. 'But he usually had the speed on me at Sheffield. It was fun but I'd put in a little extra effort and it was just, you know, being brothers and we had that little rivalry. We had some fun.'

By this time Richard Harrison was Shawn's regular mechanic and he recalled: 'It was frustrating going to Eastbourne because Kelly would beat our asses all the time. When Kelly came to Sheffield, Shawn would beat him. It was so ironic. But Kelly used to pass Shooey on his back wheel; it was one of his favourite tricks to pass him on his back wheel. I think sometimes they were too clean. If you watch some of the old video clips that are around, they'd give people too much room sometimes.'

Kelly may have enjoyed taking some points from his little brother, but Kenny Best believed that he was happier if Shawn won. 'Kelly would always want Shawn to beat him, that's the way he wanted it, he would never lay down for him or give it to him, but he always wanted Shawn to beat him – that's the way it was.'

The big carrot for riders of Kelly's class in 1981 was that the World Final was being staged at Wembley, the spiritual home of the World Individual Championship. World Final nights at the venue were something special, a magical experience both for the fans and the riders. Many aspects combined together to make it unique: it was held inside a world-famous sports stadium in the country's capital city, an arena that also had a long history in the sport from its earliest days and had been the home of the dominant Wembley Lions; 60–80,000 supporters generated an electric atmosphere; and the prestigious nature of the competition and the attention of the world's media meant that Wembley showcased speedway like no other place did on earth. And it was the perfect setting for a showman like Kelly Moran: his flamboyance, his spectacular style and silky skills were made for a stage like Wembley.

In order to qualify he had to finish inside the top eleven in the Inter-continental Final in Vojens, Denmark. No World Championship qualifier was easy, yet given that he had scored two maximums in his last four meetings, he was in top form and was among the favourites to make the cut. Everyone was excited; the rider, fans, management and everyone connected with the club wanted to see the charismatic little Californian – who they had taken to their hearts – qualify for speedway's greatest show.

'He paid the fare to go over there for our family, car, trailer and two bikes, the lot,' said Richardson.

Unfortunately, the importance of the meeting and the prize on offer at the end influenced some of his rivals to exploit Moran's reputation and take advantage of his weaknesses. He had gone to his room and was getting rested for the big meeting the following evening, when he heard a knock on his door.

'I was suckered,' complained Kelly many years later. 'A bunch of them got together and said, "Hey let's go out and have a few drinks and get a few girls." They were egging me on and the temptation of these beautiful, blonde Scandinavian women was too much. So I went along, had a few drinks and thought to myself, I hope I get on the podium tomorrow. But they sure messed me up for the meeting the next day. The rain and the trouble didn't help, but I was definitely suckered by my rivals.'

Kelly was in the very first race, but his opponents had done a good job on him because he wasn't really at the races and he crashed out on the first bend – which wasn't a good start. Then the rain interrupted the meeting and the action was delayed as safety was called into question by running the rest of the event in soaking conditions. Moran's mechanic, Eric Richardson and boss, Bob Dugard were both hoping it would be stopped so their man could recover and be at his best for the re-staging. Furthermore, being such an important meeting, many felt that it should be called off. However, Vojens was owned and run by Ole Olsen, who also happened to be at the meeting, and it was alleged that he had too much influence and it would have been abandoned if it had been held anywhere else. Therefore, despite the protests, the event resumed and the competitors splashed their way through the rest of the meeting and Kelly failed to score – his World Championship dream had gone for another year.

Dugard later described the Vojens disappointment as one of the 'worst memories' from that era. Richardson, too, was not at all impressed by the behaviour of some of their rivals.

'I was furious – livid!' said Eric. 'They got him absolutely drunk. They took him into a caravan and got him plastered. They didn't bother with anyone else, just him. They were frightened to death of him, that's the truth of the matter, scared to death of him. It was a great shame.'

Four days later, England was getting itself prepared for the marriage of their future king, Prince Charles, to Lady Diana Spencer. It was big news across the world and invitations had gone out far and wide to fellow royals, heads of state and other dignitaries. One invitation went to the Queen of Denmark, Margrethe II. She accepted and the riders found themselves on the same boat heading to England where she was due to attend this great state occasion.

Belle Vue and England team manager, Eric Boocock, was on the boat and recalled: 'She was with her entourage. There was a lady-in-waiting and these three big blokes who were obviously forces, bodyguards, because they had all the badges and the rice pudding across their chests. They roped this bit off on the dance floor for her and it was a big ship, and Kelly said, "Later on, I'm going to ask the Lady Queen for a dance." I said, "Don't talk stupid!" "I'm gonna do it," he said. She was about 6ft 6in and Kelly was 5ft 4in and his head would probably come up to her bust.

'As the night wore on and there were a few that was on the dance floor, he went over to ask her if she wanted a drink. I can see him now, he took tiny steps didn't he? He got within three good paces of her and these three stiffs stood up so fast you wouldn't believe it – they were on the ball. They stopped him and asked him what he wanted and we were on the other side of the room just creasing up with laughter – I couldn't believe it. Anyway, the chap came back to Kelly and said, "The Queen would like to thank you, but no thank you." He had a big grin on his face and I said, "Well I must give you credit for being so cheeky."'

Returning from Vojens, little Julie Richardson was tucked up asleep on the ferry back to England when the Americans' boisterous behaviour got a little out of hand.

'We were all partying, so I don't know who said it, or whatever, but there was a fire extinguisher hanging on the wall and someone said, "Let's pull that thing and let it rip!"' recalled Dennis Sigalos. "So Kelly did it, he grabbed the fire extinguisher and squeezed it and all that white powder just went all over whatever level we were on. I was like, "Holy shit, switch that thing off man!" But at that point it wouldn't switch off, so he threw it on the ground and ran – it was like a fog bank! I want nothing to do with this, I thought. So they just followed the footprints back to the room. I was in the room with Kelly, but I played dead, or whatever, and they didn't bother me.'

Eric Boocock recalled: 'We went for breakfast and then it came over the tannoy, "Would the occupants of so and so and so and so, please see the purser." Everyone was giggling and laughing, and I said, "That's quite near us, who's that?" Kelly's! So I said, "Kelly, you better go and see what it's all about." They got in while they were having breakfast and got their passports. He disappeared and came back, he was still laughing, and he said, "Oh they want about £280." I asked him what it was all about and he said, "Oh well, the cabin took a bit of a pounding." So we went and had a look and it was wrecked, the shower was wrecked, the mattress was soaked and there were even kick marks in the bloody door. We went to see the purser and he said, "The easiest way to help is to get these morons to pay the bill. That would save a lot of bother because the police have been notified and they'll get arrested as soon as they get off the boat. They'll get done for drunk and disorderly, criminal damage and they'll still get fined. They'll have to pay for the damage." I suppose high spirits got out of control.'

They confiscated Moran's passport until he paid the fine or came up with the money for the damages. However, Richardson believes his accomplices left him to take the rap for it even though the rest of the group were not blameless.

'They stitched him up, it wasn't Kelly, he was just being soft,' he said. 'He was way out of it and, in their fun, they took advantage. He was one of the nicest blokes that you'll ever meet in your life.'

Boocock agreed with Richardson: 'I felt a bit sorry for him because Kelly ended up paying. No one had a whip round, so he left England with nothing and came back with nothing.'

Kelly, along with Marice and Pete Rovazzini, were among the audience that watched as Bruce Penhall won the world crown in what turned out to be the last ever Wembley World Final. However, whoever that 'bunch' was that took care of him that night before the Inter-continental Final not only prevented him from taking his place in the sport's biggest event, but they also deprived the huge crowd that evening of the opportunity of seeing one of speedway's most spectacular talents in action in what was a very special night. Nonetheless, he was, at times, his own worst enemy, as Penhall explained:

'It's not that we forced Kelly to do anything, you'd turn your head and five minutes later he had disappeared to the pub when it was time to go. I can guarantee that the American boys knew when it was a time and a place, and they also knew when it was time to go to bed and get ready for race day. I can guarantee you that I was probably along there and enjoying my own fun, but not to get Kelly inebriated so that I could take advantage of him the next day. That's not the way you approach any sort of big meeting in my eyes. You go there to win, it's too bad if he decides to partake longer than he should, so I know we were all having fun, but I can guarantee that no one in the American team wanted to put Kelly into a bad position.'

The following day after Penhall won the World title, Rovazzini was at Arlington Stadium with Bruce and were still celebrating as they watched Eastbourne race against Poole. The Eagles defeated the Pirates, 41–37, and Moran was undefeated. However, during a second half race, Rovazzini witnessed a cheeky incident that summed up Kelly's approach to life and racing, yet his attitude unintentionally upset his team-mate.

'Kelly won the second half and defeated Gordon Kennett. Kelly tugged his leathers when he passed him, while at the same time waving to all of us in the bar! Kennett got really upset with us all, "Don't you embarrass me like that in front of everybody again." He wasn't trying to embarrass him, he was just putting on a show for us. We were in the bar watching and we gave him the thumbs up when he passed him and then he waved to us – that's all it was. When he was in the mood no one could beat him.'

Kelly Moran finished his first year at Eastbourne with an average of 9.54, marginally behind Kennett. Immensely popular with the supporters, the club had enjoyed a much more promising year in the British League than they had previously experienced. Given their lowly finishing position, though, it was expected that changes would be made during the close season. However, as Dugard told the press, Kelly was there to stay.

'Kelly is the best thing to have happened to Eastbourne for a long time. The public love him. If he left us I hate to think what would happen to our support. He treats the public as those who pays his wages, which, of course, they do. A lot of riders don't appreciate the public and then they wonder why the American riders are so popular.'

# 9

# WHERE ANGELS FEAR TO TREAD

'If you run before the wind, you never want to stop.'

Anonymous

It was late when Lars Hammarberg heard a thump on the door. He expected it to be Kelly because he'd often forget his key, had lost his key or couldn't find it on his person because of the state he was in. He opened the door and was astonished to discover him slung over Scott Autrey's shoulder and drunker than a skunk.

'Here you go,' said Scott as he passed over a groaning, paralytic fellow racer who stirred briefly from the movement. 'Good luck!' he added cheerfully as he disappeared into the night.

Autrey had been to Deanland with Kelly and the rest of the riders after the Eagles had defeated Poole, 46–32, earlier that afternoon at Arlington. Kelly had got carried away and had over-indulged. While no one could really prevent the little American from doing what he wanted, there were times when his rivals used his weakness for a good time to their advantage. Scott had too much liking and respect for Kelly to have encouraged him in a way that group did at Vojens, but he wasn't responsible for him and Kelly was a grown man. Therefore, if he'd over-done it, well, that was too bad.

There was a bit of rivalry between the southern coastal clubs – not to the level that it would grow to in the late '80s and '90s when the two teams were highfliers in their respective leagues – yet, nonetheless, a healthy degree of local needle existed. The following evening, the Pirates were due to take on the Eagles in the return leg at Wimborne Road and Scott found his US team-mate to be bright and breezy and seemingly none the worse for wear. However, from what he saw and knew from the previous evening, he felt confident that he wouldn't be a threat at Poole that evening.

'It was one of those deals when he showed up and I didn't pay any attention at first because I was getting my own bikes ready,' recalled Autrey. 'I always showed up with two bikes and like most people back then we, my mechanic and I took a lot of time with our preparation. After we had everything warmed up, covered and everything, I decided to go over and say hi to Kelly. I walked over and I was talking to him and he was doing something to his bike and it was just like he hadn't done anything. He hadn't done the chain, he hadn't cleaned it, he hadn't oiled them and he didn't even take a rag to his bike and he showed up with his bikes still dirty from the night before. I was sort of taken aback by it. In reality I should have got some confidence from it like, well it shows that he doesn't really care. I think his leathers were still wet where he'd hosed them off. Everybody is different, but I was ticked off that he showed up to a meeting with a bike that hadn't been prepared from the previous night's racing. I thought, well, if he hasn't done his clutch, that's 3 points for me.

'We went out to the race and I'll be darned if he didn't out-trap me! I was trying everything I could to get around him – it was everything I could do. I was with him, but I couldn't gain an inch on him. He beat me out of the start and I realised after about the third lap that I wasn't going to get round him. So I sat back and just enjoyed watching him ride because he was a fun guy to watch. He was hanging off the bike and the things he was doing … There was a lesson there for me, I guess, that everybody has their different approach. After it was said and done, I had to laugh at myself because, like he beat you on that bike – so much for that! I really don't know why I got ticked off with him because it was none of my business, maybe it was because I had raced with him in the USA team, I don't know. It's only when you think about it that it was funny.'

Kelly topped the Eagles scores with 13 points but the Sussex club struggled on a slick surface, the quality of which 'dumbfounded' Dugard and they lost 51–27. That defeat had come after a promising start to the 1982 season that included a double victory over King's Lynn in which Moran was unbeaten in both encounters. His performance at Saddlebow Road was even more remarkable given the chaotic journey the American endured to get there. The car he was travelling in broke down at the Dartford Tunnel. A phone call was made to Dugard and the promoter dashed the sixty-odd miles to the rescue in order to ensure that his rider made it to the match with minutes to spare. Typically, Kelly quipped, 'I don't mind a panic. It takes my mind off racing.'

Autrey's recollection of Kelly's bike is at odds with Eric Richardson's careful preparation. Maybe his role at Clifford's Dairies had taken priority over that busy weekend or perhaps he hadn't quite agreed a deal with the club as he explained:

'In that first year I was using my car to run him all over the place, I never got paid for anything – all he paid for was the petrol. I paid for the servicing and all the rest of it as it went on. I used to ask him for petrol money and, to be honest with you, nine times out of ten he had spent it. Or he'd give you the money, then a week or so later he'd be asking for it back. He'd lead me a right merry dance. The second year I said to Bob Dugard, "Look Bob, I'll do Kelly, but I want £1,000 for the season." And Bob said, "Okay, I'll pay you," but that didn't even cover what I had lost the year before.'

During the winter, Bob received a phone call from Moran, who informed him that his good buddy and fellow American, Ron Preston, was looking to move away from Poole. Preston, who was the first American to win the European Under-21 Championship in 1979, spent most of the '81 campaign on the side-lines with a knee injury. He was hoping that a different club would bring him a change of luck. He made his debut on Good Friday, almost stepping off the plane and straight onto the club's spare bike.

Preston, along with Kelly and their two new Swedish signings, Hammarberg and Borje Ring, shared a house together in Brighton. It was what Ron described as a 'den of iniquity'. 'We ruined those guys,' he said of the Swedes. 'Those poor suckers never knew what him 'em!' These days Brighton is known for its gay community, but back then it was notorious for the location of one of Britain's first nudist beaches. As it was within walking distance of their accommodation, this obviously provided the boys with much entertainment!

In the middle of trying to settle into his new surroundings and getting his equipment sorted out, Ron had barely been in the country twenty-four hours before he learned that his buddy hadn't curbed his wild ways.

'I was still getting adjusted to the time, I was jet-lagged and I started getting these calls asking me to help them find Kelly,' recalled Preston.

Panic had set in because the car that he had borrowed, Margaret Dugard's Volvo (Bob's wife) had been discovered crashed and abandoned in a ditch. Worryingly, there was blood everywhere inside, but the racer was nowhere to be found. Deanland was out in the countryside and there was a sharp right-hand corner that he failed to negotiate and he headed straight on with serious consequences.

'He was with this girl who was hanging out with him and they left Deanland together in this car,' said Ron. 'He drove it into the ditch at the side of the road and she stuck her arm through the window! He hauled her off to hospital and somebody drove up and recognised the car. They saw all the blood but nobody was there. So the police showed up, Bob showed up; they were all really worried that Kelly was hurt. Then they found out that she was in the hospital, but not him. I can see Bob now sat on the edge of the bed with Margaret, he shook his head and complained, "That little bastard!" He didn't drive anymore after that.

He should have waited for the cops to show up. That was my first day, and we had a whole season of that sort of fun – geez!'

Moran didn't stick around because not only did he not have a driver's licence, but subsequently he had no insurance and even if he did he was in no fit state to get behind the wheel of any vehicle – and he knew it. It took a lot of diplomacy from the club and the apologetic charm of Kelly to smooth things over, but Tony Millard recalled that he 'bounced up the next day like nothing had happened'.

Deanland certainly attracted what some might call 'groupies'. Sunday evenings were often filled with international racers from both teams taking advantage of the relaxed surroundings before they would head off in different directions for their next racing commitments. The image of glamorous sports stars proved a magnet for many in the area seeking some desirable excitement. With different accents, broken English or no English at all, Deanland on race day was a honey pot for all sorts of bees to gather around and a few wasps too.

Ron Preston witnessed Kelly returning to their Brighton home with some of these girls – a few were of a very dubious reputation. Moreover, as he recalled, they were often far from bronzed Huntington Beach babes, more like Brighton broads of the darker order.

'He was always dragging home something from the clubs, I mean scary-looking things, gothic-looking girls, back when gothic wasn't gothic, you know. It was all piercings and weird things. When he showed up with these two lesbian hookers at the house, man, that was too much! It was about 11 o'clock and we were just flipping through the channels, we only had BBC1 and 2 and ITV – that was it. He showed up with two women and the Swedes just sort of went, "Cool." I don't know where he found them. We didn't ask any questions, he just went up to his room and they were probably five inches taller than him and stayed all night. The next day we woke up and they were gone. It was about noon when we woke him up to go to the races and I said: "Where did your girlfriends go?" "Oh, did they leave?" Typical Kelly. He'd always make some snide remark. He didn't talk much about it, but we teased him a lot. Aside from speedway races, I didn't really hang out with him after. When I got to England he had his own entourage, he partied and I didn't.'

Kelly was a sweet-talker though. So much so that he persuaded Paul Woods' wife, Kay, to trim his hair prior to the home matches – free of charge of course!

However, his one-night stand, love 'em and leave 'em approach to night life wasn't very romantic and those decadent situations sometimes clouded Kelly's judgement as well his memory. Julie Richardson received a glimpse into this excessive lifestyle one afternoon at Arlington.

'I remember once there was a girl he had met somewhere and she'd followed him. He told her to get a taxi and come to Eastbourne and he had to pay a £130 taxi fee and he didn't know her from Adam! But that's what he was like; he loved everybody and some of them in the fullest sense of the word!'

That incident wasn't the only one that cost him dearly. He'd been out somewhere the night before he was due to race at Reading. Eric Richardson lived twenty minutes away from there, so he took the bikes direct to the track while Kelly was to make his own way to Smallmead Stadium. Due to his chaotic lifestyle, not only was he running late, he was also without transport. So he hired a taxi to take him the 2-hour journey from Eastbourne to Reading. That in itself was an expensive undertaking but, as was usually the case, he had no money to pay the driver. So he made him wait outside the pit gate while he raced; he scored double figures, got paid at the track and then paid the driver!

'Kelly would get up and catch a ride to the races with us,' recalled Preston. 'All the way there it was like, "Stop, I gotta get my laundry; stop, I need a pack of smokes," it was like baby-sitting a rock star. He would show up at the track and he wouldn't have any goggles, tear-offs and he'd have to borrow them off of everybody, but he always managed to get on a bike and haul ass.'

For all his faults, he was still a young man and still maturing. Few twenty-one or twenty-two-years-olds at that point were earning the sort of money that he was. He once revealed that he could race at Arlington, compete in one away fixture and fulfil an engagement on the continent and he could take home approximately £1,500 for that week when the average monthly wage was around £500–600 in the UK at that time.

'That would be about right,' agreed Dugard. 'He was on top money. Kelly was never cheap to employ, I promise you that! Pete Rovazzini came over and stayed with him for months and we did all the business deals with Pete and he seemed to be a good friend to him.'

Rovazzini recalled an amusing telephone call from Dugard. 'He called me one time and said, "I didn't think it was going to cost this much." "Is your grandstand full?" "Yeah." "Did you get what you paid for?" "Yeah." "Then what are you bitchin' about?" "I'm not bitchin', I just called to moan!" Bob really looked after Kelly. He was really fantastic and gave us everything we negotiated to a tee and Kelly really respected him.'

When it came to racing Moran could hardly be described as selfish, but he wouldn't sell himself short and he also understood where he was in his career.

'One time Bob Dugard was running down the riding order for the team and he said: "Kelly I want you to ride at No. 4." "I'm not riding bloody No. 4, who d'ya think I am, I'm not a No. 4 rider!" he replied. Bob says: "I want you to ride in heat 13," because there were only 13 heats in those days. He stopped and said, "Oh, is that what you want it for?" And Bob replied: "Yeah." "Oh, okay," and he just got on with it. That was a typical of him,' remembered Richardson.

However, Kelly's revelling was getting out of control. When he was staying at Dave Kennett's, he decided to strip off and ride a motorcycle up and down the street in the nip! Understandably the neighbours complained of his raucous behaviour to Kennett, who did likewise in Dugard's direction. Bob therefore took measures to restrain the Californian's crazy off-track conduct with very positive results.

'He came to live with me under strict rules: one pint of lager per day and not allowed out forty-eight hours before a meeting. During the time he lived with me he rode in thirteen meetings and got eleven maximums,' Bob claimed. 'Kelly had a weakness for booze, and if you could keep him away from that he was a super little character. Unfortunately I couldn't let him out of an evening [because he didn't have a driving licence]. So he was a prisoner in my house. If he wanted to go out anywhere I had to take him. So he was quite restricted in his nights out. He wasn't a problem staying with me at all and he was great with my children.'

Eldest son, Martin, who went on to become a World Finalist and Grand Prix winner, was only thirteen when Moran came to stay. 'He was like a big kid himself, wasn't he? I can remember when I went out on my bike, he'd be out there as well, pulling wheelies, showing me tricks and fooling around. He was a lot of fun, like a big brother really.'

For such a free bird, being under house arrest soon became a frustration, although Bob believes that he did calm down a bit after that. 'He just had enough of it after about three or four weeks. He asked if he could move out and I said, "Yeah, if you've learnt your lesson." And that's what he did. And he was a lot better after that to be honest. He realised that he probably had pushed things a little too far.'

Dugard had more patience for his wayward star than some and it would be tested thoroughly over the course of the year. Yet they both maintained an admirable respect for each other, a high opinion that they retained to the very end.

'He had a few run-ins with the police, just stupid behaviour really, but again all related to drink,' said Dugard. 'One thing that I would always say with Kelly was that he was always genuinely sorry afterward. In most cases he was genuine and sincere. If he had done something wrong he would put his hand up to it. He wouldn't lie or try to wriggle out of it. I've never, ever met anyone quite like Kelly in my life actually.'

The signing of Preston considerably strengthened the Eagles and to start with the two Americans were partnered together. Having not raced for most of the 1981 campaign, 'Rapid' Ron's body was finding it tough.

'To ride with Kelly was great,' he said. 'At King's Lynn early in the season I came in and my arms had started to pump up. Kelly said, "Don't hold on so hard to the bike. Let it go and relax." I always remembered him saying that.'

In an interview at the time, Moran added: 'Bob asked me to ride with Ron and I'm happy to. At the moment I'm telling him to have his choice of gate to help him out. When Ron gets in the groove and his confidence is high then we'll swap over gates and so on.'

When Preston signed for Eastbourne Dugard wasn't aware that he and Moran were such close friends. 'I didn't know that. Outwardly all the Americans were quite friendly with Kelly, but they were all a little bit resentful of him. Ron seemed to be a totally different lad, very quiet, very serious about his speedway. He was really in charge of that house in Brighton, they had two Swedish riders there and Kelly and it actually worked really well, they all got on well together. And Ron, in fairness to him, he did try very hard to keep Kelly under control and he did a pretty good job generally. From what I understand he was probably the best friend a man could ask for to Kelly, wasn't he? He did a lot of good things for him at the end.'

Preston's mechanic, Keith Lewis, also stayed there and he too would get roped into trying to curb Moran's excesses. He could be stubborn, yet he discovered that Lewis could be just as determined, which developed into a battle of wills.

'Keith and Kelly went round and round,' recalled Preston. 'Bob Dugard used to say to Keith, "I need you to help me to stop Kelly from getting shit-faced tonight, because there's a big match tomorrow." So he'd walk up to the liquor cabinet at about midnight and lock it so that he didn't drink all night. One night Kelly got really belligerent with him and got it open, and Keith slammed his hand in the door! It was all swollen up and he had to ride with a swollen hand the next day.'

The introduction of the Carlisle tyre would have an influence on the outcome of some major meetings in 1982. When the England v. USA Test series got underway the Carlisles came into their own. However, on a rainy night at Wimbledon for the first match, Kelly had a difficult evening and crashed in his opening ride as England won the meeting. Later he said that he wasn't using the new tyre.

'The English boys were a bit quicker out of the gate, most of them were on the new Carlisle tyre – although Kenny Carter was trapping well on Dunlops. It seems the Carlisle may be a bit better on the start, but although I want to try them, it won't be in the middle of so many internationals.'

Big crowds flocked to see the five-match international series, and the Moran brothers were paired together during the competition. Although most of the attention was on the reigning World Champion and US skipper, Bruce Penhall, the brothers were in top form and Shawn ended the series as his nation's highest scorer. America eventually won the series 3–2, but the Moran brothers' team-riding had a huge influence on the final outcome. Over the five matches they averaged 21 points and registered nine 5–1s and six 4–2s in their twenty-five races – the Moran phenomenon was underway. *Speedway Mail* noted that the brothers' racing had particularly pleased their team manager. 'Their respective performances this year have provided team manager John Scott with probably the greatest satisfaction,' it reported.

James Easter, who would follow Scott as US team manager and was also a close friend of his, recalled: 'He used to say, "If ever I am in a hole, old boy, Kelly would come along with a spade." And it's perfectly true. If you're really in a hole, those two boys would get you out of trouble. Underneath it all, they were exasperating and they used to drive him absolutely scats, but he loved them.'

'It was magical to watch them anywhere,' said Penhall. 'When you had a serious day on, and you had Kelly or Shawn coming up, you'd make sure you'd go to the fence and watch them guys because you knew that it was always going to be enjoyable. Most of the time Kelly could do things that no one else could pull off and you'd look at each other and go, "How did he just do that?" It was amazing.'

Important as these meetings were, he didn't let that get in the way of his flamboyance and showmanship. Scott Autrey remembered an incident at Poole during the fifth and deciding match against England when he turned what looked like being a potentially serious racing situation into one of his party pieces.

'He made the start and was leading the race. He had completed a lap and he got halfway round the corner and the bike reared up on him – he didn't do it on purpose. The bike reared up and a lot of the times, in a place like that, it would be very easy for the bike to turn right and go straight into the wall. At first I thought, oh my God, he's going to centre punch the wall, but he just shifted his body weight and turned it around the corner on the back wheel. My mouth was open, and as he came by he looked right over at us and waved with his right leg! This was in a Test match, a full crowd and a lot riding on the outcome, but it was no big deal to him, he just shifted his weight around. It was like how cool was that, hanging off the bike waving his foot at us! We were all laughing about it … typical Kelly.'

Penhall remembered that he would shake his head as he passed the pit gate, nodding as if to say, "Yeah, yeah, we've done it." It was one of these sorts of incidents that Bob Dugard remembered with great fondness.

'There was so many matches that he pulled out of the fire for us. Probably my best memory of all was when he came from last to first and went by the pits gate on the last lap and waved to me! He knew what he'd done and that was it. He waved with his left hand and was looking directly at me.'

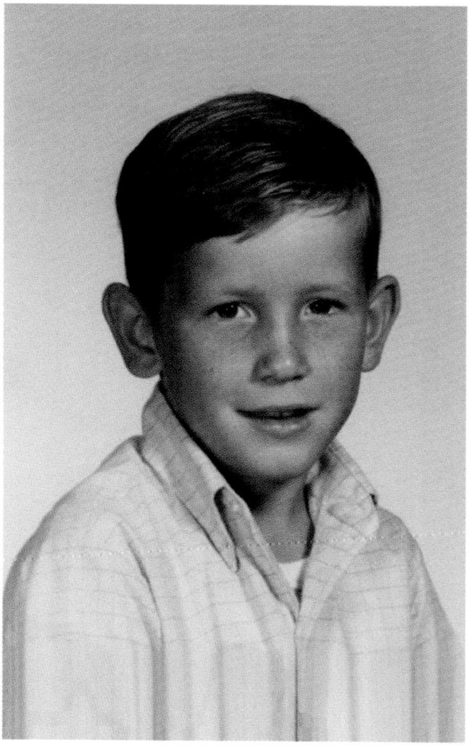

Kelly Moran (Photo by Susan Murray-Bridges)

The young Moran brothers (Photo by Susan Murray-Bridges)

Tom Moran and his sons (Author's collection)

It was an American phenomenon – Kelly mini-bike racing in the Indian Dunes (Courtesy of Susan Murray-Bridges)

Team Shamrock, the boys resplendent in their distinctive green/white suits (Author's collection)

'We're through!' Kelly receives congratulations from Steve Gresham after defeating Gordon Kennett in a soaking qualifier at Reading. Left is Barry Briggs with Bobby Schwartz. (Photo by Mike Patrick, courtesy of the John Somerville Collection)

Bobby Schwartz is the recipient of the 'Jelly Man Kiss', shortly before the 1979 Inter-continental Final (Photo by Mike Patrick, courtesy of the John Somerville Collection)

Being enthusiastically congratulated by Ian Thomas at White City after he had qualified for his first World Final (Photo by Trevor Meeks, courtesy of the John Somerville Collection)

'As he came by he looked right over at us and waved with his right leg!' Having fun at Katowice, Poland, during practice for the 1979 World Final (Photo by Trevor Meeks, courtesy of the John Somerville Collection)

On parade before a huge audience at the 1979 World Final in Katowice, Poland. On his death, this photo, and the black and white version, took on an iconic status among his fans
(Photo by Trevor Meeks, courtesy of the John Somerville Collection)

'I remember looking at his leathers when he came back from Poland and there were tyre marks all up the back.' Leading Zenon Plech during the epic heat 7 of the 1979 World Final
(Photo by Trevor Meeks, courtesy of the John Somerville Collection)

World Final action in 1979: Leaving the starting line on the inside of heat 19 alongside, Eddie Jancarz, Finn Thomsen and Christoph Betzl (Photo by Trevor Meeks, courtesy of the John Somerville Collection)

'I only got fourth. They wanted to put me on the rostrum.' A rare occasion when the fourth placed rider was invited onto the podium with the medal winners, left, third place, Michael Lee, Ivan Mauger and runner-up Zenon Plech. Next to Mauger is his wife, Raye.
(Photo by Mike Patrick, courtesy of the John Somerville Collection)

Kelly Moran celebrating his nineteenth birthday with Marice Supry at the Boulevard (Photo by Marice Supry)

Greeting Cradley and Denmark's Erik Gundersen while riding for Birmingham in 1980. John Hack is centre with Alan Graheme far left looking on (Photo by John Hipkiss)

Signing his Eastbourne contract in 1981 while watched by Danny Dunton (Photo by Rik Spiers)

Early days riding for Eastbourne (Courtesy of Mike Hinves)

On the inside leading Dave Morton (Sheffield), Eric Dugard (Eastbourne) and Mark Fiora (Sheffield) (Photo by Rik Spiers)

On the plane to Holland with (left to right) John Cook, Dennis Sigalos, Bobby Schwartz and Paul Johnson (Photo by Mike Patrick, courtesy of the John Somerville Collection)

'Anybody that could stay with Kelly long enough had to babysit him.' Bobby Schwartz running out of patience in Amsterdam! (Photo by Mike Patrick, courtesy of the John Somerville Collection)

'Everybody loved Kelly, there was no ifs and buts about it, that's for sure.' With Eric Richardson at Arlington (Courtesy of Julie Clark)

'I was suckered.' Exiting the 1981 World Championship at Vojens. (Photo by Mike Patrick, courtesy of the John Somerville Collection)

With his brother at Sheffield in 1982 (Author's collection)

'I sat there for hours getting sore fingers cutting all his Perspex for his tear-offs.' A rare pic of Kelly cutting his own tear-offs at Eastbourne (Courtesy of Julie Clark)

'When you see what he did during those four laps with the bike, he shouldn't have been able to do that.' Chasing Peter Collins during the run-off in the 1982 UK Qualifying round of the World Team Cup at King's Lynn (Photo by Trevor Meeks, courtesy of the John Somerville Collection)

Probably the best friend anyone had, with Ron Preston in Eastbourne colours in 1982 (Photo by Alf Weedon, courtesy of the John Somerville Collection)

America's victory over England in the final Test at Poole was a massive success for the team. It set them up nicely for what would be one of the best years in the nation's short speedway history. Kelly knew how important it was too and, along with his brother, he put in a sterling display, yet the importance of the trinkets that come with success held little value for him beyond that moment.

'After the presentations, he came in and gave Julie the winning medal – she's still got it,' revealed Eric Richardson. 'All the trophies and race jackets that he had at Eastbourne he gave them to her. He never kept anything. He had no value for anything at all. He never thought tomorrow would ever come, he lived for the day, that was the kind of guy he was.'

The USA team was going so well that Preston didn't get to ride in the series against England, but he did ride for America in a three-match contest in Sweden. Penhall, Schwartz and Kelly were the only regular members from the victorious side that defeated the English to ride in the Swedish series, so this meant that Preston, Brad Oxley, Lance King and Steve Gresham all pulled on the Stars 'n' Stripes to face the Scandinavians. America won the series, 2–1, and Kelly more than fulfilled his role as a third heat leader, scoring double figures in two of the matches and 9 in the other.

Tony Millard reported on the series for *Speedway Star* and he was somewhat taken aback by the American team's penchant for partying, which was certainly at odds with the quieter Swedes.

'Kelly said, "We're going to Sweden, why don't you come along." So I did. That was another four or five days of bedlam!' Millard remarked. 'The Americans were certainly fond of partying. When you think today that sportsmen are discouraged from drinking, the American speedway team was quite the reverse! They say speedway machines run on alcohol, well not the riders necessarily.'

Experienced Gresham was paired up with Moran in all three matches, and along with the captain, Penhall, went to collect him from his hotel room for the journey home, only to discover that he wasn't there.

'We were going back to England and I can't remember how we found him, but we found him in some girl's room,' Gresham grinned. 'He was still liquored up from the night before and we had to get him dressed to get him on the plane. He was really carefree, easy to get along with and had a really congenial attitude – you couldn't help but like him.'

However, as important as he was to the team, keeping him in check was a demanding job. Even though everyone was doing their bit to keep tabs on him, he would still give them the slip and disappear. In fact he would almost sink into his surroundings and vanish before you realised it. As captain, that responsibility often fell to Penhall.

'He could meet anyone in the street and he'd be gone for two hours, and you'd never know where he was. Literally, at the team stuff, we had to babysit him, we had to put him on a curfew, make sure that he was going to bed and a lot of times it became a big problem. He would get irritated because he wanted to keep going and we had put a stop to it. Don't get me wrong, he was valuable to us, he really was, but there were many times when he didn't know when to shut it off.'

Dugard remembered another trip to Sweden when he suffered another wardrobe malfunction that had financial consequences that left him broke.

'He lost his trousers somewhere or the other and had to come home in a pair of shorts. He suddenly realised that in his jeans was £600 and in those days that was an awful lot of money. It wasn't until he got back to England that he suddenly realised that not only had he lost his jeans but that's where all his money was.'

However, his off-track antics were tarnishing his reputation and overshadowing what a special talent he was. Undoubtedly this went against him when he was put forward by Bob Dugard as a challenger to compete for the then much-coveted Golden Helmet Match Race Championship. Amazingly, only once did he get the opportunity to race for that shiny headgear in 1986 – losing to Jeremy Doncaster. He should have faced Mitch Shirra at Swindon the following year except the race was eventually cancelled when they realised that the helmet had gone missing and the championship was stopped.

As a team, America were hitting their peak. While Shawn had shone in the Test series against England, Kelly once again showed his liking for the King's Lynn track when he scored a spectacular maximum for the USA in the UK qualifying round of the World Team Cup – it included a sensational pursuit and pass of Dave Jessup, of which ITV sports commentator Dave Lanning admiringly enthused, 'You won't see a better last lap of speedway than this one – a masterful piece of overtaking.' The top two nations progressed to the next stage and the USA and England had finished the match tied in first place on 39 points each – Australia and New Zealand were outclassed and some 29 points adrift. Therefore, a run-off was required to decide the winners and the Yanks nominated Kelly to represent them while Peter Collins rode for England. PC won the coin toss for starting positions and chose the favoured outside, much to Kelly's disappointment. Although neither was renowned for their starting ability, it was Collins who took the lead from the tapes and managed to hold off Moran's persistent challenge. He may not have clinched victory for his nation, but it was undoubtedly Kelly's day and he illustrated that, when he was focused, he had the beating of anyone.

'There were some great riders around and he made them look like fools at times. He had so many great races and I took so much joy from each one because he rode the bike and I did the bike – it gave me a tremendous amount of pride. He was an excellent motorcyclist, personified,' said Richardson.

Like most of his fellow countrymen, Kelly stepped up another gear when he was riding for his country, but Penhall believed that he especially responded when his nation's fortunes were on the line.

'We chose him for that run-off against Peter Collins at King's Lynn and PC got it but Kelly was our go-to guy. There was several, several times when we relied on him, World Team Cup, Test matches, he seemed to come alive when he was riding for America.

'The camaraderie was always uplifting and he was a big part of that. Sometimes it would get quite serious because that's the way it is, and here comes Kelly. It would change the whole attitude in the pits or the dressing room – he helped us so much, he really did. But it was sometimes hard to turn him around and get him serious on the motorcycle.'

The USA team's team spirit was notorious. It was so uplifting that guys would come into the side that wouldn't even be considered in other nations with more choice, and they'd turn in a match-winning display. Dennis Sigalos also believes that Kelly was instrumental in creating that special atmosphere.

'He was an easy-going guy, he could defuse just about anything. He could tell a joke, talk dirty about something to get our minds off of it, do something stupid or funny, yeah he was a bit of a clown, but big-hearted – that's the thing that comes to my mind. His attitude was, hey, it's a race; it's just a race. If he did get a little nervous, he didn't let anyone know. I think, for the most part, we were all s★★★★★g ourselves with nerves, all running to the bathroom and all that sort of stuff, and he'd just show up as happy as he could be, sit on his tool box, smoke a cigarette and be just fine.'

Around this time Moran gave an interview to Bob Radford, who asked him why he had excelled at Eastbourne. 'I love the place and it's a better climate on the coast,' he replied. 'I've got the backing and the atmosphere to help me along. I'm lucky to have Eric Richardson looking after my bikes. He is like a father to me. He knows how I ride and he's so enthusiastic, and then Trevor Hedge is helping with my motors.'

Nonetheless, Richardson revealed that while Kelly responded positively to his surroundings, it was his raw talent that raced through any shortcomings that he had mechanically or otherwise.

'We used to walk the track. I used to go round with him, and he'd be laughing and joking, he wouldn't be looking at the track at all. I used to say to say to him,

"What gear do you want on?" "Oh put what you want on." He used to pull an 18 sprocket on the front and 59 on the back around Arlington. He just used to go out and ride it. He'd come in and say that it was spinning, so I used to alter the gearing and he never knew what gearing was on there, he never had a clue. There was nothing in Kelly's bikes that was special, it was all standard. Trevor Hedge tuned his engines and it was just bog-standard stuff. If he had good equipment, really good equipment and paid the sort of money that Penhall did to have special cams and what have you put into his bikes, he'd have wiped the floor with the lot of them.'

When the Americans would get together for international events, they'd be in each other's pit, sharing stories and experiences and there would be a lot of jokes and banter going back and forth. Also they'd check out each other's equipment and Sigalos was amazed when he tried Kelly's clutch.

'He'd have the old three-spring clutch on there and we'd have the NEB six-spring clutches. They'd feel like butter, and Kelly's would be like "crack, crack" when you'd pull the clutch in, but he didn't care, he just loved riding. We used to pull in his clutch lever and it was like, "Jesus Christ, Kelly, man oh man! What's this …?" "Oh f**k it, I don't care, I'll out-gate you anyways!" he'd say. And yeah he probably did – the little bastard!' Siggy laughed.

For a rider of such immense talent, this could account for the fact that he wasn't always the force that he should have been at World Championship and international level. The fact that he didn't invest great sums into his equipment didn't go unnoticed and with national honour at stake, this had to be rectified, as Bruce Penhall explained.

'Most of the big races we'd brought a bike for Kelly because he didn't have any reliability or dependability on his equipment. So in the end we built a bike especially for him and he ended up riding a lot of my stuff in the big events because he didn't have the equipment. We ended up building a bike for him because we knew that he wasn't going to show up on great stuff. We could switch anything for him and he could ride anything that you'd put under him.'

Machine issues threatened to prevent success for Kelly when he was raced in America on a 'rider return' appearance in California. He eventually won the Scratch Main Final at San Bernardino on 25 May 1982, but he used three different motorcycles in the process, a Weslake, a Jawa and finally he had to borrow Mike Curoso's spare to get the job done.

However, when he arrived at Arlington Stadium on 30 May for the visit of Wimbledon, he wasn't quite at the races. When he got no further than the first turn in three attempts, the visiting riders became concerned over his condition. Malcolm Simmons was the Dons' captain and he published this account in his biography, *Simmo: The Whole Truth*.

'He turned up for the meeting pissed. He came up to me in the pits and his breath stunk of whisky. He started three races but never got further than the first corner before falling off each time. All the Wimbledon riders were concerned about Kelly's condition – it was clear to us that he was pissed out of his head – and, as captain, I reported him to the referee. The ref called for a track doctor to give Kelly a breathalyser test but the doc – obviously employed by Eastbourne boss Bob Dugard and too frightened to do anything to upset him – declared that there was nothing wrong with him. Funny, but Kelly was too far gone to take his last two rides. That was Eastbourne for you – you'd never get the better of Bob, no matter what.'

Simmons' recollection isn't entirely accurate because he did ride on in the meeting, winning heat 9, and finished the afternoon with 4 points. Furthermore, Moran may have 'stunk of whisky', yet according to Tony Millard this probably wasn't the reason why the American wasn't 100 per cent fit.

'I was doing the announcing that day. I helped Bob out by sending someone to Gatwick to pick Kelly up after he had flown in from America, and he'd flown in overnight from Los Angeles. Allegedly, he had decided to smoke some joints in the car, and in three races he failed to get past the first bend once … but he wasn't drunk.'

Simmons admitted that he liked Kelly a lot, but in a book that was revealing and sensational, he also accused the Americans, Kelly in particular, of having a corrupting effect on England's Michael Lee. 'I think he was badly influenced by the Americans, particularly Kelly Moran who I saw as his worst influence during his younger days,' he wrote and added, 'Whether [Bruce] Penhall and [Dennis] Sigalos dabbled in substances away from speedway, I don't know. But Shawn and Kelly Moran, Cookie [John Cook] and Bobby Schwartz … it was a known fact that they were involved with drugs.'

Even with today's more liberal attitude towards substance abuse, that is still a damning statement. It requires a little more qualifying than it reads, though. In 1982, the drug culture in Britain wasn't as prevalent as it is today, and although drugs were not uncommon you still had to go looking for them; whereas these days – certainly since the mid-1990s – not only are narcotics of all sorts more widespread, the generations that followed the '80s are more open and blasé about their use and their whereabouts. In Britain in the '70s and '80s – perhaps unluckily for Kelly – pub culture ruled the social scene. He once remarked that he used to travel through the back roads on his way to meetings during a Bank Holiday weekend in the UK, and feel a little envious of people sat outside in the sunshine drinking pints of beer and glasses of wine, while he was clocking up the miles, basically, going to work.

By contrast, America was a different story. Recreational drugs became extensive in the 1960s, particularly marijuana, and its use was rampant among servicemen in the Vietnam War. It became so common in the US that in 1970 Congress passed the Comprehensive Drug Abuse Prevention and Control Act, which reduced the penalty for the possession of marijuana – also known as cannabis, weed or pot. Therefore, when the Californians hit the speedway scene in the UK, they had a very different attitude toward cannabis than Britain, which still viewed it as harmful as any other type of narcotic – although it is still the most widely used drug worldwide.

Did Kelly do drugs? Given that he was caught at Heathrow customs, along with Bobby Schwartz, bringing the contraband substance into the country in April 1983 when the duo arrived for the England v. USA Test series, you'd have to say yes. Customs and Excise prosecutor, Mr Ian Philips, said that the drugs were found in the riders' leathers and they told the court it was for their own use. They were both fined by the Uxbridge Magistrates Court for being in possession of cannabis. Kelly had twenty-four grams and was fined £50, while Bobby had ninety-two grams and was fined £200. Afterwards Moran apologised and said, 'I am very sorry for everything, especially hurting speedway.'

As was often the case, Kelly had no money on him to pay the fine, which caused a bit of a panic as Bobby remembered: 'He only had sixty-nine cents on him or something, but because he didn't have the money he was facing sixty days in jail and he pointed at me and exclaimed: "No, no, no, he's got the money! He's got the money!" We stopped at McDonald's in Uxbridge on the way home and on the sports page it said, 'Speed Aces in Drug Shock!' And I go, "Kelly, look … that's us!" We hardly ever made the newspapers, except for that little article.'

However, Schwartz indicated that someone in the States had tipped off the officials. They searched for two hours until he told them to look in the kneecaps of their leathers.

'When he found what he found he said, "Is this all you have?" I go, "Yeah." And he goes, "We thought you had cocaine or something and were trafficking." That's what they were told and they couldn't believe that was all it was. I didn't know Kelly had anything on him and he didn't know I had anything on me. We didn't have much, just a bit to smoke.'

Moran wasn't a junkie by any stretch of the imagination. Given the circles that he was moving in on both sides of the Atlantic, you have to be pretty naïve if you think that someone wouldn't have dabbled a little bit in that area. Personally, I never saw Kelly take anything other than weed and Kenny Best didn't see anything of that nature either.

'I never saw it. There were times when I thought there was something more going on, but they were few and far between and I never saw it. I only saw him smoke marijuana but no hardcore drug use.'

He was exonerated of Simmons' suggestions in Michael Lee's biography, *Back from the Brink*, when Lee's mother, Valerie, revealed that he was trying to have an opposite effect on the rider he called 'The Champ'. 'No, it wasn't Kelly Moran. Kelly was a great character, a lovely guy and you couldn't help but like him. I know he did things but I think Kelly had a talk with Michael about what he was doing, although he didn't make much headway. Kelly also had a quiet word with me and expressed his concerns about Michael.'

Nonetheless, Moran didn't get away with his behaviour from Eastbourne's boss, Bob Dugard. At the time he described it as a 'serious matter' and supposedly sought legal advice. Unfortunately, the Eagles management hardly had time to digest the situation when another arose.

Moran once again headed to America to contest the American Final of the World Individual Championship. This time the event was held at a new venue, Long Beach, a track that met with the racer's approval. If anything, qualification was even more important to him than it had been previously because the World Final was being staged in America, at the Los Angeles Coliseum.

'I'd like to make the World Final again, it seems a long time ago since I was fourth in Katowice,' he said. 'My qualifier is at Long Beach Memorial Stadium. It's a quarter-mile track, wide and with plenty of dirt. I've got special motors and I can almost taste the World Final atmosphere, but if I make it, I want to get into the top three this time.'

And the top three was also the target for the US qualifier because, as reigning World Champion, Bruce Penhall was seeded direct to the next round, which meant that instead of four places there were only three. Once again, Tony Millard headed over to cover the meeting for *Speedway Star*.

'They organised a special bike for Kelly to use to qualify for the World Final. That was an adventure because he had his agent, or friend, Peter Rovazzini, with him. The thing was we did everything properly for Kelly, his bike was in perfect condition and everything, but he wasn't! But he still rode well and qualified.'

A near capacity of 10,000 crowd witnessed Kelly tie for second place with his brother Shawn and Scott Autrey on 13 points – Dennis Sigalos won the meeting with a faultless maximum. A run-off was required between the Moran boys and Autrey to determine the qualifying places and who would travel as reserve. Shawn drew the inside gate, Autrey was third and Kelly had the outside. However, the Morans both trapped together and arrived at the first corner side-by-side and, crucially, ahead of Scott – and that's how it stayed. 'It's so good to get it over with,'

Kelly said of the tough qualifier. 'I feel great for my brother but I feel bad for Scotty. He pioneered the sport as it is now.' While on the rostrum he enthusiastically shouted to the assembled press, 'Let's kick ass in England!'

Eight days later, the Eastbourne team prepared to take on Ipswich at Arlington Stadium. New American Champion Sigalos was there for the Witches, but Moran was conspicuous by his absence. After cancelling his original departure date from Los Angeles, he'd telephoned the club just hours before the start to say that he couldn't get a seat on any flight to London. It was confirmed that there were no seats, but the Eagles management were angry that he didn't fly when he was supposed to and the side had to field a National League rider in his place, Keith Pritchard, who failed to score. The remaining team members put in a determined display and managed to salvage a draw from the disorder that their team-mate's absence had caused – they surely would have won had he been there.

The truth was that he had some personal problems, which were such that he felt he had to change the departure date to allow him time to sort them out. But he didn't get them resolved and Kenny Best remembered that he had great difficulty getting the little racer on his flight to England.

'Things were going on with Marice and there were problems there. He didn't want to leave the US, so I practically had to drag him on the plane. She really put a lot of stress on him when he was racing in England and she was one of the reasons why he wanted to stay. She was his big love.'

Despite the years that they'd been an item, Marice revealed that they would often break up and get back together again. Kelly's party lifestyle was part of the reason but their feelings ran deep. This time it was different, it was a personal issue between them that caused him to alter his flights. Preston remembered some of the long and expensive transatlantic phone calls during this period.

'Kelly talked to Marice for hours, international, and in those days those calls weren't cheap. I remember Bob Dugard giving Kelly the phone bill and it ate up most of his pay cheque! It was a serious phone bill.'

Following the Wimbledon episode and this absenteeism, the club's management fined him £1,000 and impounded his equipment – which they owned – and once again he would have to borrow Bruce Penhall's machinery for the vital World Team Cup round that weekend. You can understand Eastbourne's frustration because not only had Bob Dugard been very patient, but the club also allowed him more time at home than most when he had to fulfil rider return engagements.

None of these problems affected his performances. He scored 10 for America as they booked their place in the World Team Cup Final with Denmark. *Speedway Star*'s Richard Clark described his performance as 'exuberant' and went on:

'There he was, minus his own bikes following a dispute with Eastbourne, and he rattled off three superb wins on Bruce Penhall's mounts.'

Before his next match for Eastbourne he had a long, clear-the-air meeting with Dugard. 'I would never have dreamed that he would have let us down like this, he has always been 100 per cent for us,' he said.

Kelly took to the microphone on the centre green to apologise to the Eagles' fans and then repaid them in the best way he knew how – by scoring a paid maximum as they defeated Wimbledon, 51–27 – the fact that it was the Dons and Simmo probably sweetened the unbeaten score. His charisma, his exciting and entertaining style ensured that the supporters easily forgave him. On the way to the starting gate he would often shake hands with the fans and high-five them.

'They pay our wages,' he said. 'They're great people and in my way I like to show them that they are important and that I do have time for them.'

'He was totally and utterly relaxed about his speedway,' Dugard added. 'It was just like going to work really and nothing seemed to faze him. If we could have got him to appreciate the seriousness of it sometimes, then who knows? The public loved him. He could really turn it on when he wanted to.'

However, over the next few months things would get very serious indeed. For Kelly and the US team they had experienced a lot of fun and were enjoying themselves, but in the midst of what should have been a day of celebration, they were about to be brought down to earth with a massive thump.

England's John Davis wasn't happy. In fact he went into the press to complain about the British fans supporting the Americans during the Test series. JD had raced all over the world representing his country and when he was doing so on home shale he expected to find the majority of the crowd backing him and his team. Sadly, this wasn't the case when they raced against the Yanks. This was especially galling at a time when England was a major force on the world's stage and Davis himself was a World Finalist. With his glamorous looks and blond hair, he was considered in some quarters as the 'British Penhall', although he didn't enjoy the same degree of success.

The Americans' popularity in the UK was at its peak at this point. Their fun-loving approach to racing, their flamboyance, colour and their unique team spirit was a breath of fresh air for speedway racing in Britain and the world over. Scott Autrey, who was the first of the Californians of the modern era to make a mark on the world scene in the 1970s, also recognised what an impact this new generation of racers from America had on speedway.

'I think they changed the sport. The second wave of Americans that came over, Penhall, Sigalos, Schwartz, the Morans, it just went on and on and they shook it up. I don't think, in the history of speedway, you'll see such an influx of talent in such a short space of time.'

Bruce Penhall's World Championship triumph at Wembley was regarded as the most popular victory of recent times, certainly as popular as Britain's Peter Collins was in '76 and some even suggested it was on a par with that of England's double World Champion, Peter Craven. However, the bubble was about to burst, and in a major way.

The scene couldn't have been staged better for their downfall. It was Sunday, 4 July, Independence Day in America, a national holiday; and Penhall, Sigalos and the Moran brothers lined up at White City for the next stage of the World Championship, the Overseas Final. On this occasion the top ten qualified for the next round, the Inter-continental Final, the last qualifier before the big one in Los Angeles and with the final in LA it was important that as many Americans as possible made the cut – preferably all four. As well as the usual US team manager, John Scott, Harry Oxley, the Costa Mesa promoter and one quarter of the Coliseum's promoting team had flown over from California to be at the meeting in order to offer encouragement.

It was a typically competitive meeting. After all the riders had completed four rides, Penhall and Dave Jessup led the scorers with 11 and Bruce's arch rival, Kenny Carter, was third with 9. They were assured of their places in the next round. Not so for the rest of the field; the next eleven riders were all covered by 2 points and only Phil Collins with just 1 point to his name was definitely out of the running for a qualification spot. Therefore, with seven places available, no one was safe and there were going to be some broken hearts.

The Americans looked to heat 19, the penultimate race when, ironically, all four would be pitched against each other in one of the most vital races in US speedway's history. To pile on even more importance, apart from Bruce, the remaining trio all needed points to be sure of a place in the next round. As the last group of programmed races began, it seemed certain that heat 19 was going to make or break someone's day unless there was some help.

They eagerly watched the next two heats, hoping the results would ease their dilemma – they didn't. After those races were over, the Morans remained in their qualifying places, but Sigalos had slipped outside the top ten and with another race to follow heat 19, the brothers weren't safe either. Given the Americans' celebrated team spirit and their friendship, most people in the stadium wondered if Penhall would sacrifice a chance of another trophy and prize money in order to help his buddies, or whether he would race for glory. Bruce was in a no-win situation: he was the reigning World Champion, he was the US captain, his actions were under the media's microscope and he recognised the importance of getting as many Americans through to the LA final as possible. Consequently, he was seen in deep conversation with Oxley and Scott studying the scores in the programme before he pulled on his helmet.

What happened next is still talked about to this day. It was one of the most infamous races of the period and one that would help Kelly as well as vilify him.

As the tapes went up and the riders headed for the first bend, Penhall was at the back. And that's where he stayed. Sigalos led from Kelly with Shawn in third, while the US skipper unwisely popped wheelies in fourth. Perhaps he thought he was entertaining the audience, but the crowd knew that he wasn't competing and they viewed his wheelies as insulting. A chorus of boos and jeers filled the stadium as the chequered flag fell and the once hugely popular Yanks were stunned to be greeted by missiles.

Kelly reacted to the crowd by returning their gestures with, among others, a two-fingered salute. Skipper Penhall was disappointed with his actions, which only inflamed the situation.

'He was somewhere else that day, I hated to see him give the fans the bird at the end,' said Bruce. 'We all got upset. We didn't realise the recourse and it irritated the crowd that bit more because of the wheelies that I was doing – and that should never have happened. I shouldn't have done that. It didn't look good. I had a chance to put the Americans in front and I did that, I don't regret that, I regret the way I went about it.'

For someone who was a fans' favourite and went out of his way to make time for the supporters, Kelly was shocked and hurt by their reaction. And he let his emotions get the better of him when he burst into tears in the pits.

'He broke down actually, he did get quite emotional and he didn't like the idea at all,' recalled his mechanic, Eric Richardson. 'He accepted it and took it because he wanted to be in the World Final the same as anybody else, but he didn't like the situation.'

Initially he stopped short of admitting that a few tears fell when he spoke to press. 'It was such a hard afternoon and to end like that, well, I felt close to crying, it was like that emotionally.'

This wasn't the first time that Kelly had reacted to the crowd. Earlier that season at Reading he was being interviewed on the centre green and was answering a question when a Reading fan shouted a remark that questioned his ability. This comment stopped him in mid-sentence, he turned to the direction of the voice, glared, 'Oh yeah?!'

Sigalos and Kelly both had 8 points and were through, but Shawn had to face the Collins brothers, Peter and Les, for one of the last two qualifying spots.

This time family loyalty reigned over patriotism and PC held off Shooey, who had to make do with reserve in the next round.

'It was the hardest meeting yet and I am just glad I got through, though I am sad that my brother, Shawn, will only be reserve. The track was very slick and that made it even more difficult for me,' said Kelly.

Kenny Best was among the group of Americans that was helping out the mechanics and he admitted that they didn't expect the reaction they received from the public.

'It was something that I don't think any of us in the pits expected. We should have because it's true fans in England and they know what's going on. I've seen riders drop a point here and there to help people out, but it was obvious when Bruce did it. Boy it turned ugly. Kelly didn't like that because it was so blatant. The fans were booing and it really upset him. It really affected him because he was such a fan person. I think everybody knew what was going to happen. I knew what was going to happen. But it didn't look good because it was so obvious. It was like a jockey standing up and pulling back on the reins of a horse. Just letting the horse slow down a little bit would have been one thing, but when everybody could see what you were doing … That's what was special about the Americans that were over there at that particular time – I can't imagine a tighter group of guys.'

Penhall preferred to forget that day of infamy but he later said that they finished in the wrong order. However, Kelly denied that they were given any instructions beforehand.

'I don't know why he would say that, because whatever order we finished in, one of us was going to have to have a run-off,' he countered. 'Bruce said that he was just going to let us race for it and he'd stay out of the way. Siggy was first and I was second and I remember looking back at my brother and thinking, dang, if I let him through I'll be in a run-off situation. We didn't know he was pulling wheelies behind us, and then after the race, on the slow-down lap, the crowd was throwing stuff at us. Of course when we got back to the pits, took our helmets off, we could hear the crowd booing. I don't mind telling you this, I broke down. And Kenny Carter came to my aid, he came over to me and said, "Hey, don't worry about it, you guys stick together – we don't do that." That meant a lot to me and I was very grateful to KC for that.'

Brother Shawn doesn't remember any instruction either. 'There were no discussions between the riders, only between Bruce and Harry Oxley that I remember. Bruce just let us go for it, but we knew, well I knew, what was happening when we got to the first corner because Bruce wasn't there!'

Supporters bombarded the sports press with unforgiving criticism of Penhall and his fellow countrymen. The USA had qualified for the World Team Cup Final, which was due to be staged at White City and because England had failed to make the final they may have counted on the encouragement from their English fans. But they soon realised that any backing would be greatly diminished when many supporters indicated that they would boycott the final in protest over their actions in the Overseas Final. Not only had they severely damaged their reputation with the British public, it would also mark the beginning of the end of an era.

If, collectively, the Americans needed any convincing that times were changing, or that things would never be the same again, then the death of their fellow countryman, Denny Pyeatt, rammed home the fact that racing wasn't always fun. Pyeatt was riding for Reading at Hackney on Friday, 16 July when he crashed heavily and was sent hurtling through the safety fence and struck a lamp standard. He was rushed to hospital with head injuries. Sadly, he never regained consciousness and passed away early Saturday morning. The tight-knit Californians were stunned by the tragedy, and so was the sport as a whole that was still reeling from the deaths of both Brett Alderton and Zdenek Kudrna earlier in the year. Bobby Schwartz was particularly affected because he was his team-mate at Reading and was close to him.

'I didn't realise people could get killed,' admitted Kenny Best. 'Zdenek Kudrna got impaled on a post during a grass track meeting. That was my first experience that someone could actually die from doing this stuff. We were all young and thought that we were invincible. That was the first time that I had really known someone who got killed racing, not that I knew him well at all, but just knowing and seeing someone and knowing they had died … Kudrna's death and Denny's did affect Kelly.'

'Denny was a great guy,' said Kelly. 'It was hard. I remember calling Kenny Carter and Mike Lee and asking them what was going on? It was tough to take in. You know we think we're Superman when we put that crash helmet on and we're wearing all the protective clothing, but something like that makes you realise how vulnerable you are – it makes you think.'

According to his brother, it doesn't do to think too much, though. 'Denny had a more conventional style and he always had a smile. I have to say to you, during our racing career, people used to get hurt, you read about people breaking bones and stuff, you kinda go, shit that sucks, then you've got to get it out of your mind straightaway. You've got to do that when you're racing – you've got to get over it in seconds. Even when you ride, you see it happening and that's bad, but you've got to get over it – you've got to get on with the job. It's one of those things.'

The dust had hardly settled on that tragedy and the White City controversy when attentions turned to the next World Championship qualifier on the fast Vetlanda track in Sweden. Disappointed with the slick surface at White City,

Kelly's Swedish housemates gave him cause to feel optimistic for a better circuit. 'It's big like Belle Vue and should have a lot more dirt than there was at White City. It should suit me,' he said before leaving.

In the same interview, for the first time in print, he also gave out a timetable for his career. 'When I came here I gave myself three years to get to the World Final; I did it in two. I gave myself six years to win it. This is the fifth year now. I am having my best season so far, so let's just see.'

Memories were still fresh in his mind of how his rivals took advantage of his flaws during the corresponding round in 1981, and with the final in his own country he wasn't going to make that mistake again. This time the Inter-continental Final took place on a Friday evening. Julie Richardson, his little good luck charm, remembered him departing for Vetlanda. 'I can see him now, leaning out the car window and waving at me with both hands and shouting, "See you at Belle Vue." He was very confident.'

The top eleven scorers qualified for the final and yet this round was even more competitive than any of the others. Drawn at number 13 again, he won back-to-back races to put himself in a commanding position for a qualifying place. He found himself scrapping with Penhall for third place but ended up pointless in his third outing before booking his ticket for the LA final with a victory in his fourth ride. Fellow countrymen, Penhall and Sigalos, also joined him in a close meeting that was won by Les Collins on 12 points.

With a match the following evening at Belle Vue, he shouldn't really have celebrated like he did … but what the heck, he was in the World Final and it was in his home country. Such achievement was a once-in-a-lifetime experience.

'Martin Hignett was driving Kelly back and he had to catch that ferry to make the race at Belle Vue,' said Sigalos. 'We showed up and it was like, "Where's Kelly?" He didn't make the ferry so he was late getting to the meeting.'

'He just got off the boat, and Lars Hammarberg drove him. He was just absolutely pie-eyed and he was trying to get on his bike and ride – it was comical!' Julie smiled. 'But he was just so happy that he had made the World Final and the way that he celebrated was to drink – that's the way he was.'

'I had the bikes there ready, Kelly turned up and the doctor wouldn't let him ride – he was out of his mind,' said Eric. 'Arthur Nutley couldn't make it so I ended up managing the team.'

Already without Ron Preston, the track doctor declared Moran was unfit and the Eagles drafted in Newcastle's Rod Hunter as a late replacement. He was fined £10 by the referee and reported to the Speedway Control Board. The Eastbourne management issued a warning over his future conduct and released a terse statement to the press the following afternoon, which read: 'The rider had been celebrating reaching the World Final the previous night in Sweden and not slept for more than twenty-four hours and was obviously in no fit condition to ride. We agree with the action taken by the Belle Vue management.'

At the time he showed little remorse and supported his actions by underlining his achievement. 'You can't expect somebody to go home and have a night's rest after they have just got through to a World Final. But basically the whole thing was due to a big mix-up in Sweden. There was a lot of confusion about the homecoming arrangements. We seemed to be driving around Sweden for half the night. I was tired, burned out and a little hung over. But I was only half as tired as I was when Wimbledon made their protest.'

However, in an interview with the author in 2006, he showed more maturity and regret when he was asked about that incident at Hyde Road.

'I was okay, but I wasn't in a fit enough state to race at those speeds at the old Belle Vue. Stuart Bamforth [Belle Vue promoter] shook my hand for pulling out and there was no way that I wanted to be a danger to anyone on the track. I regret those incidents, I didn't mean to let people down like that, but I was young and having too much fun. You think you're invincible at that age.'

With under a month to go before the World Final and the World Cup final only weeks away, he faced a race against time to get fit after he crashed at King's Lynn on 31 July and sustained shoulder and rib injuries. His immediate thought was that he had jeopardised his World Championship chances. 'I thought, oh no, I've done it now. The track doctors wouldn't say anything except that nothing was broken,' he said later. He underwent intensive physiotherapy at Brighton and Hove Albion FC and made his come back on 8 August in a league encounter at home to Birmingham. Showing no ill-effects from his injuries he scored a paid maximum in their 46–32 victory.

He wasn't the only American to fall foul of injury. Dennis Sigalos sustained a broken ankle a few days prior to Kelly's crash and was out of the US team that was due to contest the World Cup. His place was taken by Bobby Schwartz and Scott Autrey filled the reserve berth to join the regular trio of Penhall and the Morans. They were racing in memory of Denny Pyeatt and a picture of their fallen compatriot hung in their pit. They also raced with small toy koala bears on their person or machine as a tribute – Pyeatt was likened to a koala for his knack of sleeping anywhere and at any time.

America faced defending champions, Denmark, West Germany and former Czechoslovakia at White City. True to their angry supporters' word, even allowing for England's absence, the crowd was well down on what was expected. This didn't bother the USA, they had a job to do, whether there was 1,000 or 10,000 in the stadium.

With a gold medal up for grabs, Kelly took the meeting very seriously. In fact, if anyone doubted his determination that day, it wasn't Eric Richardson.

'We lived not far from Ascot [horse] racecourse. He stayed here with us and we were going to White City for that meeting and we passed Ascot to pick up the M4 motorway to get into White City. I said to him: "There's Ascot racecourse over there, Kelly." He replied: "Ascot racecourse? I'm not bloody interested in Ascot racecourse! I'm going to a bloody speedway meeting and that's what I'm concentrating on. Ascot racecourse is nothing but blue grass in America." He cut me dead. He took the wind out of my sails and I never spoke to him from then on throughout the meeting. I put the gears on, he rode the bike, I took the bike home, and he went home with Ronnie Preston.'

Rain threatened the meeting and a sharp shower shortly before start time made the track a bit heavy – which possibly played into the Americans' hands more than the slick-loving Danes. Kelly was in the first race and finished third behind Hans Nielsen and German Georg Hack, but after that he was undefeated, finishing with 10 points. They sewed up the gold as early as heat 13 when Shawn Moran won the race to clinch the trophy. And the unbeaten Schwartz unselfishly handed over his last ride to reserve Autrey so that he could feel part of their triumph. The USA stamped their authority on the meeting by finishing 13 points ahead of silver medallists, Denmark.

Kelly regarded that meeting as one of the highlights of his career. He said: 'That one stands out. I guess it was because it was a team effort, it was the first time that America had won the team cup in their history and we dedicated the win to our buddy, Denny Pyeatt. It was a bit wet to begin with, but the sun came out and it was a memorable day. Denmark were the reigning champions and it was neat to beat them. It wasn't often Denmark were beaten.'

Even though the US speedway team went on to become only the second nation in the history of the sport to complete a Grand Slam of all the major world championships – Schwartz and Sigalos won the World Pairs in Australia – the AMA still treated the sport with indifference. This was illustrated to Kelly when he was waiting for his World Team Cup medal – an award that obviously meant more to him than the average cups and trophies he'd won.

'Unfortunately winning the championship was the easy part, the hard thing was collecting my medal,' he later wrote in his column in *Speedway Magazine*. 'It appears the AMA goofed and gave my medal to Dennis Sigalos [who wasn't in the team that day]. Now Dennis may be a fellow rider and a friend, but I want my medal. I earned it the hard way and they are so hard to come by.'

When a stadium is empty, a perfectly prepared oval speedway track can be a beautiful, tranquil thing. The red dirt that lay almost like a carpet around the symmetrical 437-yard (400-metre) circuit in the Los Angeles Memorial Coliseum was as eye-catching for its rich colour as much as it was for its unspoiled visage. And under bright Californian skies that lit up the stunning white Olympic-style concrete arches with its dormant cauldron on top, that ghostly, expectant peace was shattered when Kelly Moran's specially prepared Weslake tore up the track during practice and its engine growled like an angry bear within the empty stands. Purists may have had their misgivings about holding the sport's premier event out west, but they couldn't argue about the grandeur setting for the 1982 World Championship Final.

The Coliseum wasn't new to speedway because it had held the American Final the previous year, but the third and fourth bends were quite sharp then, whereas now they were perfectly proportioned, as one would expect under the experienced eyes of Briggs, Mauger, Milne and Oxley. The venue had staged the 1932 Olympic games and it was due to do so again in 1984. Yet on 28 August the Coliseum, which conjured up images of ancient heroes from myth and legend, had its arena taken over by gladiators of a different kind: sandals had given way to steel shoes, horse-drawn chariots were replaced by snarling 500cc motorcycle engines, and the lightning quick reflexes that earned the old combatants another day in this world were superseded by the combined skills of rapid reactions and an instinctive twist of the throttle by sixteen of the world's best speedway riders.

Kelly had warmed up for the big meeting by scoring a 15-point maximum against Sheffield and defeated his brother twice in the process. His specially tuned machines by Trevor Hedge were boxed up after the meeting and taken to the airport for transportation to LA by Mike Hinves.

'I did the bikes to ride in the World Final in the Coliseum,' said Eric Richardson. 'He had a meeting before the World Final and Mike took them up in a trailer. I had them sent over because I couldn't go. But he did me the great honour, well I thought so, of putting the family's name in the programme as his mechanic. If you see the programme you'll see it there, it says: "Mechanic: The Eric Richardson family."'

Bruce Penhall, the defending World Champion who had quit British speedway the day after the USA had won the World Cup, was the favourite to win again. His arch-rival, Britain's Kenny Carter, was expected to provide him with his strongest challenge. However, Penhall said that Kelly was definitely a threat.

'Who did I worry about most? Obviously 75 per cent of those riders could have won it that night, but Kelly, absolutely – he lacked consistency, that was the only thing. He could have four good rides and one really bad ride, not talking about a second, but a dead last. Every time I lined up against him I would worry about him because he could win at any given time. And he did, quite often. It was nice to see him there and Dennis too. Kelly had some good races he put together and a lot of people didn't. That's the hardest thing about a one-off World Final, you have to have a superb night and you can't really drop one point; if you do, it's a good chance that you're going to have to have a run-off. You have to be utterly perfect on the night. Unlike the GPs now and I'm a GP fan, you have room to make a mistake and you have time to fix it, but you don't in a one-off World Championship, you have to be great,' Penhall assessed.

Most pundits knew that Moran had the ability to be the best in the world, but few tipped him as the 1982 champion; he was a contender, though, a dark horse, and Ivan Mauger believed he would finish in the top four. Eric Linden said that he could be 'a shock merchant' in his preview for *Speedway Star*, while *Cycle News* noted that he wasn't favoured to take the trophy but 'can always be a danger to the more fancied riders'.

Kelly himself was under no illusions what a big occasion it was in his career, and his life. 'It's going to be a really special time. To race in a World Final in front of your own countrymen, your friends and family, will certainly be the pinnacle of my career. In my second season over here I came fourth in Poland. Since then I have improved a hell of a lot. This is going to be a big occasion, but nerves won't eat me. In fact I go better in that type of situation. I know I can do it.'

The presentation had all the colour and the razzamatazz that one would expect of a big sporting event held in America. In the field were riders from the Eastern bloc, in particular lone riders Edward Jancarz from Poland and the Soviet Union's Mikhail Starostin. According to KK who, along with Kenny Best, was Moran's mechanic for the meeting, the Pole's Polish mechanic had his head turned by the vision of the Wild West coming to the World Speedway Championship.

'The funniest thing I remember was, they had a stage coach, the Old West-style stage coaches, Wells Fargo, to take the riders around on parade. Penhall and some of the top boys of that time were on top of the stage, and we were right next to this Polish guy in the tunnel. And he looked at us and goes, "Woah, a stage coach!", threw his wrenches and ran after the stage coach, and I killed myself laughing. He got all excited when he saw that coach, the cowboys and horses. It was an interesting night, we did fairly well.'

Moran was drawn at number one, which meant that he was in the very first race and each of his five rides would be evenly spaced out, although they were all races that could take place after a track grade. Therefore, he had to keep his eye on conditions.

He faced Dennis Sigalos, Peter Collins and Mikhail Starostin in the opening heat. Despite starting from the inside, it was Siggy from the outside who took the lead that he never relinquished and PC slipped into second with Kelly third. Before the opening lap was over, Moran had forced his way past Collins for second and finished with 2 points. Kelly watched as the first shock of the meeting occurred in heat 4 when, in a titanic battle, Britain's Les Collins defeated Penhall.

Moran faced Penhall in his next race and Jan Andersson and Vaclav Verner. Penhall started from the pole with Kelly in gate two but, still reeling from that opening heat defeat, he made a determined start and grabbed first place. Meanwhile, Jan Andersson also headed Moran. On his day Andersson was a world-class rider, but he relied on his starting and didn't possess the same degree of natural ability that Moran had at his disposal. For a racer who rose to the occasion, was on home shale and fed off the support he got from his fans, finishing behind Andersson, the perennial middle-order Swede, was an early blow. It didn't put him out of the contention, but it did place him in the chasing pack instead of snapping at the heels of the early leaders. That third place was certainly viewed as a setback by his pit crew, as Moran noticed when he returned to the pits.

'I'll never forget this. After two races we only had 3 points,' Best said. 'I don't know about anyone else but I was feeling so bad inside. Apparently KK did as well. Kelly turned around and looked at us, it was the opposite of the way it should have been – he gave us a pep talk! He said, "What's the matter? What's these long faces for? We're not done, we've just got started. We're starting brand new, right now, don't worry about it." And in his third heat he won the race and finished the night okay, in fact I think he only dropped one point in the rest of his races. KK and I had long faces and Kelly came over and gave us a pep talk. He ended up fourth in the world again. I really wanted him to win it, though; I wanted him to do so well.'

Like 1979, he ended the meeting with 11 points, with the highlight being a characteristically spectacular pass of Hans Nielsen to win his third race. However, after finishing second to Les Collins in his last ride in heat 17 he was actually lying in third place overall. Only his fellow countryman, Sigalos, could deny him a bronze medal if he won the final heat. Kelly could be accused of many things, but selfish – when it came to racing – wasn't one of them.

'I remember I was cheering Siggy on and my mechanic (KK) said, "What are you cheering him on for?" And I said, "Well, look, it's Siggy and he's in front." Then he told me that if he finished second then I would have a run-off for third place with him. I didn't realise.'

'I totally believe that, that's just the way Kelly was,' said Sigalos on hearing that particular tale. 'He wanted to see everyone do good; if you beat him you beat him, that's just the way racing is. It probably helped a little bit that I'm an American also and he wanted to see as many Americans on the podium as possible.'

'He would always be rooting for them, especially Denny [Sigalos] or any of the Americans,' Best added.

Bruce Penhall retained his championship with Les Collins second and Sigalos third. It was a controversial night when Kenny Carter was excluded after falling during an intense battle with Penhall. Furthermore, Bruce made the night his own when he announced his retirement from the sport to become an actor in the television show, *CHiPs*. Although it was a massive disappointment to have the World Champion retire, rumours that he intended to pursue a career in Hollywood had been rife for most of the season.

Kelly believed America's first World Final was a big success, although he would have liked to have finished on the rostrum. 'I know I could have done better, but the track was dreadfully slick,' he said afterwards.

His machinery was damaged when it was shipped back to the UK; the repair bill was estimated to be in the region of £100. There wasn't much time to get it ready though, because he was in the British Open Championship at White City on 5 September. The World Final line-up had been assembled to compete for a £5,000 first prize, albeit without the retired Penhall. Promoters tried to hype-up the event as the 'alternative World Final', claiming that the victor could describe himself as the World No. 1 while the sport had a non-riding champion.

Suffering from a flu bug, Kelly did well when he finished third behind Sigalos and Nielsen. He admitted that the adrenalin of competition was enough to get him through a 70-odd-second race but as soon as that chequered flag dropped it was a struggle to ride back to the pits.

Unfortunately, during Eastbourne's home match against Poole, he was an innocent victim of a crash caused by Vaclav Verner. While chasing Eagles' Paul Woods and Moran, the Czech rider straightened up as he entered the third bend and missed Woods by a whisker, but rode straight into the American – he had no chance. He was the darling of the Eagles fans and pandemonium broke out at Arlington with supporters directing their anger at the hard-riding Czech. The situation got so heated that Verner was involved in a scuffle with supporters, was fined, suspended from the meeting and was escorted to Hailsham police station where assault charges were considered.

Meanwhile, Kelly left the hospital with a broken collarbone and a cracked shoulder blade. It looked as though his season could be over and hopes of pipping Gordon Kennett to the number one spot so that he could represent the Eagles in the British League Riders' Championship were definitely scuppered. Luckily, in the crowd at Eastbourne that day was a local bone specialist, Derek Richards, who accompanied him to the hospital. His expertise no doubt helped him to make an earlier than expected track return for the Eagles' remaining fixtures. A month after the accident he was back in action, but a little tentative by his standards.

Despite the top-end power of Kennett, Moran, Preston and Woods, Eastbourne finished in twelfth place in the league. The top-four lacked any real support from the remaining members of the team and, subsequently, they were absent when the trophies and medals were being handed out.

For Kelly though, it was his best season yet. He finished with a 9.62 average, but he had been registering a figure of over 10 before injuries interrupted his run. In fact, he regarded his seasons in Sussex as the best of his career. 'I think 1981 and 1982 were my best years and my happiest,' he reflected many years later. 'It was such a great team spirit, especially the second year when Ronnie Preston joined us – we had a lot of fun. Bob Dugard was a great promoter, being an ex-rider he knew what it was all about. Win, lose or draw, he always stuck by his riders.'

Dugard was pleased that Kelly felt that way and believed that he responded to the family atmosphere at the club, the tight knit community that personified Eastbourne Speedway.

'I think it did help him, in his own words he had the best two years of his career, didn't he? A lot of that was to do with the environment he was in. He was treated as a family member. He was an immense talent, but he did tend to go a bit wild when he was released from house arrest!'

When Kelly left Britain for California he had every intention of riding for the Eagles again in 1983. He left his houseplants with his fan club secretary, Sue Lovett, which, surprisingly, attracted the attention of the local constabulary. She wrote in the newsletter: 'I am "plant sitting" for fourteen pot plants that are scattered about my home. It was quite a job transporting them from Kelly's house in Brighton to my house thirty miles away. Actually we were stopped by a police patrol car because they thought the car was overloaded with passengers! It was quite funny when they looked in and saw only four passengers and a lot of plants.'

Gordon Kennett was seeking a transfer from Arlington and, initially, the club's management intended to build a team around their Yankee duo of Moran and Preston. However, shortly before Christmas it was reported that the Wizard of Balance wasn't coming back to England to race. The news sent shock waves through Eastbourne speedway, and the ripples could be felt throughout the British League.

He had attended the 'King of Concrete' meeting at the Long Beach Sports Arena on 3 December and, although he wasn't racing himself, as a member of the USA's victorious World Team Cup team and ranked fourth in the world, his presence generated quite a bit of interest.

'I was interviewed on the infield by Larry Huffman and he asked me if I would like to ride in California instead of racing in England and, on the spur of the moment, I said, "Sure, I'd love to race in America." Afterward I remember thinking to myself, you've just made a commitment in front of 5,000 people, you idiot. Then I started getting these calls from people saying, "Are you really going to stay in America, Kelly?" and pretty soon I was getting offered help here and there to do it. It was gathering momentum. I was offered sponsorship and everything.'

Speculation over the festive season was rife about his future with Eastbourne. Eagles fans refused to believe that their star would turn his back on their club. Furthermore, it was reported that the club lost just under £1,000 a meeting during 1982, putting the team's future in 'serious jeopardy'. When Gordon Kennett moved to King's Lynn, the Eagles could ill-afford to lose Moran as well if they wanted to field a competitive team in the top flight.

Dugard moved to quell fears over the club's future and that they would be without their charismatic star. 'We have talked to Kelly and what he meant was that he would stay in America if Eastbourne weren't able to run in 1983,' he assured them.

However, less than a week after that statement, a letter appeared in the 12 January 1983 edition of *Cycle News* from Kelly Moran, which was described as 'a letter to his English fans'. He said: 'My racing career in the US, although successful, was very short and I find myself almost unknown in my home country. As much as I want to be World Champion, I feel it would be a hollow victory unless I receive the recognition from my home country that I feel I would deserve. So 1983 will be spent here in the US, trying to get as much exposure as possible. In 1984 I want to return to the United Kingdom and Eastbourne.'

Nonetheless, Dugard and Eastbourne still refused to believe it. Soon the club's immediate future was linked to the return of their Californian stars. Bob said: 'I don't expect to have too many problems with Kelly. He has always been happy at Eastbourne and we are hopeful he will return. I wouldn't go so far as to say the track will close if he doesn't come back.'

Moran then confirmed that he wouldn't be racing in the UK and, as the Eagles' future hung in the balance, the American's decision was attacked by supporters. Even when Ron Preston also failed to re-join, fingers still pointed at Moran for the club's plight. As far as Bob Dugard was concerned, it was the end of an era.

'He got talked into staying in America, quite a good sponsorship deal and everything, but that never materialised into what it was supposed to have done. Really, that was the end of Kelly Moran that we all knew in England, wasn't it?'

# 10

# RIDE OUT THE PAIN

'Y'know, you've got to grow yourself a hard shell and
learn to wear it; maybe cry a little bit along the way,
but it ain't gonna help a man to look back.'

Tap Henry, chuck wagon cook

Facing the KM Video cameras following the first Test at Wimbledon between England and the USA on Thursday, 21 April 1983, Kelly Moran explained to his many fans, Eastbourne in particular, why he had decided to concentrate on racing in California instead of continuing his career in the British League.

Speaking in a low, humble voice, he said: 'I have a baby boy now and I am just trying to settle down – settle down, that's a hard word to say for me – I'm just trying to re-establish myself with sponsors and people back home. I enjoyed myself in England and that; I just wanted to try something different so I decided to stay home this year. I am really enjoying myself now playing the family man part.'

Kelly first saw his child when he returned to America to ride in the 1982 World Final – he was born just under a fortnight before. Unfortunately, due to his racing commitments, he didn't get much time to bond and get re-acquainted with his mother, Marice Supry. Undoubtedly that was one of the prime motivations behind his decision to forego racing in Britain, but he also took into account a number of other factors, not least that he had left behind him a chaotic trail.

'I was still trying to get money out of Kelly for petrol but, well ... by the end of the season we were good friends, and we stayed good friends. But if it ended differently, I believe he would have come back in '83. He was going to try and sort himself out,' said mechanic, Richardson.

As his housemate, Ron Preston also saw a side of Kelly that few outside his professional circle would see, which went beyond the usual 'hangers-on' that flocked to him like crows and were the more worrying kind of predators. 'He had another side to him that nobody knew but his party crew. The chicks he hung out with over there, the non-racing people, they knew who he was and what he did, but he was just somebody who always had a way to get money for something. Speedway was one world and the party life was another, the underworld.'

A couple of years later, Moran acknowledged that his decision to remain in California also helped him to break his involvement with the midnight movers and other jackals from the streets.

'I spent three quarters of my time getting drunk. My buddies were mostly on the dole and I was spending all my money on buying them drinks in the pub. I'm not blaming England. What I did, I did to myself. It was all out of sheer boredom.'

In another interview with the author, he pointed out: 'I had got in with the wrong crowd you could say. Staying at home enabled me to break from them and concentrate on racing.'

The Wimbledon fixture was his first meeting in Britain since announcing his intention to remain in the USA. He had come over to race for his country in the five-match Test series and the World Team Cup UK qualifying round. Although the Yanks had won the first match, 64–43, and he was riding his brother's machinery, critics thought that his lack of racing in the world's toughest league at that time was a factor behind his lowly score of 3 points. It was a theory he soon blew out of the water when he followed it with two double-figure returns in the next two Tests.

'I wasn't sure how everybody was going to take me because we've had a bit of a problem since we've been back. I was a bit disappointed with my own performance but I was equally happy with Shawn's and the team's,' he said.

He was wise to be concerned about the reception he would receive when he arrived for the Test matches against England, because he had good reason to be. The press and some supporters had attacked the American, accusing him of leaving the club in the lurch and laying the blame at his door for the Eagles' sorry state.

Since he had made his decision to remain in the USA, followed by his buddy, Preston, Eastbourne had failed to sign a suitable number one to replace the firepower that the top three from '82 had brought to the team. It was left to Paul Woods to fulfil the number one's obligations and, although the signing of Danish rider, John Eskildsen, was considered a success, he wasn't yet in Moran's or Preston's class.

Therefore, his former club was languishing near the foot of the southern section of the League Cup table and had only won two matches. The absence of Moran in particular had hit attendances hard at Arlington, so much so that while searching the world for riders in order to strengthen his team, Bob Dugard commented wryly, 'My only fear is that if I sign any more, I will have more riders than crowd!'

Dugard had a lot of time for Kelly Moran and exercised more tolerance than many would have done. However, he was also known as a passionate character who didn't suffer fools gladly. So given his club's struggling situation, combined with the press speculation that a rift had developed between them, some expected their inevitable meeting to be something akin to *High Noon*. As a result, many watched anxiously as the talented Californian and the sometimes hot-blooded promoter viewed each other for the first time since the end of the previous season.

Kelly said that he knew that look in Bob's eye and he thought that he 'had it coming to me'. The tension was palpable, but Dugard just extended his right hand and said, 'Hello Mr Moran,' and offered him a cigarette!

'It was totally unprofessional of me not to call him when all that was happening,' he admitted. 'I could understand him being angry with me and when I came over for the Test matches I wouldn't have blamed him if he decked me.

'The press always blows things up, but I told Bob my reasons. It's not anything personal, it's not money, but after five years, and I am only twenty-two now, I just wanted to spend one year in my home state, or my home country if you want to put it like that,' he told KM Video. 'I know I put Bob Dugard in a really bad position and I am very sorry about that, but when I spoke to Bob three months ago, he was the first one who told me that Ron Preston wouldn't be returning. That was a complete surprise to me, and he said that he hadn't been able to contact Ron and I haven't seen Ron at the races myself.'

Optimistic supporters hoped that, having Moran in Britain and away from the influences in California, Bob could persuade him to ride to their rescue and save their season, but it wasn't to be. In fact, hopes of him pulling on the Eagles race jacket in 1984 were virtually ruled out as well.

'I don't know if I am going to be returning next year or not,' he continued. 'I am really happy at home. I'm sorry I've disappointed people and made some enemies now. Maybe some year, or someday, I can hopefully please people as much as they please me by coming out and watching me.'

During his stay he played an integral part in the five-match series, which they narrowly lost, 3–2, after a thrilling fifth and deciding match at Sheffield. By scoring 9 points, he did help his nation win the first qualifying round of the World Team Cup at Reading, before, to the disappointment of his British fans, he boarded a plane bound for California.

He hadn't really been performing on the Californian circuit in the way a superstar racer, world number four and world team champion was expected to do. Sure, he had to adjust to the smaller tracks and other things, yet part of it was due to a piece of news that he hoped he wouldn't hear when he got back from England. Kelly loved having kids around and always made time for their honest, raw view of the world. At the races he used to make sure he'd accommodate them for autographs and pictures and, as many people have observed, he was a big child himself at times. Therefore, having a son of his own made him particularly proud. A week after the World Final in Los Angeles, when he jetted into Britain to race in the British Open at White City, his rivals and friends were all shown photos of him; he was as pleased as any doting father could be. He even expressed his delight in his fan club magazine when he wrote: 'I must say it really is a great feeling to be a dad to such a super son.' And then the worst happened ... he absorbed the news like a sponge, but he was crying on the inside and was devastated. He wasn't his son.

He wasn't the only one who was distressed by the news, though. 'I did let him know that there was a possibility that he wasn't the father. I thought for sure it was Kelly's and I wanted it to be his. But, yeah, I had to do that, have a paternity test,' explained Marice. 'That was hard for him. I think he took it hard. We stayed together, but we ended up not being able to stay together.'

Even though he could be a perfect gentleman, he wasn't always good to be around. Like many, Marice found it hard coping with his excesses and at the time of conception they weren't an item. Besides, there were occasions when he operated by using an 'out of sight out of mind' philosophy, sometimes by design yet often influenced by the inducement of stimulating refreshments.

'He wasn't an angel, he was partying a lot and we went our separate ways,' she said. 'And he wasn't that faithful either. He used to always send me cards and stuff saying, I'm keeping my promise, I hope you are – about being faithful. I guess I was the only one keeping the promise. It was devastating, still, to find out that he wasn't keeping his promise.'

Despite it all, there always was a place in his heart for Marice, and in turn there was still a place in hers for him. True love never really dies. While the flame became an ember, their love never really burned out ... but many years would pass before circumstances would stoke up the fire and it would ignite again.

One of Kelly's friends said that he was 'crushed' by the news. The father turned out to be a rival, one that he raced against and alongside, someone he respected and counted as a friend and would continue to do so. He didn't blame him because he knew full well that the good time atmosphere that surrounded the US team at this stage allowed for boundaries to be crossed and for inhibitions to fall. However, he also surprised others by his philosophical attitude toward the whole affair.

'We were living there [in Brighton] when he found out that Marice was pregnant,' Preston recollected. 'Me, Kelly and Keith [Lewis] and all us guys were in that house when Kelly found out and he thought it was his. I think it was up until a year after he was born that Kelly found out that he wasn't the father. I remember thinking to myself that he's liable to kill himself. It was such a huge thing, we didn't know, I remember talking to Keith about it and saying, "We're going to have to keep an eye on him when all this crap hits the fan."

'Even somebody that wronged him like that, he'd just say "Oh they're a bit of a wanker" or something like that. I never saw him go totally off on one. It was terrible, man. As far as all of us were concerned, we were all blown away with the way in which he handled it, he was very casual about it. It was like it didn't bother him, but I can't see how it couldn't. I remember talking to him about it, he was really calm, amazing really, and he said: "Well, it is what it is." That's a bumper sticker right there!'

He found his pressure release valve in his partying and drinking – his 'escape' he'd call it decades later. His anger and pain was drowned in the flow of alcohol, hidden in his crazy antics and concealed in the arms of willing women that would come and go. All the while he still presented that mischievous smile to the world that would shield any anguish locked away inside.

When the subject was brought up he'd respond with an uncharacteristically terse reply and change the subject. While it was still painful, his words and actions made it clear that he'd packed it away in a box marked 'not to be opened' and put it to the back of his mind and moved on. After all, as he used to say, 'There are plenty more fish in the sea.' Wisely, he didn't dwell on it, and neither should we.

# 11

# THE MAGICIAN ON A BIKE

'God gave me my talent and I was afraid of
facing him one day if I didn't use it.'

Jack Sorenson, artist

As he slid into the corner, Kelly Moran had already decided that it would be for the last time because he was getting tired of pounding around the Indian Dunes like a circus act. He did his best to give them what they wanted and after he had exited the corner, he shut the throttle off and his Godden's engine note subsided as he rolled to a stop by photographer, Jim Brown, publisher/editor Robert Fitzpatrick, and Paul Heffernan. Brown enthused, 'That was great, but can you hang off the bike more?'

Ever polite, he used his charm and diplomacy to explain that he couldn't do it to order and after spinning more laps than he could remember during even the busiest of meetings, he'd had enough.

They were carrying out a special photo shoot for a unique magazine cover to launch a new speedway publication in the US, simply titled *Speedway Magazine*. They realised that they required something unusual to capture the attention for the front of their first issue.

'One thing for sure, it had to be special. If it was a rider he would have to be the most spectacular rider we had. Finally one name stood above the rest, that of wonder boy, Kelly Moran,' reported the mag in their title page.

But to do this on the eve of a new season was no easy feat, in fact taking the photos was the less stressful part. A new bike had to be flown in from the Godden factory in England by Jim Busby, and Kelly's new red STP suit was made in three days by Z Leathers especially for the occasion. Brown used three different cameras, four various types of film, several different settings and lenses, never mind the number of positions, in order to produce 100 top quality photos from which the mag's staff had to choose just one. Reportedly it took them ten hours to decide on the final shot, but that wasn't the end of the task.

To make it even more exceptional required further creativity. 'We had taken him to a racetrack that was out in the middle of nowhere; it was dusty and dirty. We got this picture of Kelly, but it didn't look any good because of the background,' recalled Heffernan.

It was decided that the spectacular Moran should be depicted flying through the air – 'Cloudy Kelly', as Shawn called it. Therefore they needed a suitably bright, blue sky with the appropriate white clouds to form a realistic background, which they obtained from a holiday shot taken in Kenya by their managing editor, H.R. Wrenn-Meleck. This cover was even more of an achievement when you realise that this was done in a pre-digital and pre-Photoshop age and it's subsequently become one of Kelly Moran's classic action shots.

'I remember doing that photo shoot for the magazine and Jim wanted me to hang off the bike more. But it was a natural thing; I couldn't just do it to order. I think they got what they wanted – it was neat to be on the cover,' said Moran.

The return of Kelly Moran was big news in America. After Bruce Penhall's retirement from competitive racing to become an actor, having a non-riding World Champion was a blow to the sport worldwide, but particularly in the USA where his success had done much to put the sport on the map in his home country. Therefore, charismatic Kelly, who was every bit as engaging as Penhall yet even more spectacular to watch, was the ideal choice to go on the cover of the new periodical.

Friends, rivals and experts are mostly in agreement that he was one of the most talented riders the sport has ever seen, yet his dazzling and pleasing style added an alluring elegance to such a degree that he made the sport into an art form. Moreover, many artists have put to paper, or canvas, their interpretations of his appealing, neat style and although he wasn't the first or the last to employ a hanging-off-the-bike spectacle, his method was arguably the most attractive. It was, as Billy Hamill once observed, 'sheer aggression with so much finesse'.

According to Kelly, it was Costa Mesa promoter Harry Oxley who first used the phrase 'The Wizard of Balance' to describe him, which the racer thought was original – it wasn't. The saying was first used to describe Britain's double World Champion, Peter Craven, another rider whose style was such that a photo taken by Wright Wood is still regarded as the image that best depicts the sport. And like his American successor, Craven also hung from the bike when cornering, which was especially impressive when you consider the machines they were riding in the '50s and early '60s. Without doubt he was the pioneer of this way of racing.

Furthermore, when cornering, he would seemingly disappear and it would look as though he'd fallen off, only to emerge in perfect control. Kelly too would sometimes appear as though he had come to grief, especially during his early career as a pro, but being a bit taller than Craven his 'now you see me, now you don't' act didn't carry the same level of jaw-dropping astonishment. They were both small racers: Craven was 5ft 1in, which was three inches shorter than the American. Those extra inches did make Kelly's style more defined – prompting a Yorkshire TV commentator to once describe him as having a 'Cossack style' – but their lack of height made it look as though they were moulded to the bike, like they were part of it. Of course, Peter Collins, Chris Morton and Jan O. Pedersen were also vertically challenged racers who also raced at the highest level and, again, looked the part and their styles have also been reproduced to illustrate speedway in various forms. But only Craven and Moran share the magic that sets them above everyone else and are the supermodels of speedway.

It was this exciting way of riding that caught the attention of photographer, Mike Patrick. For forty years he photographed speedway all over the world and said: 'He was a world apart from anyone else. On the track he was just the king of balance. He was fantastic to photograph. If Kelly was in the race, I'm sorry to the other guys, but my camera was always on him. He would provide such spectacular pictures.'

'I didn't plan to ride like that or show off. Speedway is about forward momentum and it's important to get your wheels in line as quickly as you can. I would hang off the bike like that because I wanted to stand the bike up because the more lean you've got, the less grip you have,' Kelly explained.

Scott Autrey, who had raced in other disciplines including circuit racing before settling on speedway, was astounded by Moran's ability. 'He was the first one I ever saw take his right foot off the peg and that's to get the bike more up and down – stand it up. Even if his body had to shift to the inside a bit, he'd still have the bike up and down so he had the wheels in line so he went faster.'

Such was Kelly's talent that some wondered if he had obtained some dark knowledge, because his skills stretched beyond the spectacle and would regularly reach into the unknown and pull off passes and moves that, to his rivals, were seemingly impossible to carry out. He could find grip where others found none; he could turn his machine on a sixpence while in the thick of the action; and he'd seamlessly transfer his bodyweight to change direction. Sometimes it was just a subtle movement that you'd miss unless you were paying attention.

'On a bike I don't think I've seen anyone as exciting at the top level,' believes Bob Radford. 'Kelly could do anything. He had that little bit more talent and he could just flick his hips or whatever in the middle of the corner to turn the bike.'

When occasion demanded it, he would almost freewheel into the corners and then pick up the pace when he had to. In fact, he had been seen in the middle of the corner, turning his front wheel left so that the machine was momentarily straight, wheels in line, but on the edge of the tyre he'd slow up sufficiently so that he could change his line, or direction, in order to challenge his rival.

'I picked up a technique of trying to scrub off speed. When you turn that wheel to the opposite side that thing goes left on you,' Kelly explained. 'Yes I know I have a knack for racing speedway. I'm one of the very few. I don't sit on the bike. I sit with the bike. We both make ourselves go. I'm sure people with practice and patience can ride a motorcycle but not many people can ride a bike without brakes and make it slide into the bend. It's a natural thing with me.'

Especially during the early years of his career, Kelly would transfer his weight to the back of the machine and as he exited the corners his front wheel would lift from the traction he was getting. He never weighed much more than eight stone so one might wonder how his weight transfer could have been so beneficial. Mechanic Richard Harrison may have the answer.

'Kelly and Shawn ran different gear ratios to anybody else because of their ability. We could get away with a lot of different gearing than most of the others did. We were always a couple of teeth higher than anybody else because they were so light and they had the ability to turn. A lot of the guys you watch now, they're kind of waiting for the corner to come up. They're going down the straight and you can see them waiting to turn left; they don't run the corners hard enough whereas with Kelly and Shawn, because we'd run their gears higher, they'd go into the corners really hard because they knew they could turn the bike.'

Paul Heffernan watched Moran weave his magic on California's tiny circuits and he believed that the progression of machinery has dulled the appreciation of what he could do on a speedway bike.

'He was probably the first rider I saw who took my breath away and that's what Kelly would do, he would suck the breath out of you, you would gasp because of what he was doing. There was a picture I used for my company for some time of Kelly on the back wheel, looking under the handlebars, you could see my logo on his leathers, and that wasn't a show. That was a true racing shot, it wasn't staged. Scott Daloisio took that photo. That photo is almost iconic with the way he came here and rode. He didn't just go out and win races, he'd have the front wheel grasping for air, hanging off the side of the bike and it was not like he was trying to do wheelies, he was so light he would get so much drive. Today's bikes will do a wheelie because of their lower centre of gravity, but these were real, in-your-face, hard stonking wheelies. He was coming out of the corners at Costa Mesa, with his wheel grabbing for air and he didn't even miss a beat.'

Kelly may have lost the run-off to Peter Collins during the 1982 UK qualifying round of the World Team Cup at King's Lynn, but Autrey was watching from the pits that day and has since studied a TV clip of the race and believed that Moran was breaking all the rules of technique.

'When you see what he did during those four laps with the bike, he shouldn't have been able to do it. He crossed over the back wheel down the back straight and missed it by a quarter of an inch, or half an inch. If he would have hit him, it would have been a horrendous crash. If you watch him on that last lap, the last corner, he almost kills the bike, pulls it so tight and almost stops it, and that back wheel got a hold. He'd just got up on the back wheel and that's his last attempt at a slingshot. That was a very tough thing to do with those bikes back then because they didn't have the horsepower like they do now and it was a good way of coming off and landing on your lid! You can see he did that on purpose. I had never seen anyone do it like that before. I've seen Peter Collins do a lighter version of it, but I've never seen anybody like Kelly.

'Another thing he'd do,' continued Scott, 'and he used to do this on slick tracks, he'd pull his Weslake almost to a stop in the middle of the corner. He'd get that drive all at once and it would just launch him, that's when he'd get on the back wheel. He was also very good at riding on the top of the tyres, keeping the bike stood up so you get as much rubber as you can on the track.'

His style of racing could make him vulnerable sometimes because of his low weight, plus he relied on his balance, and his propensity for pushing the envelope could be his downfall. However, Dennis Sigalos recalled a race in Holland that left everyone open-mouthed. Understandably, it's a race that sticks in his mind.

'The track was really, really rough. Kelly came down the back straightaway, hit a bump, which knocked his legs up into the air to where he fell off the left side of the bike; he's hanging on to the handlebars, the bike was dragging him, but he stayed with it. He hit the next bump, and then "whoop!" his body came right back onto the seat and he kept on going! We all just looked at each other going, what the hell just happened? Was that Kelly's luck, experience, or he wouldn't give up? Anyone else would have let go of the handlebars and just rolled away, but he stayed on and probably still won the race!'

Bruce Penhall recalled that riding with him in team events was entertaining to the point where you'd get a bit distracted.

'If it was a team event, it was a bit grippy or whatever, you had your eye on him. It was actually an art what he was doing on a bike, because he could get himself out of certain positions as quickly as he could get into them. You were watching him more than the guys behind you. I loved riding with him.'

Rivals couldn't believe what he'd get away with and would accomplish as a racer. His brother was also capable of stunning his opposition – he wasn't called 'The Miracle Worker' for nothing. Inevitably, tired of eating their dust, other riders began copying their visible set-ups, believing that they too could run the same things and achieve similar success.

'Kelly and Shawn were the ones that started riding with smaller and flatter handlebars and everyone tried to copy them but it didn't work for them because not everybody else was 5ft 4in and weighed 120lbs,' observed Autrey. 'Their size was perfect for the scale of a speedway bike, but they rode that much different. Erik Gundersen was another one. After the Morans did that, others followed by having their handlebars lower and sitting back farther on the seat; some guys could pull it off and some couldn't. The Moran brothers were both natural born racers.'

By sitting back further on the seat they would press on the left foot peg with their foot. Their continuance with this method eventually caused a mechanical defect, though, as Harrison revealed.

'The gear wheel on the clutch, if we ran any big clutches, the way they used to put their left foot up, they used to push the chain guard in and put the chain off-line and that would wear the teeth away – Shawn more than Kelly, although they both used to ride that way. They used to ride a lot with their left foot up and press on it and put their weight on the footrest.'

While that racing trait was shared by both of them, the other equipment issue was caused by Kelly's racing style alone. Racing with higher gears enabled him to take the corners hard and at speed, but that would cause problems with the handlebars, frame and front wheel. After he had left the pit gate, he'd make his way to the start line and would coast toward the fence, stop, and then knock his front wheel against it.

'I do that to straighten my front wheel. It gets bent because of the way I ride the corners so hard, and it causes the frame to bend,' Moran explained in a Q&A in his fan club magazine.

'Kelly used to twist the forks like nobody's business,' recalled Harrison. 'He always used to go up to the safety fence and tweak the front end, or he'd tweak the front end and also kick the clutch – they were his little quirks. The way he rode, he did twist the forks and they are quite soft, so he'd just twist them back straight. But, yes, he was straightening them and that was because of the way he would ride.'

A combination of lower forks and better technology meant that as his career progressed, Kelly didn't often knock his front wheel against the fence. But right up until he quit racing he'd still kick the clutch at the start line. That was his ritual.

From 1986 to 1991, he used Comet Frames as built by Gordon May – his brother did as well. May doesn't recall Kelly bending frames unless he had a crash.

'He was pretty good actually, he didn't bend many and he didn't come off a lot. It was through another American, John Cook, that we brought out this twin-top tube frame, which we called the Flexi-Flyer, and I believe Kelly rode them most. His brother also used them and it was through Shawn that he came to me. Kenny Carter was my main test rider for experimentation, and him and Kelly was about the same weight. He was wild but there were no problems at all. He didn't used to come back moaning or anything – he was a great guy. He wasn't a technical sort of lad. Once he got the frame that was it, unless there were any problems. He was the sort of lad that could get on a bike and ride it no matter what it was. You'd get others, specialists, who want things altered, but he'd just get on a bike and ride it. I believe he went to PJ frames for his last few years.'

Other riders couldn't believe that Kelly could be so much better and suspected that they had some sort of technical advantage. However, like the rest of his machinery, his Comet Flexi-Flyer frame wasn't developed especially for him.

'I had one rider who said that he had bent the diamond, did I have one? I used to do six at a time, so I said to him, "I've got this one. This is what Kenny Carter uses, but you can have it." When I saw him again, he said, "Oh what a difference Kenny Carter's frame is." Well it wasn't because they were all alike – it's just in their head. It's surprising what thoughts they had, they believed that Kelly was on something special but he wasn't. They were made on the same jig and there was probably half a dozen frames done at a time and when they wanted one they just used to take the first one. I hate to dispel this speciality thing, but that's how it was.'

Pete Rovazzini believes that had his lifestyle been different, he could well have followed his mini-bike rival, Wayne Rainey, into circuit racing and, eventually, the then Blue Riband event the 500cc World Championship. Kenny Carter's brother Alan did participate on the tarmac, which could have led to an opportunity for Kelly to try it.

'He actually had an offer from Kenny's dad, Malcolm; he had an opportunity to go and test on one of those motorcycles. If his lifestyle was more conducive and he was more focused, he would have been great on a road bike, maybe even 500cc World Champion. Kenny's dad saw that too.'

In 1984 he had the chance to test his skills against some of the stars from other disciplines by representing speedway in the Superbikers Championship in the USA. Champions from road racing, motocross and dirt track racing took part. It was an annual competition that was put together mainly for television purposes – ABC's *Wide World of Sports*. Held at Carlsbad, the circuit uniquely reflected the disciplines by incorporating tarmac and dirt surface split into road, motocross and dirt track segments – some say it was a pre-cursor to the modern day supermoto. There were three qualifying heats, one each for dirt track, motocross and road racers, then a semi-final and a final. He found himself lining up alongside former mini-bike rivals, Ricky Johnson, Wayne Rainey and Jeff Ward.

The machinery they used was motocross bikes and while Kelly's height was ideal for speedway, it wasn't such an advantage on these machines. Riding a Honda, not a Maico 500 as Kelly once said, he could barely touch the ground with the tips of his toes. Nonetheless, in his first heat, he showed his talent when he roared off into the first corner.

'The bike flew!' Moran enthused. 'I was in the first corner first but crashed into the hay bales they had around the track. I closed my eyes when I fell and when I opened them there was straw everywhere. I got back on but those guys were gone.'

Watched by his father and his friends, he completed the course in his semi, but didn't transfer to the final and the event was won by Kent Howerton for the second time.

Kelly enjoyed pitting his skills against racers from other forms of bike racing and he said he had a lot of fun mixing with guys that he'd raced against as a kid in the Indian Dunes and Saddleback Park. However, speedway was where his true talent lay.

His unique artistic style was more pronounced on the smaller circuits, especially in California. It has been said that he was better on the smaller tracks while his brother excelled on the bigger, faster raceways. Dennis Sigalos doesn't subscribe to that view.

'No, I don't agree with that. Kelly was well-rounded, he was dynamite on a small track but he could ride any track. He could probably ride around there faster than most people could on his first lap. Kelly could turn on a dime, turn the light switch on and off, ride a big track, a small track; put a track in front of him and a motorcycle and he could ride it. He could ride somebody else's bike better than they could.'

He was more than a spectacular and fast racer. His personality apart, what endeared him to thousands of supporters was his exciting and entertaining style. Although occasionally he could make decent starts, he couldn't do so consistently, especially not when he lined up alongside riders like Erik Gundersen or Dave Jessup, who had lightning reflexes from the tapes. Therefore, he achieved his victories the hard way, from the back. He was so adept at this that multiple World Champion Barry Briggs once described him as 'the best passer in speedway'.

'He wasn't known for his gating, he was known for passing you on the outside, with no room, six inches of dirt, and just hanging on like a freaking flag on a flag pole,' Dennis Sigalos laughed. 'That was Kelly and everyone loved him for it and all the riders admired him for it. He was never a dangerous rider, he wouldn't put anyone else in a bind, but he could ride that darned motorcycle.'

Phil Crump finished third in the world in 1976 and was one of the most consistent riders of his era. He thought that the American could be a bit too accommodating on the track. 'He wasn't hard on anybody because he had so much ability he didn't need to be. If you passed him, you passed him and then he'd pass you back. He was certainly a bit special.'

Few knew him better than his brother. Being of a similar age, they shared many speedway adventures together, representing their country and riding in the same teams. For all of his brother's raw ability, Shawn believes he also had a good racing brain.

'He was good at thinking ahead; meaning you could see if you were going to pass someone, even if you didn't know him, you could tell if he was going to run with ya or not. Just as he was thinking what he was going to do to keep you out, or keep you wide, Kelly was already thinking of his next manoeuvre. I'd call it a set-up. The other rider would be thinking that he'd be coming through a particular way and move to cover it, then he'd cut under him and pass. I can't say much for his gating! He had his times, he was like a PC or someone like that, but he could do the business from the back. If you can't gate, you've got to do it from the back.'

For sponsor Jim Busby, who himself had won Le Mans, he was in no doubt about Moran's place in motor sport, not just speedway.

'Seeing Kelly ride was like watching the race in slow motion. He would almost effortlessly move around the bike using his bodyweight to find balance and traction, and traction he did find with drives off the corners that seemed almost unreal. Following his virtuoso performances he would simply step off the bike and smile like he knew something we didn't. He was right. I have spent the last forty years of my life around some of the world's best racers – drag racing, Indy cars, Formula One, Nascar, Sports cars at Le Mans – and won a few races myself. When looking back at all the racers I have known, raced with and against, I must say that the two most naturally gifted and impressive I have ever known are Michael Schumacher and Kelly Moran.'

During his professional career racing against the best in the world, Kelly raced upright engines of various manufacture. The modern-day lay-down engine was just beginning to make an impression in the shale sport during his later years. These days speedway racing is more about maintaining your momentum during four laps; closing the throttle and scrubbing off speed, or locking up in order to radically change direction, isn't recommended. And due to the higher power band such actions can have a disastrous outcome. However, such was his ability it seems likely that he would have been just as competitive in the modern environment. In fact, Billy Hamill believed he was ahead of his time.

'Speedway is more about momentum instead of a cut and shoot like it used to be. It depends on the situation too and the track size and the way the track is. When the lay-downs came out that's when everything changed from the way the tracks are ridden. Not totally different, but significantly different; now it's more about getting your momentum going. The first guys I saw do that was probably Kelly and Hans Nielsen – that I've seen do it very well. I had never seen anyone go as fast around Cradley Heath as those two. I remember wondering how the hell they could carry so much speed going into the corners. Obviously Hans had that lanky style to kind of counterbalance it with his legs and stuff; whereas Kelly would do it with his upper body and he'd be in the bike more, more part of the bike; he kind of looked like a fairing on a motorcycle more than a rider on top of it. That technique – I've never seen anyone perfect it as well as Kelly. The majority of the riders couldn't even do it.

'I looked at him when I was learning how to ride the lay-downs – what would he do? When I was adapting my style I thought well that's more of a Kelly Moran style, you're getting into the bike, but you're still getting the bike up onto the tyre. It's a different way of riding. Kelly was very much about finesse, instead of aggressively riding the bike like myself or [Tony] Rickardsson would. He would have learned to get the maximum potential regardless.'

America's speedway invasion began as a trickle in the early '70s with only Scott Autrey and Steve Gresham sticking it out in Britain. Then the flood of talented riders began in 1978 and Kelly was at the head of it. Moran was more than a match for any of them and often he'd make the very best look ordinary. Autrey believed he really was a unique talent. 'Out of all of those guys, how great they were, and every single of one of them were great riders, Kelly stood out above them all, above all of us, he was just something special.'

# 12

# GOING HOLLYWOOD

'Their riding they say, had turned to art,
at three little tracks, only an hour apart.'

Robert 'Five Flavors' Pfetzing

STP (Scientifically Treated Petroleum) is one of motorsport's best known brands. It's synonymous with NASCAR racer Richard Petty and his famous number 43 Dodge Charger. Its presence has also been prominent in other forms of racing too, most recently the Bloodhound SSC land speed record project, which is headed by Richard Noble and driver Andy Green – a pairing that produced the first ever supersonic land speed record in 1993 with their Thrust vehicle. However, in 1983, STP expanded their involvement with speedway racing in a big way with the Moran brothers.

Until this point, STP's main association with the sport was with Alan Christian, but now the company was exploring diversification and sought to extend their name into more areas of motor sport – speedway being one of them.

'They got to hear about me possibly staying home,' said Kelly, 'and Ralph Salvino of STP got in touch with me through KK and he said that he liked my style of racing or whatever, and that they wanted to sponsor my brother and myself. When I told them that my brother was definitely racing in England they said, "No problem, we'll do a worldwide sponsorship deal." Shawn and myself both received a five-figure sum.'

Paul Heffernan, who had developed the Carlisle tyre, was brought in to obtain sponsors for Kelly. He remembered being summoned to the Rovazzini's when news spread that he was going to stay and race in California.

'I got summoned to Pete Rovazzini's house and there he was lying by the pool acting like Al Pacino! I thought, Oh my God, this guy is hanging out like he's right out of *The Godfather*. It really was like that. But when I spoke to him I could see that he really, really cared about Kelly. It wasn't bravado, they genuinely cared. And then I spoke to his father, he said to me, "Look we really want you to help Kelly." My next question was how much or what did they want me to do. To be honest, I was pretty busy, but I really liked their attitude toward Kelly. They wanted to get him into an environment that was conducive for him to do well. I put him on the Carlisle deal and I had brought STP into speedway with Alan Christian. So I got Kelly sponsored by STP, I tied in Super Seer, NGK, Z Leathers, Sam Tanner got him Arai helmets – I mean, he was sponsored to the gills. He was covered with everything.

'Kelly's first STP deal was not very big, Alan Christian's was bigger,' Heffernan revealed. 'He would say "see ya" to people so we had "see ya" put on the back of the leathers. He was managed like a rock star, he didn't have to do anything but ride. Rovo never showed up, but I would stop by and see Mr Rovazzini once in a while. It was almost like a seamless management.'

Kelly was delighted with the arrangement, as he said in *Speedway Magazine*: 'If you fans only knew what it does to a rider's programme when he has the backing of one of motor sport's leading sponsors. So on behalf of Shawn and myself, we thank you STP.'

Nigel Tubb was STP's co-ordinator in Europe and believed that their sponsorship was ahead of its time. 'Up until this point all speedway sponsorship had been a product-based deal. But the decision was made to sponsor the Morans on a cash sponsorship, a healthy retainer if you like. It was the first of its kind in the sport. We had the "Team STP" concept going ten years or so before the "Team Exide" thing which was so successful with Billy Hamill and Greg Hancock. If we did it now, we would be in the Grand Prix as "Team STP".'

Moreover, they both had access to plenty of STP's product and because of their success on the track their rivals once again thought that their use of STP goods was part of the reason for their achievements. Therefore, they also began to use STP, which not only increased their sales but also expanded the company's profile.

'We had a product called AP75, which was our equivalent of WD40, and the riders found that it was significantly better. So STP's reputation on the speedway scene grew,' said Tubb. 'Soon various parts wagons around the tracks carried STP's products. They [Kelly and Shawn] were very marketable. They were unique. Not only were they brothers, but they were both very successful riders. It wasn't that one of them was good and the other was average, both of them could win titles, left, right and centre. They were excellent ambassadors for the sport and the product. It was a great success and interest in the company was phenomenal.'

There were occasions though when, inspired by the facilities that corporate hospitality provides, Moran's actions and judgement were impaired. STP was heavily involved in Indy Car racing at that time and Rick Kelly recalled an incident when the company had invited them to one of the big races.

'We went to an Indy Car race because Rick Salvino invited us and Kelly walked up to Gordon Johncock and he goes, "Where did you get those handicap shoes?" Well Gordon was recovering from a big crash at Indy [Indianapolis 500]! He'd get smashed at these things and walk up to people and make an ass of himself.'

The Morans, and the other subsequent sponsored riders, all took full advantage of the stickers provided in order to market the STP brand at every opportunity. Kelly even took a personal risk to lead the way, as Ron Preston recalled.

'On the way down to one of those Denny Pyeatt memorial races at El Centro, he stopped in the middle of the freeway, got out and put a big STP sticker on this big boulder. So everyone that was coming down would see it and go, "Oh I know we're heading in the right direction because there's Kelly's STP sticker!" That was a pretty dangerous thing to do.'

With the new sponsorship came a new colour scheme that matched STP's colour branding, red, white and blue – red being the dominant colour. To start with, Kelly wore leathers that were mainly red and white, with blue trim and blue and white chequers that ran up and down the side of each leg. They were distinctive and he admitted that he had to look twice when he caught a reflection of himself.

'For the very first time I will be wearing red leathers,' he said at the time. 'You get so used to wearing one colour that when you put on a new pair you don't believe it's you. So remember, I'm the little one in red.'

Later in the season he altered his colour scheme to incorporate blue bottoms (one of his favourite colours) to his suit, with red and white chequers running up his legs, which contrasted nicely with the red and white top and the bold STP oval on his chest. When he changed his crash helmet to blue the following year, this became the classic Moran colour scheme, one that varied only slightly over a six-year period, which would be revisited much later in life in a bid to recall the days of yore.

The changes didn't end there, though. After six years riding Weslake motors, he switched to Godden engines. His brother had already been riding them and other international riders were also using them, including Hans Nielsen and Simon Wigg. The Italian-made GM had also entered the sport and, while Weslake was still a leading choice, the sun was beginning to set on the marque from Rye, but Kelly's association with that machine wasn't quite at an end.

Godden was manufactured by Don Godden, a British long-track racer who had also worked for Weslake, but Jim Busby imported the machines and sponsored Kelly.

'They were good engines,' he said. 'I was sponsored by them in terms of never having to pay for a repair, a re-build, or even if I blew one up – which I never did. The power band was different on the Godden to the Weslake. It wasn't quite as responsive as the Wessie from the start, but once you got up to top speed they were great. Jim sold out to Tom Cirello at the end of '83, but the arrangement was still honoured.'

A few weeks into the new campaign another sponsor came on board, the card game UNO. Moran said, 'I have personally been playing it in Europe for quite some time. First STP, now UNO. If my luck keeps on going this way I may take up acting!'

All these positive changes only enhanced Moran's optimistic frame of mind when he was quoted as saying, 'I feel the changes at this stage of my career could give a tremendous boost to my World Championship hopes.'

Having already uniquely adorned the cover of the new American publication, *Speedway Magazine*, inside he was also given a regular column, entitled 'Kelly's Kolumn'. To start with, Paul Heffernan ghosted the column.

'I ghost wrote his column for about six issues and then he said, "Can I do it myself?" and I said, "Of course you can." I never helped him after that at all and, as I understand it, he did his column for the rest of the time.'

Even the casual observer was left in no doubt as to how important the sport in America viewed the return of the Wizard of the Balance. However, not everyone shared that enthusiasm and perhaps they felt that all the attention he was getting was a bit over the top. He may have been ranked fourth in the world and won the World Team Cup, but he was one of many riders competing on the Californian circuit and, at national level, some had more honours beside their name than him.

Characteristically, he didn't play on his reputation but after he retired he admitted that he had to win over some of his Californian rivals. 'I just wanted to be an ordinary racer. I just hoped that the other guys didn't look at me and think, oh Moran's here, 'cos he's been over to Europe, world number four, I'll show him what racing's all about here. At first I would win a race and then I'd look back to offer my hand of well done or whatever, like I would in England, and they had already turned back into the pits and I used to think, oh okay. And when they used to beat me I used to go over to them and say, "Hey, good race buddy," and they used to look a bit surprised, like oh thanks, maybe he's not so bad. That was the main concern. I didn't want people to think I was anything other than an ordinary racer, even though I had raced in Europe and been in World Finals.'

Kenny Best and KK would wield the spanners for him. They were both excited about having him racing in the US again. However, Best recalled that some of his rivals certainly did try to give the little superstar a reminder of what racing, Californian-style, was all about.

'The only thing that I didn't like was that his reputation had preceded him and there were a few guys over here who wanted to make a name for themselves and were pretty wild riders anyway,' said KB. 'I used to get pretty upset because if they could beat Kelly that was like the highlight of their career. They would do some stupid stuff and cause some really bad crashes that didn't need to happen. Kelly knew about it and it didn't bother him, but it used to bother me.'

While Best did mechanic for Kelly, he saw his role differently, more of a good friend who would look out for him. This meant that he'd often get into disagreements with others when he'd seen a less experienced rider put Moran in a dangerous situation.

'People used to say to me, "Well, look at Kelly, he does the same thing," but I couldn't explain it to them, he was different, he could do things on a motorcycle that other people couldn't. It may have looked like he was out of control but he never took anybody out like what was happening over here during the first year. They would drive for the corner way too hard and there was no way that they're going to make the corner. Kelly was driving in so deep they thought that they could, and they would go even deeper than him to pass and take him out. That used to scare me because they were in over their heads. I can remember Guy [Sam] Ermolenko – I got into him one time, but we patched it all up – but he made a couple of dangerous moves and was out of control trying to get around Kelly and that could have crashed him. I didn't like to see him crash because he had those injuries that were pretty bad at other times.'

Ermolenko had been part of the Gaston & Dillon team set-up with Kelly's old buddy, Danny Becker. While Becker wasn't the force he once was, his reputation on the track was still fearsome. Therefore, a typical daredevil move from the Wizard of Balance reminded his competitors what a rare talent he was, and it helped thaw the cool atmosphere he had encountered from some of them.

'I passed Danny round the outside and some of the other riders couldn't believe it – "Hey you passed Becker round the outside, how did you do that? No one does that," they said. I always got on okay with him and I've always had respect for all the riders. It's a dangerous sport – if you're fair with them, then they're fair with you.'

Having to win over some of his rivals may have been caused by a disappointing and slow start to his new era. During the Spring Classic meetings at Costa Mesa and San Bernardino he failed to reach double figures in either meeting – although his showing at IMS may have been affected by seeing his brother break his arm. He finished down the order at Hemet and at Ron Preston's new track at El Centro; luck deserted him while he was leading the scratch semi-final by a mile when the heavy track caught him out and his machine reared and he was deposited onto the track. His trip to England to represent America in the Test series and the World Team Cup also called a halt on his campaign in the Golden State, and he was aware that he hadn't hit his top form yet, as he acknowledged in his column.

'The transition from the European quarter-mile tracks to the American tracks is such a difficult task and I guess it showed during the Classics,' he wrote. 'But be patient, I have adjusted to the Goddens and have practised as much as possible. I feel confident that you will see my European form very shortly.'

The format in the USA of employing a knockout system was a tough one. If you finished third in your first scratch race, you were out of that segment of the meeting; and should you experience a fourth or worse in the handicap (there were six riders in a race), your night could be over after just two races. It was akin to the knockout system that was used in the Grand Prix from 1998 to 2004, a format that wasn't liked by its competitors and which produced some desperate manoeuvres.

'I think riders like Hans Nielsen and Erik Gundersen would take some time to get used to it, especially the handicap racing, but from scratch they'd be gone, man, because they were such good gaters – not like me,' Moran said. 'I can remember asking Harry Oxley, "Don't put me in the first two races, Harry," and that was because the track was so heavy in the early races. When you'd start off the fifty-yard line in the handicaps, you'd use all your tear-offs by lap three.'

Critics of his decision to remain stateside pointed at the lower standard as the main reason why Moran's decision was unwise. By lacking the top competition he would face in the British League, it was viewed that this harmed his World Championship chances. He wasn't the only American to remain in California. John Cook and Brad Oxley also elected to give the UK a miss and with national stars like Mike Bast, Alan Christian, Mike Faria, John Sandona and Dubb Ferrell all capable performers on the US circuits, Moran wouldn't be able to rest on his laurels. There was some up and coming riders, too, who would later appear in Britain like Robert Pfetzing, Buddy Robinson, Bobby Ott and Steve Lucero, and they didn't lack characters either. Keith Larsen was known as 'the Snakeman' because he brought his pet python to the races with him. He also took his dog, which led to a comical tale of Kelly having an almighty struggle trying to contain the strong animal – Moran adored dogs. Speedway in California might not have scaled the level it enjoyed in Britain, but it didn't lack quality or excitement.

There were even a few characters in the stands, too. Most notable was 'Gene Gene the Dancin' Machine'. He was a regular at Costa Mesa and would be seen jigging on the crash wall of turn two in between heats.

One thing Moran didn't lack was meetings, because there were three tracks that operated on a weekly basis – Costa Mesa, San Bernardino and Ventura – plus short seasons at other venues like Auburn, Hemet and Ridgecrest.

There were other benefits to racing on the west coast, not least the famous Californian girls. He may not have had the Hollywood-style looks of his friend, Penhall, but what he did have was a courteous charm, a fun demeanour and a cheeky grin that was matched by a mischievous glint in his eye. While he may not have been tall, his lack of stature only added to his appeal; young girls found him cute and the more mature ladies wanted to mother him. When he wanted, his success with the opposite sex could be just as good as his racing. Indeed one of his sponsors' PR men once remarked that he could 'charm the knickers off a nun!'

'There seemed to be more girls than supporters,' Kelly admitted after he had retired. 'The other riders were always trying to get off with my girlfriends. Being a little guy, with a big heart, I chose not to take it out on them off the track, but to beat them on it. So the Jelly Man was still king!'

Mike Faria (also backed by Jim Busby Racing) was one of the leading riders in California and resisted a very good offer from Swindon in '83 to continue his career in the USA. He said: 'There was nothing at the time like sunny southern Californian action. Everything was right here, local, you didn't have to travel too far, the tracks were all an hour and a half, or two hours away, it was good money and it was sunshine all the time.'

However, on 20 May at Costa Mesa, Kelly faced an unbeaten Mike Bast in the Scratch Main Final. Bast led going into the first corner, but suddenly No. 31 Moran slipped through on the inside and grabbed the lead. Bast regained it on lap two, but Kelly wasn't going to be denied and he re-took first place on the back straight, only for his rival to nose ahead on the home straight, yet Kelly accelerated away for his first main victory of the season – the real Kelly Moran had arrived.

'After winning the main at Costa Mesa I knew the hard work, uncertainty, and verbal abuse from Europe was worth it all,' he said in his column. 'To win my first Scratch Main of the season, although I am considered a world-class veteran, was a great feeling! You may not know it, but this is only my second full season in the States and everything seems to be getting better each week. My Goddens are working so good and ran really well for the World Team Cup qualifier. I sure hope they run as well for the American Final.'

Once again four World Championship places were up for grabs from the US round and he expected nothing less than a hard meeting where dropped points and mistakes would prove costly. 'My mechanics have been working day and night for two weeks on my equipment for that one night,' he said. 'Believe me, the race at Long Beach is by far the toughest race to make the World Final and everything has to be tuned to perfection. I don't care who else makes it as long as brother Shawn and I do.'

Shawn did qualify, Kelly didn't. He ran a third in his opening race, which put him under pressure. However, having gathered 6 points from three races, he was leading comfortably when his bike caught too much grip and, seemingly in slow motion, his machine reared and he fell off the back. Dennis Sigalos slipped by easily but Kelly's machine flopped end-over-end and Dubb Ferrell was forced on to the infield to avoid it. Moran was down for several minutes but eventually returned to the pits unaided – his World Championship dream was over. He was very disappointed because he was aiming to become the first American to qualify for the World Final without racing in the BL.

US team manager John Scott was a level-headed sort of chap, but close observations would reveal that he was becoming nervous. He tugged at his sleeve to check his watch, and in between talking to his riders he looked hopefully at the pits entrance for the arrival of Kelly Moran. This was the semi-final stage of the World Team Cup at Wimbledon, where the USA was due to face England, Denmark and Sweden. Although Scott knew that Kelly had flown into Britain, he hadn't arrived and no one, not even his brother, seemed to know where he was.

Signing-in time came and went, yet Scott still held on, believing his diplomacy would be sufficient to ensure that Moran could take his place in the meeting. Unfortunately, the clock seemed to have gained wheels and the officials were pressing him for a decision. He couldn't wait any longer and with the inexperienced Rick Miller in the pits, he decided that he would promote Lance King into the team and draft Miller in at reserve. He was just crossing out Moran's name on the team sheet when he suddenly appeared, strolling into the pits with his usual grin and without a care in the world. However, as far as the officials were concerned his arrival was too late to participate because he hadn't signed in on time.

For all Kelly's faults, Scott realised that his team was going to be up against it facing the hosts and Denmark, therefore he had to get Moran re-instated if they were to qualify.

'Nobody found out where he was, although we all had a fair idea of where he was, it's probably more diplomatic not the mention it,' said James Easter, who was a close friend of Scott's. 'He had to beg and plead to get him back in and the way he did it was to say this: "Put it like this, dear boy, everybody is here to see Kelly Moran ride, and you're denying them the pleasure and I don't think that's a good idea" - very diplomatic. And he got him in.'

Denmark won the meeting with the USA second – thus qualifying direct to the final in Vojens with the Danes. But Kelly scored 2 points and after a fall in his second ride he was pulled out of the meeting and his remaining rides were taken by King. *Speedway Magazine* described Moran as 'strangely out of it', it doesn't take much imagination on the reader's part to have a fair idea of what he'd been doing that caused him to be so late.

Although he never said anything publically, Scott was disappointed with Kelly's unprofessionalism and had already decided that he wouldn't be including him in the team for the final. Therefore, he returned to California unaware that his international engagements for 1983 were at an end. On his return he won the Fair Derby at Costa Mesa and at Long Beach – scene of his World Championship exit – he excitedly battled his way through from the back to win the Scratch Main in the US National qualifier – he had stated that his ambition was to win the National that year, a title held by his brother.

Meanwhile over in England, at Hackney's Waterden Road stadium where Kelly had suffered multiple injuries and Denny Pyeatt had lost his life, Shawn Moran had crashed and broken his leg. Therefore, he was ruled out of participating in the World Team Cup Final. Realising that their World title was under threat, Scott tried to persuade Penhall to make a comeback before he recalled Kelly from California.

They faced Denmark on home shale, England, who had to negotiate another round for a back door entry, and former Czechoslovakia. This time Miller was in at reserve from the outset, joining Kelly, Lance King, Dennis Sigalos and skipper, Bobby Schwartz. But the loss of the younger Moran and being in Denmark's backyard was too much of a mountain to climb and America slipped to third behind champions Denmark and England. This time Kelly scored a more creditable six, winning his second ride, but he was not at all happy with what he viewed as Denmark's gamesmanship and even suggested there was some a conspiracy that preyed on the nation's Hackney hoodoo.

'They cheated, we were robbed,' he claimed in his column in the September 1983 edition of Speedway Magazine in the US. 'Ole Olsen led Denmark to a so-called victory by being the promoter and grading the track whenever it suited his team instead of every four heats [it was, and still is, standard practice to grade the surface after every four races]. They ripped us off and I hope we all remember it. When they won the Danish crowd went nuts. It was then that I realised how mad I was because it was a Dane, Finn Thomsen, who was involved in that incident at Hackney with Shawn that has all but wrecked his year. I, for one, will not ride there [Hackney] again. It's nothing but a dangerous cesspool that has done more damage to US speedway than anything else. So please AMA, you issue our licences, please do something about Hackney before the cost rises anymore.'

He returned to the USA to be confronted with some resentment from his fellow riders; the AMA had awarded him 6 points because he missed a National qualifier at Auburn while he was representing his country. Kelly was unashamed. 'I have worked very hard for my international standing and have never received any special treatment and I feel I was cheated by receiving only 6 points.'

Pete Rovazzini was waiting for Moran at Ventura and, like John Scott, was getting concerned as the clock ticked away. It was an important qualifier, but Rovo didn't expect his friend to be taking advantage of the sights from a unique view.

'My mom had chartered a helicopter ride to take him from LA to the race track at Ventura. I was waiting in my car and when he finally arrived I said to him, "Where in the f**k was you, dude?" "Oh, we were looking at … you'd be amazed how many swimming pools there are in southern California!" "You're taking a tour and we've got to qualify for the US Nationals?!" That's our Kelly, get out of the helicopter and then go out and race.'

It was during this qualifier at Ventura that confusion over paperwork saw him pick up a $50 fine by the AMA for supposedly failing to appear in the US Best Pairs meeting there. He successfully appealed, but it appears that he could have been experiencing some backlash from the press because he was disappointed by the amount of publicity that the affair attracted, which threatened to dent his reputation. In his column he demanded an apology.

'I want to make it clear that I never committed to that race and the decision to fine me was reversed once the true facts were known. When I was racing a qualifier at Ventura the sign-in woman asked me if I was doing the Best Pairs race. I gave her a "tentative maybe". The only reason I did that was so that she'd leave me alone and not bother me the rest of the night. The week after, George Rich handed me a suspension notice saying I'm fined $50 for not showing. I didn't even know what it was all about. He told me I had signed in for the Best Pairs. The only thing I had signed was a sheet saying I was present for the qualifier. I don't like to race at Ventura, so I didn't sign up for the Best Pairs. We pleaded our case and won. They screwed up, not us. We won because we weren't guilty. The Ventura people were supposed to get in touch with my manager but they never even bothered to call him. Hopefully we can get a public apology out of them.'

KK was mindful that Kelly hadn't really got into his stride during his first full campaign in the USA for five years. He realised that perhaps his rider was taking the laid-back lifestyle in California a bit too seriously and felt that he had to impress the importance of qualifying for the Nationals on him in order to maintain the future well-being of their racing programme. He needn't have worried; Kelly performed his party piece and put in a performance that was burned in McGoldrick's memory for the rest of his life.

'He hadn't had a lot of success and he needed desperately to be in the National Championships and he was way behind on points. I spoke to him about it and said, "Look Kelly, you've gotta do this because if we don't make it to the National we don't have a chance of getting sponsorship in any way, shape or form after coming from the British League for all those years." He pulled his finger out and he went after it. We had an IMS qualifying race and, man, he raced unbelievably. Jim Busby was there, the guy who helped us with Godden, and Kelly wheelied to get in between two guys who were blocking him and they were so close that he had room for his bike, but not the handlebars. So he picked the bike up at the end of the straightaway, and wheelied high enough to get his handlebars over the tops of those two guys and then dropped it again, went into the corner, and beat them both coming out of the corner! He did several things of that type, like he'd go deep into the corner and would pull it out so hard that he just rocketed past everybody down the back straight. That was probably the most impressive night I have ever seen him race.'

Kelly had qualified in fourth place with 47 points; Mike Faria led the qualifiers on 64. However, approximately a month before the National, an incident occurred that may have provided him with the inspiration for his impressive showing. On 2 September at Costa Mesa he was running wheel-to-wheel with Leni Faas when they touched – the report described it as a tap from Kelly – and Faas crashed. The referee, Irwin Moon, excluded Moran and, unusually, Kelly got quite angry over the decision. With his night curtailed by what he viewed as an unfair call, there was a lot of discontent in his pit. He declared to whoever would listen that he'd show everyone who the 'real champion is' when they staged the Nationals.

Therefore, he lined up for his first US National Championship final since his debut season in 1977 in a determined mood. He believed his brother was the rider to beat (he'd sensationally won the World Long Track Championship with a broken leg) and stated that he hoped that there would be some dirt on the track. 'It's always exciting to see someone go from fourth to first,' he said.

Prior to the big night at Costa Mesa, Kelly paid tribute to his supporters in the States: 'I'm really happy a lot of my fans stuck with me. I am enjoying my racing immensely this year. One reason I enjoy it so much is the fantastic fans. It was always my plan to give myself three-quarters of the season to get used to small tracks again. Even though I started out here in 1977, it still changes you a lot racing in Europe on the big tracks for five years. Every time I came home I felt like a third division rider. We gave ourselves this long, and it's working out.'

He set out his intention from the very first race, which he won convincingly by defeating one of the favourites, Mike Faria, who turned out to be his closest rival on the night. In fact he reeled off three more victories with such speed and superiority that observers believed that if they timed the races in the US he would surely have had the track record – an unofficial time of 44.4 seconds had been recorded by Moran earlier in the season, which was regarded as the fastest time. As the last round of races began, Faria was the only rider who could prevent him from winning his first US National and Kelly required just a second place to clinch the crown, which he achieved easily – although a shoulder-to-shoulder tussle with race winner John Cook indicated that he wasn't playing it safe. Naturally he was delighted; winning the US National was one of his pre-season goals and he'd done it. Kenny Best was in the pits with him that night and was equally pleased.

'He was so happy, the highlight of his career at that point. I couldn't really talk to him because he was having so much fun talking to the fans, family, and friends – he was smiling from ear-to-ear. That first title, I remember I just pretty much stayed away from him, packed away all the equipment and took off in my van, while he took off with some friends.'

Years later, though, Moran reflected that winning the National wasn't quite the earth-moving experience that he thought it would be.

'I remember I made four out of five starts, which is unusual for me,' he laughed. 'It was really cool to win it, and neat to keep it in the family. But it was a case of, oh I won the National. It was good and everything, but it felt like a bit of an anti-climax – I hate to say that. There were a lot of congratulations and celebrations but, I don't know, I expected more I guess.'

The news of his triumph had hardly reached the UK when rumours circulated that he would be returning to the British League now that he had won the biggest meeting in the USA. How these tales started is anybody's guess because in his column he told everyone that he intended to remain in California for 1984 and this was repeated again by Paul Heffernan in another part of the magazine.

'I don't know where they got those stories from,' said Moran. 'When Shawn won the National one of his biggest regrets was that he couldn't spend another year here defending the title. So there was no way I was going to go back when I was the defending champion.'

Nevertheless, the gossip wouldn't stop. So much so that Kelly became quite annoyed with the stuff that was being reported in the British press – this was when he began to get disenchanted with the media in the UK. A few weeks prior to the 1984 American Final at Long Beach, he took up the pen himself and in the June edition of his column he described the reports as 'outright lies'.

'There have been some totally false and libellous statements made about me in the British press lately. I would certainly hate to have to tell everybody that they can't believe anything they read in the British press about me, but that is beginning to look like what I have to do. Unfortunately there are certain writers and publications that persist in printing total lies about me and my intentions and my personal life. They are totally unconcerned with the truth – even a semblance of the truth – and make no attempt to check out what they write about me.

'Of course this isn't the first time they've ignored the truth. The British press constantly and continually reported that I intended to return to the British League in 1984. Those of you who read this column know that I never intended to return to the BL this year. No one even tried to contact me and find out my true intentions, nor was there ever an attempt to report the true facts.'

A month later, however, in the July edition of *Speedway Magazine*, they printed a statement from Kelly's personal manager, which seemed to close the door on any future involvement in the BL for the foreseeable future when it said: 'Kelly has considered going to Europe but we are at an impasse. Their offer [Eastbourne's] is so short of what we need that we are not even able to use their offer as a starting point for negotiation. If Kelly Moran goes to Europe it will be for the largest contract in British League history. He has made it in America and for us to move Kelly and our operation to England is going to cost a great deal of money.'

# 13

# KING KELLY AND THE MAIN DANE

'He was a racer from the bottom of his feet to the top of his head. He had a heart of a lion, a small man, but a man of great stature.'

KK (Ken McGoldrick)

As Kelly gazed at the leaden grey clouds and felt the spots of rain strike his face, he realised that this was one of the things that he didn't miss about competing in Europe – the weather. He once said that in California they called it off even if it looked like it could rain because the people wouldn't come … a situation they seldom had to deal with due to the west coast's agreeable climate.

He was in the tiny town of Mariestad, Sweden, to ride for the USA in the Inter-continental Final of the 1984 World Team Cup. Dennis Sigalos had broken his ankle in the American Final – an injury that all but ended his career – and he was called up as a replacement. He looked around at his team-mates and fellow riders from the opposing teams of Denmark, England and the hosts, and could see the look of resignation on their faces. If it was anything other than a World Championship event, the meeting would be off; but because of its importance safety was put aside and they were expected to race. He joined his team-mates Bobby Schwartz and Lance King under a makeshift shelter of a bike cover and looked across the gloomy stadium at the sparse crowd – the weather was that miserable that not even the rare chance of seeing some of the world's top racers was bringing out the locals in sufficient numbers to allow the club to at least break even. Rain or not, America was there to do a job: to win and progress straight through to the final at Leszno, Poland, and avoid having to do it all again with the addition of the Czechs and the Germans in a last-chance round.

The slimy conditions produced sixteen heats that were largely processional, except that one rider did provide the small audience with something to remember. Kelly began the meeting as reserve but when John Cook finished a distant last in the opening race, team manager John Scott put Kelly in his place for heat 8. The talented Yank breezed past England's Simon Wigg for victory and defeated Hans Nielsen for another win as the USA made light work of the adverse conditions and won the meeting on 41 points – 18 ahead of runners-up Denmark. Captain Bobby Schwartz would never forget that meeting because what he witnessed lived long in his memory.

'It was really wet and we blew everybody off and, in the mud, Kelly went around Hans Nielsen with no problem, while pulling a tear-off off with one hand. Him and Shawn had to ride the same bike in all the heats. I've never seen anything like it. All these extra bikes we had, everybody had two or three bikes, but Shawn and Kelly had the one between them. One of the bikes blew up so they both rode the same Godden bike; they came in, fuelled and oiled it, never changed the rear wheel, the tyre, just put him back on it for the next one and shoved him out to race. We offered them the spare, mine, but they just rode the same Godden and never changed it. I was really amazed by that; how he could just get on the bike and go!'

If there was one rider that got under Kelly's skin it was Hans Nielsen. It was not as if he didn't get along with him – he could get on with everyone – but there was just something about the Dane that made the American step up his game when he met him. Perhaps it went back to his spell with Birmingham when he didn't want to leave the Midlands club, but when Nielsen arrived he was transfer-listed – as it turned it out it was a good thing because he had two awesome seasons with Eastbourne – or maybe it was because he was the direct opposite of Moran, a total professional, quiet, rarely seen in the bars and dedicated to being the best. Their rivalry never spilled over into anything as bitter as the Carter/Penhall one or as intense as the one that Nielsen would experience with his fellow countryman, Erik Gundersen – Moran's absence from BL racing prevented that. Nevertheless, when Kelly lined up alongside Nielsen, he made a special effort to defeat him. Indeed, as late as 1989, after a particularly impressive showing in a league match for Belle Vue when he was the only rider to lower the Dane's colours, Kelly proudly told the author, 'I passed Nielsen from the back!'

Dennis Sigalos had also had a run-in with Nielsen during the Inter-continental Final at White City the previous year. He offered this assessment of why Kelly may have taken an aversion to him.

'Hans was a hell of a rider and he was one of the guys to beat. He was a hell of a starter. Most of the time he'd sit around the inside there and take up some room.

He used his head a lot. I don't think there was any real drama between them, but maybe Kelly was joking and kidding around and Hans didn't take to it – you know how Kelly could be sometimes. They were opposites.'

'He just wanted to beat him,' said Kelly's future wife Lorna. 'But yes, when he raced against Hans he used to be determined and there was a bit of rivalry there.'

However, his antipathy toward Nielsen wasn't helped by an incident on the ferry when they were returning from Mariestad and a clash when racing, as Schwartz remembered.

'Hans had bumped him during a race in Sweden and he was mad about that, and then he got mad at him on the boat. He was playing the pinball machine when Hans did something to it – I don't know what exactly, he knocked his arm or something. Kelly had a little bit too much to drink and he got all pissed off with that "Danish bacon head" as he used to call him! He was angry and getting in trouble with the other people on the boat. He wouldn't behave and they wanted to put him in the brig. We managed to save him from that. They said, "As long as you can contain him in his room, that'll be fine." So that's what we did, we got him to his room and he was fine. He was mad with Hans, though. He wasn't that bad, but whatever was happening they had enough of him!'

'I can't remember having any major disagreements with Kelly, unless he was a bit pissed,' Hans Nielsen pondered. 'He was really easy-going unless he was pissed, then he could be a bit of a pain.'

Nielsen was also riding Godden machines and this may have also added to the competition between them. In '84, though, Jim Busby had sold out to Tom Cirello and Kelly had taken delivery of a Mark IV Godden engine. He may not have been the most mechanically minded racer out there, but he knew a good motor when he got on one.

'The bike is very fast – very fast!' he emphasised. 'When you're idling the motor to when you stab it, it just pulls all the way and keeps going. It doesn't want to wind out. Gene Woods has two of these. He put his together stock. We haven't. We had ours stripped all the way down. We found an oil line that was kinked. Like when you're drinking Pepsi with a straw. That's how the oil line was inside the motor. Dennis Briggs went through it and he replaced all the little stuff like that. It's like night and day over the old bike.'

It was this machine that he used at the American Final at Long Beach. He qualified in an impressive second place with 14 points but was unable to defeat a flying Schwartz, who won the meeting. Brother Shawn also qualified and Lance King. Once more, Kelly headed to Britain to race in a World Championship qualifier, the Overseas Final at Belle Vue. The next round – should he be successful – was five days later in Denmark, which was the last qualifier before the World Final itself.

Therefore, they planned to make it into a bit of a holiday and took in some meetings prior to the event at Hyde Road by visiting, among others, Poole and Sheffield. As well as his usual stuff, he only brought with him some spare tyres and an engine that was ready to bolt into his brother's bike. Kenny Best accompanied him and once again they got into an adventure involving a car.

'Kelly crashed some cars and he wasn't supposed to be driving. The funny thing was he never had a driver's licence – that was kind of strange. He never had one of any sort, not from the United States. I rented a car and I was still learning about driving on the wrong side of the road and Kelly and Shawn were screwing around with me, fooling about, turn this way and that at all these roundabouts and stuff, and I looked the wrong way at a roundabout and I ended up hitting this guy. I'll never forget that guy for the rest of my life, because his name was Peter Mycock!' laughed Best.

'It tore the front bumper off this rent-a-car and we took it back to Shawn's house. And they got those big STP stickers that they used to have, two feet long, and used them to tape that bumper on. But it kept falling off. I'll never forget when Kelly and I took it back to the rental agency and I was the one who was responsible for it. We took it back and we had the rear windows rolled down and had the bumper sticking out of the window laying in the back seat. We drove up and the guy said, "How'd everything go?" and we said, "Well, we kinda had a problem with this bumper." When he looked and saw this car was destroyed, he went nuts!

'They were always doing things to me, like saying, "Look out!" when there was nothing to worry about. And Shawn's favourite thing was sticking his arm out of the window, raising it up and slamming it against the side of the door just as I was making a corner, like I had hit something when I was looking the other way. That's how I ran into that Peter Mycock guy.'

There was some criticism when neither of the Moran brothers was present for practice for the Overseas Final. Kelly defended their decision and said, 'We know that track. I'm not saying we were so confident that we knew we'd get through the round, but when you know a track and you've ridden it enough times there should be no need to ride it over and over.'

He described that meeting as the hardest of the two qualifiers and complained about the slick surface. In fact, he had to defeat Les Collins in a run-off to secure his place in the next round – he nodded 'I've done it' to his watching brother on the pit wall as early as the opening lap! For Shawn, his passage to the next round was easier when he finished third overall behind Lance King and Phil Crump.

Ole Olsen had retired as a racer, but he still owned the Vojens track where the next round, the Inter-continental Final, was being staged and he was biased toward his countrymen – as Shawn would discover. Such was Olsen's standing he held considerable influence with the nation's federation, the DMU and the FIM – too much influence, some critics believed. Nonetheless, overall the race track was a good one although it was nearly always slick because the venue received more than its fair share of rain. For someone whose starting wasn't his strong point, the slick surface didn't always suit racers like Kelly, who would rely on a bit of grip to pass his opponents.

However, this wasn't the same Kelly Moran who was eliminated at this venue in 1981 after some of his rivals allegedly got him deliberately inebriated to a point where he wasn't fully fit on race day. Neither was it the crazy Californian whose talents on the tracks were often overshadowed by a series of off-track antics that invariably got him into hot water with the authorities. This Moran was on a mission, and was more relaxed and happier with his lot than ever before; he had good sponsors, good equipment, a good team of helpers and a new woman in his life – a pretty lady called Lisa Metzler. His supporters in America claimed that he was riding better than ever and after a particularly successful month in May when he won nine main events (including three doubles) across all three tracks, it was hard to disagree with them. His form had been so good that they were calling their National Champion, 'King Kelly'.

US team manager John Scott wasn't convinced about this reformed version of the diminutive star, though, as he revealed when he was speaking to James Easter. 'I had arranged all the transport and what have you and I asked him, "Where do you want to sleep Scotty, which hotel?" And he replied, "As far away from f*****g Kelly as possible!"'

To help him in his quest to qualify for his third World Final, former World Champion Barry Briggs joined Moran in the pits for these important meetings. Briggo knew Kelly from his mini-bike days and, with four titles to his name, it was hoped that his influence could be the additive he was looking for to transform him from super talented racer into world number one.

'I wanted to help him because I thought he was going to be a talent who would never be recognised for how good he was,' said Briggo. Motivation didn't seem to be one of his roles because he was quoted as saying that all he had to do was 'pat him on the back and away he goes'.

'Having Barry in the pits with me made the other riders look at me and know I meant business,' Moran reflected. 'I was enjoying my racing, it was great to come over to Europe, race for America or in a World Championship and then fly home to the sun again.'

Moran laid down his intention when he passed Erik Gundersen to win in heat 2. He was feeling very confident when he lined up for his next race, but he didn't reckon on rival Nielsen who, after failing to score in his first race, was eager to get on the score sheet. After a tight first corner that typified these qualifiers, Kelly clashed with Nielsen, fell and was excluded.

'I was on gate three and Hans was off the inside. I was always told that the thirty-yard line meant you had to maintain your line to the best of your ability before turning in for the corner. Hans just took me out before then and I was lying there on the track with the front wheel wrapped around my neck wondering what the heck had happened. Then the ref excluded me!' complained Kelly.

The American was incensed by the decision and the actions of Nielsen. Having the support of most of his rivals, he couldn't believe he was excluded. It was one of the rare occasions (the only one in my memory) when he dashed off to the telephone to protest to the referee, Swede Torre Kittlesen. 'I tried to protest about it but he wouldn't speak to me on the phone. This other guy said, "He doesn't want to speak to you." Even John Scott couldn't get the ref on the phone for me. So I went out onto the track and made gestures at the referee to pick up the phone. Then I shook my crash helmet at him, pretending I was going to throw it at him through the glass and I could see him duck under the table!'

Kenny Best was his mechanic and he believed that the odds were stacked against his buddy when it came to expecting a fair decision. After all, Hans was Danish, they were in Denmark and combined with the rivalry that was beginning to take root between the Danes and the Americans, it didn't matter who agreed with him, the decision was never going to go against Hans.

'I thought there was a bit of home track advantage going on there myself,' Best said. 'There were words in the pits with Olsen about that; Kelly complained to him. I couldn't believe that Kelly was excluded. When you're with someone and supporting them you do have a slanted view. I was sticking up for him, but they [the Danes] would say that there was no way that Hans did anything wrong. From where I was, my vantage point, I couldn't see that well. But Kelly wasn't the type of guy to bail out like that, he wouldn't back off. I was kind of wary of Hans Nielsen and that was one thing with him, in a lot of races he would come down on Kelly sometimes. He'd be on the pole and Hans would come right down on him and put his elbow into him. I don't know if that was because I saw Olsen go over and talk to him at certain times, whether that was something that Ole taught him, but I saw him do that a few times.'

Nielsen said that he didn't remember the clash, but defended: 'I'm not saying I wasn't hard at all, but when I first came to England I learned the hard way and quite often I was on the wrong end of it. I suppose that made me pretty tough as well – if they do it to me then I'll do it to them sort of thing. From then on, after my first two or three years in England, I got pretty hardened I suppose with the experience that I'd had. So sometimes you'd shut the gate on people to make sure they don't pass you, so that may have been the case with Kelly.'

Kelly wasn't, by nature, a vengeful person, but he committed Nielsen's actions to memory and marked him down for payback at some point in the near future when the opportunity arose – and it would come during the Dane's most important race of the season. After all, his exclusion had put him back into the chasing pack, whereas before he was among the leaders.

He won his third race and it was plainly obvious that his brother, who was second, wasn't exactly pushing him for the lead. On the contrary, it seemed more likely they were team riding and keeping their rivals behind them. A second place in his fourth race ensured his place in his third World Championship.

Shawn, meanwhile, won the meeting with 13 points and was expecting to receive one of the impressive-looking trophies that he saw on the centre green prior to the start of the meeting. Instead he received a puny piece of silverware, which was hardly befitting a victory in one of the hardest meetings of the year. Although disappointed, it did underline the partisan approach employed by Olsen and his staff at Vojens.

The Moran brothers' impressive display went down well with the assembled press, in particular *Speedway Star*'s Philip Rising, who pondered, 'Perhaps speedway is about to become the age of the Morans. They have the ability to become superstars in speedway and how we need them.'

America's domination in the Mariestad round made them pre-meeting favourites for the 1984 World Team Cup, especially as holders, Denmark, were weakened by the loss of Tommy Knudsen through injury and, likewise, England were missing Kenny Carter. Moreover, held in Leszno, Poland, the hosts weren't the force that they once were.

The Yanks arrived with the same side that demolished the opposition in the rain in Sweden, but they were in an over-confident frame of mind. Kelly's derogatory term 'bacon heads' was bandied about in a bid to put off the Danish team, but it hardly registered on the ultra-cool Scandinavian riders. In truth, prior to the event itself, there were members of the US group who seemed to think that victory was a mere formality. They were in for a hard lesson.

Later, Moran regretted coming up with that phrase, which he probably adapted from the Danish bacon produce that was widely available in Britain and Europe. He said, 'I love those guys to bits. I wish I never called them bacon heads. It began because when they were talking it sounded like they had a mouthful of bacon. Those were the days when we got into a big rivalry between the Yanks and the Danes.'

He needn't have worried because they didn't take it to heart, as Erik Gundersen explained: 'It was okay, it didn't worry us. He was such a comical character and he would say so many different and funny things to stir things up a bit – it was just the way he spoke. We were always laughing and joking with him, and he was good company.'

'I didn't take much notice of that. I just got down to business and did what I had to do,' agreed Nielsen.

From the moment Lance King finished last in the opening heat and Denmark's Bo Petersen roared to first place, the writing was on the wall. The Danes dominated the meeting and they won thirteen of the sixteen races – Shawn Moran was America's only race winner. The Yanks finished third overall and Kelly scored 5 as the USA's failure to make any impression on the Scandinavians saw tempers flare and it was reported that they were fighting among themselves. They were, though, aggrieved by the ref's handling of the starts.

'Some of us were really over-confident,' Kelly admitted. 'It was good to be confident, of course, but there is a limit. There were little quarrels but nothing out of the ordinary. Tempers were short because it was such an important race. When it started to go wrong, they started to panic. And the Danes were playing games at the tapes – really cheating. The referee didn't help out at all either. We were told at the riders' briefing that the referee knew who the rollers were, and he said that whoever pushed the tapes, the tapes would go up and he'd put on the red light and he'd warn them once. That never happened. There was no warning whatsoever, so that was really unfair, I think. The track was so slick, there was no dirt on it at all, and unless you were making the starts, you couldn't get on terms with the Danes, who were always so fast from the tapes.'

The Danish celebrations provoked a determined reaction from skipper Bobby Schwartz. With the '85 final scheduled for Long Beach, he predicted that they would win in their home country – an outburst that Kelly certainly didn't agree with because he believed that only made them even more resolute.

Although he was unable to ride, Dennis Sigalos was with the team in Poland to encourage his fellow countrymen and he recalled that the importance of the meeting didn't get in the way of the riders enjoying themselves, even in ascetic Polska. He found Kelly to be in his usual fun-loving mood.

'Kelly was going up in the elevator, and there was this little glass strip on the elevator that you could see as it went from floor to floor. You could see through this strip as it went from the bottom to the top. And so, Kelly being funny, he presses the button and sticks his bare ass against the window, presses the button and it goes up, so it's going, squeesh, squeesh, squeesh, then it's coming down and he's got his tongue on the glass as he comes down, so he's licking his own ass! I've got a picture of him all bent over, no one would know who the hell it was but we all knew it was him. We laughed our asses off!'

Post meeting, the initial sombre atmosphere in the US camp soon gave way to a more buoyant mood, so much so that journalist John Chaplin and Kenny Carter – who was there as a co-commentator for TV – had to take cover behind a curtain when they wandered into a champagne fight orchestrated by the Californians. More destruction followed and, initially, Kelly received the blame even though he was angelically and blissfully asleep.

'They wrecked the motel with the moat around it, threw furniture out of the windows and they had the fire extinguishers going off in the hall,' said Schwartz. 'Kelly was in his room, he wasn't involved, he was passed out. Lance King, Ronnie Scopellite – their faces were pure white! They tried to act like they were asleep. You'd pull back the sheet and they're just f*****g white!

'Meanwhile, you'd go down to the end of the aisle where Kelly was, his door was open, and there was all this chalky white stuff floating around, and he's passed out on the bed and looked like an angel in heaven!' he laughed. 'And he had nothing to do with it, but there was this fluffy haze around him – he looked just like an angel. He had nothing to do with the ruckus; he was just passed out asleep. I'll never forget the sight of him lying there, it was funny.'

Journalist Graham Baker carried out an interview with Kelly for *Speedway Star*'s World Final preview special and he observed that he had 'calmed down a lot since his hell-raising days in the British League'. History shows that wasn't necessarily the case, although he was more relaxed and content than perhaps he'd ever been and a degree of maturity had come with his age of nearly twenty-five years. However, what seems more likely is that he did more of his partying away from the public gaze of race tracks and stadiums. One occasion in California, he turned up at a bar by himself and got talking to a couple of guys and they couldn't believe that Kelly Moran was in the same bar as them and conversing with them like he was a regular fella. In fact, their disbelief was such that he had to produce some ID to prove that he was who he said he was!

'There were times when he was teetering on the edge,' said Heffernan. 'Rick Kelly was instrumental when we could have had problems. He went to stay with Rick for a while and that got him away from it.'

However, it appeared that his calmer exterior was down to his girlfriend, Lisa Metzler, from Colorado, as he explained: 'She's beautiful, not the usual Californian type of girl around the speedway scene. She's the type when you get up in the morning, she asks you what you want for breakfast, what you want for lunch and whether you've any washing to be done. That's just what I need. She's been tremendous for me. I'm a better person than when I was in England.'

'I have had some personal problems,' he told *Speedway Magazine* before leaving to ride in Ullevi. 'Mind you, speedway is a very open sport, unfortunate as it is. Everybody knows everybody else's business. Me, I have learned to be pretty much a private person. I believe what you do behind closed doors isn't anyone's business. It's no one else's business to intrude on. I feel I have grown up a bit.'

Inevitably the question of when he would resume his career in the British League was never far away, but by now Britain's weak pound against the US dollar was enforcing his decision to remain Stateside and would also encourage more Americans to stay at home the following year – Lance King and Sam Ermolenko among them.

'No matter how much they offer me, I don't think they can ever get the pound back up again and that's the big problem right now. We make all these pounds but the problem is when we exchange our pounds to dollars we lose out,' Kelly explained.

Well sponsored, he didn't pay for anything with regard to his racing and now that he was US National Champion his earnings doubled. He was enjoying the high life and life was pretty good. 'It was a good time for me,' he told *Backtrack* magazine. 'And look at the weather I had to deal with back home … poor Kelly!'

Understandably, he regarded his brother as the rider he feared most in the World Final and he said, 'If we're both in a run-off for first place, we'll cross the line shaking hands. We really will do that.' And responding to a question about how he would handle the pressure of being the World No. 1 he remarked: 'I'd love it. But I'll do it my own way with a laugh, a joke and a grin – not a flashing smile! If I could win this World Final, I think it would really change me all round and make me a lot better person.'

Correctly as it turned out, most pundits believed that his lack of top-class competition throughout the season would prevent him from lifting the sport's biggest prize. That little bit of sharpness that comes from frequently riding at world level was a vital ingredient, not only for Moran, but also for the Eastern Bloc riders who didn't compete in the BL.

When he arrived at the Ullevi Stadium for practice, he certainly noticed Barry Briggs' influence. 'I was walking into the pits and looking at my engines and thinking, I don't remember having "HZ" on my engines. Barry had got some engines from Hans Zierk, who used to do Wiggy's [Simon Wigg's] engines so I knew they were fast. Zierk was stood at the side, arms folded, looking proud and said, "Super fast motors – good." Barry just said that he knew that I wasn't that good off the start and would need some quick motors because the ones I had he didn't think were quick enough. And they were very fast.'

In the stands was the boys' proud father, Tom, and their grandmother. 'I was told that during the meeting, when either Shawn or myself was riding, he sat there with his American flag and his Moran Brothers Racing jacket, cheering and going, "That's my boys." So I think everyone in that section knew who he was supporting!' he remembered.

'It was great that he was there, but we were so focused on our racing,' smiled Shawn. 'I think it was because we got to the World Final and he'd talked to Grandma about it and it was open to go with work. It was neat.'

Once more, Shawn was one of the pre-meeting favourites and Kelly was expected to be a contender as well. Little brother was making his debut in the biggest individual event, but he didn't fare too well. Kelly, on the other hand, was in the mix but the slick nature of the track wasn't helping his cause. He could have gone into the interval stage in a stronger position had he not suffered a misfortune. While chasing Swede Jan Andersson for the lead, his white helmet cover had come loose and was flapping annoyingly. As he removed it, he inadvertently tossed away his goggles in the process! Therefore, his challenge for the lead was ended by shale and dust stinging his eyes. He managed to remain in second, though, and was equal fourth on 6 points behind the unbeaten leader Nielsen (9), and Gundersen and King on 8. He would, though, have an opportunity to play his role in the destiny of the World title in his next race, heat 15.

Danish rivals Nielsen and Gundersen lined up alongside him and it was a pivotal race. If Erik was going to take his first World title he had to lower Nielsen's colours, while his rival knew that with one programmed ride left he couldn't afford to let Erik finish ahead of him; perhaps, though, neither considered the little American who was sandwiched between them on gate three – Nielsen was in gate two and Erik was starting from the outside.

As the green light went on, Czech Petr Ondrasik pulled back from the tapes. Predictably, the swift-starting Danish duo left the start like a whirlwind to compete in what was a hectic first corner while Moran waited for his moment to pounce. As they clashed, Kelly deployed his skill and cut underneath them; he passed Nielsen and for a moment it looked as though he had the speed on Gundersen too, but the little Cradley Heath racer just beat him to the third corner. Despite getting close, he wasn't able to overhaul Gundersen for the lead and he finished second. Crucially, Nielsen was third and his championship hopes took a massive blow as he slipped to third overall behind joint leaders Gundersen and Lance King.

Dennis Sigalos was watching the action in Gothenburg and, knowing of Kelly's anger over his exclusion at the hands of Nielsen in Vojens, he smiled when he saw him zip by on the inside and mess up his World title hopes and remarked,

'Payback's a bitch, isn't it!' In his biography, Nielsen said, 'That incident lost me the World title.'

'I knew those two would be going for each other on the first bend and they probably knew I was crap off the start,' Kelly laughed. 'I just did that cut back underneath them, got a bit of drive and the bike just hooked up. I got by Nielsen and I knew I had the speed, but Erik just had the edge.'

'I wouldn't say I was shocked,' Hans reflected in this book, 'because I always had the greatest respect for him on the track and he was good enough to do that. Obviously I wished he hadn't, but I couldn't stop him doing it and maybe I expected him to go around me, so I moved out, but he cut back and he was good at that. I don't recall the details but he was always pushing hard to beat us and had the capability of beating anyone on the day – and he was very good from the back. I never took it easy when I had him on my back wheel – I knew I had to be at my best.'

'That was a tough race and him beating Nielsen helped me a lot,' Erik conceded. 'It was a tense first corner; when Hans and I bundled, he sort of hit my rear end and I took off into the dirt. Then when I came back in, Kelly had seen the opportunity to hit the line and he nipped inside Hans and me coming out of the first corner, so it was tough, but he did me a big favour in that particular race. I wasn't aware of any issue he had with Hans but, of course, it could have been that.

'He was pushing me all the way as well. I managed to beat him but he was going fast. I felt him behind me all the time. His balance and the way he could turn the bike was unbelievable.'

Erik went on to win the World title, while Nielsen defeated King in a run-off for silver. Kelly won his last race to finish on 11 points and was fourth again. Briggo found it hard trying to get the happy-go-lucky Californian to fully concentrate on the meeting.

'Nielsen lost the title because of Kelly and he had the drop on most of the boys,' he said. 'You can't rely on passing in every race. When you go to the start you've to go there and concentrate, otherwise you're last from the start. He had so much talent but you couldn't get him to focus. He always wanted to shake hands with everybody and be friendly when he needed to be focused.'

'At least I qualified for the meeting without riding in the British League and I was the first American to do that,' Kelly said proudly. 'Hindsight is a wonderful thing, but at that time I did feel that if I raced in the British League for a few weeks before the World Final, I would have been sharper, then maybe I may have got on the rostrum … but who can say? What was special about that final was that both my brother and myself had qualified and our father was in the stands watching, and he was so proud of us.'

Kelly's disappearing act during the close season was a source of fascination and intrigue to Mike Patrick and the cause of some incongruous amusement from his friends and rivals. Mike travelled to the USA to snap some West Coast action and was flying to Ron Preston's Imperial Raceway at El Centro, close to the Mexican border, for the Denny Pyeatt Memorial race, which was one of the first meetings to open the 1984 season in California.

'I was flying with Bruce Penhall, Bobby Schwartz and Jeff Immediato and I had been staying at Bruce's at the time. They were talking about Kelly and Bruce was saying that nobody sees him all winter, nothing at all, and then he'd just turn up for the meeting ready to race. He did, he was there, and he was okay. People wouldn't hear from him for months on end and then he'd arrive ready to go,' Mike chuckled.

Kelly finished second to Dennis Sigalos in the Scratch Main but didn't enjoy the best of Spring Classic meetings by failing to transfer to any of the main events and finished in a lowly twelfth place. It wasn't long, though, before he was back in the groove. On 3 April he won his first Scratch Main at Ventura since his debut season back in 1977 and a week later defeated Mike Faria in a match race.

Previously, during the US Best Pairs controversy in '83, Moran indicated that he didn't like to race at Ventura – whether it was the track, the location or because of that disagreement, he didn't make clear. If anything, with his experience of the bigger circuits in Europe, it wouldn't have fazed him, yet it was puzzling that it took him so long to visit the top step.

'It all depended on whether he'd put his race face on. If he put his race face on he would be a factor, but if he didn't he was just having a good time – that was Jelly Man,' said Mike Faria.

Ken McGoldrick noted that although he had curbed his impulsive ways on the track, he wasn't able to do so off it. He believed that contributed to the fact that sometimes he couldn't find his 'race face' because his head was still swimming with the spirits.

'I didn't mind his all-or-nothing attitude because he was smart – as he got older he learned not to go for all or nothing. He'd prefer to start after everyone else and work his way through from the back so that he didn't get caught up in the front, and have some young guy trying to make a name for himself by knocking him off and hurting him. The fact that he drank so much was the biggest problem I had with Kelly. He couldn't control it to the point where after the meeting he could have two drinks, or two pints, and tomorrow after the race he would have two pints; he wanted to go and have fourteen pints all at once and the next day he was obliterated as far as being sharp and quick with his moves and actions.'

Nonetheless, Mike Faria was one of the circuit's top riders and he was especially effective around Ventura. He was in the middle of an unbeaten run at the 'Commotion by the Ocean' and just when it looked as though Moran was going to end that sequence, his bike failed. In fact, the opening weeks of the Californian season were something of a frustration for him as he was continually hit by mechanical problems. His initial enthusiasm for the Mark IV Godden was starting to wane when another engine failure denied him that victory at Ventura.

'I don't know what it is. At first we thought it was the magic box; we tried a slow charge and all sorts of things, but now we're finding metal shavings under the pan. Whatever it is, I'm tired of it.'

However, he persevered with it and won a double victory at Costa Mesa, losing just one race on his way to glory and beaming, 'Guess we finally have this new motor sorted out.' He repeated that double success at San Bernardino. Bobby Schwartz remembered seeing him complete one of the doubles. 'He won every single race, handicap and scratch, semis and final, and won from the fifty-yard line – that was amazing. He just blew them all off.'

Then on 22 May he finally ended Faria's winning streak with another double success. Moran said that he'd just started a winning streak of his own, while Faria countered that he intended to start a new one next week!

'I think the bigger tracks suited us better, whereas someone like Alan Christian preferred the smaller ones,' said Faria. 'Ventura was a big track then, almost a quarter-mile; the other guys kinda liked the smaller tracks and weren't too sure, but me and Jelly Man, we kind of let it all hang out. He was the Wizard of Balance and I was Flyin' Mike!'

Both of them figured prominently during '84 at all three tracks. Starting from the fifty-yard line in handicap racing, they thrilled the crowds as they battled their way through the pack to transfer. It was one of the most spectacular sights in Californian speedway. However, any rivalry between them was only ever friendly.

'We go way back; he was just a good lad,' Faria reflected. 'When we diced on the track we were pretty even with each other, no foul riding or anything like that. We'd congratulate each other when we won because we were the good guys and not dirty, you know. After the races we'd go and have a beer and have fun – he was always good for a laugh, believe me! We took care of each other and, at the time, me and Kelly were pretty much unstoppable at any of the race tracks. If he was on one night, I was on another night, we just gave each other a good run for their money. Kelly earned those wins and I earned mine back, they weren't given to us. We rode really close together all the time.

'I know technology has changed, but back then we had upright engines and the competition was closer and tighter and guys weren't being taken out left and right; you could actually trust your opponents. Nowadays I give the riders five feet because the lay-downs are so much faster, they spin so much more. If you hook up it's hard to control it and you can take off and nail somebody. Back then it was just so much better, so that made the competition tighter and you could trust riders.'

America's small tracks, skilful riders and powerful bikes made speedway a more intimate experience than it was in Europe or Australia. Riders were rarely spread out and it was often exciting handlebar-to-handlebar stuff. Match races were frequently held but were viewed by some critics as suspect, to say the least. However, after Kelly's death a TV clip emerged on YouTube of an impressive demonstration of close-quarter action between him and Bobby Schwartz. It was so graceful and exciting it almost resembled a choreographed ballet with bikes on dirt.

'We didn't know who was going to win exactly, but we knew we would look after each other in each corner, one would go inside and one would go outside and it just flowed. We weren't really racing hard,' said Schwartz. 'It was staged to the point where we wanted to put on a good show; it was done at full-blast, but we knew that we were going to be able to move around – I guess we were just expecting it to happen. We were at top speed, but you could use your art and do it. It was a bit surreal, but at the same time we were having fun and just doing our thing. We were going for it and you can't do that without having confidence in each other and I believe they were some of the best match races that anyone got to see in America. Mainly guys just go for it, they're not trying to put on a show, they just go out there and try to win the race. But it doesn't look as good as what we were doing, even if you knew we were out there having fun – it was beautiful. It was speed, it was poetry, it was calculated and we could do it because you couldn't do it unless you both knew what you were doing and knew what to do – we both did. That's how it worked out.'

As he was the reigning US Champion, was chasing World Championship glory in Europe and in fine form domestically, Kelly attracted a lot of column inches. Despite all that, there were still some who resented the publicity he was receiving. *Speedway Magazine*'s editor, Robert Fitzpatrick, had to defend the mag's position when they received complaints about the number of times Moran had been featured on their front cover. He wrote: 'I've already heard the comment, "Kelly's on the cover again?" Kelly has been a fantastic ambassador for the sport internationally, as well as nationally. And, of course, anyone who has seen a race will know that Kelly Moran is "The People's Choice" – the rider who evokes the most crowd response in this country.'

However, when the publication staged the Speedway Magazine Cup at San Bernardino, Alan Christian defeated Moran in a run-off to win the event and after pulling off his crash helmet, he turned to Fitzpatrick and demanded, 'I wanna be on the front cover!' He did make the cover – the back one.

With the number one on his back, Kelly did notice a change in attitude from some sections of the sport compared with previous years. But he was nobody's fool and didn't forget the animosity he was faced with at times during 1983.

'When I was here riding last year as number 31 I tried talking to people and they didn't want to know me as such. Now that I'm number one I've found that I have had more people coming up than I expected saying, "Hey buddy pal," supposedly acting as my friends just because I have number one on my back. But I like being number one, it's neat.'

As well as being the US No. 1, Kelly's talent and speed still attracted incredulous comments from his rivals, who couldn't believe what he was getting away with and how.

'Being a small guy I was able to pull a higher gear than the other riders and lower tyre pressures and stuff,' Kelly explained. 'I would pass people round the outside and people would come up to me and say, "How did you do that, Moran? I can't run what you're running, I'd be in the fence." It was cool. Dennis and Wendy Briggs were doing my engines and Mark Snyder was mechanic, and we had it working really well and had a lot of fun. My reactions were good and it was just flowing.'

Speedway in California was booming, crowds were up and the enthusiasm was infectious – so much so that an ambitious promoter, Robbie Klima, tried to expand the sport beyond its southern Californian heartland by staging a series of races in Las Vegas, Nevada. Kelly, Christian, Faria, John Sandona and Brad Oxley were among the West Coast stars who travelled to compete in the Silver Bowl football stadium – now known as the Sam Boyd Stadium. Unfortunately, the elements conspired against the event and freak desert thunderstorms washed out the first two meetings. However, the third meeting did go ahead and Moran won on a difficult surface.

Faria often found himself on some of those sorts of trips with 'King Kelly' and they were always enjoyable. 'We did a few tours together and he came up to Sacramento when I did an ice race up there and pitted for me. He'd stay with me in the pits for a while then he'd have to go and get some sauce – he was back and forth. He was trying to tell me about a set-up and I said to him, "I've got my set-up, Kelly, you need to go and sit down." He tried to tell me a few things but he was on the sauce a little bit, so I'd listen but not do it, because everybody has their own way of doing things. What he did suited his style of riding, what I did suited my style of riding, everybody works the throttle different, everybody goes into the corner different, so you find something you like. We stayed at my mom's house and she said, "The only beer you're getting is root beer, Kelly – no drinking." He looked at me and I go, "Hey, it's her house, Kelly." He liked to hug and kiss, and I'd go, "Kelly, no more hugs and kisses, bro – I don't do that stuff. You do that to those other guys, don't do that to me!" He still did it anyhow! He'd been around the world by that point and everybody loved him. He was a fun, loveable guy and was personable.'

When Moran and Faria teamed up to compete in the US Best Pairs at Ventura, given their form they were one of the pre-meeting favourites. Anyone who had any doubts about Kelly's ability around that raceway was soon silenced when he won the Ventura Track Championship three days prior to the AMA Pairs event – albeit Faria wasn't in the line-up.

'When I looked at Kelly, how good he was going, I felt as though we had that one in the bag,' Mike reflected. 'He was such a talented rider, we were on our game and we wanted to win. I thought: this is ours. What did he weigh? 115lbs? – so he was lighter. And he was able to be a little bit faster, but I was able to stay with him and we ended up winning it.'

They actually tied for first place with the Lance King/Robert Pfetzing pairing on 26 points (Kelly 16, Faria 10). As this was an AMA competition, it was run in accordance with international rules, which stipulated that in the event of a tie in a pairs meeting, a run-off would be staged featuring one rider from each pair. This didn't please the crowd, who felt that both pairs should have contested the decider. Many began to leave as Moran and King rolled up to the start line to a chorus of jeers. Kelly made the start and hugged the inside line and clinched the title. 'He loved that Best Pairs title, he talked about that until the day he died,' said Mike.

'We got a nice trophy for the cabinet, but we also got an AMA medal as well, which was a total surprise,' Moran recalled. 'I got on well with Mike. He was great to race with. He was always a top rider at home and did very well when he went to the British League.'

Kelly's starting abilities, especially at world level, could never be described as his strong point. But Danny Becker believed that he was a much better gater than Kelly would have us believe and that he played on that myth for his own entertainment.

'Even with me he would do it. He'd make a really bad start on purpose, just so he could beat us from behind because it was so boring for him to do it from the gate. He could beat us in any way that he wanted. He said that he was a bad gater – that was pretty funny! He could make the gate anytime that he wanted to, but he didn't do it. He'd let the clutch out, everyone would be gone before he'd let it out and he'd always smile when he did it. I don't think he fooled too many people.'

Mark Synder spent the season as his regular mechanic. Kenny Best and KK filled in when their other commitments allowed. It didn't matter who he had alongside him, he still didn't pay much attention to the technical side of the sport.

'We got Mark to help Kelly out with some of the qualifiers and big meetings over here. Then when he wasn't racing here he went over to England with him. He was a real nice guy and still is.'

As the reigning champion, Moran was one of the pre-meeting favourites to retain the US National Championship. However, possibly because of his carefree persona, the general opinion was that his heart wasn't really in it, which, considering the success he had leading up to that event, seems a serious misjudgement.

Mike Faria had finished runner-up to him in '83 and the year before that he was second to his brother, so he was eager to take that final step – amazingly he didn't win his first National title until 1990. Making the trip from England to compete was also Shawn, Bobby Schwartz and Sam Ermolenko. When Schwartz defeated Kelly in their opening race, it was clear that Boogaloo was going to be the man who was most likely to prevent him from taking successive titles.

Interestingly, Faria's chances were virtually over when he finished last in the only race in which Schwartz dropped points – third behind Alan Christian and Mike Curoso in heat 6. Watching from the pits as he prepared for his second outing, Kelly couldn't believe it and later commented, 'When Bobby finished third in the race with Christian it changed the whole thing.'

Nonetheless, Schwartz kept the pressure on him throughout the evening. When he won his next two races, Bobby won his third; when the defending champ won his fourth race, Schwartz won his next as well. As they entered the final round of heats, Bobby was 1 point behind him and then won his last race, which meant that Kelly had to win the final heat of the night to retain the crown.

He faced two riders who were in with a chance of a rostrum finish, John Sandona and Christian – another rider who had been waiting a long time for a National title and someone who excelled around the Costa Mesa track. Sam Ermolenko completed the line-up.

When Schwartz glanced at Moran before he was pushed off for the decisive race, he noticed something that gave him hope. 'He went out and he had three broken spokes in his wheel and I remember thinking, "maybe his wheel will break!" I wanted him to do good because we were buddies, but I also wanted to win the National.'

Christian determinedly told the announcer beforehand that there was no way he was going to lose that heat. As the tapes went up, Christian and Kelly banged handlebars and elbows in the first corner, but using his experience, the diminutive No. 1 roared away into the lead and never looked back to retain his championship.

'I sure felt those vibrations in the first corner with Christian,' he smiled afterwards. 'It was neat to win it a second time and to keep it in the family for three years. Everyone was ecstatic and Bobby Schwartz was really pushing me that night and kept the pressure on.'

His success had finished off what had been one of his best seasons, arguably one that could have been even greater if he had spent a little more time racing in Europe in preparation for the World Championship. As the champagne celebrations kicked off, KK had already decided that he would take a step further into the background. Sadly, Moran's happy-go-lucky, party approach was burning him out.

'I kind of quit working with him because I got a little tired of his lifestyle. He didn't seem to want to advance himself in any way; he just wanted to have fun and race. I knew it was going to end [the success] and it wasn't going to stay like that forever, so I quit working with him pretty much as a coach and started working with Billy Hamill and Chris Manchester.'

Inevitably there were a lot of celebrations and congratulations, yet unlike twelve months previously, he didn't rush off with friends and family to rejoice long into the night. Instead, armed with his trophy, medal and some liquid refreshment, he planned a more sedate evening and left with his good friend, Kenny Best.

'He spent some time at the track talking to people and stuff. There was a party going on here and a party going on there, but for some reason he was different, he didn't want to do that. We stayed until everyone had gone and he was telling people that he'd see them here or there, wherever they were going to be, and we just went back to my house. He was deep in thought, very thoughtful, and the two of us sat there, had a few drinks and talked all night with the trophy on the table in front of us.'

# 14

# TURNING POINT

'The sheer challenge of life on the edge, whether actual or vicarious, keeps us young our whole lives.'

Barrie Palmer

Kelly sat up and caught his breath. He looked across at his stricken mountain bike that lay beside him with a buckled wheel and thought to himself, something is trying to tell me something here – perhaps it's time I went back to race in England. He'd been making preparations to defend his US National title when he decided to take off to the beach on his bike and negotiated a route through a dry lake bed. Instead of following the usual path, he veered off to the right and up and over a ridge to gather some speed – as he had done many times before. He was pedalling away when he hit a rock embedded in the sand and suddenly he was flying through the air and landed heavily. Luckily he wasn't injured, but it wasn't the best preparation.

'On the day of the Nationals something didn't feel right,' he said. 'I was going for the treble and I was thinking, wonder what the track will be like? Oh it don't matter, I like that track. It was such a hard year, every time I crashed I seemed to hurt myself.'

The '85 campaign had begun so well: he won the Denny Pyeatt Memorial at El Centro, won the opening night Scratch Main at a new track at Carlsbad – a venue that he helped design – and recorded a double at the other new track at Ascot. He was also chosen as a test rider for a new silencer, what they called a 'Pig's Nose', in preparation for it possibly being introduced the following season.

Then it started to go wrong; first of all his winning streak at Ventura of four successive Scratch Main victories was ended by flu. He won the Bruce Penhall

Classic and thought he'd also won the Speedway Magazine Cup, only to have the result amended afterwards when it was discovered that John Cook had used an illegal tyre and the title was handed to Alan Christian. A fall during the American Final in a run-off for the last qualifying spot ruled him out of the World Championship, and then he broke some ribs after a heavy crash at Carlsbad on 23 June. His season really hit the buffers on his return when he sustained a painful foot injury at Costa Mesa that prevented him from riding for the USA in the World Cup at Long Beach – his popularity was such that his absence from the team warranted half a page of explanation in the programme.

'Brad Oxley crashed and the push bar on his bike hit my left heel and bent my steel shoe upwards. I was sat on the track looking at my toes pointing up at me! Mark Synder, we used to call him "Mr Muscles", got hold of it and bent it back – what a relief. There are more little bones in your foot than your hands and I fractured them all along my foot. That pretty much ended my season,' he explained.

His brother Shawn qualified for the World Final at Bradford and Kelly jetted over to support him – he was fifth. The following week there was a three-match Test series between England and the USA and during the second Test at Ipswich, Kelly pulled on a spare set of his brother's leathers, jumped on his bike and rode in a couple of races. But even that was doomed because he contracted bursitis, which was a swelling that appeared on his elbow like a golf ball. Not only did that prevent him from racing in the third Test, it also ruled him out of competing in the Californian State Championship at IMS.

By the time it came round to defending his National title, he hadn't ridden regularly for some time and scored just 6 points as Alan Christian grabbed the championship. 'A horrible year, I broke seven bones in six months,' he said. Therefore, with no number one on his back and with his inner voice trying to tell him that it was time for a new beginning, he planned a return to the British League. 'It seemed like a good idea,' he said later.

It wouldn't be with Eastbourne, though, as the Eagles had switched to the lower division, the National League, and riders from outside Britain and the Commonwealth were excluded from racing in it. So Kelly sounded out Shawn about joining him at Sheffield, although according to his brother he took some persuading to swap the sun and fun for rainy days and the pressures of league racing again. Besides, such was the complexity of British speedway's rule book that it wasn't quite as simple as that.

Kelly's final calculated average with Eastbourne in 1982 was 9.62, which was a stumbling block when it came to fitting him in the side with his brother. It could be done but to do so would have compromised the overall strength of the Tigers. Therefore, Sheffield's boss, Maurice Ducker, applied to the authorities to have his average assessed at a lower 7.50 figure and argued that it should be re-assessed because he hadn't raced in the BL for three years. After much discussion, the new average was agreed and they could go ahead and finalise the contract with him – once the small matter of Eastbourne's transfer fee of £25,000 was addressed. Although Sheffield's supporters and Moran's fans were just happy to see him racing in what was then the world's toughest speedway league and his return was a boost to the sport in the UK, many felt that lopping over 2 points off his average was an absurd decision because it was obvious that he was going to make a mockery of that lowly average.

Ducker was delighted to have one of the most spectacular riders in the world in the team. Alongside his brother, Shawn, the Tigers also included Neil Collins, Peter Carr, Martin Hagon, David Walsh and Peter McNamara and they were expected to be one of the main challengers for honours in 1986.

'Enticing Kelly back to ride in this country is a big step forward for the British League,' said Ducker. 'From Sheffield's point of view, it is a good show and it has taken a lot of wrangling over the past three months to set up a deal with him. He may take a few weeks to settle down with the Tigers but I'm sure he will prove a big asset in our determination to win the British League this year.'

But Paul Heffernan didn't think that the deal was good enough and still doesn't think it was a wise move to this day.

'The worst thing for Kelly was to go back to England without an entourage, without a programme that completely took care of every issue. He should have had a mega deal,' he said. 'Had that happened for him back in England, he would have won a World title – I'm absolutely sure about that. There were deals made for him that were just wrong. I didn't want to be involved and I wouldn't have let him go under the circumstances that were being offered. He spent three years racing in a system where he didn't have to do anything. He just had to put his leg over a bike and he didn't even have to think – and he thrived. He won two National titles, back to back, and that was at a time when it was really hard to win it. Look at the talent; if you blinked the title had gone. If he had that set-up in England, he would have shone beyond what people could have imagined.'

However, probably due to the fact that he missed 71 meetings out of 120 scheduled races because of injury, Kelly was a little short of funds and took a job during the winter as a fork lift driver for Rick Kelly's roofing company. As someone who was used to working in the twilight hours, initially he found it a bit difficult coping with the early starts.

'It was hard getting up so early in the morning to go to work, but now I feel guilty if I sleep until noon and it's like half the day is gone,' he said in his final column before departing for Britain. 'Getting into the habit of waking up early sure helps me get a lot of things done these days. My friends can't believe it – they think I've been up all night!'

'He worked for me for quite a few years, usually during the off-season,' said Rick. 'We had street sweepers, what they would call Tennant Street Sweepers, and he'd get on them and show the kids how to get them up on two wheels!'

While a difficult, problem-strewn season was one of the reasons that influenced his decision to return to British racing and although his approach was questioned throughout his career, he was still ambitious. He realised that if he was to be a serious World Championship contender, he had to race in Britain.

'Let's face it, the best riding in the world for experience is there,' he said. 'You're racing against riders of different nationalities in practically every event and they too all have their different experiences from their respective countries. When you race the same guys day in and day out, you don't seem to learn anymore. But when you get the chance to get around the country racing different tracks and different riders, that's when you get experience and you start learning a lot of different things. There are five or six riders in this country who've beaten everybody else – we've beaten ourselves. Where do you go from there? I'd rather start getting back on climbing up the ladder rather just stay down on the lower rungs. Going to England will improve my chances in the World Championship.'

Before leaving America for a new career with the Sheffield Tigers, Kelly signed off by winning the 1986 Spring Classic Series. Three exciting and entertaining years riding the Californian circuit were at an end. He left as a champion, but he couldn't have known what fate had in store for him over the coming months.

When Kelly and Shawn entered the Pinegrove Country Club in the Stannington area of Sheffield, it was a very quiet evening. In fact, there were only two people in the public bar, both attractive ladies who instantly caught their attention. Being sociable guys by nature, they didn't feel it was appropriate to leave them drinking alone. Therefore, they offered to buy them a drink. The Californian accent attracted the girls to start with because, clearly, they were not local lads on the pull and they were intrigued. Kelly and Shawn introduced themselves and learned that their names were Lorna and Lynne.

'We were just having a quiet drink when they both came to the bar and said, "Can we buy you a drink?" recalled Lorna. 'We'd never met them before, ever, and since we were the only people in the bar they asked us if we'd like to join them, so we said okay. And with their accent and everything, it was oh right, nice to speak to an American. We didn't know anything about speedway, we didn't have a clue who they were, what they did, or anything like that, because I had never been to speedway at that point. Kelly said that he'd come over to race speedway and my impression of speedway at that time was that Elvis Presley movie, where he went round on the Wall of Death (Roustabout) – I thought that was it!'

Kelly wouldn't go so far as to say that it was fate, or love at first sight, but he believed that some higher force was at work that evening because 'The Walk of Life' by Dire Straits was playing on the jukebox when he began talking to Lorna Brindley and, ever afterward, when he heard the opening bars to that song, he would be transported back to their first meeting. 'We got chatting and we hit it off from there,' he said.

'After they'd called last orders, they asked us if we wanted to come back to their place. We thought, no chance!' laughed Lorna. 'I asked them where they were living and Kelly said, "Over at Goodison Crescent," and he told me the number, I think it was number six, bang opposite where my brother lived. And my brother was 6ft 4in and built quite big, so I thought any funny business and I'd run across the road to my brother's. So we took them up on their offer and went for something to eat. At that time they brought Mexican food with them in their suitcases. So they made Mexican food, which I'd never had before. And that was it. It was a really nice night and then we went home. There was no funny business. At first, what attracted me to him were his impeccable manners. I had never met anyone with such impeccable manners. He opened the door for me and was an absolute gentleman. I just thought, wow! Lynne? She just thought they were really nice, well-mannered brothers, but that was it. She never had much to do with them after that. And then Kelly asked me if he could take me out again. I said, "Oh, okay."

'Later that week he called at my mum's house, which was where I was living at the time. At that point I thought I was really trendy because I had this bright pink cat suit; I thought I looked wonderful with a lovely perm. And Kelly turned up in a pair of clogs! I thought, oh my God! That was my initial impression. I thought he was going to do a clog dance or something. But looking back I was in this bright jumpsuit … so fashion wasn't brilliant back then, but nobody wore clogs, except Kelly – clogs and white socks! So we went out on our first date, he came and picked me up and met my mum and dad in his clogs. He also wore like a bomber jacket and he was growing a pony tail at the back and my dad was like, right. After our first date we were kind of inseparable.'

Lorna couldn't have known that being with Kelly Moran was going to be very different to anyone else she had met at that point. She had no idea that he was a double National Champion, had won gold for America and had been fourth in the world three times. In fact, such was his performance when she first saw him race that she thought he must have been starting out and certainly not the talented racer who Sheffield had gone to great lengths to bring to Owlerton.

'When he took me to speedway for the first time he scored 3 points and fell off about three times. I thought he must be learning and thought that he wasn't very good!' she giggled. 'Afterwards I said to him, "Are you just starting? Are you learning?" and he said, "Yeah, I am kind of." I didn't know anything about his past at Hull and Eastbourne, but as time went by I realised that he was quite good. I remember going into the bar prior to my first speedway meeting and I didn't have a clue who people were or anything, and he asked Michelle Lee – who was Neil Collins' girlfriend at the time – he asked if I could sit with her and Samantha, who was Peter Carr's girlfriend, and so I did. I think they just sat and talked about me all night! I'm still best friends with Michelle but we didn't hit it off at first.'

There was an element of truth when he agreed that he was 'learning', because after three years away from British racing there had been a few changes – not least a much smaller league, which, in turn, meant fewer meetings. Furthermore, since he last raced in the UK they had tightened the rules at the starting gate and you were no longer permitted to touch the tapes. If you did you were excluded, whereas when he was there before you could bend the tape and would only suffer exclusion if you broke them. And much to the discontent of some of the top riders, the sport's authorities had introduced a rule where only the Czech-made Barum tyre could be used.

'I find it so strange with so few tracks in the top section,' he said. 'As far as less meetings are concerned, I have been lucky in the fact that my average has been quite low so there have been guest bookings looming, left, right and centre. I have done pretty well in those meetings – so as to not let anyone down. But they should be a bonus. As for starting, I don't know how to roll at the tapes anyway! As a rider I know the only reason a rider rolls and touches the tapes at the start is to cheat, and I can't condone that, but excluding him is a terrible idea.'

He also noticed that the atmosphere had become more serious since he'd been away. 'Everyone used to have a laugh and a giggle at meetings. Now when I arrive nearly everyone seems to have his "speedway" face on. Surely we can still get some enjoyment out of it?'

Just as he made machinery changes when he decided to remain in the USA, he did likewise when he moved back to the BL. He switched from Godden to the Italian-made GM, which, at that stage, had already powered both Egon Muller and Erik Gundersen to World Championship glory – these days GM is the dominant engine. 'Shawn has got me fixed up with GM and a Comet frame,' he said. 'I thought I would have trouble with the Barum tyre too, but so far I've been alright on them. Too many people are frightened of change. I don't know why because if I can't get on with the GM I at least know that I can go back to Goddens.'

He also had a new mechanic. Ex-rider from New Zealand, Alan Mason, picked up the wrenches for the Jelly Man and the American was particularly pleased with his contribution, describing him as 'really good'.

When Lorna first saw Kelly race for Sheffield, he was still getting used to his new surroundings but it didn't take long before he was starting to fulfil the faith that Ducker had shown in him. Actually, the Sheffield boss was particularly pleased with the way he performed on and off the track for the Tigers.

'I couldn't have hoped for a better rider. He has helped enormously since his arrival – with team spirit, advice for the lads, helping out wherever he can. Kelly keeps the lads aware of the score, goes around the pits geeing them up, and with lads like Neil Collins, Peter Carr and Peter McNamara they can't help but respond. Shawn is the more business-minded of the two but, don't get me wrong, Kelly also means business this year. And don't forget, this deal is not just for one year, it is for longer than that.'

Perhaps the most exciting and interesting aspect was having the brothers ride in the same team together. Memories of their telepathic partnership during the Test series against England in 1982 and 1983 that had been so productive were still fresh in some people's minds. Therefore, the prospect of them reproducing that amazing team-riding was very exciting and the Tigers' fans soon got used to seeing them come out together, often to save the match.

'We got on well together,' said Shawn. 'We didn't have a problem with gate choice. Just getting out there together we knew what we would do. Let's say if there was someone in front of us we'd try to catch him; one of us would be on the inside, the other on the outside, whichever way it worked. One of us would have a go, if Kelly was on the outside and I was on the inside, if I couldn't get drive I wouldn't go on the outside, Kelly would have his chance to go for it. You'd let him go, you wouldn't get in his way because it wasn't about winning for us, it was team riding. Obviously we wanted to win, like everybody else, but we'd give each other a chance to have a go.'

'It was really cool riding with my brother, we were both so light we could run small gears and just fly,' said Kelly.

It didn't always go according to plan, though. During a Test match at Poole against England in 1983, an on-track misunderstanding saw Kelly switch to the inside, expecting his brother to come alongside him on his outside. Instead, he tucked in behind and this allowed Simon Wigg to swoop around them both. There were words afterward from his team-mates and Kelly was hurt by the criticism he received. Underneath it all, he could be quite sensitive.

All forms of motor sport are dangerous. That risky side brings an unspoken bond between its competitors, so when one of their own pays the highest price for his sport, it's felt by everyone. However, when it happens outside the business of racing, it's especially difficult to comprehend. When Kenny Carter killed himself after murdering his wife, it sent shockwaves throughout the speedway community. Furthermore, as he was the last British speedway star who would regularly attract column inches from the wider sporting press, that tragic episode was fast food to the notorious British tabloids, which lapped up the story.

The Moran brothers attended the funeral. Kelly was quite unprepared and slightly taken aback by the sort of attention that this solemn occasion was attracting and expressed his displeasure at the media vultures that had descended upon the funeral. Upset and emotional, on-lookers saw the usual happy-go-lucky Californian get very angry at the assembled hacks and photographers, so much so that someone had to place a light restraining presence on his arm. On such a sad day, he felt their intrusion was unwarranted and distasteful.

The Carter tragedy did give Gary Havelock an early opportunity to sample the selfless generosity of the American, as he recalled: 'It was my first ever meeting for Bradford in 1986. I think it was just after the Kenny Carter incident so they had a guest, and that guest was Kelly Moran. I was starstruck, you know – I'm riding with Kelly Moran! Kelly Moran! I always remember because it was in the days when you could choose your gates between your team-mates, so if you had one and three you could decide who was on one and who was on three. As a seventeen-year-old, even back at Middlesbrough, I was only ever told what gate I was going to have, you're off gate three or gate four, usually whatever the worst one was. And Kelly came up to me and said, "We've got two and four, dude. What do you want?" I was just completely gob-smacked, here was this megastar asking me what gate I wanted. I just said, "You have what you want mate, I'm not bothered." So I had gate four and got absolutely blasted by the rocks on the first corner. That always sticks in my mind – what a fantastic guy he was to offer this kid the best gate in heat 1. That was Kelly all over.'

His form improved quickly as each meeting passed and it wasn't long before he was challenging Shawn for the number one spot in the team. Therefore, US team manager John Scott decided to select him for the World Pairs Final to partner his brother. Unfortunately, Shooey crashed at Oxford and broke his ankle and was ruled out of the final in Pocking. Sam Ermolenko was chosen to replace him and would use Shawn's equipment. Having got used to Kelly's laid-back approach to preparation, mechanic Mason wasn't prepared for Ermolenko's meticulous planning. During practice Sam found it hard to decide which machine he was going ride; it was Shooey's unfamiliar clutch set-up that caused him to deliberate.

James Easter was also managing the Aussies at Pocking and he remembered the pre-meeting riders' briefing when Moran illustrated his playful attitude towards big meetings. 'We were outside because the weather was so good. Television cameras were there covering this meeting, plus all the FIM big wigs, and TV was filming the briefing. I can't remember who the referee was but he asked, "Any questions, ladies and gentleman?" And Kelly put his hand up and we all go, oh no, and the ref says: "Yes, Kelly, what's the question?" And he goes, "Where are all the good time girls around here?" We all died!'

Erik Gundersen laughed at that tale, and added, 'There were times when he would say things when you'd think, did he just say that? Sometimes you didn't know whether to laugh or cry. That's the way Kelly was.'

Nonetheless, Sam's preparation paid off because they came very, very close to grabbing the gold medal ahead of pre-meeting favourites, Denmark (Gundersen and Nielsen). They were also faced with a new challenge in this competition of six-rider races. It was a controversial decision and it made team riding that much harder due to the extra men on the track. However, despite the reservations, it was quite something watching Kelly in particular pick his way through the traffic on the German circuit.

When Gundersen got into a tangle with Roman Matousek and couldn't take his place in his third race, it looked as though it was going to be America's day. However, Erik did continue and somehow they clawed themselves back into contention and at the conclusion of the meeting they were all square with the USA on 46 points. Therefore a run-off was required to decide the destiny of the gold medal. Kelly was first choice for the Americans while Denmark chose Nielsen. Following eighteen heats of racing, the track had slickened off and gating was vital; it was Nielsen who got to the first corner ahead of Moran and it was all over – silver for the Americans.

'In that final he was racing well that day,' said Nielsen, 'and I knew that I would have to be at my very best to beat him in the run-off. I was very pleased because I didn't take anything for granted because he could pass you from anywhere.'

Moran regarded this meeting as one of his best, certainly the best of that season. 'Neither Sam nor I had ever ridden there before and having six riders in a race was an experience. I was really happy to get second because the partnership was such a last-minute thing. Coming back from the meeting was pretty memorable too.

Alan Mason and myself drove back, and everyone told us to stay away from Brussels – we tried, but we still managed to hit the middle of the city. We drove around lost for at least three hours!'

The brothers lived next door to each other in Sheffield, but for the first few months Kelly's house was being re-decorated and updated. Meanwhile, his relationship with Lorna had blossomed, in fact it could be said that they fell in love quickly. Moreover, he especially enjoyed the environment with her family.

'Either he was at my mum's house or Shawn's, and when he went back to America for a race, a rider return, he was there two weeks, and we missed each other a lot and that was it, we were always together then,' she said. 'When we moved in next door, we'd be in bed, Shawn would come in and he'd lie on the bed chatting. It was really lovely actually; there was a proper bond between them. He is very different to Kelly, different personalities, but they bounced off each other. He was very close to my mum and dad, my whole family really. He used to go to my mum and dad's every Sunday for lunch. He liked his Sunday lunch and my mum used to cook it. He used to go to the pub with my grandfather, dad and my brother before, and I used to pick them up and bring them back for lunch.'

Now living together, Kelly revealed his race-day routine in *Speedway Star* and Lorna had evidently slipped straight into the new lifestyle.

'My girlfriend, Lorna, will fix me my main meal of the day at lunchtime – and that can consist of all kinds of things! For the rest of the afternoon I probably check up on a few phone calls and generally keep a check on the house next door. Before I leave I take a shower, pack my bags and leave at around six. When we arrive, I'll just take it easy, look at the track and check that it doesn't resemble the North Sea! After the meeting, we'll pop out for a meal and wind down.'

Seemingly quite settled, he qualified from the American Final while his brother heroically won the meeting with a broken ankle. In the next round, though, in their very first race, a tough first bend saw Shawn crash and re-break his ankle. Seeing his brother fall out of the corner of his eye, Kelly dropped his own personal ambitions, laid down his machine and rushed to his brother's aid. Shawn's championship hopes were over yet his big brother successfully qualified for the next stage and was just five rides away from another World Championship.

That year's World Final was due to be staged at Katowice, scene of Kelly's memorable fourth place as a teenager. In almost every interview he expressed his desire to make speedway's biggest competition. He had a chance to get some experience in Poland when he agreed to race in the

JMS All Stars Farewell meetings held for Edward Jancarz at Gorzów and Ostrów. He was joined by other world-class riders like Phil Crump, Chris Morton, Kelvin Tatum and Tommy Knudsen.

The tour's departure was delayed. They had to wait for him because he had been arrested. Lorna recalled: 'He went to court for drink-driving and he was like, "They can't take a licence off me because I haven't got one!"'

15

# DANCING WITH ST PETER

'To appreciate heaven, well, it is good for a man
to have some fifteen minutes of hell.'

Will Carleton (1845–1912)

## Mieszko Hotel, Gorzów, Poland, 13/14 July 1986

Phil Crump was an early riser. He emerged from his hotel room to head down for breakfast, and was astonished when he opened the door to discover that the hall was full of furniture. He had absolutely no idea about the drama that had unfolded in the next room, where Kelly Moran had been fighting for his life.

Crumpie had won the previous day's meeting at Gorzów, defeating Kelly in a run-off. They were due to travel 173 miles south-east for their second event in Ostrów, but the Australian discovered that Moran wouldn't be racing because he had an accident in his room.

The whole group, who had travelled to Poland as part of John Smith's JMS All Stars troupe, indulged heavily that evening to the point where it would have been a memorable night if the various beverages hadn't obliterated most of their recollections. Actually, as it turned out, it was a night that would live long in the memories for some.

Rick Miller was also part of the travelling band of riders and he recalled: 'For some reason we all got pretty drunk that night. I don't think I've ever been that drunk in my life except for that one time in Poland and I don't remember ever being that drunk before. It was a stupid, stupid night. I don't know if people were pouring it in my drink and I wasn't noticing or what, but I had way too much vodka and so did everyone else. The way I remember it, a lot of people were like that. It was just one of those crazy trips.'

Unsurprisingly, Kelly had also been enjoying the amenities provided by their hosts and other distractions that, to some, are the fringe benefits of being an international sports star. He had returned to his hotel but he was having some communication problems at the reception desk, which were obviously further complicated by his happy state and the language barrier. Chris Morton and his wife Jackie, and FIM referee Graham Brodie, arrived on the scene and they decided to help out. While they too had been enjoying their evening, they hadn't indulged to the same level as their American friend; besides, what happened next had a rapidly sobering effect on all involved.

'Kelly was completely pissed and not making much sense,' said Morton. 'We suggested he should go to bed, but it turned out he was trying to get his room key. So we found his room number, got his key, and Jackie and I agreed to take him to his room and join the others in the bar in about ten minutes.'

During the short journey to his room, Brodie's attention was diverted by a naked racer, who was merrily roaming the corridor. Trying to maintain the sport's reputation, he gently persuaded the rider to return to his room. As he guided the drunken rider, suddenly he heard a crash followed by a few curses and he immediately rushed to Kelly's room.

'The three of us were pretty merry,' Mort admitted. 'We got to his room and Jackie unlocked the door. As we went past the bathroom on the left, there was a second door that had a wooden frame surrounding a plain glass panel. Kelly flung his arm back saying, "I don't wanna go to bed." He smashed his arm through the plate glass door panel and it shattered loudly and splintered everywhere followed by a fountain of blood, which squirted from his arm like a jet, spraying blood on the ceiling and the walls. Kelly was flapping his arm around like a loose hosepipe spilling its liquid for fun.

'I grabbed hold of him and threw him on the bed and pinned him down. He had a look of fear in his eyes and I had a hold of his arm, which was pumping blood at an alarming rate and draining the life out of him. He had severed a main artery.'

Faced with this desperate scene, Chris sobered up straight away and set about saving his friend's life. Meanwhile Jackie rushed down the stairs to call for an ambulance while her husband attempted to stem the blood flow.

'My body had kick-started me with an adrenalin rush that gave me amazing clarity. I stopped the flow of blood by moving my hands down Kelly's arm and applied pressure with my thumbs as near to the wound as I could until the flow of blood stopped. Kelly looked at me and said, "I've f****d up this time, haven't I?" I saw the look of shock and fear in his eyes and he looked scared. I said, "You'll be all right Kelly, just keep still, Jackie's gone to get help."'

With Brodie now also in attendance, Jackie informed them that the ambulance was on its way and she would wait in reception and bring the paramedics up as soon as they arrived.

Soon the gravity of their situation was beginning to sink in, especially because of their location. Communist Poland in 1986 wasn't as developed as Western Europe and economic reforms only brought austerity to the Polish people and its infrastructure. Polish politicians may have had access to superior medical treatment, yet in the main facilities were far behind those enjoyed in the West – arguably things hadn't moved forward much since the 1960s. When time is of the essence, waiting for an ambulance always seems an age. They may have taken some comfort from hearing its siren wailing in the distance and they probably dismissed their concerns over the length of time it seemed to take to arrive because the important thing was that it was coming. And then, of course, there was the language barrier.

'The main paramedic indicated to me to move out of the way. At this stage they had no idea what the problem was. I gestured at Kelly's arm but the paramedic just wanted me to move. So I reverted to international sign language and visual aids. I released the pressure on the wound, which sent a jet of blood splattering up the wall! Both paramedics emitted a loud "Aaah!" and they proceeded to put a tourniquet on his arm to stem the blood flow,' recalled Morton.

After some basic treatment, a shocked Moran was put on a stretcher and taken downstairs to a waiting ambulance. Morton and Brodie followed and were stunned to find no ambulance! They didn't expect to find a high-tech, specially equipped, Mercedes-Benz Sprinter-style emergency response vehicle, but they were scanning the car park for a Soviet-type 'Latvija' vehicle at least. They exchanged disbelieving glances when they saw the two paramedics hurriedly carry Kelly toward what looked like a Lada estate car with its back seats folded down! It was like something out of a Monty Python sketch. If the situation hadn't been so serious they would have probably laughed at the absurdity of it. Meanwhile, the two medics hastily slid their patient into the back as if he was a piece of awkward shopping.

Fear began to creep over Brodie and Morton as they followed the 'ambulance' in a taxi to the hospital. Instead of a busy accident and emergency department, it was quiet with seemingly just one nurse and doctor on duty. Moran, who was unconscious at this point, was placed on a wheeled bed so the doctor could look at him.

Immediately the doctor began to get to work on his severed artery in order to save his life. Suddenly Kelly stirred and started shouting and fighting off the doctor and wouldn't allow him to help. With only the tourniquet stemming the blood flow, his movements only increased his heart rate and the loss of blood was increasing again. The struggle continued for a few seconds before the frustrated doctor turned to the astonished and scared Morton, summoned some English, and said, 'I cannot help if he does not stay good!'

Chris stepped forward and spoke to Kelly who, according to Brodie, was kicking up a fuss because he didn't want an injection of anaesthetic due to his fear of AIDS from needles. Unfortunately he wouldn't listen. This was no time to be stubborn and Chris found himself pleading with the American to allow the doctor to fix him. With his life in the balance and his blood flowing more rapidly again, he was begging him to behave. As he implored him to be sensible, he realised that his condition was becoming desperate and his emotions began to flow. Tears spilled from his eyes and lined his cheeks and finally, to Mort's relief, he relented and agreed to let the doctor treat him. He was whisked into theatre so they could stabilise his condition.

It was around 2 a.m. when, exhausted, Chris sank into a chair next to Brodie with his favourite shirt stained red with blood. Approximately twenty minutes later, the doc returned to inform them that he had only managed to plug the artery and dress the wound and, oddly, had placed the American's left arm in a cast. More specialist treatment would be required when they returned to the UK, but he was safe and would be kept in overnight. Although he was too modest to admit it, Morton had been a hero. Brodie commented: 'If I have a crisis like this, I want you to be there to look after me.'

When Kelly awoke in the hospital ward, the first thing he wanted was a cigarette. 'I made this gesture to this guy who looked like Roger Johns [Wimbledon rider] and he gave me a ciggy. After losing all that blood, one of those strong Polish cigarettes was like getting a huge rush of something we shouldn't mention!' he said.

The hotel accident wasn't something that he liked to talk about and he'd often make light of it. However, following Chris Morton's account in his biography, Kelly dispensed with his cheery persona and said seriously: 'I thought I was dying. I had severed my artery, tendons, nerves and guides in my wrist and I needed a blood transfusion. I had lost over four pints of blood in ten minutes. But being in Poland and with all the AIDS stuff that was happening at the time, they didn't know how much blood was infected because it was still a new disease back then, so I refused. Zenon Plech was my interpreter and he said that I should have it. But I thought it was best to get back to England. It must have been terrible for

Chris because the hotel had to replace the bedclothes, the carpets and the curtains because blood was pumping out everywhere. If it hadn't been for Chris and Jackie, I wouldn't be here.'

The next morning, after hearing about the drama, Crump was even more amazed to see Moran arrive during breakfast and announce, 'They're not stitching me up with horse hair!' This bravado was a combination of shock and his sometimes OTT wit that, given the serious nature of what he'd done, didn't elicit much laughter.

Miller, who was nursing the worst hangover of his life, said: 'He was lucky to be alive. I remember I went to his room and someone stopped me from going in, they said, "You don't want to see it in there." And then, wow, there he was! We were all pretty worried about him because he was as white as a ghost.'

Kelly was overwhelming in his gratitude to the Mortons, though. It was something that he would never forget. He boarded the bus for the trip to Ostrow and was surprisingly bright considering what he'd been through over the previous hours. Marvyn Cox was another rider who was part of the group, and he didn't know of the accident until he boarded the coach and saw him.

'When I got on the bus to go to the next track he was sat on the back seat with a Walkman headset on and his wrist was all strapped up. If it hadn't been for Chris Morton he would have been dead.'

Communications weren't as widespread as they are today, especially so when you were in the Eastern Bloc. Therefore, neither Shawn nor Lorna had any idea about the trauma that Kelly had been through until he arrived back in Sheffield.

'I came back early in the evening and he was sitting in the chair and had this big bandage wrapped around his arm. It looked like a robot arm and it was red – it wasn't dripping but soaked red,' recalled Shawn. 'It was spooky. I didn't know how bad it was at first. I knew he was away racing but I didn't know he was back and there he was sat in my place with this red, bloody, bandage on his arm. I asked, "What happened?" He started to tell me a little bit about what had happened, and I went, "F**k!!! How bad is it?" And he said that he couldn't move his fingers very well. We talked for a while and I didn't want to see that sort of thing, I am a sissy on that side. He looked a little pale. All I knew was that he put his hand through a plate-glass window and Chris Morton was there. He said it was just squirting all over and I went, "Oh God! F**k!" Then I began to wonder how bad it really was – yew!'

Lorna remembered his return slightly differently, but typical of him, he understated how serious the cuts on his left wrist really were.

'Me and Shawn were both waiting for him at his house and he came in with a cast on his arm and said, "I've had a bit of an accident." He didn't go to hospital because we didn't realise how bad it was. That night we went to bed and in the morning he got up and the cast was soaked with blood, and he said, "I feel a bit dizzy." So we went to hospital and they took the cast off and they operated that afternoon. He was quite lucky.'

Initially it was reported that he'd be out of the saddle for three months. That proved to be a hopeful estimate because it was six months before he could even think about racing a speedway machine again.

'When he cut his arm, he'd cut what they call guiders, which make your fingers move,' added Shawn. 'He cut his tendons too and whatever else is in your arm – he did a lot of damage. The guiders took a little while to heal. He ran a rubber band from his thumbnail to his arm to keep it mobile. It was just a band until he got his movement back. He was fully recovered, though.'

Eight-hour microsurgery was required and he also had to have two skin grafts at the Northern General Hospital in Sheffield. Not only was his season at an end, but the accident occurred just a week before the final World Championship qualifying round. He was temporarily released from hospital and bandaged up with his arm in a sling, so that he could attend the qualifier at Bradford as a spectator.

'I'm really grateful to Chris, I guess he saved my life,' he said. 'It's really disappointing to be out of the World Championship, I thought I was on my way to the World Final. I'll miss riding for Sheffield, but I'm just glad to be alive!'

Kelly's gratitude to Chris extended to a long track meeting in Mühldorf, Germany, the following year. He was riding one of his brother's machines that he described as 'a rocket ship' when he came up behind his saviour.

'I prepared to go round him but I thought, shit, he's the guy who saved my life in Poland. So I backed off. I transferred to the final in third but the magic box broke down in the final. After the meeting we were sat around having a meal and a drink, and this and that, when Chris said to me, "Your bike was so fast, why didn't you pass me?" I replied: "I couldn't pass you because you saved my life in Poland." I remember Chris giving me a little wink of acknowledgement.'

# 16

# IF IT WEREN'T FOR BAD LUCK

'Racing is life. Anything that happens before and after is just waiting.'

Steve McQueen, actor (1930–80)

Kelly's accident did have a silver lining: he'd get to spend more time with Lorna Brindley. Their relationship was allowed to blossom and deepen during his enforced lay-off because it wasn't subjected to his sometimes hectic racing schedule, when he'd be heading off in different directions around England and overseas. Therefore, accompanied by Lorna, he took off to America.

Travelling to California was quite an exciting experience for her at this point in her life. She was nineteen years old, a student studying hairdressing, and although she had holidayed in Europe this was the first time she'd been to a long-haul destination. They stayed at the home of Kelly's grandmother, who he called Nana, at Paramount. Unfortunately, their stay didn't get off to the best of starts.

'While we were there, the first night she had a stroke,' recalled Lorna. 'We found her on the floor in her bedroom. Tom came and she went to hospital. We stayed at his Nana's and we were there for months. When she came out, I looked after her. I took care of her, cooked, cleaned and bathed her – everything. Kelly was brilliant, although he used to disappear now and again, but he was great.'

On the eve of the new season, Kelly said: 'She had two strokes. When she came out we took it upon ourselves to look out for her. She's made a miraculous recovery. Now she can walk and cook for herself again. It was good to know that the winter was spent doing something really worthwhile.'

This unhappy episode meant that Lorna got to meet Kelly's father, Tom, in the less-than-favourable circumstances, but she could see straightaway where her boyfriend got his manners from. 'He was a lovely man and a reliable person.

He did a lot for his boys; he loved them. He was with Kay Rutherford at the time, and they welcomed us into their home and we spent Christmas with them. We'd spend a lot of time at his Aunt Joy's, his Aunt Joy and Uncle Tom Murray – he was very close to them. When I used to go over there that was the most comfortable for me. Another time, they fetched his mum and we had Thanksgiving and Christmas there. Kelly loved having family around him.'

Nonetheless, his recovery was slow. He also became a bit frustrated at sitting on the sidelines again while the business end of the racing season was played out without him. An optimistic estimate that he could race in Australia during the winter proved to be wildly inaccurate.

Once again, just as they had when he suffered multiple injuries at Hackney in 1978, many supporters sent him get well cards and letters and he thanked them for their support at his earliest opportunity in the press.

'It was a few months before he got proper movement back,' Lorna said. 'I don't know if he was embarrassed, but he didn't say much about the accident. It was early in our relationship and I hadn't got a grip on just how much he drank at that particular time. I knew what he used to be like when he got drunk, though.'

While she noticed that he would vanish for long periods, in an interview that he gave to the *LA Times* he revealed just how frustrated he was waiting for his injury to heal until he could get on a bike and compete again.

'It was hard sitting out with nothing to do,' he said. 'I had a bad disposition. I was chewing on people for no reason. I was difficult to live with. The doctors gave me stretching exercises to do while I was recovering, but I was climbing the walls. That's when I started riding a mountain bike. I was living with my grandmother and whenever I got bored I'd ride to Huntington Beach and back. I was riding forty miles a day, usually three or four times a week. It was the only thing that kept me from going nuts.'

However, he lost his sense of direction during one of these trips, took a wrong turn and ended up in Compton – which was like LA's version of The Bronx. Needless to say, he pedalled very fast to get back onto the correct road!

Throughout his three years concentrating on racing in California, he would often be quoted as referring to England as that 'bloody country'. Given the number of attacks that supposedly came from Britain in his direction when he concentrated on racing in America, it's not surprising that he felt some antipathy toward the UK. He told the *LA Times* that he had to 'make myself like it over there'. His many British friends and supporters would be shocked to hear that because, beyond his moans about the British weather, he maintained a sunny disposition. Moreover, his chameleon-like adaptability meant that he slipped into the English way of life much easier than some of his fellow countrymen, yet, underneath it all, he also endured England for his career – after all, sunny California it's not.

In a one-off column published in *Speedway Star* in April 1987, his feelings toward Britain appeared to have softened. 'I really missed Britain when I was in California. I like the living and I like the racing and I believe you've got to be happy off the track as well as on.'

As his wrist slowly healed and he ticked off the days before a new season started, something happened in the US that, at the very least, may have re-balanced his views. Even though the sport's glory days were behind it, US promoters didn't give up trying to expand and develop it. They made ambitious plans to take it to Hawaii for the first time. Naturally they intended to take their crowd-pleasers and Kelly's name was mentioned along with other racers like Faria, King, Schwartz and even his brother. Whether the organisers thought that he wouldn't be fit enough to race or that he wouldn't be interested in travelling to the island is not known, but the fact was that he wasn't asked to ride in the meeting. Kelly, who had been the darling of the Californian scene just a year or so before, took it personally and felt that he'd been snubbed.

'I was hurt that I didn't get invited to ride in Hawaii, but rather than sit at home and sulk I decided to go to England early and get my bikes and equipment sorted out for this season. There was nothing left for me here, so I left.'

Once again he was paired with his brother at Sheffield in a team that was largely the same as 1986 except for the addition of two new faces at reserve, Ian 'Egon' M. Stead and Adrian Stevens. His early return to England certainly paid dividends because he started off in flying form – and so too did the Tigers team.

Over eight months after his hotel accident, his wrist wounds still required protection. He wore a special plastic guard to prevent stones and dirt from getting into the wound or aggravating it. Rain forced the postponement of Sheffield's first match of the season, so he travelled to Coventry and scored 9 points. Concerned about how his wrist would hold up, he admitted to a few butterflies.

'I was really nervous before my first race but I couldn't believe it when I made a super start. I had no idea I'd return to this sort of form I've enjoyed so far, I hope it keeps going,' he said.

A series of encouraging scores peaked over two days in late April when he scored his first paid maximum of the season at, of all places, Hackney – proving that although he disliked the Waterden Road venue, he wasn't intimidated by it. The following evening he scored a full maximum at King's Lynn. Sheffield then entered a purple patch as they surged to the top of the League Cup table. Once more Kelly registered another full maximum, 15 this time at Ipswich as the Tigers came away with another victory and Moran got to challenge for the Golden

Helmet, losing to Ipswich's Jeremy Doncaster. The winning sequence came to an end at Swindon when Kelly suffered his first mechanical breakdown of the season and then had his first fall at Belle Vue four days later while the Tigers' dominance began to slip.

Someone who was impressed with his displays was Lorna. 'When he started racing properly again, I realised he was good then! I remember thinking, Oh he is quite good, because prior to that I'd only seen him in a few meetings, and then he fell through that plate-glass window so that was it. So I didn't really know of his ability.'

Despite his sparkling start he wasn't impressed with the tyre that was in use in the British League. He complained: 'You chase somebody and you work on them, and you work on them, but you get no nearer and no further away. Who wants to watch follow-the-leader? I wish somebody would ask the riders what they want for once. It just makes me mad. You go out there and you want to win and win. But when you get nowhere you say to yourself at the end of the day, "Why do I have to deal with this?" I remember the days when I first came here, when everyone was going first to second, back to first, to third and so on. Now everyone goes around in a neat procession – who wants to see that? I'd rather watch the results on Teletext! There's a choice of engines, GM, Jawa, etc., so why not tyres? Set up a ballot vote and ask the riders what they think.'

By now Lorna was immersed in British speedway's social scene and although she was mainly interested in Kelly, she began to get to grips with the sport as a whole. 'When I first went to speedway I was only interested when Kelly was racing because I knew who he was. But when you're going week-in and week-out, and going to every meeting, you get to know the rest of the team, the girlfriend scene and everything. It was really nice. You get to know different teams and he was really good friends with Mitch Shirra. We spent quite a bit of time in Coventry where Mitch lived with Kim, his wife. We'd spend a lot of time with Bobby Schwartz. I loved Bobby, he was absolutely adorable and was so good with Kelly. They all were really. We'd go down there for the weekend, go to Bobby's and then stay at Rick Miller's. The thing was, Kelly included me in everything, so wherever he went, I went with him.'

Rick Miller was in his fifth season racing in Britain and raced for Coventry. He had a house in Sutton Coldfield and he remembered that when Kelly visited he showed another talent that he'd previously displayed when he was at Eastbourne.

'There were no cell phones in those days, so Kelly would come over to my house and he'd just pop in. He'd hang out all day or spend the night. If there was nothing particular to do that day, like we didn't have to race or get ready for a race meeting, Kelly would just start gardening in my backyard! He would just pull some weeds, tend to the garden and tinker out there. He'd do it all the time. Even when I was dating Kim – who is my wife now – he'd come over and start gardening and she was always amused by that.'

'He loved his gardening,' Lorna added. 'One time he'd come home from a night out and was in the garden working away at one in the morning!'

She also got to experience what life could be like for an international speedway rider when she accompanied him on a trip to Poland for Zenon Plech's farewell meeting at Gdańsk on 21 June, in which he finished fourth with 11.

'They thought he was God over there! I went once with John Smith, a few riders and a couple of girlfriends. We were having our soup, a starter, and then a stripper came waltzing down the middle of the table! I was like, "Oh my God!" I was covering my soup thinking, I don't want nothing falling in there! He [Plech] gave Kelly the biggest crystal vase and it is here in the house. I said to Kelly, when he was in the hospital, "What do you want me to do with it all?" and he said, "Keep it for Chelsea [his future daughter]."'

The USA team selectors chose the Moran brothers to represent the USA in the World Pairs Championship and they won the semi-final on a rain-lashed track in Norden, finishing 9 points clear of nearest challengers England. Then the pair of them jetted back to the USA to compete in the American Final. Kelly successfully qualified in second place behind Sam Ermolenko, but Shawn failed to make the top five. Disappointed, he withdrew from the Pairs and, just as twelve months previously, Ermolenko replaced him.

This time the final was staged in Pardubice, former Czechoslovakia. Kelly travelled with a group of riders and journalists. It was reported that somehow he'd managed to get lost when he arrived in Frankfurt to change planes. That was only part of the story, as *Speedway Star*'s Richard Clark recalled.

'We were due to fly from Heathrow to Frankfurt, change planes and on to Nuremburg, stay there overnight before swapping the air for motorway. This was mostly Friday night, so Kelly had plenty of time to sample Heathrow's Bloody Marys. Which he continued to do so once we were airborne en route to Frankfurt. At Frankfurt, the turnover time was not much more than an hour or so yet, in that seeming blink of an eye, we managed to lose him. "Wait in Lounge" became "Go To Gate," became "Now Boarding", all in the absence of the Wizard of Balance. A search party was assembled, England star Kelvin Tatum, myself and Lions boss Eric Boocock who, ever resourceful, somehow managed to commandeer a bicycle parked near the check-in and rode off on his quest on that!

'Kelvin and I finally tracked our fugitive down. He was hunched down behind a chair, appearing to be playing hide and seek with whatever demons had previously been lurking at the bottom of his Bloody Mary. Gently coaxing him plane-wards, it soon became obvious that the finer points of walking were eluding our Kelly. So, Kelvin on one arm, myself on the other, we helped him along as best we could. Which posed little problem, Kelly being the diminutive man he was, until the boarding gate loomed – with the airline's ground crew waiting. How to clear this obstacle?

'I will not boast of a razor-sharp instinct, cool, calm and collected in any crisis, because that would be a lie, so I'll put what happened next down to sheer inspiration (desperation?). Handing our three boarding cards over and still trying to hold Kelly vaguely upright, I murmured to the uniformed lady, "Epileptic, he'll be fine," and to my astonishment, she smiled sympathetically and waved us on to the plane! Needless to say, this was all news to Kelly when we told him of this adventure during the two or three days abroad that followed.'

However, he was very nearly prevented from riding in the final itself. His last-minute approach to any race meeting got him into hot water with the officials when he failed to arrive at the designated time of four hours before the start. Together with US Team Manager, John Smith, Kelly protested against his exclusion and was eventually re-instated but was fined 200 Swiss francs. He was cleared just in time for him to climb alongside Ermolenko into one of the vintage cars for the parade.

Having come so close the year before, the Yankee duo may have fancied their chances in Pardubice. After a promising opening race when they finished second and third behind Mitch Shirra, they faced the Danes and the hosts in their next race. Unfortunately they couldn't live with Hans Nielsen's electric start and his partner, Erik Gundersen, relished the wide-open spaces and battled past both of the Americans. While Kelly held on to third, Sam was relegated to the back with a slowing motor. That duck put them firmly in the chasing pack.

When the final race arrived, at best America could win silver if they finished first and second, but Denmark were out of reach. The other contenders, England (Tatum and Simon Wigg) were in with a chance of overhauling the Danes if they occupied the first two places. Given that Nielsen/Gundersen hadn't been defeated since their opening race, it was a tall order.

As the tapes rose, remarkably Kelly hit the front with the Danes hustling for position behind. Unfortunately, he didn't complete a lap before his bike slowed, eventually grinding to a disappointing halt and he was overtaken. Nonetheless, he felt that his efforts were restricted by yet another slick track. 'I just wish they'd put some dirt down at these places,' he said before he stepped up with Ermolenko to receive his bronze medal.

A week later, at Bradford, he equalled the track record as he finished third in the Overseas Final and was through to the last qualifying round of the World

Championship. Feeling confident of his chances and enthusiastic about the way his season was going, he had to fly back to California to fulfill a rider return engagement before turning around and jetting back to England to represent Sheffield with his brother in the British Open Best Pairs.

Racing at Ascot on 9 July, Kelly was pressuring Billy Hamill in the Handicap Main. They had both passed Jay Gianetti and were racing for the lead when Moran touched Hamill's rear tyre and they were both sent tumbling into the crash wall. Hamill was able to take his place in the restart, but it was a disaster for Kelly. Initially, it was thought that he had dislocated his shoulder. But he was still experiencing some pain when it was re-set and it was discovered that he'd broken his right collarbone – again.

The Inter-continental Final, the last qualifying round of the World Championship, was just under two weeks away and he faced a race against time to be fit enough to take his place in the event. A year after having to withdraw from this meeting due to his hotel accident, he was determined that his hopes of a fourth World Final appearance wouldn't evaporate again. Therefore, he remained in America and received daily treatment from a man who specialised in American football injuries. With under a week to go, he announced that he would be riding in the meeting in Vojens. His brother gave up two guest bookings in order to be by his side in the meeting and said, 'If he can ride to 70 per cent of his ability, I think he'll be able to put up with the pain and score enough points to qualify.'

Unfortunately, the injury just hadn't healed sufficiently for him to race and at the eleventh hour he pulled out. There was one consolation, though – his replacement was the man who saved his life, Chris Morton.

Returning to England, once again he had time to kill. On one occasion in the Pinegrove Country Club he was left sporting a souvenir from his adventures; when questioned, he used the well-worn excuse that he had walked into a door. He had got into a difference of opinion with a big rugby player over who was the best ever jockey. Unsurprisingly, Kelly believed it to be Texan-born Willie Shoemaker, who had won four Kentucky Derbies, while the rugby player thought it was Lester Piggott, who had won nine Derbies in his long career in the UK.

'Willie Shoemaker is the best jockey ever,' Kelly stated.

'No, Lester Piggott is the best jockey.'

Fuelled by alcohol, the little American became 10 feet tall and more insistent that he was right and his companion was wrong. So it went back and forth, 'Willie Shoemaker is the best,' 'No, I'm telling you it's Lester Piggott.' The rugby player became bored with it at this point and finally said: 'Listen, I'm telling you it's Lester Piggott, now drop it.'

But he wouldn't drop it, and like an annoying bar fly Kelly teased, 'Willie Shoemaker.' Standing around 6ft tall, 16 stone and solidly built like a block of flats, compared with Kelly's lightweight frame, 5ft 4in height and 8st, he had heard enough and angrily turned, 'Look, I've told you, it's Lester Piggott, now leave it alone!' However, Kelly didn't heed the warning and said again: 'Willie Shoemaker.'

This time he picked Moran up by the shoulders as if he was a small boy, his little feet dangling beneath, looked him square in the eye and said, 'Lester Piggott,' and forced home his belief by head-butting him! Kelly was sent reeling, taking a table and chair with him, and landed in an untidy heap on the floor. Bloodied, shaky, but unbowed, people watched as he determinedly got to his feet and declared, 'Willie Shoemaker!'

The audience on the back straight gasped as bright jagged lightning flashed menacingly above the main stand at Hackney speedway, which was followed by a foreboding, thunderous crack of doom. The sky was black and mean; if anyone was looking for bad omens Mother Nature was providing them. This was the second Test between England and the USA – England had won the first at Ipswich – and having chosen to move up from the National to the British League during the winter, Hackney was awarded this pivotal second Test of the three-match series and the public responded in big numbers.

The significance of Waterden Road as the venue for this encounter wasn't lost on the public or the media at large, even if the ever-positive US team tried to put their reservations to the back of their minds. Kelly had sustained multiple injuries there and had been extremely critical of the track and had even asked the US federation to step in and do something about it. His brother had also broken his leg at Hackney, but more importantly it had claimed the life of fellow American Denny Pyeatt. On a humid and sticky evening, the atmosphere was right for tensions to boil over.

Just under a week prior to this meeting, Kelly had made his track return for Sheffield and scored a maximum at King's Lynn – although he admitted that he was still sore. Nonetheless, when the Morans held off Andrew Silver for an opening race 5–1 they didn't seem unduly troubled about their location. Four points up after two races; all seemed to be going well for the USA … and then light rain started to fall.

The track surface was patchy and there were no less than six fallers in the first six races from both sides. Riders, mostly American, started to grumble about its condition. England's Jeremy Doncaster crashed heavily in turn three during heat 7 and was excluded. Shawn had immediately taken evasive action and laid down his machine but thumped the fence. He emerged clutching his ribs and when he was walking down the ramp to the pits, referee Frank Ebdon put on the two-minute time allowance! Needless to say, he didn't take his place in the re-run. However, when Kelly also fell heavily at exactly the same spot in the restart, all hell broke loose.

After checking that his brother was okay, Shawn began packing up his gear as if to quit the match, but was persuaded to stay by manager John Scott. The US team had a meeting and the referee inspected the track and ordered the third corner to be re-graded. As captain, Shawn led a meeting with his team-mates and it appeared that they didn't want to continue. Ebdon, Moran and the US manager held lengthy discussions, while slow handclaps resonated around the stadium and sections of supporters began chanting, 'Why are we waiting?' Fans close to the pits area began hurling abuse at the US team while work continued on the circuit. Half an hour later, a threatened walk-out had been averted and the racing resumed. Unfortunately, the weather deteriorated and the match was abandoned after twelve heats with the USA leading 36–34.

Disgruntled fans trudged home in the pouring rain and it was widely believed that Shooey led the revolt, although Simon Wigg stated from the start that he wasn't happy with conditions either. Shawn and Scott were fined £100 by the referee and Hackney promoter, Dave Pavitt, said, 'The blame lies with the Americans. Punters were leaving the stadium very upset.' While most accepted that the surface on turn three was a bit icy, the organisers and officials all felt that the prima donna Yanks was overreacting. England's co-team manager, Eric Boocock, who was also Sheffield's team manager, was reported to be both surprised and shocked by their attitude. But the night wasn't over yet. Doncaster, Sam Ermolenko and Kelly were all chosen for a random drugs test. What had already been a long night got even longer for the Jelly Man.

Unable to produce a sample to order, he had to drink gallons and gallons of water before finally doing the necessary at 12.25 a.m.! However, it was even worse for Ermolenko, who forgot altogether and was immediately suspended, which resulted in a ban that he successfully had overturned.

A fortnight later, the brothers were assured of a warm reception when they travelled to Hackney again with Sheffield. Kelly blew a kiss to the noisy crowd before he and his brother scorched to maximums and their team left London with a victory.

'The track was shit when Frank Ebdon made us run,' said Shawn. 'There were eight crashes in the first nine races – that's not down to the riders. That's why I wanted to walk out. Except that night, overall, the surface at Hackney was fine, it was the fence. The fence sagged, it wasn't high enough. It was an easy "going over" fence; if you slid into it you were okay, it would catch you. Of course lamp posts, you had to deal with them anyway, but when someone gets hurt then you start complaining big time – that's what it usually takes and by then it's too late.'

In between times America inflicted a rare defeat over Denmark in the second leg of the World Team Cup Final at Coventry, but were unable to prevent England from winning the third and final Test at Sheffield – so they lost the series.

Although he hadn't made it himself, Kelly travelled to the Netherlands to lend his support to the two Americans in the World Championship at Amsterdam, John Cook and Ermolenko. Tony Millard was also covering the event for the media and, unsurprisingly, they relaxed in one of the city's notorious coffee shops. 'We finished up in some café, in all my innocence. He was smoking this stuff – most people smoked it with tobacco, but he didn't, he smoked it neat!' laughed Millard. Ermolenko finished third overall and Kelly was heard to quip, 'I hope Sammy's remembered to take the drugs test!'

The international year ended in Prague where America finished a distant third in the World Team Championship and also third in the meeting itself. Kelly, though, top-scored with 10 points and inflicted Gundersen's only defeat. Furthermore, he represented Sheffield in the British League Riders' Championship and finished third after beating Kelvin Tatum in a run-off, and said, 'It's funny that this is my first BLRC. I guess my average wasn't good enough in the past or I kept getting injured. I really enjoyed it out there.'

Professionally it had been one of Kelly's best BL seasons; statistics (9.23 average) show that it was his finest since 1982. None of that meant much to Sheffield boss, Maurice Ducker, who responded to the Tigers' trophy-less season by placing all the team on the transfer list! The American was furious.

'The first I heard about it was when I got a telephone call from a very good friend of mine who asked me why I wanted a transfer. I told him that I never asked for a transfer. He said: "Look on Teletext." I did, and it told me that we were on the transfer list at Sheffield and that was news to me. Mind you, when we went to the Sheffield dinner/dance, Maurice Ducker said nothing to us. It was like nothing had happened. I don't know if that's typical of promoters, where they can go behind your back and when you see them face to face they have nothing to say. I think Bob Dugard had it right when he called promoters "demoters" – and that's just what they are! They expect to turn up at the meeting three hours before the start and see a packed stadium and fantastic racing. Have they watered the track? "No. But we are just going to." Everyone says rain this and rain that as an excuse. Well, how the hell can you cover a dog track that's on the outside of a speedway track? Do animals have more importance than a human being?'

Personally, things were moving along nicely too. In fact, during one of the quiet spells of the season, Kelly became engaged to Lorna Brindley. For all his rebellious ways, he also possessed a sense of tradition. 'His manners were impeccable,' she said. 'He asked my father, Robert, if he could marry me.'

Looking enthusiastically towards the future and putting the transfer list controversy behind him, he said: 'Next year I'm marrying my girl, an English girl, and we are going to settle down. Well, I can never settle down but I have quietened down somewhat. I'll be back as long as there is a British League. I'm enjoying my speedway and heck, if you enjoy yourself and you enjoy work, that's the two best things going for you.'

## 17

# ADVENTURES IN AFRICA

'You've got to enjoy your life – that's my motto.'

Kelly Moran

A supporter's banner hung at the King's Park Stadium, Durban, for three meetings and it read: 'The Pocket Rocket, the Jelly Man. If any man can, the Jelly Man can – KELLY MORAN.' The South Africans, like other countries where the Wizard of Balance had performed, had fallen under the spell of the charismatic racer from California and they'd taken him to their hearts. 'He did really well and he was a big hit over there,' recalled Lorna.

In January 1988, a group of international riders took part in fifteen meetings called the Champion Spark Plugs International series in South Africa, where they'd compete against the best of the local talent. As well as the individual tournament, there were also some team matches, four team competitions and a best pairs event, which took place on tracks at Corobrik, Durban and Sun City – the indoor Superbowl.

Despite being knocked out in one meeting and having to borrow machinery when his engine blew up during practice at Corobrik, his spectacular, entertaining style and his happy-go-lucky personality made him a massive success with the local supporters. Indeed it was at Corobrik – 'home of California-style racing', as its slogan boasted – that he smashed the track record. However, it was at Durban where his sense of fun combined with his confidence saw him produce a ride that has become legendary among the group of riders that were present.

'We had a bet,' revealed Rob Tilbury. 'He said that he was going to touch the tapes and start from thirty yards behind. He said he'd pass me on the last bend. We all had a £50 bet; and we thought he was never going to pass me, never in a million years, no way. Guess what? He passed me on the last bend! He was so, so talented.'

The riders were based in a hotel in Johannesburg and they were on a working holiday and in high spirits. The establishment, a Holiday Inn, had standards and the management felt that their guests needed reminding.

'All the guys were told that they had to come down in proper shoes in the morning by the hotel manager, no flip-flops, feet had to be covered is what they said,' Lorna smiled. 'So they all came down in their racing boots! Rob Tilbury wore bright, pink hot pants and racing boots! He was very unique … he made the party. We called him "Turbo", well Kelly did.'

The hotel had other problems with their exuberant guests from overseas and on this particular occasion the perpetrators were fined for their behaviour. 'It was me and Kelly and a couple of others and we ran both bath taps, put the seal in, and we put three bottles of shampoo and fairy liquid into the bath. It was a big bathroom. Well it filled from the floor to the ceiling with bubbles, literally filled it! We came out looking like Smurfs! We all got fined and had to clean it all up. They were good times,' Tilbury laughed.

Of course you can't visit South Africa without experiencing a safari and seeing their exotic wildlife. Therefore, they all made a visit to the Kruger National Park and it wasn't without incident. They came upon an elephant with her calves and she was none too happy to see them cruising along.

'It was just fantastic and we went in our combi bus,' said Lorna. 'I can remember going along and there were elephants in the middle of the road, we were driving towards them, then all of a sudden one turned and started charging! Neville Tatum was driving, he slammed it in reverse and we all panicked.'

'A car had passed us in the opposite direction,' Moran recalled, 'but we didn't think anything of it because we were having a good time. I did think he was being silly going so fast. Well, we found out that car had upset one of the elephants, so when we turned up the elephant was upset and headed straight for us!'

Rob Tilbury was on the bus with them and he remembered the very brief stand-off between the bus and an angry elephant that was flapping her ears with anger and beginning a charge. 'This elephant was so big, I'll tell you what – she would have run over us! She was massive; you'd never seen anything like it. I said to Neville: "Neville, go back, GO BACK!" And Kelly went, "NOW, NOW, NOW!" He put this van into reverse and we were doing 40mph in reverse! Kelly was laughing all the time – unbelievable.'

Tatum later quipped that during their encounter with the world's largest land animal, no one was taking photographs as they reversed at high speed! Kelly, meanwhile, fancied himself as Allan Quatermain and caused his fiancé's heart to miss a beat or two. 'We were told not to get out of the bus in the Park, but Kelly did. He got out to have a closer look at the hippopotamuses in the pool – he didn't stay long!' she laughed.

'There was a lion asleep by the side of the track and he wanted to get out,' Tilbury added. 'I said to him, "What are you doing?" He went, "I think I'll stroke him." "You don't stroke him, get back in the van, you little prat!" He was a nightmare, absolute nightmare, but a lovely guy.'

Tilbury rode for Canterbury and Arena Essex in the National League so until joining the tour in South Africa he didn't have much contact with the American – although he had heard a lot about him. He got along well with him but lost a bit of innocence along the way.

'It was the only time I know that I got drugged up!' he laughed. 'It was me, Kelly, and a few others that went out on jet skis on the lake. We came back and this bloke had a fire going called "Durban Poison". Well I didn't know anything, I didn't take drugs or anything like that. Anyway, we were all cooking, having a braai – what we call a barbecue – and the aroma from this fire, which must have been four or five feet high … all of a sudden I was laughing and joking with everyone. I thought, what's going on, my head is a bit funny. We were all high as a kite from this fire and bloody Kelly knew, the f★★★★r, he knew about it, he knew what it was all about, but he didn't tell me!

'We'd been racing in Durban, I got 12 and he got 15 or something like that, and he said, "Let's go down to the beach." I never drank at the time and he kept saying, "Have a drink," "No, thank you." "Go on, have a drink." "No, no." But in the end I did. I had about five beers and I was completely paralytic with him. We fell asleep on the beach. When I woke up, I could hear running water and I swear I was looking at a shark's face! There had been a storm that night and all these dead sharks had been washed up on the beach next to us! It was like something out of a movie. They were only baby sharks, but there was me and him waking up in the middle of these dead fish. The running water was the blacks [*sic*] taking showers on the beach and they looked at us a bit strange lying among these dead sharks.'

Somehow, though, for all his partying off the track and no matter what state he was in, Kelly could still put on the style, much to Rob's astonishment. 'One time he'd had so many pints and shorts that he was out of it. He had to ride because the fans wanted to see him. So we gave him gallons and gallons of water and got him sober. Then he went out and got a maximum! I couldn't believe it.'

From their location in Johannesburg, by road it would take around six hours to get to Durban. Not if you were an international speedway rider. Tilbury reckoned they did it in four and a half hours, driving flat out.

However, because of the difference in altitude and humidity, there were some adjustments required for their engines to be fast, as Marvyn Cox explained: 'When we were in "Jo-burg," it was over 2,000 feet above sea level so we had to run the engines very lean. Then we went six hours south, so I changed the main jet, the needle jet and the needle on the carburettor. Kelly wouldn't know about that. Somebody else did that for him. Everywhere in Europe everybody would do everything for him and he didn't have to worry because someone did something for him somewhere around the world. So he'd just sit out there in the sun, scrubbing boots and helmets and so on, while somebody would do his bike for him. He didn't know what he was doing, he'd put on a small sprocket and hopefully the thing would work. He would always be one or two teeth less, sometimes, three – it depends.'

Sun City is called 'Africa's Kingdom of Pleasure' and is to South Africa what Las Vegas is to the USA – a gambler's paradise. A luxury resort/casino located in the North West Province, it's approximately two hours away from Johannesburg. Its 'Lost City Golf Course' is notorious for having a water feature that contains crocodiles at the 13th hole – no wonder Kelly wasn't keen on golf! 'He hated it,' Tilbury laughed. 'I used to play about six times a week but he wouldn't come out with me. "No," he used to say, "too much walking."'

As well as hotels, casinos and bordering a game reserve, the Pilansberg, Sun City also contained a splendid concert/sports hall called the Sun City Superbowl. In 1988 they laid a speedway track inside – which was about the size of Reading – and staged three meetings. It was an exciting and prestigious event in such a plush arena.

Well supported, the first event was a Kelvin Tatum Select versus a Kelly Moran Select, which the former won. The Champions series was concluded the following night before they staged the Sun City Classic in which Tilbury emerged victorious, although the night before he had been successfully trying his luck at the gambling tables.

'I won £2,000 that night racing and then I went to the casino and won £18,000. I won the Sun City Classic and Kelly said, "Come on Rob, let's go to the casino," so we went in the casino all night and you can imagine, can't you, I couldn't stop losing! It happens like that though, doesn't it? And another time you keep winning.'

'We went to Sun City for a week,' Lorna added. 'The rooms they put us up in were out of this world – beautiful rooms – and then at nighttime we had front row seats for a boxing match. We were treated like we were really something – superstars.'

Kelly finished third overall in the series behind winner Rick Miller and second-placed Kelvin Tatum. Miller, though, rued a pre-tournament agreement he entered into with the rest of the riders. 'It was a great trip for me. There was a lot of money on it – I think it was 50,000 rand was the total prize for the tour. Early on, we all had a hard year racing, so we decided that we didn't want to race so hard in the whole thing and knock guys off trying to win the money. So we decided to split it. That was a big mistake for me because I won almost every event down there!'

For recently engaged Kelly and Lorna, South Africa, with its stunning sunsets and rich colours, was as exotic as it was romantic. In fact, he liked South Africa so much that if he could have, he would have moved out there to live. 'It was a wonderful, amazing experience,' she enthused. Known these days as the 'Rainbow Nation', at that time there wasn't a Judy Garland atmosphere of sweetness and joy going on in the country; it was more like Wendy O. Williams-esque chaos and mayhem.

Approximately twelve months before Kelly and his fellow riders travelled to South Africa, the British and Irish Lions rugby union tour was cancelled due to political objections to the country's apartheid policies – a system of racial segregation that had been in force since 1948, in which the nation's black people (and other groups) were discriminated against and in which at one stage whites and blacks were separated in public areas. Moreover, a state of emergency had been declared when resistance to the much-hated system flared into violence in the rural Bantustan homelands. As a sporting nation, South Africa was largely frozen out of competitions due to the international sports boycott, and even Formula One – a sport not known for taking notice of international opinion – staged its last race at the Kyalami circuit in 1985 due to people using the GP to attract international pressure to end apartheid by staging intense protests.

Furthermore, in 1980 the United Nations compiled a list of sportspeople who had competed in events in the country. Although no ban or punishment was dished out, moral pressure could be brought to bear on the individual and some sports bodies did discipline anyone found to be on the register. The UN General Assembly adopted the International Convention against Apartheid in Sports in December 1985.

However, there was a hunger for sport in South Africa and its athletes were eager to test themselves against the world's best. This was highlighted by Zola Budd, who circumnavigated the ban by becoming a British citizen so that she could compete in the summer Olympics in 1984.

Speedway, though, adopted the old adage that sport and politics shouldn't mix and carried on in spite of some difficulties. It had a long history there – for a short time they even formed a league in 1947. International riders like Peter Craven, Alan Hunt, Scott Autrey and Barry Briggs performed in the nation, but the international community continued to pressure South Africa via boycotts and other economic sanctions to isolate the country and encourage the authorities to end apartheid. Happily, unlike some sports stars, riders didn't return to face possible bans, but at this stage things were coming to the boil in a volatile nation.

'One thing that Kelly said, and we both agreed on this, was that you treat people like you want them to treat you,' Lorna said. 'We didn't see anything racist or connected to apartheid, to be fair. I'm sure there was bad stuff, but we didn't see any of it at all. Kelly and I would have been very offended if we had seen stuff like that.'

When talking to the author, Kelly agreed with Lorna. He acknowledged that there was unrest, but he never saw anything untoward and believed that any trouble was confined to the known trouble spots that regularly made the international news. 'South Africa is nothing like the image it has and all the bad press that comes across on the TV. It is no different to many other countries at all. I really love it and I've made a lot of friends out there, probably more black than white,' he said.

The following year they stayed on a plot with a family, Noddy and Charny Naude. It was a large dwelling with livestock and they had two black staff, David and Elizabeth who, contrary to the media's image of white South Africans, were treated as part of the family. Kelly included them too.

'David used to feed the animals and do the groundwork and Elizabeth used to do the cooking,' said Lorna. 'I used to make things, like Kelly would say that he'd like a shepherd's pie and he used to get everybody together to eat – David and Elizabeth were welcomed by that family. At Christmas time, they bought them a present and everything – it was like a big family. David loved the sunglasses by Oakley that Kelly had and Elizabeth liked my perfume. He was sponsored by Oakley so we gave Elizabeth and David the sunglasses and my perfume, stuff like that, we left it behind for them. We would stay in South Africa until the new season started. We adored it.'

Their second trip to South Africa followed in 1989 and Kelly began in flying form by winning the Transvaal Open with a 15-point maximum, and followed that by finishing runner-up to Richard Knight in the Buddy Fuller Trophy in Durban. Unfortunately, his trip was painfully interrupted during the third meeting of the tour, the South African Pairs Championship at Corobrik, when he sustained a broken collarbone. Paired with local rider Noddy Naude, he locked up and the chasing David Steen was unable to avoid him. However, it was hoped that he would be back in action before the end of the tour because he planned to have laser treatment on the injury in order to speed up his return.

With time on his hands he enjoyed spending more time with Lorna and they slipped into the daily routine of life in South Africa. 'Noddy and Charny were wonderful people,' said Lorna. 'They gave us a "bakkie" truck. I used to take the kids to school in the morning, Lorazel and Joeleen; I used to drop them off so that they could catch the bus for school. And the dogs … you'd go out, they'd hear the car starting and all of them would come running and jump in the back of the bakkie and then I'd go. Where we stayed there were about twenty-six dogs, two peacocks wandering around, goats, geese – horrible geese that used to chase you everywhere – six horses, and Charny used to take the horses out in the day.'

This presented Lorna with an opportunity to test out one of Kelly's boasts when he first began dating her. 'He used to tell me a load of crap when we first met. He told me he used to be a jockey. I think he was trying to impress me. While we were there I made a joke of it and said, "You used to be a jockey, you can get on the stallion!" And she brought the stallion out. He got on it and we were ready to go riding, and the horse just reared with Kelly on it and he fell off the back. I said, "What happened to the days when you were a jockey?" and he replied: "I've had enough, I'm going in," and he walked in holding his bum! He just said, "I bet no one else has pulled a wheelie on a horse," and tried to make a joke of it, but it was so funny. That was it, he said that he wasn't doing it anymore and he never got back on a horse,' she laughed.

Although he was injured he still attended the racing and indulged in the frivolities afterward. Of course, being the way he was, his behaviour was often over the top. Fuelled by liquid brew he grew 10 feet tall and that argumentative side would come out. One night, Rob Tilbury heard a frantic knock on his hotel door and he opened it to reveal Lorna who was clearly worried about her man.

'Many a night Lorna used to come and find me and say: "Can you help me get Kelly in?" and it was like, oh no what now. They had like a bar or a nightclub underneath, if you know what I mean, and I never drank at all so I'd have to go down. One night, I got hold of him and said, "Kelly, come on." "No, no, I'm having this bloke!" This bloke must have been 7ft tall and 3ft wide and he wanted to fight him! I had to apologise to him, "I'm really, really sorry," and I put him over my shoulder, I swear, and carried him back into the lift and got him back to his room. Absolute nightmare! "Nobby, Nobby," he used to call me Nobby and Turbo and then he'd pass out asleep. I had to sling him over my shoulder when he was drunk. I had to carry him out most nights! Lorna used to say, "Go and get him." He always used to come and get me, "Come on Turbo, you look after me," he used to say.'

'Turbo' Tilbury and Kelly became best pals. Their adventures in the Rainbow Nation were never less than entertaining, although the American definitely gave his buddy a few heart-stopping moments. In most cases the danger element was provided by the Californian when boundaries would be tested, but Rob unintentionally supplied the risk factor during one of their off-track escapades.

'I nearly killed him one day,' Rob chuckled. 'We were on a speed boat that belonged to Tommy Jobson. Kelly was in one of those rubber rings on the back of the boat. I was driving and we were going round this corner really fast. When you turn the corner you go faster, don't you? So if you can imagine the rubber ring with him on it, we turned the corner and he's perched in this rubber ring and with the momentum he goes skimming across the water, right past the stern of the boat at a frightening rate of knots and crashed! Well, f*****g hell, he must have done thirty somersaults and he was bruised from head to toe, and he said, "You nearly killed me, you bastard!" I'll never forget that day.

'Another time we were in this speed boat going down the river, we had one of the skis, only the left one and they were worth £500 and I dropped it and broke it up. I looked up and there was Kelly on this bridge and I said, "Kelly, what are you doing?" He was going to jump from it. It was about 80 foot high and I said, "Don't jump, Kelly, it's too high." But he jumped! I can't imagine how high it was. Down in Durban, the waves are eight foot high, you wouldn't go out there, but guess where he was? In there doing his rolls in the sea! He was a f*****g lunatic sometimes.'

However, while he stayed at Noddy and Charney's place, Kelly was far from the party animal. Quite the opposite. But once released from domesticity and within the social whirl of being with his fellow riders, plus the usual hangers-on who only viewed him as a rich source of entertainment, he did get into some bother. On one occasion he soon discovered that the South African police (SAPs), like his Polish experience during his tour with Eastbourne, were less tolerant of alcohol abuse than most of the Western countries he was versed with.

'He was okay,' said Lorna. 'He did drink but he wasn't out of hand. He had his moments after a meeting, though. Sometimes I'd come home and someone else would drop him off. One particular night he'd decided to drive himself home and I came back with Noddy and Charny. Then I got a phone call asking me if I could come and bail him out – no chance! He had been drinking and driving and I wasn't going to go to the police station in the middle of the night. Jorge Alvis went and bailed him out and brought him home. I said to him, "If you drink and drive and get caught, it's your own fault." And he said, "Mmmm, I can't comment on that." He knew he was in the wrong. He came home with his tail between his legs. I couldn't not talk for too long – I had to give in. That was the thing with Kelly; I think I was a bit too soft with him. We never argued because there was no point, so he got away with a lot.'

One occasion, however, Lorna got particularly mad with him and while he was sleeping it off she shaved off one of his eyebrows. When he discovered this, instead of an argument he went out and got his hair shaved off on the opposite side! Eventually, it was shaved completely and, along with the similarly coiffured Andrew Silver, formed 'Team Flymo'.

Kelly was able to make a return to the track before the tour was over by racing in the final meeting. He finished in tenth place with 26.5 points in the Champion Spark Plug series.

By the time Moran returned for this third and final trip to South Africa in 1991, the political landscape was changing. Nelson Mandela, who had been imprisoned for his stand against apartheid, had been released in February 1990 after over twenty-seven years behind bars. Just two months after his release a concert was staged in his honour with a subtitle of 'An International Tribute for a Free South Africa'. Music heavyweights like Peter Gabriel, Lou Reed and Neil Young performed. Political negotiations were on-going to make the country a fully democratic nation and Mandela would eventually become its president in 1994 – completing a remarkable journey from anti-apartheid revolutionary to respected world statesman.

However, this tour was shorter than before and also all the meetings were staged at Corobrik. It seems likely this could have been due to the changes in the country because SA Automobile Association was restored as a full member of the FIM again. There was a lot of interest in the international riders' arrival; television even covered some of the action, possibly seeing their presence in the country as an indication that South African sport was returning from its international exile.

Kelly retained the Transvaal Open Championship by defeating Richard Knight in a run-off for first after they'd tied on 13 points. He stayed injury-free this time and while he didn't visit the top step again during the six-meeting tour, his exciting style entertained the audiences and he always ended his racing with a double-figure return.

His popularity never wavered. 'They loved him, absolutely loved him. What a wonderful man,' enthused Tilbury, while Marvyn Cox added: 'He was so outgoing, friendly, and on a very small track like it was out there, Corobrik, it was very similar to the tracks he raced on in America. So he could do his American style of running wide, mid-track, turn the bike, pick it up on a sixpence and wheelie down the straight – very popular with everybody. And because of the likeable person that he was, he could enjoy life with everyone.'

'The idea was to go out there and put on a good show for the locals,' said Kelly. 'It was by no means a Mickey Mouse show, and there was a lot of talent and endeavour out there. We had a great time and the promoters put on a good show. I loved it out there.'

# 18

# THE YORKSHIRE YANK

'And when Irish eyes are smiling, sure, they'll steal your heart away.'

Chauncey Olcott and George Graff Jnr

Without doubt, it was a very memorable occasion. The day was Saturday, 12 November 1988 – chilly but predominately bright skies stretched out overhead as Kelly and Lorna were married at Stannington Church, Sheffield. Moreover, it was a traditional English white wedding and in the words of the bride, 'a really lovely day'. Chris Morton, the man who had saved the American's life, was their best man and Kelly's mother, Sharon, flew over from California to share in her eldest son's big day.

'Our wedding day was brilliant,' enthused Kelly. 'Boy, was I nervous. I've been to a few in the past, but your own is something else. It made a World Final look like a piece of cake. We had a great time amongst a lot of good friends and we reckon the Pinegrove Club had its biggest turnover of booze since it opened.'

Unfortunately, Mike Carver, who Kelly referred to as 'Doctor Mike', was unable to attend their wedding, but insisted the newlyweds made use of his paid-for tickets. Therefore, they had a few days' holiday in the USA while the racer managed to slot in an engagement at the Ascot half-mile for the US Long Track Championship.

'I've had to visit Mike so many times that he's become more of a friend than a doctor,' Kelly said. 'Riding in the half-mile is a bit of an ego trip back home. Everyone wants to win and there is quite a bit of rivalry between the boys who stay home in the States and those who race in the British League. As soon as the event is over, Lorna and I will be hopping on another plane where we will spend a few days with Mike and Billie Carver.'

He couldn't stop Sam Ermolenko winning the meeting and the Skoal Shoot-out, a unique event that featured eight riders over four laps. Kelly finished second to Sam but spent most of the race fending off the close attentions of firstly Lance King and then Phil Collins.

It has been said by many that Kelly and Lorna were made for each other, a good match and a sweet couple, but being married to a speedway racer was a very interesting experience. The day would start off when he'd remind her how his body had been ravaged by the consequences of his profession. It wasn't as much rise and shine, more like slow and easy. He had to carefully manipulate his movements, encourage his bones to co-operate with his sleepy muscles in order to get his day underway, and the process wasn't always pleasant.

'The first thing he did when he'd get up in the morning, which was not nice, was he used to crack his whole body, click, click, click everywhere! Everything used to crack. He was always stiff – stiff shoulders, stiff this and stiff that,' she grinned. 'He had loads of injuries, but he never dwelled on them. He'd get injured and a week later he'd be riding whether it had healed or not. There was no resting, no stopping him. "It's only a collarbone, it'll be fine," he used to say.'

In 2006, he listed his injuries: 'I have broken over 130 bones – that's documented. I've broken my left collarbone four times and my right nine and have had over thirty concussions. I've broken bones but never went to hospital because, although I knew they were broken, I could still compete and I'd carry on.'

His sleeping habits could be a bit unconventional too. This was especially so after he had overdone it with refreshments. Sometimes he would sleep where he fell and on one particular occasion he snoozed while he was cradled in the hedge outside his house. Lorna recalled him coming in and complaining about sticks and leaves stuck in his backside. However, when he was armed with a new Stephen King novel to read, that would often take priority over catching some shut-eye.

'He would read it in bed,' she said. 'Totally engrossed and I would get a bit fed up and I'd ask him to read me some. He did, but not for long, he'd say, "I'm not reading you anymore, it's not the same reading out loud." You just did not wake up Kelly, though, oh my God, he was obnoxious, rude and awful if you tried.'

Sheffield team manager, Eric Boocock, also had the unpleasant experience of trying to stir the American after he'd had a skin-full. He didn't forget that encounter, to the point that he preferred to leave him on the plane rather than face the wrath of a recently woken Jelly Man, whose reaction could be likened to disturbing a bear from his hibernation.

'We'd driven through East Germany, through the Brandenberg Gate, but we flew in the night before from Heathrow and by the time we got off the plane we couldn't wake up Kelly – he was that pissed. The stewardess said, "You'll have to take your friend with you." And I said, "He's no friend of mine," because he was so nasty when he was like that. I said, "I don't care where he stops, he's not with me." Twenty minutes later, we're waiting for the luggage, when he came flying down the corridor on a f*****g bike! They used to have them in the airports in them days. He was wobbling from side to side, laughing and acting the goat. You've never seen anything like it – and he was comatose twenty minutes earlier!'

In the time that they had known each other, Lorna had already experienced some of the excesses that could get Kelly into trouble. And as much as she loved him, she had to admit that there were times when she wondered if tying the knot was a good idea. However, the doubts that she had were soon dispelled when they were apart.

'Sometimes I did think: do I really want to marry him? Then the next minute he'd be the most wonderful-est person, yeah I do want to marry him, I do love him. Then he'd go away to a meeting and I'd totally miss him.'

Kelly especially enjoyed being part of a close-knit family. He settled quickly and that structure went some way to kerbing his devil-may-care attitude.

'We were a close family, so he was welcomed into that,' said Lorna. 'I have two brothers and a sister, and I think that helped him a lot because he loved it and loved Sundays when we were all together. I don't think he had that growing up because his parents went their separate ways when he was very young. And Sharon had to work a lot of long, hard hours to bring up her boys. The family that he did have in America was very, very close, though. He loved Christmas too. My family all thought the world of him, thought he was great, although sometimes they thought he was a bit wild, but that was just Kelly. He was very close to my mum, he used to talk to her about all sorts. So he settled into Britain and started talking like English people, adopting the Yorkshire accent, "aw reet ..." it was kind of funny listening to an American – "A Yorkshire Yank," that's what he used to call himself.'

Long after he had left England and retired from racing, that Yorkshire influence would come out during conversations – especially when he was speaking to an English person – when among the Californian speech he'd suddenly come out with the agreeable Northern term, 'aye'. It was no surprise to Kenny Best that he adapted so well to English life and being part of an English family.

'He fell in love with England and fell in love with its people. Others would say I miss this or I miss that, and some felt isolated. But I never heard that from Kelly, he fitted in quicker than anybody over there. Part of his life was that he moved around a lot, even in off-season he lived with different people. He never had one specific place really. He'd stay with us for a few weeks, then he would go with someone else for a while. He was adaptable and he didn't really need any roots. He enjoyed and got along with all sorts of people.'

'I'm very happy over here and seem to enjoy each year more than the previous one,' Moran said shortly after his wedding. 'England has a lot going for it and I've become a real fan. That's why I'm planning to stay over here for quite some time.'

It has also been suggested that he was more Irish in his approach to life than Californian, never mind American. Given the number of injuries and scrapes he got into, perhaps he didn't fit the 'luck of the Irish', but he certainly suited the 'Irish eyes are smiling' doctrine; in fact it has been said that his eyes could light up a room.

'If there ever was a poster shot for Ireland in America it would have been Kelly Moran,' believed Paul Heffernan. 'He was happy-go-lucky, he was a lot of fun and he really did always come up smiling. He almost acted more Irish than he was Californian because that was how he was. You couldn't take that away because that was an important part of his character.'

Even before she was married, Lorna had slotted into the hectic life of a 'speedway wife' very well. However, there are no manuals for such a role and as her husband didn't have a normal 9–5 existence, it could be a balancing act mixing the responsibilities of married life with that of the sometimes turbulent lifestyle that racing a motorcycle can bring. During the season the routine was that there was no routine, except that Thursdays were nearly always race night at Sheffield's Owlerton Stadium. She realised that Kelly wasn't the most organised of people and she soon became more and more involved in his profession because the better prepared he was, the better his scores were and the more money came into the household to cover day-to-day expenses.

'I used to pay all the bills and make sure the mortgage was paid. Sort out his race meetings, where he was going to race, the contracts – that's how we did it basically,' she recalled. 'I ended up finding him sponsors, negotiated his deals because he was terrible at things like that, he'd just accept anything. I'd work for him so they'd pay two for the price of one basically. I used to go everywhere. If he was racing in Poland I used to negotiate with John Smith and it was if you want Kelly, I'm coming. He was very good with his sponsors and he had quite a lot then, and he got to know the people who were sponsoring him. He'd go and have a meal at that person's house, and he'd take the time out to take them to meetings and show them a good time.'

Of course, there was the social side to attend to as well. Kelly enjoyed the social aspect of the sport and, with the way speedway was structured in the 1980s, there was time to enjoy it. While there were occasions at the end of a meeting when they had to dash off for an overseas engagement, such commitments were not quite as regular as they are today.

'We had a lovely new house in High Green, in the north of Sheffield, and after the matches, the Test matches, I used to go home early, prepare the food, and everybody used to come to our house and have a good party,' she said. 'He could be a bit stroppy on a race day. Once he got to the track he was fine. And he could be a bit snappy when he was about to get on a flight – he never said that he didn't like flying, but he was worse than me, very tense. I kept out of the way on race day and the boys were usually in the garage so I just used to do their breakfast and keep out of their way. That was their time.

'All the neighbours knew Kelly and what he did. We used to have the bikes outside preparing them and there was a guy called Eric, who was like his best friend – they were thick as thieves. We were very much part of the community there. Graham and Cath, who lived next door, were good with him; they all knew he raced and no one really got in his face. I don't think anyone went down and watched him, no one was starstruck, they were just good neighbours. He had beautiful manners and the only time he had a bit of a temper was when he'd had a few drinks after a meeting and he'd totally lost it.'

Actor Clint Eastwood once said, 'They say marriages are made in heaven. But so is thunder and lightning.' The Morans also weathered a few storms, but most of these occurred when the American was under the influence of some liquid lightning.

'If we ever had a fight, I used to stay at Roy and Betty Wilson's, around the corner. To be fair we didn't fight that often, but they were always there for us. Roy was a steadying influence in speedway. He was always there to help. We were very close to them. Every day I used to go there, get their dog, Tiger Lilly, take him back to our house and we used to take him out for walks – and Kelly used to like animals anyway. So we had their dog every day while they were at work. At speedway we used to drive Roy home because Betty used to leave a bit earlier.'

Furthermore, because Kelly would often join the supporters in the bar afterwards, she got used to hanging around while he talked to fans, team-mates, managers and rivals. This would lead to some unconventional sleeping habits.

'We had mechanics live with us as well. Darren Boocock was really patient with him and Jimmy Van Dyke came and lived with us and we got along really well,' Lorna recalled. 'We had a good laugh. Jimmy saw how difficult it could be putting Kelly to bed after meetings. We'd stay to the bitter end, he'd stay there talking to people and he could never be rude to anybody or say like, "Sorry, I've got to go now." They would wait to speak to him and he'd be there talking and signing autographs. In the end we'd be like, "Come on Kelly, we've got to go," and shoo him out the door! Nobody could tell him, you couldn't say, come on Kelly you've had enough, we just had to wait until he was ready to leave.

'Once he was in the van, he was usually sparko'd. Some nights we'd just leave him there, cover him with a blanket and leave him until the next morning. You didn't move Kelly – wherever he fell, he slept. You didn't move him. We had like a duvet cover in the van and we used to cover him up and he'd often stay there in the night. It was a lot of late nights and a lot of driving back from faraway places when everything was closed.'

During a meeting at Swindon, she found herself having to take over as driver and drive the van from the track back to their home in Sheffield. Her husband was too far gone to take the wheel and was sleeping it off in the back. Exasperated, not only did she have to get behind the wheel of a vehicle that was much larger than she was used to, she also had to negotiate the unfamiliar 176-mile journey home, in the dark, while Kelly offered no assistance whatsoever as he slept soundly.

The STP sponsorship had also come to an end. Since his return to British League racing in 1986 he'd been backed by Life's A Beach surf wear – a phrase that would be used not only as a metaphor for the way he lived his life, but also thrown at him as a criticism. With his Life's A Beach cap often perched on his head, Kelly's association with the company came to represent his second era of British League racing.

By his standards, the 1988 season was a quiet one and his average slipped to below 9 points. The Sheffield team remained largely the same and although they were among the most exciting sides in the British League, trophies still eluded them – a fact that greatly frustrated promoter Maurice Ducker.

Kelly's World Championship ambitions ended early when both he and Shawn were eliminated from the title chase in the American Final – a dropped chain dashed Kelly's hopes. Shawn teamed up with Sam Ermolenko to race in the World Pairs and they finished third. For the first time, Kelly was made captain of the Tigers team and he was paired with his brother to represent the Yorkshire club in the British Open Best Pairs at Reading.

On a heavy, grippy track, under threatening skies at Smallmead, the Morans should really have won the event but they lost out by one point to Oxford's Hans Nielsen and Marvyn Cox. The surface seemed to suit the elder Moran better than Shooey as he took the outside gates and would use the grip to power around the opposing pair. A lack of meetings due to several postponements because of poor weather, combined with the heavy surface, took its toll on Shawn. Reading's Jan Andersson pressured him for second; unusually for him, he couldn't fend off the Swede's challenge and that handed victory to Oxford.

'For some reason I always had problems with my arms,' said Shawn. 'They would ache if I hadn't raced for a while, they would get really tired. I would have problems hanging on. Usually they would get better as the meeting went on. It wasn't a big problem, after a match or two they were okay, but I couldn't really do anything about it. It was one of those things.'

Kelly's lack of mechanical knowledge was put under the spotlight when he abandoned the favoured GM engine for Weslake in the 1988 campaign. The British-made engine had powered Bruce Penhall to two World Championships and once ruled the roost. However, Weslake's days were virtually at an end. The factory, which still operates today in Rye, Sussex, as a research and development centre, had been instrumental in the development of the four-valve speedway engine. Their engineering skills had been utilised at the very top of the motor sport world during the late '60s through their partnership with American driver Dan Gurney to produce the Gurney-Weslake V12, winning the Belgian Grand Prix in 1967.

GM and Godden were the two engines that were leading the speedway world at that point, having shared the World title between them since 1983. The Czech-made Jawa had also lost ground to GM and Godden, due mainly to the fact that the factory was suffering from lack of investment and was stuck in the old business practices of Communism – a situation further confounded by a Communist regime that was in its last years as Mikhail Gorbachev's reform policies were rapidly pulling down the fabric of the Soviet Union.

However, by now the engine tuner had begun to play an important role in the performance of the engines. Although the modern dilemma of 'set-up' had yet to gain any real prominence, with a narrowing power band and slicker tracks, getting the power down on the track was becoming more difficult.

There was quite a lot of crossover between speedway and long track racing at that point and with the latter's higher speeds, technical know-how was being transferred from the big 1,093-yard (1,000-metre) tracks to the smaller ovals of speedway. Therefore, the services of tuners like Otto Weiss and Hans Zierk became much sought after and their use of 'trick bits' may have given the riders an edge, although it also drove up costs.

The new Weslake engine that Moran raced was called the Bill Davies Weslake. Essentially it was the same power plant that he'd used during the early days of his career, which contained some updates here and some improvements there. On the face of it he had a good deal. Davies promised him that he would carry out all maintenance and service the engines at no cost. If he blew an engine it wasn't going to be a big issue for the Californian ... basically, he had a 'works sponsorship'.

It was a blow-up at King's Lynn where his ability to get the most out of any bike he rode was showcased. He was making a guest appearance at Saddlebow Road on Easter Monday morning for Swindon. Afterwards he dashed down to Reading to guest for them that evening.

He'd seized his engine during his third ride. And while in sight of the chequered flag in heat 11, he crashed and handed a gift 5–1, and the lead, to Lynn with two races left. Swindon's Andrew Silver and Gary Chessell recorded a 5–1 of their own in heat 14, which meant that the outcome of the match would be decided in the last heat – a nominated riders' race.

The American was picked to represent the Wiltshire team with Brian Karger. Therefore, he asked Alun Rossiter if he could borrow his bike for the all-important final race. Having scored 4, Rosco was a bit reluctant to lend him his mount, only because he didn't think it was up to the job and, with it being a last heat decider, he thought he should have jumped on somebody else's. But Kelly insisted and said, 'Well, I haven't got anything else to ride.'

Facing the Stars' top two riders, Lance King and Richard Knight, and on unfamiliar equipment, the Robins team were hopeful that the Yank's celebrated talents would do the business. As they watched from the pits, the tapes went up and Kelly emerged in the lead and never looked back and earned them a draw – unfortunately, Karger was unable to split King's Lynn's pairing. On returning to the pits he quipped to Rossiter: 'Works fine for me, Alun!'

Weslake was found wanting during the big meetings when his rivals would arrive with the latest developments on their super-tuned GMs and Goddens. This was illustrated during the 1988 World Team Cup Final at Long Beach, when Kelly finished his night's work with just 5 points and failed to win a race. He could hardly keep pace with the slick-starting Danes, who comfortably won the meeting.

Sam Ermolenko was America's top scorer and when questioned about the wisdom of Moran using a Weslake, he diplomatically responded: 'The Weslake wasn't fast enough on that track.' Which meant that it had plenty of speed for one of the nation's fastest tracks at Owlerton because they raced there every week, so his knowledge of the circuit, combined with the fact that he would meet maybe two riders of world-class quality a week as opposed to fifteen in one meeting, meant that the Weslake's shortcomings were not exploited until the best arrived with the best. Sadly, the Weslake was at the end of its life, and it was no surprise that Moran reverted to a GM the following year – although he did use it again from time to time.

Despite Kelly Moran's sublime ability ensuring that the Weslake was among the big points on a regular basis, unfortunately his lack of mechanical knowledge didn't help Davies develop the engine as much as he would have liked. The American knew how to race – he could ride any machine and get the best out of it – and he knew what he needed, when it was spinning too much, when it wasn't pulling enough from the start, etc. What he didn't have were any ideas internally about what they could do to the engine to improve it and make it more competitive. And why should he? His philosophy had always been that he was the rider, they were the mechanics, tuners or whatever. His job was to ride the bike to the best of his ability, as Ron Preston discovered when he was travelling with him after they had both given up racing.

'We were coming back from El Centro and we'd run out of conversation, so we started talking about the old days when I asked Kelly, "What gear did you use at Belle Vue?" "I have no idea." "What? You're s★★★★★★g me!" "That wasn't my job, I was the rider," he said.'

That's not to say that '88 was a poor season, far from it. It was the first year since 1984 that he had managed to finish the campaign without picking up an injury that sidelined him. His victory in the Peter Craven Memorial meeting at Belle Vue – defeating a world-class field – and also the Diamond Jubilee at Sheffield, proved that he was still hungry for success.

'He was very ambitious at that point,' said Lorna. 'He lived for speedway, he was speedway mad – that was his total life. The night before speedway his bikes would be prepared, he'd make sure his leathers were clean and everything would be packed ready. The next morning he'd get up, he'd be really good, he didn't drink the night before, especially on the day, he did not drink, not a drop, he was very, very disciplined like that on race days. He could be snappy but he was very focused on race days.'

Kelly's success in the Peter Craven meeting was in the new venue at Kirkmanshulme Lane, Belle Vue. The famous stadium at Hyde Road had closed and been demolished, so a consortium, which included Aces star Peter Collins, saved the club from closure and moved to Kirky Lane. However, the Jelly Man's triumph in that meeting and another impressive showing in their Diamond Jubilee event, followed by three visits with Sheffield when he never scored less than double figures, indicated his liking for the new circuit.

Due to the fact that Sheffield's lease was due for renewal in November '88, there were whispers on the wind questioning the club's future. Despite fielding a tremendously exciting team, it was known within management circles that they were losing money – it was later reported that they had lost £28,000. Therefore, someone from the Aces management quietly sounded out the Wizard of Balance about making a move across the Pennines to join one of the most famous speedway teams in the world. They even offered him more money than he was getting in Yorkshire and that alone was sufficient for him to express an interest in their offer. Moreover, he realised that changes were on the cards and during a quiet moment at Owlerton he told the author, 'Keep it to yourself, but I might be going back to Eastbourne next year.'

'It's all so frustrating,' Peter Collins told *Speedway Mail*, 'because until I know where I stand on Moran I cannot finalise my team plans.' The happy couple were still enjoying the sunshine in South Africa at the time and, as usual, Kelly was proving difficult to get hold of during the off-season. However, almost as soon as PC made that statement, the situation became clearer when it was confirmed that Sheffield would not be running in 1989. That meant that Shawn was available as well.

Realising what was on the cards, Sheffield's team manager, Eric Boocock – who had also been PC's manager at Belle Vue – picked up the phone and called Collins. Booey said, 'John Perrin was adamant that he wanted Shawn and Kelly and I rang Peter and said: "Peter, get one of them, but for God's sake don't have them both." Separate, you could handle them, together they were a handful. But their racing ability was out of this world. On the right night Kelly had more talent than Shawn; no matter what manoeuvre he did, he'd make it look so uncomplicated; he was terrific.'

'When I was in charge at Belle Vue at that time I didn't want two Morans there. I knew we could only cope with one of them,' admitted Collins. 'I had a 1–7 that I'd made and Kelly was on that list. I had a lot of different plans but John Perrin and his disciples decided that they wanted the two Morans. If Kelly had been there on his own that would have been quite enough, but it was too much to cope with the pair of them. One of the biggest problems was spending all the sponsorship money we got from British Car Auctions in one hit on them two – I really didn't want to do that. It was what John Perrin wanted, so I went along with it to some extent, then John and I fell out not long after. We had to sacrifice the bottom end of the team because we had two number ones.'

Nonetheless, both of them started off their new careers in the Aces' colours in sparkling form – especially Shawn, who was rejuvenated by the move. Chris Morton was among their team-mates, which also included Peter Ravn, Paul Smith, Gordon Whittaker and a young lad who was a sensation that year, Joe Screen.

Shooey was granted a Testimonial at Belle Vue, becoming the first American to receive a benefit meeting. However, it was during this special occasion when his brother's season was rudely interrupted. He crashed with Ronnie Correy during his first ride and broke his finger. When compared with some of the big injuries he had sustained, the breakage doesn't seem like a major issue, but it proved to be problematic to heal. His missed the World Championship qualifier and the Test matches against England.

It was while visiting Belle Vue for the second Test that he met Eric Boocock, who enquired, 'Are you still out with a broken finger?' 'Yeah.' 'My brother broke his finger and he was racing again after a couple of weeks.' Eager to know how

Nigel had managed that he asked, 'How did he do that?' 'He had it chopped off!' 'I don't fancy losing a limb,' the American fearfully replied.

'When it shattered they took the three biggest pieces and screwed them together,' he said. 'After five sleepless nights, the hospital put an aluminium brace on it to immobilise it altogether because the screws had moved. And they warned me that any further movement could result in amputation or a permanently dead finger.'

During his lay-off he boasted that his garden was tidy and filled with life, so much so that he said it looked like Kew Gardens. Finally, he made his track return on 18 August and scored a paid 15 points. However, two weeks later he trapped his hand in a garage door and cracked a bone. Fortunately, he was fit enough to take his place in a decimated USA side for the World Team Cup Final at Bradford on 17 September.

To this day, the result of that event is almost immaterial for it will forever be overshadowed by a first corner crash in the opening heat that was of such severity that all four riders were ruled out of the rest of the championship. Moreover, it almost claimed the life of Denmark's triple World Champion, Erik Gundersen – one of the most popular and likeable champions of all time.

As was his routine, Kelly was on the scene following the crash and watched his fellow countryman, Lance King, being removed from the track in a neck brace. But it was Gundersen's condition that caused most concern; he was in a very serious state. Moran was clearly shocked by the whole affair and was very emotional. He was seen hugging Denmark's team manager, Kjel Lund, and had to dig deep to find the reserves within himself to throw his leg over his motorcycle and race for the USA – he scored all but two of the team's total and provided their only race winner.

England won the championship but any celebrations were quickly muted once they learned of the extensive injuries that Gundersen had sustained. America had finished last out of the four competing nations and faced qualifying for the following season's championship for the first time in five years. In many ways, that black day in September marked a line in the shale, since then nothing would ever be quite the same again.

'We've never been to Hungary before!' said Kelly of the prospect of qualifying. 'It could be a blessing in disguise having to travel all over Europe to race in the qualifying rounds next year. It could be the kick up the pants we needed. I'm still not fully fit, I only took the pot off my wrist last weekend and it still hurts.'

Stories of Kelly's off-track antics were starting to take on legendary status – and also attracting interest from outside the sport's circle. Eastern Europe was changing and beginning to break the shackles of Communism. Nowhere was this more evident than in Poland, where in June 1989 the Solidarity movement scored a resounding victory in the legislative elections, which paved the way for the fall of Communism across Europe. In Gdańsk, where the Solidarity movement had begun in the shipyards with Lech Walesa as its figurehead, they decided to stage the Solidarity Games, of which speedway would be part of the entertainment.

Organised by Barry Briggs, Gary Havelock found himself on a flight to Poland with Kelly Moran, Mitch Shirra and a very young Leigh Adams. 'Lech Walesa laid on his private jet for us to make the short flight to Gdańsk,' recalled Havelock. 'We found ourselves in the company of officials from the PZM and they were all suited and booted, but very serious. Kelly reached into his bag and pulled out a bottle of duty free vodka. He started doing shots with these officials and by the end of the flight they were all his best mates. Leigh Adams had his eyes opened!' Havvy laughed.

'We took our own kit bags and leathers but were riding standard Jawa bikes that were supplied at the club. It was so wet that during the first two races we were just aquaplaning down the straights. They had to call it off. In Poland whistling is booing, and they'd just announced that Lech Walesa was there in the stadium and about the same time they announced that the meeting was off. There were 15,000 people whistling and I believe Lech Walesa got pissed off and went home because he thought they were whistling at him!'

They had an early flight to catch next morning for England. A bus picked them up from their hotel. Havvy was amazed to find that Moran was already equipped with refreshment for the journey ahead. 'He'd bought a bottle of Bacardi in the shop the morning after the meeting. We were getting on the coach to go to the airport for a 6 o'clock flight in the morning and by the time we got there he'd drunk the lot!'

On arrival at the airport, the driver got out of his seat, only for a very happy American to jump in and take off! The driver watched in horror and was almost apoplectic as this crazy Californian departed with the coach he was responsible for. Fortunately, it was returned quickly and intact, but there was no pleasing the driver, who really didn't see the funny side.

On Sunday, 8 October, Belle Vue travelled south to compete in a special Inter-league Challenge match at National League, Rye House. The Aces promised to bring both of the spectacular Moran brothers and the Rockets' fans were excited about the prospect of seeing the much talked about Americans race around their circuit. But they were to be bitterly disappointed. Shawn couldn't get back from a racing engagement in California in time and was replaced by Andrew Silver.

Meanwhile, Belle Vue's boss, John Perrin, telephoned Kelly at 8 a.m. on the morning of the meeting and learned that he was staying in Warrington at Roland Danno's home. Kelly also informed him that he didn't want to ride for the Aces that day and planned to go to Sweden with Danno. 'I told him he is a professional and should abide by his obligation to ride at Rye House and he promised me faithfully he would appear. But when we got to Rye House he was nowhere to be seen,' said Perrin.

The Aces lost the encounter 49–46 and meeting referee, Will Hunter, fined Moran £100 for his non-appearance, while an angered John Perrin acted swiftly by reporting him to the BSPA and penalised him a further £500. 'Later, when I returned North, I found his van and bikes parked in Warrington where I guessed they would be. On making enquiries I found out he had gone to Sweden, so I had no alternative but to report him to the BSPA. He will not be riding for Belle Vue again this year.'

Kelly always maintained that he had never agreed to do that meeting. 'At no time did I agree to ride at Rye House. I told John Perrin that I would let him know because the meeting wasn't in the original contract I had. But he took it for granted that I would do it, and then decided to sack me for not riding in a meeting that I had never agreed to be in anyway.'

Whatever the rights or wrongs of the episode, having already missed a large chunk of the season because of injury, he couldn't afford to be sat at home when he should be racing. Therefore, he made his peace with the Aces' management and apologised. John Perrin wasn't known for being soft-hearted – he was considered to be a gruff straight-talker whom some found intimidating – but even he couldn't resist the Californian's charm and humility and he was back in the Aces side to face Coventry. 'I couldn't find it in my heart to kick him while he was so obviously down,' he said.

Despite his transgressions, he received a warm reception from the supporters. However, the American may have received a premonition that something unpleasant could be occurring when he made his return on Friday, 13 October. The match had to be abandoned after seven races because of rain. Unusually the conditions were not the talking point in the pits; instead it was the heavy security that surrounded Kelly's pit. His rakish lifestyle had caught the attention of the wider national press and a journalist was poking around for a story. While the Californian was able to sweet-talk Perrin, the hack from Fleet Street couldn't be charmed.

'That bloke came specifically to see Kelly – to "hound him" was what he said – so we wouldn't let him in unless he paid his admission. As far as I know he didn't come in,' said a satisfied Perrin. 'The security was assigned to keep any harassment to a minimum because, after all, the matter was an internal one between Kelly and Belle Vue.'

Having peddled their sensational journalism at Kenny Carter's funeral, the 'Red Tops' had really unleashed the hounds on the public since that sad day in 1986. Although their careless writings and photography had yet to reach their sleazy peak, the story about the Moran couple still turned out to be a little truth smothered by a few lies.

In their 22 October 1989 issue, *The People* ran a story about Kelly's absence from the Rye House meeting with the headline: 'On Yer Bike, Wife Tells Romeo Speedway Star.' Inside, it claimed that he had disappeared to Sweden 'with a leggy blonde'. It went on to suggest that Lorna had put their home up for sale and was living with her parents; she was also supposedly quoted as saying that her husband was the 'George Best of the speedway track'.

'I wouldn't have thought to say something like that,' Lorna denied. 'I'll tell you what happened: someone came knocking at my door asking to put my side of the story forward, and I said, no thank you, and closed the door. I've never ever said anything to anybody. Apparently somebody did. They offered me money, but no thanks. I never spoke to anybody. I never said, "On yer bike." We tried to work out who told them this stuff because Kelly said he hadn't said anything. We had our ideas, but I'll keep that to myself. We can't prove who it was but how did they get a wedding photograph? Whoever it was got paid for it, so I should have told them a load of rubbish and got the money.'

Many years later, when asked about this episode, Kelly took a moment to reflect before he answered: 'I totally blame myself. I don't know if I was falling out of love with my wife at the time or what, I couldn't really say because I'm no psychologist. I went to Sweden with Roland Danno, his girlfriend and her friend. But she wasn't leggy or anything, in fact she was smaller than me! I wasn't interested in her. I just wanted a drink or two with Roland. And that's all there was to it. But the papers got hold of this story and blew it all out of proportion.'

'He just buggered off somewhere,' added Lorna. 'He went off with somebody for I don't know how long. Apparently Roland had got a girl that he set him up with or something. I didn't ask too many questions after. But I had him back, didn't I? I didn't divorce him.'

Although the Aces had retained him, as the season ended there was plenty of speculation about the charismatic Californian's future in Manchester. However, on New Year's Eve, he called Perrin to wish him a Happy New Year and struck a deal for 1990 before hanging up. As he and Lorna travelled Down Under where he rode in a series of meetings, including Phil Crump's Testimonial, John Perrin announced that he'd re-signed and said, 'Kelly is back with Belle Vue now and he has informed me that he intends to do his best for us. That's good enough for me.'

# 19

# YOU AIN'T SEEN NOTHIN' YET

'Action speaks louder than words, but not nearly as often.'

Mark Twain, author (1835–1910)

Kelly pulled off his crash helmet, glanced at his mechanic, Craig 'Craiger' Cummings' annoyed and disappointed face and said: 'You think I'm shit, don't ya?'

'No, I know you were shit there!' replied the burly Scotsman.

'Just watch this!' the little Californian determinedly announced.

The American had just run a last in the first race of the 1990 World Team Cup Final at the legendary Pardubice track in the former Czechoslovakia. It was a disappointing last and given his wayward behaviour the night before, he returned to the pits to be greeted by some irritated faces. In one of the most open finals of that period, to begin their challenge with a zero wasn't the sort of start that the USA team were hoping for and their team manager, John Scott, was also displeased with him. So much so that he considered dropping him from his next ride and replacing him with their young reserve, Billy Hamill.

Moreover, the build-up to the event hadn't been good for Kelly. His equipment – and his brother's – had been lost en route to the track somewhere between Amsterdam and Prague, so for practice they had none of their own apparel to wear. Having previously raced on the Czech track before, Kelly had planned to skip practice. But given the importance of the event, combined with the fact that Craiger had done some 'DIY tuning' on his engines before leaving England in order for them to be competitive on the big circuit, he was urged to take to the track. He wore a spare set of Sam Ermolenko's leathers that were much too big for him and he looked like an anorexic on the comeback trail. Nonetheless, practise he did.

With the rest of the evening and night to go before the main event the following afternoon, there was ample downtime available to socialise and have some fun. He spent part of it enjoying himself in the company of former Czechoslovakia's Roman Matousek. Encouraged by Moran, the muscular Matousek's party piece was to pump up his muscles to the point where they would strain against the confines of his shirt until – Incredible Hulk-style – his muscles would eventually rip through the material! The downside to this remarkable spectacle was that he'd have no shirt to wear and would usually have to borrow one.

Predictably, Kelly over-indulged and missed most of the FIM banquet that evening because he was sleeping it off in his room. Unfortunately, the local vodka and other beverages had taken its toll on him when he finally surfaced on race day. He was seemingly bright enough, but being an afternoon event his normal recovery time was sliced in half and it was clear that he was much the worse for wear.

The good news was that all of his equipment had arrived in time for the final, but Shawn was still minus his leathers and would wear a spare set from a Czech rider. Craig Cummings got to work on getting his machinery ready for action and although he was used to his rider letting him do most of the mechanical requirements, he was annoyed by his lack of professionalism. 'I wasn't particularly happy with what had happened the previous evening,' Cummings admitted. Luckily other members of the US team helped out during these hectic hours by getting everything prepared for a World Championship event.

Gary Havelock rode for England, and having witnessed his antics the previous evening, he was astonished by Moran's performance. 'Before the meeting he was selected for a random alcohol test. We all thought he'd fail but, amazingly, he passed!'

Lining up in the first race, Kelly wasn't at the races at all. 'He had an absolutely shocking first race,' recalled Cummings. 'He was not even on the pace in the first one and then all of a sudden he came to life.'

He had to persuade manager Scott, though; some said he even pleaded with him not to drop him and to give him another chance. Of course Scott knew what astonishing ability he possessed and, besides, he'd always had a soft spot for him and he agreed. He wasn't disappointed.

Over Kelly's next four races he was unbeaten and finished as the USA's top scorer with 12. It was also a performance that debunked some of the myths that had grown up around him. At 427 yards (391 metres), Pardubice was a big, wide track and on the day it was slick, thus making the starts important. This combination wasn't supposed to suit the Californian because he was thought to shine on the smaller circuits and gating wasn't his strongest point. Unusually, he won those four races by making starts, including the long drag from gate four across the pack to hit front in his second race – 'just watch this' indeed! Even Nielsen failed to do that on one occasion.

During a very competitive meeting, the USA won the championship for the second time in their history by finishing 3 points ahead of nearest challengers, England, and Denmark were further back in third, while the hosts – who stole vital points off everyone at some crucial stages – were better value than their fourth position suggested. Sam Ermolenko clinched gold in the last race, but there was little doubt who the star of the show was, as *Speedway Mail* proclaimed 'Kelly's Heroes!'

Lorna recollected that when he returned to their home in Sheffield he was particularly pleased with his achievement. 'He brought this big, crystal vase thing back and he was really proud they won it. He was very proud of that.'

Unlike previous seasons when they had been seeded, America had to qualify for that World Team Final in Pardubice. That meant that they had to see off the challenge of an emerging Australia, Sweden and West Germany. They raced in two meetings and clinched their place by winning the second round in Mariestad, Sweden.

It was during the return trip from that qualifier that Kelly displayed his total disregard for money, which was as comical as it was wasteful, as James Easter recalled. 'I was Aussie team manager in 1990 and we were all coming back through Stockholm. There was this gorgeous lady at the duty free shop who had a large chest – a magnificent specimen! Kelly latched on to her and he worked out that if she bent down to get the cashmere scarves out of the bottom drawers, he got a right eyeful of her tremendous knockers. He then went on to buy five or six! He bought five of these things, which, in Sweden, were a lot of money. He'd won £400 or something and he blew the lot on these scarves, just so that he could see the lady's chest, and then he gave them all away! This lady was absolutely distraught, John [Scott] didn't know whether to laugh or cry, and it was highly amusing to us looking on, but then we weren't on the end of things like that.'

His indifference to financial matters became a problem for Lorna, who was managing the household bills. Representing your country has never been a particularly lucrative undertaking, especially in speedway, but it was all income nonetheless. Having her husband riding all over Europe was no use to her if she didn't see some of the reward so they could keep a roof over their heads. Therefore, she had to make a private arrangement with John Scott, as Easter explained: 'She rang up John and said, "Look, we absolutely have no money. He's winning money all over the place, but every time he gets it he spends it on booze and parties." So John had to enter into an agreement with her that, when he was on international duty, John would get the money, pay Kelly some pocket money and keep the rest to give to her – it was that bad at one stage.'

Craig Cummings was an experienced mechanic. He had wielded the wrenches for Shawn and Bobby Schwartz before helping the elder Moran, and he would go on to be an influential figure behind Billy Hamill's success. Therefore, Kelly was catered for in that department and it showed on occasions when he was fully focused on the job in hand. He was rewarded by being picked to ride for the USA with Ronnie Correy in the World Pairs Championship and they qualified for the final at Landshut, Germany.

'They were the best times,' recalled Correy. 'Kelly and Shawn were my heroes growing up. They were so talented and being small like me they were an inspiration to me. Back home they'd help me out with little bits here and there. Riding with Kelly was so good because he was one of the best when it came to team riding; he was so talented. I remember the semi-final in Prague, we pushed the Danes, Nielsen and Jan O. Pedersen, pretty hard and we finished second. Yeah, the first corners were crowded with six-rider races – they're always crowded even with four – but we found our way through. Before the final in Germany, Kelly and Mitch Shirra just partied so hard the night before. They filled up this big bowl with booze and drank it until they fell down. I left them to it and went to bed. The next thing I knew, someone was carrying Kelly over their shoulder and putting him to bed!

'Next day, he had breakfast and was ready to race. I was amazed that he could do that and be so good. So many times he'd be passed out drunk and then the next day he'd score a maximum. Supremely talented, a super guy and we had a lot of fun, but when he had too much to drink he could be a pain in the ass. He'd always pick on the biggest guy in the bar to fight with. I used to say to him, "Why don't you pick on someone your own size?" "I can take him," he used to say. Many, many times I would have to break things up when someone had him in a head lock or whatever.'

Correy wasn't the only one who had witnessed this side of him. Ron Preston had also seen it on more occasions than he could remember. 'I don't know how many times I saw him standing in front of a guy who's two feet taller than him, he's drunk and he's poking him in the chest calling him a wanker, saying, "Yeah, you just think you're a big shot," and then the next thing you know he's flying across the room. That happened a lot.'

The policy of running six-rider races in the World Pairs hadn't been a popular one with the riders. And with memories of Erik Gundersen's horrific crash still uppermost in the minds of most of the competitors, when Britain's

Simon Cross sustained a career-threatening back injury and Gerd Riss also had to withdraw with an ankle injury, Kelly had seen enough and hit out at the sport's authorities.

'Why do they always wait until someone is killed or maimed before they start changing the rules?' he said after the meeting in which America finished sixth. 'The only track I know which is safe enough for six-rider races is Pardubice. Now the FIM have agreed to drop six-man races, but they have done it too late because there have already been three serious injuries. Why can't they let the riders decide what is safe and what isn't? We're the professionals, we can judge these things, not some blokes who have never ridden a speedway bike but sit around a table and say, "Hey, wouldn't it be a good idea ..." They should let the riders make the rules because we know what will pull the people through the turnstiles.'

In what was described as a 'rare interview' in *Speedway Star*, Moran also called for more dirt on the tracks to make it more entertaining and safer. 'Every rider agrees they should put dirt down. I don't mean the sort of shale that is like sand on tarmac, but properly prepared dirt on tracks where a lot of work has been put in. Our pleas for dirt always fall on deaf ears – I might as well be talking to my feet. We are into the nineties but we are just going backwards when we should be going forwards.'

Although he had a carefree persona and was a joker to some, Moran could be outspoken and he would have another pop at the authorities later in the season as well. 'If something was desperately wrong he'd say something, but most of the time he was an easy person,' said Lorna. 'He wasn't an argumentative person. He was quite laid back with things like that. A lot of them were his friends and team-mates.'

Once again, his World Championship hopes were dashed in the first round. Shawn won the meeting while Kelly lost a three-rider run-off for the last qualifying place. However, the race was awarded when Greg Hancock crashed out with a broken arm, which elevated Ronnie Correy to fourth and Kelly to the first reserve position.

When Shawn crashed heavily in Sweden, it looked for a little while that Kelly would take his place in the Overseas Final. As it was, only his machines raced that day in Shooey's hands and he watched his brother finish third in the meeting. Indeed, he went all the way to the World Final itself and finished second, losing a run-off to Per Jonsson for the crown.

Behind the scenes though, all was not as it seemed. Following his fall in Sweden, Shawn had been prescribed a painkiller that contained a banned substance. When he realised this he informed the authorities and offered to pull out of the Overseas round at Coventry rather than face potential problems.

BSPA chairman, Maurice Ducker, acted on his behalf and he was cleared to ride – but still they tested him and, of course, he tested positive. Almost three months had passed, yet he was allowed to progress all the way to the final at Bradford and compete in the sport's showpiece event. Even his explanation and efforts beforehand were not enough to prevent the authorities from harshly stripping him of his silver medal.

Obviously, the FIM knew all along and seemingly chose to make an example of him. During the World Final itself the relevant authorities were in full knowledge of the facts and the likely consequences. Armed with that knowledge and feeling extremely angry over the treatment his little brother had received, Kelly chose to display his displeasure in no uncertain terms during one of the biggest events for the US authorities, the AMA Awards Banquet. With the men dressed in tuxedos and ladies in sequins, it was a glamorous occasion that included motorcycle racers from all disciplines – not just speedway.

When the US team were asked to come forward to collect their medals for their World Cup victory, Kelly took advantage of this moment to let them know what he thought of the FIM, and the AMA, for hanging his brother out to dry.

'I got up to receive my gold medal and I told the American Motorcycle Association exactly what I thought of them,' he said. 'People were trying their best not to burst out laughing; they were putting their serviettes by their mouths hoping that the big dignitaries wouldn't see them. A week later I got fined $1,000 but it was suspended for twelve months. I told Lorna, "You might as well sign the cheque now." I couldn't keep my mouth shut. What they did to Shawn was crap, absolute crap! If they had done it to me I would have taken legal action. I wouldn't have let it drop, no way. I'd make sure everyone found out how stupid they had been.'

Disillusioned, Shawn Moran hadn't made the trip to California for the awards ceremony, but he heard about his brother's outburst and admitted that it felt good that he had stood up for him. 'I heard about it and felt that it was cool. It was touching what he did.'

Even though Kelly was keen to have his say on some controversial matters, he still enjoyed his racing. During a visit to Wolverhampton he had been riding particularly well and lined up in a last heat decider alongside Chris Morton, but the Wolves duo of Ronnie Correy and Graham Jones out-gated the Aces pair and took the lead. With victory slipping from his team's grasp, Kelly tried hard to pass them and then pulled a full-locker on the first turn of the third lap and was hit by the following Morton. They crashed heavily and at first it was feared that the American may have done some serious damage. Happily, he escaped injury and when the track announcer asked him how he felt he replied: 'I landed on my head, I'm always alright when I land on my head!'

Martin Morley, whom Kelly called Nicky, used to help the brothers out during race nights and he remembered another crash involving the elder Moran at Kirky Lane. 'He had a big crash on the top turn at Belle Vue – he got tagged from behind by someone. I was running along with Shooey on the centre green and he said, "Bloody hell, get going, it's my brother!" So I sprinted up there, he's lying down by his bike and he's got his knee up and I said to him, "Kelly? KELLY?" He opened his eyes and said, "Oh f**k, Nicky, I'm alive!" We got him up and walked him back – he could be so funny.'

Despite the fact that he didn't have a driving licence, he continued to drive in England. However, that situation couldn't go on and when a sponsor came forward Lorna advised him that it was about time he took his test.

'He used to drive everywhere, then he got sponsored with a van, a hire place, so I said, "I think it's about time you got a licence, Kelly, and drove legally." So he had private lessons and took his test discreetly. I think he only had about four lessons and passed first time.'

He enjoyed a good season for Belle Vue and the club finished third in the league, but were thrown out of the Knockout Cup on a technicality. The SCB ruled that their use of rider replacement for Peter Ravn was unlawful and they amended the result against Reading and they, instead of the Aces, qualified for the final. All in all, it was a season of contradiction for the club and their slump in September finished any outside chance they had of challenging for the league championship.

Individually, though, Kelly took part in his third British League Riders' Championship and, with home track advantage, he was hopeful of a good result. He put in a battling performance to finish runner-up to Hans Nielsen, defeating Correy in a run-off.

By this time Cummings' patience had run out and he'd quit being Kelly's mechanic. As a result, his form wavered from inconsistent to downright disappointing. For the final match of the year, he provoked the wrath of John Perrin by arriving without a bike and had to borrow Joe Screen's!

'Anybody who could stay with Kelly long enough had to babysit him,' said Lorna of their string of mechanics. 'They did have to put up with a lot of crap. It wasn't just mechanic-ing, it was looking after him afterwards, it was waiting for him to the bitter end, to drive him home and wondering what state he was going to be in.'

Triple World Champion, Erik Gundersen, also noticed that he'd give as much time as possible to the supporters, sometimes too much.

'I admired him for his ability on the bike and for what he used to do off the track with the fans as a whole. He always had time for everybody. He would come in with his cap on backwards, cigarette hanging out of the side of his mouth, and the kids would approach him for his autograph and he would sit down with them. He was always behind with everything that he had to do because he had time for everybody.'

'He used to do some crazy things,' added Morley. 'He would pull people out of the crowd to mechanic for him. "You lad, come and mechanic for me." I'd be like, what's going on? And there would be a mass of mechanics around his bike and they would be saying, "Did you do the back wheel?" "No I didn't do it, did you?" I didn't do it, I didn't do it, and then I had to run like bloody hell, jump the fence and run onto the centre green and Kelly would say: "It's okay, it's okay." And off he went. He'd know if it was loose or if it wasn't as it should be. Wherever we went he had to steal a bottle of tabasco – everywhere he went,' laughed Morley.

At the conclusion of the season there were a lot of rumours circulating about the future structure of the sport in Britain. Once more, Eastbourne indicated that they wanted to return to the top flight, only this time Bob Dugard had an application form from the British League and bank surety that appeared to guarantee the club's future if they moved up. He even named riders he'd earmarked for the side. Unsurprisingly, Kelly's name was at the top of his list.

However, Dugard was let down by politics. A new constitution was adopted and in the end not only didn't the Eagles compete in the top league, they didn't come to the tapes at all to start with and Kelly remained at Belle Vue.

'We were told by the BSPA that we would get up into the senior league because there were two clubs that couldn't afford it and it would all sort itself out. But it never did,' Bob explained. 'I think it was Berwick that wanted money from us to buy their licence and I said no. We had an arrangement with the BSPA and Kelly was part and parcel of that plan.'

'It would be neat to be World Champion at least one time. It would be neat to think that I was the best that year,' said Kelly Moran shortly before competing in the 1991 Overseas Final at Bradford. He'd qualified from the American Final for the first time since 1987 in what turned out to be the final speedway meeting at Long Beach.

His motivation had been renewed to have World Champion by his name at least once in his career by becoming a father. Lorna gave birth to a girl they named Chelsea on 7 June 1991, and Kelly was as proud as any father could possibly be. Although he was 'at work', he did manage to get there to witness the birth – just.

The victorious USA team that won the 1982 Test series against England. *Back row, left to right*: Shawn Moran, Dennis Sigalos, John Scott (team manager), Scott Autrey and Ron Preston. *Front row, from left to right*: John Cook, Bruce Penhall, Bobby Schwartz and Kelly Moran (Photo by Trevor Meeks, courtesy of the John Somerville Collection)

'He did get quite emotional.' Kelly Moran being consoled by Eric Richardson following the controversial Overseas Final in 1982 (Photo by Mike Patrick, courtesy of the John Somerville Collection)

His third place medal from 1982 British Open (Photo by Alan Clark)

World Team Champions 1982, a victory that Kelly said stood out in his career. *From left to right, standing*: Scott Autrey, John Scott (team manager), John Smith (team manager) and Kelly. *From left to right, kneeling*: Bobby Schwartz, Bruce Penhall and Shawn Moran (Photo by Trevor Meeks, courtesy of the John Somerville Collection)

Kelly Moran with Ron Preston (right) after scoring a 5–1 with Eastbourne (Author's collection)

Even during the World Championship, he still found time for his fans at the Los Angeles Coliseum (Photo by Scott Daloisio)

'He just extended his hand and offered me a cigarette.' Enjoying a joke with Bob Dugard at Wimbledon in 1983 for the opening England v USA Test match (Photo by Trevor Meeks, courtesy of the John Somerville Collection)

Crossing the finish line to clinch the 1983 US National Championship at Costa Mesa (Photo by Scott Daloisio)

The 1983 US National Championship. *Left to right*: Mike Faria (runner-up), Kelly (first) and Dubb Ferrell (third) (Photo by Scott Daloisio)

'He had the heart of a lion.' Seven-times National Champion, Mike Bast (right) and Ken 'KK' McGoldrick (left) listen to Kelly at Costa Mesa (Photo by Scott Daloisio)

'He was very good at riding on the top of the tyres, keeping the bike stood up so you get as much rubber as you can on the track.' (Photo by Scott Daloisio)

*Right*: A rare occasion when Kelly protested to the referee after he was excluded during the 1984 Inter-continental Final in Vojens after a clash with Hans Nielsen. Looking on behind is Barry Briggs (Photo by Mike Patrick, courtesy of the John Somerville Collection)

*Below*: Everyone's friend, no matter what nation, colour or creed, Kelly crossed all the divides to be friendly with everyone. This time he jokes with the Polish team during the 1984 World Team Cup Final at Leszno. *Left to right*: Zenon Plech, Roman Jankowski and Boleslaw Proch (Photo by Mike Patrick, courtesy of the John Somerville Collection)

Kelly was always the first to congratulate his opponent: this time Lance King during the 1984 World Championship (Photo by Trevor Meeks, courtesy of the John Somerville Collection)

Kelly with Barry Briggs during the 1984 World Final after he had accidentally ripped off his goggles during his second race (Photo by Trevor Meeks, courtesy of the John Somerville Collection)

Offering encouragement for Shawn ahead of his debut ride in the 1984 World Final in Gothenburg. Kneeling to the right is mechanic Richard Harrison. (Photo by Trevor Meeks, courtesy of the John Somerville Collection)

'He was different this time, he didn't want to party.' At home with Kenny Best and the US National trophy on the table after retaining it for the second successive year in 1984 (Courtesy of Kenny Best)

The staggered start in a handicap race in the USA: Kelly (1), Alan Christian (2) Rick Miller (10) and Lenis Faas at the front (Photo by Mike Patrick, courtesy of the John Somerville Collection)

Kelly with Sam Ermolenko and trophies after finishing runners-up to Denmark in the 1986 World Pairs Championship in Pocking, Germany (Author's Collection)

'Glad to be alive.' Kelly with Chris Morton (centre), who saved his life, and Andy Smith at Odsal Stadium after his hotel accident in Poland (Photo by Ken Carpenter/Retro-Speedway)

Leading Robert Pfetzing and Jeremy Doncaster at Bradford during the 1987 Overseas Final (Author's Collection)

*Right*: The happy couple
(Courtesy of Lorna Brindley-Moran)

*Below*: Kelly with Lorna and canine friend in California
(Courtesy of Lorna Brindley-Moran)

'He could pass you from anywhere.' Leading Hans Nielsen in Prague in 1987 (Photo by Mike Patrick, courtesy of the John Somerville Collection)

Neat and tidy riding style for the Belle Vue Aces in 1990 (Author's collection)

Kelly, Chelsea, Lorna with Rick Kelly and gold Rolls Royce at Chelsea's christening (Courtesy of Lorna Brindley-Moran)

Wearing his 'Life's A Beach' hat while waiting for the racing to start in Prague (Photo by Mike Patrick, courtesy of the John Somerville Collection)

Proud father with his daughter Chelsea (Courtesy of Lorna Brindley-Moran)

'Kelly heroes.' Celebrating with his brother and the World Cup trophy after a match-winning performance following the USA's success in 1990 (Photo by Mike Patrick, courtesy of the John Somerville Collection)

Watching the action at Coventry in 1990 (Photo by Jeff Davies)

The USA team at practice during the 1990 World Team Cup at Pardubice. *Left to right*: Rick Miller, Shawn Moran, Sam Ermolenko, John Scott, Billy Hamill and Kelly who is wearing Sam's 'roomy' leathers and sporting his 'team flymo' haircut. (Photo by Alex Alexander)

Leaving the start during his last season for Swindon in 1992 next to Morten Andersen and Justin Elkins (partly hidden) at Oxford (Photo by Mike Patrick, courtesy of the John Somerville Collection)

'I was honoured.' As captain, Kelly accepts the silver plate for the USA from series sponsors Alf Crawshaw of Coal Products Ltd after they defeated England 3–0 in the 1992 Test series (Photo by Mike Patrick)

On the outside of Tom Sephton during his comeback season in Owego, New York in 2003 (Photo by Ian Charles)

Pictured with his mechanic, Merle Craven, after winning his last Scratch Main event at Owego, New York, in 2004 (Courtesy of Jason Bonsignore)

During his enforced stay in a variety of care facilities he was able to see many old friends and reconnected with his first love Marice (Courtesy of Marice Supry)

Chelsea Moran with her father in 2010 (Courtesy of Lorna Brindley-Moran)

'He was at speedway, so I had to phone my mum to come and be with me. A friend of ours, Darrell, collected him and took him to the hospital – let's just say he had a lot to drink. So he slept, while I laboured!' Lorna recalled. 'He woke up at the crucial point, just when Chelsea was coming and he watched his daughter being born. He was a very proud dad – he used to carry her around the pits and stuff. My sister and myself had Chelsea and Ross just a day apart; it was quite fun really because we were in the hospital together. That was really nice.'

In a humorous 'Loves/Hates' Q&A that he gave to the short-lived magazine, *Speedway Now*, he said in his loves section: 'I love having to get up at 4 a.m. in the morning, after getting in at 2 a.m. from a meeting, and changing my daughter's nappies!'

With the World Championship qualifier on the horizon, Kelly stared proudly at his daughter and told the press, 'I'd love to have that gold medal to show Chelsea and be able to tell her that her dad wasn't such a bad rider after all.'

Rick Kelly, who Moran had known since his mini-bike racing days, was given the honour of being Chelsea's godfather and he spoilt her. 'Rick doted on Chelsea; there was nothing she didn't get from him. When she was young, it was Christmas time, and Rick spent a fortune on Chelsea. Me and Kelly were so jealous because he never bought us anything,' said Lorna. 'He's still got her first pair of shoes, which I think he had done in silver. He came over for the christening and somehow he managed to get a gold Rolls Royce for us to travel in for the day. It caused quite a stir at the time.'

'I just called everybody I could to find one and everybody came out to see it. In those days it was still quite something to see a gold Rolls Royce,' said Rick.

Married and now a father, there were some who believed that this change in personal circumstances had altered him, but Kelly didn't agree. 'I don't think so. Five years ago you could have got whatever odds you wanted on Kelly Moran being married and having a baby. Now it's happened and I am as proud as can be. Have I changed? Yes and no. It will make me more of a home-type person, but when I am out with the lads I'll still be the same.'

Following the painkiller controversy, Shawn had been banned from competing in all World Championship and international events, but took out an ACU licence and still raced for Belle Vue. He joined his brother in the pits at Bradford for the Overseas round. 'That's a boost right through,' said Kelly. 'We get on pretty good, Shawn and myself. We would do anything for each other. When it comes to World Championship events you have to ride that much harder. Maybe you will take someone a little wider than normal or you close the gap instead of leaving room.'

Kelly used his brother's machinery in the meeting and battled hard to get through the tough round with 7 points – his situation was made a bit more precarious by a last race duck. 'Typical Moran performance, leave it until the last and cause a sweat!' he joked. 'I would have liked a better final ride, but I missed the start and the wet conditions at that time didn't help.'

He was drawn at Abensberg, Germany, for the semi-final on 18 August, but things started to go wrong when, while travelling with his brother, he missed two ferries at Dover and arrived at the venue an hour after official practice had ended. And then his machines were late for examination and he faced being thrown out of the meeting.

'They've told me I can't ride because I was late but I spoke to Günter Sorber on the Saturday night and he told me I didn't need to be at the track until 12 o'clock.'

Meeting referee Graham Brodie became involved and eventually he was cleared to ride, but was fined £100 because his bikes were not available for inspection. He began the meeting with a last place in his opening ride, which left him with a lot to do. However, two second places followed before he found himself chasing Sam Ermolenko for the lead in his fourth race. Then, suddenly, his engine blew a hole through its crankcase with such force that he almost stopped dead and Gert Handberg ploughed into the back of him and tumbled down the straight. Characteristically, Moran ran the length of the straight to his fallen rival to offer his apologies and to check on his health. With 4 points to his name, he added a further 2 to his total but his chance of appearing in the World Final again had gone. He was disappointed but was typically philosophical and commented: 'There's always next year, I've still got time to get there again.'

His relationship with the press, especially the wider sporting press, wasn't that good. Clearly the sports pundits and critics had run out of patience with his sometimes less than professional approach and although they acknowledged his talent, they perceived that he was shamefully wasting it. No doubt still angry over the authorities' treatment of his brother, from his standpoint there was some disillusionment creeping in, as can be seen in an interview he gave to Peter Oakes. He said: 'At one time or another there has always been someone knocking what we are doing. It seems the only time anyone wants to speak or write about Kelly is if there's something bad.'

Unfortunately, that view was only underlined when Philip Rising wrote about his performance in the semi-final in Abensberg in *Speedway Star*: 'Kelly's participation was something of a sick joke. He had missed the previous day's practice, reaching Abensberg with brother Shawn late in the day. He ambled out on parade, in dirty leathers, failing to take his place with Ronnie Correy on the pick-up truck taking them to a designated spot in front of the stand. "Win or lose, the beer is always here," says Kelly and, regretfully, that will be his speedway epitaph rather than a chronicle of achievements as long as those of Nielsen. The two could not be more different.'

Normally not given to responding publicly, Kelly had his say when he was being interviewed for Aces on Video/JSD Videos. Conducted after scoring

13 points at home to Coventry, the interviewer, Darren Fletcher, observed that it was an engine failure at 'exactly the wrong time' that cost him a place in that year's World Final. He said he was disappointed with what he read and harshly likened the magazine to a tabloid.

'I had second place, no problem, and had I got another second, 8 points would have got me through. These things happen. Look at Ricky [Miller], he won the American Final, and then goes out in the Overseas. It was a bit of a disappointment.'

Politics prevented him from riding for his country in the first England v. USA Test at Bradford. The AMA showed their total disregard for the sport and their country's fortunes when they insisted that he fulfilled a rider return engagement at Costa Mesa instead of representing his nation. This time not even the diplomatic skills of John Scott could persuade them otherwise. 'I had a series of telephone calls and sent a series of faxes to Bill Boyce at the AMA to let Kelly stay in England and represent his country, but the American authorities refused to bend. They have insisted he goes home so that means we only have seven riders for the first Test at Bradford.' One can only speculate what their motivation was for such a bizarre decision.

Kelly was also disappointed to be omitted from the USA's World Team Cup side. His form was just as good as it had been the previous year and after virtually winning the trophy for them in 1990, he expected to be considered for a place.

Unfortunately, Scott had grown irritated with him, especially when he failed to arrive for the second Test at Wolverhampton seemingly without providing an adequate explanation. And with a new generation of riders coming through who were keen to make their mark on the international scene, understandably Scott chose to go with them instead. However, while the American team participated in practice at Vojens, Kelly made his point by winning the Peter Craven Memorial Championship at Belle Vue with a perfect score. The Yanks finished a distant third behind the winners, Denmark and Sweden. 'That was to show those people who decided to leave me out of the side for the World Team Cup,' he said.

In the week leading up to that meeting, Shawn returned from a racing trip in Sweden and announced his retirement. 'It just hit me all at once. I've had enough of speedway,' he told Richard Frost of the *Manchester Evening News*. And Kelly's season also ended on a painful note when Ronnie Correy clipped his back wheel and the Jelly Man was sent bouncing down the track. He was temporarily knocked unconscious from the fall and had broken his collarbone, some ribs and punctured a lung.

'It was just one of those things that happen in speedway,' he said. 'I've broken my right collarbone eight times but this is the first time I've done the left one. I thought I'd broken my shoulder blade, but it's the rib in my back and I've done two more at the front.'

# 20

# RUNNING THE RED LIGHT

'It just amazes me that he never won the World Championship, because he definitely had the talent – more than most of us.'

Dennis Sigalos

Kelly Moran didn't like to spend long periods of time by himself. Many were the occasions when Lorna would come home from an evening out to find the house lit up like a Christmas tree. When she enquired what was going on, he'd simply reply: 'Just waiting for you to come home.' On occasions he would also sleep with the light on.

He was making the long drive back from Swindon to his home in Sheffield after he'd been part of a winning team for a change. 'It was nice to hear the supporters cheering instead of booing for once,' he said. It was 1 October 1992 and the Robins had ended a shocking run of defeats by winning at home against King's Lynn. Maybe, just maybe, he thought, the club could do enough to avoid relegation.

With only the stereo, the open road and a bottle of what he shouldn't have for company, he lit a ciggy, turned up the van's heater to insulate himself from the chill of the night, and put his right foot to the metal. The red taillights of the vehicles in front of him lit up the night and helped him tick off the miles as he sped past them on the motorway. And he had a lot to think about. As usual he presented a smile to the world, and in fact he didn't dwell on his problems, preferring to lose them at the track, hide them in a joke or in the pursuit of a good time. But late at night, on his lonesome, the various setbacks and problems he was experiencing would chew on him like demons from his dungeon of despair. Therefore, he couldn't help but ponder what the future would hold.

'After the meeting, that's when you'd get thinking. There's nothing on the road and you've heard every cassette in the world. I'd light up a cigarette, start driving and start thinking about stuff,' he revealed.

Moran had been transferred from Belle Vue to Swindon in late April 1992. His brother had indicated to John Perrin that he wanted to make a return to racing. Eager to accommodate him, especially as the Aces had made a slow start to the season in the Gold Cup, to Kelly's immense disappointment he suddenly found himself shipped off to Wiltshire. In some ways it had worked out well for him because the doors of opportunity opened when John Davis was ruled out for the season with a broken leg, so there was a space for the Californian in the Robins' nest.

It all happened so fast, though. He raced at Oxford for the Aces on Wednesday, 29 April, and the following night he became a Robin and made his debut for them in a cup match against Wolverhampton. There was hardly time for him to get adjusted and this showed when he scored just 3 points. Privately, he was very disappointed to be transferred; publicly he put a positive spin on his move.

'I'm hoping a change of track will help me recover my form. This is the longest bad run I've had; it can't get worse. Of course, the position of my brother has played on my mind a bit and that's doesn't help.'

After he retired he was more open about his feelings toward the move. 'It upset me to be transferred to Swindon like that. John Perrin came up to me and said, "You're riding at Swindon tomorrow." I never understood it, as I thought I was doing okay for Belle Vue. I know I had my disagreements with John, but we got along fine. I never had any problems over contracts – once it was done, then that was it. We clashed a bit, but I thought, oh well I like the Swindon track,' he shrugged.

The truth was he probably wouldn't have been the one to make way for his brother if he hadn't made such an indifferent start to the 1992 campaign. Nonetheless, he enjoyed riding the Swindon track and, given his form over the previous years, he'd nearly always finished ahead of Davis in the league's averages.

Richard Crowley was a young journalist making his way in the media when Moran joined Swindon, a move that surprised him. 'Kelly's signing came out of the blue for me, as it was against the general grain of what appeared to be the BCA/ADT way of bringing in young talent (along the lines of Leigh Adams, Brian Karger, Peter Nahlin and Andrew Silver). The club as a whole was going through a difficult time, with a disastrous season in 1991. There seemed to be a great deal of pressure on Swindon manager Ron Byford and growing unrest on the terraces.'

For his last Aces match at Oxford he wore a new set of leathers that caught the attention because it had a Jelly Baby on the back. That set began life designed by Lorna Moran. 'I remember sitting at the table and drawing them out, the colours and everything, and said to him, "I'm not a designer," but he just said I was doing fine. We designed one pair where the American flag was wrapped around his leg, "See ya" on his bum and then you had a Jelly Baby on the back. It wasn't a reference to Chelsea, though.'

Unfortunately, the press soon jumped on him when he failed to arrive for the Robins' local derby match at Reading on 4 May, even though he had a valid reason. His van really did break down en route and its gearbox had broken – 'Thank God it was still under warranty,' he said. But there was no doubt about the tone that the press adopted when they suggested he was unprofessional and unreliable.

It was a pity that the press as a whole didn't show the same amount of enthusiasm when it came to reporting the American's good deeds, which he carried out to promote his and the sport's image. Swindon's match day programme of 30 July 1992 included a letter from Mrs J. Shields of Rotherham, near Sheffield, who was a teacher at Ecclesfield School. She sang the praises of the Californian's general style and attitude towards the pupils of Form 8E.

'They both [Kelly and Lorna] very kindly came to school to help some of my pupils with an English assignment. It involved being interviewed by the youngsters about their lives in speedway and about the sport in general. The visit was a great success,' she wrote. *Speedway Star* also printed a version of it in their letters page and it added, 'They are an extremely friendly and likeable young couple and both answered questions with honesty and a great deal of humour. He is in my view a great ambassador for his sport and his country.'

While it was obvious that some of his critics had grown frustrated with his off-track antics when he had the ability to be among the very, very best, this communication was a reminder that, despite his faults, he never meant any harm and a large part of his popularity with the public was due to his accessible persona – something that a lot of world champions could have learned from.

As a young reporter, Crowley remembered that the American instantly put him at his ease with his approachable demeanour. 'My memory of him in the pits is that he seemed pretty cheerful and usually enjoyed a laugh and a joke. Compared to some riders that I can remember feeling a little bit intimidated by during my early years of reporting, I don't ever recall any problems with Kelly. Even though he was past his best during his season at Swindon, it was still clear at times to see his undoubted talent on a bike.'

While he was in the throes of white-hot competition he was able to put his problems to the back of his mind. However, he soon realised why the club was dropping so many points – the track, which was prepared by Tom Shirra, wasn't providing them with a home track advantage of any kind.

'When the green light came on all I would think about was 5–1, 5–1; in the pits it was nothing but racing,' said Kelly. 'When I used to ride there for other clubs I loved being a visitor. But riding week-in and week-out, it wasn't a home track. A few of the other riders had gripes about it and they used to say, "Heck Jelly Man, when you used to ride for Sheffield or Belle Vue you'd kick backside here, how come you can't get to grips now it's your home track?" You would think the track staff would let you know where it was wet, but every time we felt like visitors. There were too many bumps on the track and we used to say to Tom, "You've got to do something about the first corner." And that caused arguments with Mitch, which wasn't good.'

Initially it seemed that a change of track was having a positive effect when he scored a paid 11 as he helped the Robins defeat Eastbourne. Then the next day he had an early opportunity to remind John Perrin what he was missing when he raced at Belle Vue and registered another paid 11 – this time, though, it was only him and the fast-emerging Leigh Adams who stood between the Aces and total humiliation.

Among his team-mates was long-time buddy, Shirra. He partnered him during the team's visit to Poole on 13 May and all was going well until his last programmed ride, when misfortune struck a painful blow. His chain snapped, his bike stopped dead, and poor Kelly was catapulted over the high side and he landed heavily … snap! Another broken collarbone.

It was during his recovery period when he realised just how the Swindon management were running scared, scared of finishing at the foot of the league for the second successive season. They had avoided relegation on a technicality in '91 and at the time of Moran's crash they were once again flirting with the lower regions of the First Division. Therefore, they weren't prepared to take any risks by having one of their star men on the sick list when they had the wonders of modern medical science at their disposal.

With the atmosphere at the club at an all-time low and restless, disgruntled supporters that were in need of appeasing before too many drifted away in the face of disappointing results, Kelly was sent to Brian Simpson in Ipswich to undergo laser treatment on his shattered collarbone. In his own words Simpson 'welded the bone together'. This treatment may have been beneficial to a younger rider and one who hadn't had so many collarbone injuries as the Jelly Man, but for him it wasn't a triumph.

Just twelve days after his crash, he was due to return to the track for the morning and evening clashes with Midlanders Cradley Heath, a side that was one of the pre-season favourites for honours. From the moment he arrived at Dudley Wood in the morning he experienced problems. His new leathers were too tight and they caused him pain in his shoulder once he'd pulled them on. There was no way he could ride wearing them. Instead, he used a spare set loaned to him by Cradley's young American, Greg Hancock. His suit was older, so the material wasn't as restrictive as a new one, plus he was bigger than Moran, so it was more comfortable.

He retired from his first two races, touched the tapes in his second – probably deliberately so that manager, Ron Byford, could replace him with a reserve – and then withdrew from his last race. Steve Masters was one of the reserves and he recalled a frightening drive to Mitch Shirra's place for urgent repairs before tearing off to Blunsdon for the return match.

'Mitch had gone through so many engines, six or seven, and they kept blowing up all the time. He blew the last one at Cradley so he had run out. He had to go home. We were going to clean all the bikes and stuff at his house, then drive to Swindon and he was going to get another engine off of Peter Schroek. I remember that trip from Cradley to Coventry, which was where Mitch's house was – it was the scariest road trip I've ever been on. There were three of us and Kelly was in the middle and he had a little black midget van, and Mitch was at the front. And he'd just be overtaking on bends, blind corners and stuff, and they'd indicate to say that it was okay to overtake, but it was frightening.'

Still wearing Hancock's leathers and looking far from comfortable, Moran scored 1 point before having to withdraw after just two outings in the evening match – Cradley won both encounters. At the conclusion of the meeting he emerged quietly from the back of the pits and looked drawn and pale. With his right arm and shoulder wrapped up tightly in a sling, it was clear that riding with a broken collarbone at the age of thirty-one was a lot tougher than when he did so at twenty-one – and it showed on his strained face. Needless to say his 'comeback was very premature and he told the author how the Robins' management had pressured the Californian to ride. It was obvious even to his harshest critics that he shouldn't have been racing.

Furthermore, Kelly wasn't as fit as he should have been. The highlife off the track was starting to take its toll on him and his body was warning him that he couldn't continue with that lifestyle if he wanted to retain good health in the future.

'He was ill and he was bleeding out of his back passage,' said Lorna. 'He had tests and stuff and he had liver damage at that point. That was the first time that it was identified that his liver was damaged. He wasn't poorly, but he could see the signs, things happening, but he didn't take it seriously because he was still young, wasn't he? He was still a boy. If he had stopped then he would have been fine. But he said that he couldn't stop.'

Kelly made a return and started to perform like he should. He scored a 15-point maximum at Arena Essex as the Robins won a rare victory on the road and there was a glimmer of hope that they could climb out of the lower reaches of the league table. He also passed Peter Nahlin on the back straight at Swindon in a last heat decider to give Swindon a draw against Eastbourne and finished third in the Super Pink Pizza Classic individual. However, such was his poor start to the 1992 season that he found himself at reserve for the first time since he arrived in England in 1978. It was good news for the Robins team to have such an experienced rider in that position, but not so good for a rider who had been just five rides away from the World Final the previous year.

His upturn in form was helped by having ex-Shawn McConnell and Ronnie Correy mechanic, Rod Young, twirling the spanners for him. He lived locally and the American would pick him up at a motorway junction for home matches and continue to the track.

Moran had another opportunity to remind Perrin and the Aces what they had lost when he produced a spectacular display to top score with 15 – the sibling rivalry was still evident as he passed Shooey for a win in one race – but he couldn't prevent his side from losing the encounter, 43–47. Team manager, Ron Byford, criticised his riders after the defeat but Moran was exempt from a roasting and he described him as 'superb'.

However, he continued to pay no heed to his health scare. At Blunsdon it was said that he was one of the few who marched into Ted Nelson's office to help himself to the Hine cognac bottle that was hidden in his drawer. His dependency was also demonstrated to Peter Collins' wife, Angela. She had always found Kelly to be utterly charming and a complete gentleman. She'd got to know Lorna well while her husband was racing for Belle Vue and she met her in Sheffield in order to attend a concert together with a few friends. They returned to discover that Kelly was missing. Later she saw a dishevelled man, wearing a cap, shuffling along the street clutching a bottle, who resembled the British cartoon strip character, Andy Capp. She was stunned to learn that it was her charmer, Mr Moran.

Martin Morley recounted an earlier incident where he was inexplicably left to his own devices in the Pinegrove Country Club and Martin was left wondering what the hell had happened to his friend. 'I used to go and play snooker with him. One day, he just buggered off and left me there. He went to change all his German money and there was a pub next door or something, well that was it – straight in! He left me stranded. Overall we did have a bloody good laugh, though.'

This lifestyle was putting a huge strain on his marriage and with a young child to consider as well, the extra pressure of his irresponsible behaviour only added to the tensions. Nonetheless, Kelly's feelings for Lorna remained strong and he loved his family, so he tried to mend his ways.

His wife recalled: 'I said to him, "I can't carry on like this; it's just ridiculous with a small child. I don't want people making fun of her at school over her dad." So he went to AA [Alcoholics Anonymous] and I went with him. He went in one room and the family went in the other. When it was over he went straight into the bloody pub! What the hell was the point of that? Fair enough he went to a couple, but he only went for me. He did it for me because he loved me. He didn't do it for himself and that was his downfall.'

'I was splitting up with Lorna. It was one of those things,' he said with his typical philosophical attitude and then acknowledged: 'I think it was inevitable what was going to happen in my personal life. It was going to more or less happen and it did happen.'

Journalist John Chaplin, who had his own battles with the demon drink, recognised the signs very early and also witnessed the strain that Moran's drinking was having on his marriage. 'I cannot recall how or why we were first in touch, but I do remember Lorna's distress because Kelly's drinking appeared to be out of control. Over a period there were many calls, some of them tearful because of Kelly's problem and her despair at trying to cope with the effects on their relationship. I tried to act as a sounding board for her to pour out her feelings. I hoped, in some way, I could be a help to her and offer her some sort of comfort because, after a long personal battle, I was a recovering alcoholic and understood what she was going through. I have no way of knowing if I succeeded in easing her obvious pain.'

'The decision to separate was my decision because I couldn't cope with his drinking, especially with a young child as well,' Lorna said. 'In the end I loved him; I loved him to bits, but a care love, not an "in love". I was always caring for him, looking out for him, always, in case he opened his mouth and somebody punched him. I think he thought that I'd be there forever and put up with everything. In the end, what I said to myself was, can I see myself in ten years' time with the same person, in the same boat and feeling like I feel? The answer was: no, I can't. He said that he couldn't change and that he wouldn't be able to stop, so that was my decision and I stuck at it. I did love him. I was a little confused because I was thinking, shall I or shan't I, so it wasn't a clear cut split. We didn't argue or anything like that, it was purely because he drank and I couldn't keep up with the aftermath of it all. And that was it, that was my decision and he totally understood it. The split put him off everything, though.'

His form began to drop and according to Ron Byford he found a kindred spirit in Mitch Shirra. 'Him and Mitch were going about together, and they were off drinking and what have you. If I had my way I would have taken the bike away from Kelly when it came to repairs and maintenance and given it to somebody else to deal with, because he'd go away from the track after the meeting and he'd come back with the bike in the same bloody state as he left it the week before! Him and Mitch went through this period where I don't think that they were that bothered. I was pleased to sign Kelly but I did have trouble trying to motivate him.'

Young had left and he was without a regular mechanic and resorted to asking the author to help him out one night. 'You're helping me in the pits tonight,' he announced. Talk about the blind leading the blind! Having told him from the outset that the most I could do was clean, the club arranged for someone else to help Kelly with the basics of changing the rear wheel, oil, chain, clutch, etc., but I wasn't off the hook and I ended up doing a lot of cleaning! Cleaning wheel rims, brushing off the shale, fetching, carrying and mastering the refuelling process and handing tools to this chap whose name I never discovered, while Kelly did what he always did – ride the bike and watch on from his seat in the pits as he made observations about our mechanical abilities, some amusing, some critical. 'Don't worry guys,' he grinned, 'I'm not out again for another three races.' The match was against Oxford and Hans Nielsen got hot and bothered over an exclusion – something that Kelly found amusing. He scored 7 points that night. It was very interesting, but not a career move.

Understandably, given his sorrow over the breakdown of his marriage, he had lost his drive and motivation. 'It really hit home. I lost all interest,' he said. Speedway scribe, Bob Radford, met him at Malcolm Holloway's pub, The Dolphin, in Swindon where he was staying and found the Jelly Man to be far from his usual happy self. 'He came in and I said to him, "Would you like a drink?" and other than, "A double scotch please, Bob," that was about all I got out of him. He was visibly down, visibly at the end of his racing career and that was a rather sad way to see him for the last time.'

However, in the midst of this turmoil he agreed to pull on his country's colours again and ride in the England v. USA Test series. Having ruled himself out of international racing, the ever persuasive John Scott called and convinced him to represent his nation once more. Even in his enthusiasm to pull on the Stars 'n' Stripes again there was a distinct trace of disillusionment. 'We had a long chat and I agreed to change my mind, partly because they asked me and partly because all the meetings are here in England so there's no international travel involved. I've had enough of all that.'

Partnered with his former Aces' team-mate, Bobby Ott, he scored a paid 12 points in the opening match which America won, but didn't fare so well in the second match at Wolves where he failed to score. Then, for the third and final Test, he was honoured to be made captain of the team at Swindon. Modestly he said that he didn't think he deserved it and it was a personal highlight in his final year of racing. 'I don't know how it came about. I guess it was because I was riding for Swindon. But yeah, it was nice to go up and receive the silver plate for winning the Test series, it was neat.'

His club, though, were desperate for him and his fellow riders to re-discover their form and stave off relegation. Their supporters were restless and concerned that they would have to face the embarrassment of being relegated for the second consecutive year – and this time there would be no escape. They vented their anger at Byford who, as he lived locally, found it quite difficult to deal with. Their victories over King's Lynn and Oxford had given the club a glimmer of hope, but they had to win their last home fixture of the season against Poole on 15 October. Four days before this important match, Kelly and Shirra had made guest appearances for Coventry at Arena Essex and helped the Bees to a win. Moran was in brilliant form scoring a paid 15 and Shirra also finished with 9. At the end of the night he turned to his Kiwi friend and said of his work on their engines, 'I wish you found that earlier in the season.'

This gave Swindon and Byford renewed hope for the Poole match. He arranged for Kelly to use Leigh Adams' workshop to prepare his bike for this vital fixture. Already a very professional racer, Adams was a young rider who had taken over the number one race jacket at Swindon and was taken aback by his lack of mechanical expertise. 'He stripped down an engine and seemed to be okay so I left him to it and went into the house. About an hour later, having rebuilt the engine, he came in, had a glass of water, then after a minute or two he produced this carburettor part from his pocket and asked, "Do you know where this goes?"'

'I'm not Mr Technology,' Kelly defended when speaking to *Cycle News*. 'When I first started I would strip down an engine and I'd put it back together and I always had extra parts left over. To me, that just meant there was excess weight in there!'

With everything prepared and feeling confident on the motor that Shirra had built, which had served him so well at Arena, he left for Blunsdon to compete in one of the most important meetings in the club's history. After two races the scores were level when Moran was bumped off to race with Jimmy Nilsen in the third heat. The tapes went up and, to the delight of the home supporters, the Robins pairing led the way for a 5–1 … only for disaster to strike. Kelly's engine seized solid.

For the rest of the night he used Adams' spare bike. The Australian was bigger and taller than Kelly and he was famed for his smooth, armchair-like style, as opposed to the American's more spectacular, drop-handlebar approach. At 100 per cent motivated and confident, Moran's ability would usually have been enough to score well but he could only manage 3 and Swindon lost and were condemned for the drop. Afterwards he took to the radio microphone and apologised to the bitterly disappointed fans. He said that he found it hard to believe that Swindon wouldn't be running in the top division in 1993. 'I was just too light for the bike. I knew I had the power to catch riders but I was just not heavy enough to put weight on the back wheel to pick up grip to get by.'

His last speedway meeting was at Bradford on Saturday, 17 October, where Swindon lost 50–40 – he scored 2. It was the end of an era for the Wiltshire club and also the end of the road for Kelly Moran. There was no big announcement, no fanfare, a farewell meeting or anything like that. British speedway was going through one of its many catastrophes and a new rigid pay structure was brought in for the following season. When the American heard of what the rates were likely to be he laughed, 'I'm not racing for that sort of money.'

He remained in England for the rest of the year, finalising a few things with his wife. Rick Kelly came over from California to spend Christmas with them and he took Kelly back with him. 'It was sad,' Lorna admitted. 'He just went home. I never stopped loving him but I fell out of love with him. Rick was here at the time and it wasn't long after Christmas they left. We did everything, the divorce, by post.

'He used to phone up quite often and send birthday cards and presents. He didn't forget Chelsea, put it that way. I tell you what he did, and I respected him for doing this, he didn't support me financially with money, but what he did was he signed the house over to me and Chelsea. He didn't just leave us in the lurch and he didn't demand half of the house or half of this and that, he just signed the house over and I carried on with the mortgage.'

Although he had experienced the worst season of his British career, he still showed some of the talent that made him such a huge star. At thirty-two, there was still some racing left in him, or so it was thought. When it became clear that he wasn't coming back to race in Britain, many expected him to ride on the southern Californian circuit again – but he didn't. Midway through the '93 season there was a report that Oxford had considered approaching him, but that turned out to be press speculation. 'I never heard anything from them,' he said. His brother continued to race for Belle Vue and helped them to a league championship, but for the Jelly Man it was over.

'My heart wasn't in it and if your heart's not in it it's no good carrying on. Mine wasn't in it. Why waste the promoter's time, the sponsors' time and the fans' time? It wasn't a matter of quitting. I don't know, possibly it was something to do with my break-up. I just lost all interest.'

Steve Masters noted that the sport's policies were not sitting well with him. 'Kelly said to me, "When the politics get on top of you, it's time to call it a day."' On another occasion before a meeting at Reading he turned to the author and observed, 'Here we go again, drugs and alcohol test. I can tell you now that it's going to be me and Mitch that's picked, it always is, and it's supposed to be random.' In the press he complained: 'At every World Championship event I know I'm going to be tested. They don't need to draw names out of a hat! Sometimes I feel like saying, "What did you do, have my name 100 times in that hat!" I can get blotto when I'm not racing but I'm okay the next day and I'll not fail an alcohol test.'

It has been suggested that his earlier than expected demise was partly due to the sport's drug testing laws that were introduced around 1987, which did catch a few of the sport's big names. He'd smoke cannabis but this was one of the banned substances. Therefore, because it still shows up in your system a few days after taking it, he could no longer have a puff with a meeting on the horizon. So he drank instead; and the demon alcohol slowly began to grab a hold of him and before he knew it, or would admit to it, he had developed a problem.

His wife believed that, although the party attitude was ingrained from the often wild atmosphere of Californian speedway, it was in Britain, where pub culture was part of the UK's way of life, that his dependency got worse.

'I think it was definitely over here where it happened. When we were in America we didn't used to go to bars, it was always people's houses – you don't tend to go in bars. Over there it was okay, he'd get a buzz and things but he wouldn't go too overboard while we were there. It was when he was here, after race meetings, he'd get so tanked up because everybody was his best friend, everybody would buy him hard drinks and I'd be there glaring at everybody. I'm sure they used to hate me, but I had to take him home that night. It was part of his whole sportsman's job, but I do think it got on top of him and it took over. It wasn't just his drinking, it was his smoking too. He used to smoke cigarettes as well and it was all part of it. Smoking was never dwelled upon, no one ever asked him to quit that, it was never an issue – never. The thing is, he's always had his own mind. I don't think he wanted to stop drinking.'

Nonetheless, Ron Preston remembered the early days of speedway on the West Coast, especially in 1976–77 when a young Moran was starting to make his mark on the scene. 'Danny Becker, Ed Williams, all those guys, they took Kelly to Irwindale, a track that was a little bit north and they used to race on Thursday nights. There was a tavern, Irwindale Inn, it was called, and Kelly was sleeping in the back door, smoking weed and chasing girls at sixteen years old and then going home with whoever. How could you do anything but go off a cliff when you started at that age?'

As each generation of racers and teams rides into the misty shroud of history, it is the champions whose achievements shout the loudest from our past that stand out. But there is a select group of racers that didn't win the same amount of medals or trophies, whose talents and charisma also echo from speedway's history, and their notoriety can reverberate just as loudly.

Kelly's professional speedway career ended when he was thirty-two, yet he is one of the few from our sport whose reputation not only shines through speedway's past, but can also send a shaft of light among the wider motorcycle racing world and beyond – more so than most World Champions. If talent alone was enough, he should have achieved more than he did, especially during the height of his fame when he was heavily backed by STP and others.

'If only he could have been more serious he could have been World Champion, probably more than once, and his whole lifestyle might have been different and he could have been alive today,' said Bob Dugard.

'His downside when it came to becoming a champion was that he was too generous, he would always put everyone else ahead of himself,' Bruce Penhall assessed. 'You can't be; you've got to be ruthless at times. If you allow them an inch, they're going to take a mile. And then you're going to come out on the wrong end of the stick every time. He was truly one of a kind, though.'

'It would be fair to say that Kelly had the potential to be World Champion,' Dave Lanning added. 'If he had applied himself and never had that happy-go-lucky, scatty attitude, the most consummate party animal in the history of speedway, he could have won the World Championship, probably more than once. He was just totally and wonderfully irresponsible.'

During 1988 the author sat with him in the Panorama Room at Owlerton Stadium when he responded to an observation that he was as good, if not better, than the Danes that were ruling the scene at that point. 'You've got to remember, they haven't really had the injuries like I've had, or some of the guys have. It can knock you back,' he pointed out.

Two years after he retired, the one-off World Final was scrapped in favour of a Grand Prix-style championship. When it was first mooted in the early '90s, his reaction was a nonchalant one and he merely contemplated the financial reward for extra meetings and shrugged, 'More money.' These days it's a season-long competition and some feel that such a tournament would have been more suited to him than having to be perfect on one night.

'I guess it would be like ten World Finals,' he pondered. 'I would have liked to have tried it; it would have been neat to race in Cardiff's Millennium Stadium and stuff like that. The GP? Well, yeah, I guess it would have been kind of interesting.'

Ivan Mauger and Barry Briggs have both stated that he 'wasted' his talent, which is a strong statement to make, yet it is one that illustrates their frustration as well as their admiration.

'I know people say that and I think they expected more of me,' he responded in 2006. 'Obviously I would have loved to have won the World Championship, but heck, I was fourth three times. A lot of riders never get to compete for the World title. But I could never be ultra-professional like some of those riders were, that's not me, and to be like that would have driven me bonkers!'

# 21

# DIVINE INTERVENTION

'I'm just a stray on this broken down highway.'

Tony Clarkin

Many racers find it difficult to adjust when they finally retire. For riders like Kelly Moran, who had been riding a motorcycle from an early age – at the expense of an education – when it finally comes to an end it's extremely tough to get used to a normal, mundane 9–5 existence. Usually the financial rewards in Civvy Street are not nearly as good as they're used to and then they have to deal with the fact that they're an Ordinary Joe. Being an ex-speedway racer doesn't have the same appeal as a current racer; and as each year passes by, if you're not involved with the sport on the other side of the fence, your star soon loses its shine – usually eclipsed by the glare radiating from the new riders. Therefore, adulation disappears, your popularity fades and you're yesterday's hero.

For Moran, he'd also left his family behind in England and had to deal with that break-up and being apart from his daughter. His brother continued before he too would retire from the sport in mid-1994, yet he remained in England with his partner. While Kelly may have welcomed a break from the sometimes crazy routine of dashing off here, there and overseas for a race, his new life meant that he had more downtime to think.

No matter how good you are, falls in motorcycle racing are part of the business. Therefore, broken bones are a by-product of that risk. Away from racing, tumbles are less frequent and the threat of sustaining injuries is greatly diminished. Given the number of times he'd smashed his collarbone alone, that was one side of racing that he wasn't going to miss.

As well as living with Rick Kelly, he also took a job in his business as a roofing contractor. Unfortunately, it was during a visit to carry out some work at a ranch when his propensity for accidents struck again.

'We were going to a big ranch in Valley Central. There was a big arch with the name of the ranch underneath,' Rick recalled. 'We have these lift trucks and the boom wouldn't go underneath. So Kelly jumped up on the arch to hold the sign up. Well, the guy pulled through and Kelly figured he was going to stop so he jumped down, but he didn't stop – and he broke his femur. That was about the only job he had after he quit racing. Kelly had broken so many bones. That's why he said he drank because he was in so much pain.'

Kelly's version was slightly different, though: 'I fell off the roof, three storeys up, and broke my right femur and right ankle. They were even considering calling out the helicopter ambulance for me. If I was racing at least I could roll a little bit but when you drop from three storeys up there's not much you can do about it.'

It was a bad break and he spent a long time in hospital recovering. When he got out he returned to Rick's house near San Diego. Since Moran's death, Rick Kelly's image has been tarnished somewhat and he's become a controversial figure in the former racer's life. However, they go back a long way to his mini-bike days and Lorna Moran recalled that, as they both drank, the combination of alcoholic stimulant and sharing the same space for years on end would often cause friction and ignite a barrage of harsh words – or worse.

'They fed off each other. They were drinking all the time. The thing was, Kelly wasn't earning any money, Rick provided all the food and everything. Even though they both drank, he was there for him. Rick and Kelly were always having fights and then they were the best of friends the next day. When you live with somebody 24/7, both drinking and the other one is not earning any money, they must have got on each other's nerves. One time when I was there they started arguing and I left them to it. When it was over I came out of the kitchen and said, "Right, what shall we have for dinner?" because they were friends again. I've known him a lot of years and he did welcome him into his home, and he lived there for many years and never worked.'

'He was like a little brother to me, that's what he was,' said Rick. 'We fought like brothers and one of his friends accused me of abusing him, but they didn't understand what he could be like and was like with me! We had some good times, though. I used to arrange limos to go from the races to here. Everybody called me Kelly and him Little Kelly. I painted his first helmet when he first raced at Irwindale, because I used to work for Crown Helmets. We sponsored Rick Woods. I was involved with speedway back then.'

Lorna and Chelsea would fly over to see him at Rick's and one visit in particular came to mind. 'We bought this huge Christmas tree but we had to cut it to get it into the room! We went to Disney Land and Chelsea had her eighth birthday there. When she was about one, he bought her a little baby walker and she just zoomed all over the house in this walker. Rick couldn't wait to get home at night to see her – he absolutely adored her. A lot of people have a lot of bad things to say about him, but he wasn't that bad. He was a really good friend and he was there for Kelly. We thought a lot of him and he's Chelsea's godparent. And he never forgets her.'

Moran tested his friend's patience on a number of occasions. He used to refer to himself as a 'house mouse' and while the cat was away, this particular mouse would take every opportunity he could to play.

'The minute I would leave for the airport he'd start arranging parties. He used to call people and say, "Rick's leaving on Friday for ten days," and he'd invite everyone for a party. One time I got back early and there were all these people at my house. I'd come home from work one day and there was all these Jehovah's Witnesses sat around my table. Kids used to sell magazine subscriptions and he'd sign me up for newspapers and magazines that I didn't want. He'd invite anyone in. Then when I was away he'd call me asking where the booze was and I used to tell him it was locked up and he'd call me a son of a bitch. He'd take care of the dogs, though.

'I went to Costa Rica and I had to get someone to stay and babysit him. Her name was Rose. Well, he invited all the neighbours over to have a barbecue and the poor woman ended up doing everything because he got drunk and passed out. The minute I would leave for the airport – I'd leave some cash for day-to-day things – he'd start arranging parties.'

The parties provided a welcome distraction from the fact that he missed his family and his old way of life. But the more time passed, the harder it became. So he'd pick up the phone to talk with old friends. 'He'd call England, Australia, all over and I had a bill for $900,' Rick revealed. 'So I put a block on international calls, but somehow he got around that. So I had to change my plan to include international calls. When I'd get home from work in the evening he'd be passed out, and then he'd be up at three in the morning making all these international calls. He'd be on the phone for hours.'

Ron Preston noticed that his drinking was out of control when he talked a company he was working for into hiring a suite for a flat track race at the Del Mar Fairgrounds in 1997. 'I invited Rick Kelly because we used to do a lot of business together then and said, "It's your choice whether you tell Kelly about it or not. If he comes I'm going to be having customers so Kelly can't be acting like Kelly, so it's probably best not to tell him." Race day came and I go into the suite and there's Rick and Kelly Moran! I said to Rick, "He's your responsibility." The next thing I turn around and Rick's gone but there's Kelly nursing a keg – sucking on like a hose that's coming out of it!

'Then he ran into Danny Becker and they started hugging each other like they were long-lost friends. They were like Danny DeVito and Arnold Schwarzenegger in that movie, *Twins* – those two together was a nightmare. The next thing I knew, someone came and got me and said, "Hey, there's a guy in the bar, you said you know him," and it was Kelly and he was totally shit-faced. We carried him back to the suite and immediately he starts telling the chick of one of my business friends that she's got nice titties! And this guy said to me, "I know she's nice, but he can't be saying that stuff – that's not cool." Then he passed out so they just parked him in the corner and left him there.'

On 18 October 1999, Tom Moran died. He'd been married to Kay Rutherford, who was known as the publicist for San Bernardino Speedway. Sadly, she passed away before Tom, following a difficult battle with cancer. Needless to say Kelly was upset by these events and it was felt that a trip to England to see his family for Christmas would be a good tonic for him. Rick's neighbour, who had previously worked with the movie mogul, Howard Hughes, in his airline business, arranged a VIP ticket for him on TWA. Rick took him to the airport, gave him some cash and waved him a fond farewell.

Strangely, Moran's luggage arrived at Heathrow Airport but he didn't – in fact, he was nowhere to be found. When flight after flight came in and no Kelly, Lorna and her family became concerned. After a whole day had passed without any word, understandably this sparked a flurry of worried transatlantic phone calls.

'I didn't know what happened, but he missed his connecting flight and the next thing you know is we have to find him. Lorna and her mum and dad were looking for him, and were calling all the hospitals – no Kelly. And because I was the last person to see him when he boarded the plane, I had the police here, Interpol and the FBI – it was insane!' laughed Rick.

'He was missing for three days – we called it "Clueless in St Louis",' continued Rick. 'St Louis was his connecting flight to London. It was LA to St Louis and then to London. He got hammered or something while he was in first class, so they got him a hotel in St Louis because he was that bad and then he missed his plane. Finally he called me and I had to pay for his ticket from St Louis back to here. He never made it to London. He must have had a good time for three days because he was broke! All the neighbours were going, "Oh my God, he's flying under this guy's first class credentials!" So he never made it to England for Christmas.'

Kelly did make it for Christmas 2000 though and stayed with Dorothy Brindley, Lorna's mother. It was while he was in the UK that he spoke to Peter Oakes of *Speedway Star* magazine and said: 'We are all good friends, it's not what you all read about with divorces. I just took all my clothes and left quietly and that was that. But it affected me, probably more than I knew at the time. They still come over to America and stop with me at San Diego. That's a bitter divorce, is it? I'm able to see my little girl, there's no visitation type of stuff, I can come and go as I please more or less. Obviously I'd phone ahead and say I'm flying over for so many days and I can see her.'

'Even though we were divorced, we'd still talk on the phone, we never fell out or anything like that,' Lorna agreed. 'He used to give me advice on boyfriends, that's how bizarre it got – I used to say, "Kelly, you can't do that!" He always used to call me Lorn ... we did laugh and we'd be on the phone for hours talking. We kept good friends.'

But it wasn't like it was before. While he continued to be the happy-go-lucky little fella that he always was, with his career at an end, combined with a reputation that wasn't always flattering, he was often barred from the sport that he graced with such flair for so many years. Sometimes he would be refused entry unless he paid like everyone else and could be found left outside the pit gate – a forgotten hero. Without his bike and crash helmet, his popularity with speedway's administrators had fallen almost to the point of exclusion. The massive role he played in US speedway's success mattered little at that point.

His frustrations, disappointment and even anger would manifest itself in his wild ways and he found an exit strategy in the bottom of a bottle. 'It was my escape,' he said later. 'Although my marriage ended amicably, I missed Chelsea and alcohol was my escape. It never quite makes it better, but you continue thinking that it will.'

Ron Preston had finally done it. He'd managed to get the Jelly Man to agree to do something about kicking his drinking habit. It had taken a lot of persuasion, patience and determination to get him to see that he couldn't continue abusing his body in that way.

'My father had died and his wife – it was a tough time. I was bad at that point. I just felt like I was spiralling, not so much out of control, but I felt that I was in dire straits,' Kelly said. 'Only Ron Preston and Rick Kelly knew how bad I really was during the '90s. I wouldn't wake up wanting a drink because I always felt so rough, but, as I said, it was my escape. I was constantly in a drunken stupor, just killing myself daily, and I realised that I needed to change that.

'But what really convinced me to try and do something about it was when I thought about my daughter. I just thought about the day when she might get married. I didn't want her to get married and not be able to have her daddy there. The thought of not being able to give her away – I hate that expression – really made me decide to do something about it.

'I can't remember some of the things that I've done but I do know that I upset some people and you don't want to lose your family,' he said regretfully. 'I'd like to think that you can make new friends every day, but you can't get a new family. I was in such a self-denial thing, but by the time that I realised that, I'd lost my marriage. So I remembered this place that Ronnie told me about and I thought I'd give it a try.'

Nikki Sixx, the founder member and bass player with that uber-excessive '80s rock band, Motley Crue, once said, 'When you can't climb out of a hole, you crouch down and call it home.' Moran's home was the bottle and he'd used that as his 'escape' from his troubles. He told *Cycle News*, 'By the time I realised it, I'd lost my family.'

It is said that someone with an addiction has to hit the very rock bottom before they'll seriously do something about it. Whether he had reached that stage or not, only time would tell, but having the courage to admit that he needed help was a big step towards getting his act together.

This would be the beginning, his first step on what would be a long road of rehabilitation to not only sobriety but also a healthier lifestyle. However, he didn't have the finances for a stay in a fancy clinic like the Betty Ford one in Beverly Hills where famous people go for treatment, so it would have to be somewhere less prominent and more spiritual. A place, in fact, that Preston felt would not only be productive but also instructive for him because peace for the soul is just as important as a healthy body.

It was 2002 and they were in New Creations, El Centro, in Imperial Valley and they were gathered in Pastor Walter Colace's office. New Creations' mission statement read: 'The goal of Christ Community Church is to glorify God through making disciples.' Despite the good intentions from all involved, and it really did appear that Moran was sincere in his wish to dry out, it soon became apparent that this wasn't going to be easy and he wasn't ready for his faith to be tested.

Colace, who had been through his own personal demons, looked at Kelly sitting across from him and asked: 'Kelly, do you know who God is?'

'Yeah, me and the Big Guy have a real good understanding.'

The expression on Colace's face was such that Ronnie had to disguise his grin. 'Ahh, okay, what do you mean by that?'

'Well, he knows who I am and I know who he is – we have a good understanding.'

Sensing some opposition to the idea, he added: 'You've gotta realise this rehab is a volunteer thing, you're not going to jail, you're here because you want to be here and you want to get help.'

'Yeah, I understand,' Moran replied.

Seemingly he was set to make a fresh start when Preston left him, but he immediately felt uncomfortable. He called Ronnie and said, 'You've gotta come and get me, I can't stay here.' Moran may not have realised how important this was, but Preston did, so he didn't go and retrieve him and hoped that he would at least give it a chance because it had taken a long time to get him there and even longer to admit that he had a problem. Unfortunately, not only was he stubborn, he was determined too and he'd made up his mind that he wasn't staying and left.

Colace warned him that if he walked out he couldn't go back. This didn't worry the little Californian. With his bag of belongings he hit the road. 'The next thing you know he's called Scott Autrey and told him I've got him in a cult,' Ron chuckled.

'He called me up and the first thing he said was, "Scotty, Ronnie's got me in a cult! I'm in this treatment centre in the middle of nowhere, he's got me in a cult. They're like Biblical fanatics man!" I said, "Kelly, just go back, you'll be done with it in a few weeks."'

There was no persuading him, though, and he eventually arrived in the border town of Calexico and needed a ride. Rehab, it seemed, wasn't going to work after all. And once again it was Ron Preston who had to sort something out for him.

'Kelly called me and goes, "Hey I got a ride to a Greyhound Station in Calexico." This is like four and a half hours from Huntington Beach and two and a half hours from San Marcos and on the Mexican border. So he's standing at the Greyhound Station and he tells me where he is. So I called this friend of mine who lived in San Diego, George Williams. "Hey George, you don't know anybody in Calexico do you, who can pick up Kelly?" This is when I knew that God was involved. He asked: "Where is he in Calexico, I'm right by the border right now? I'm right in front of the theatre." I replied, "Turn around, you see the Greyhound Station, there's Kelly right there." And he said: "Kelly's the only white guy and he's sitting on his bag with everything he owns in it."'

George turned his truck around and drove over to where Moran was, rolled to a stop, wound down the window and said, 'Hey Kelly, what are you doin', man?'

'Hey George, I need a ride.'

'Where d'ya wanna go?'

'Back to San Marcos.'

'It ain't going to happen today, but get in with me, I'm taking this barbecue to a men's rehab.'

George had volunteered and was helping these people set up a barbecue at this centre. When they arrived, Kelly helped out and engaged in conversation with the people there, one person in particular.

'The pastor of this rehab centre came up to Kelly and started talking to him,' said Preston. 'He convinced him that he needed to go with him, said something like, "You need to come with us, you'll like it up here." Within an hour of talking to this guy, Kelly got into his van and went to Calipatria and stayed at that guy's rehab for six months.'

The establishment was called Victory Outreach and it's part of a larger international organisation that has spread to twenty-eight countries. Part of its mission statement said it's 'dedicated to instilling within men the qualities that transform them into Godly men needed today in the home, community, church …' and further stated it was 'committed to equipping and training men from all walks of life from all over the world to respond to the call of God.'

'It wasn't a rehab centre, it was a men's Christian home,' Kelly pointed out. 'You could check in for six months or a year, and I decided to go for six months. It was free and you could leave whenever you wanted to, it wasn't a prison or anything like that.'

He dwelled in a home across the street from its church and it was managed by pastors – in particular Joe, whom Kelly would speak fondly about. This place didn't just cater for people suffering from the effects of alcohol abuse, it also assisted those who had issues with substance misuse as well. Consequently, Moran discovered that keeping company with addicts of all kinds meant that he had to respect their needs and issues and adjust his own behaviour accordingly, just as they had to for him. Of course, being in a house of God also required a certain cordial behaviour that was expected at all times.

'When I got there I knew I had to dry out and I remember thinking: okay, well at least I'll be able to have a smoke. But that wasn't allowed either! They said, "No Kelly, no smoking." So I went what they called 'cold turkey' and that was very hard. It wasn't too much of a problem for me, I wasn't seeing pink elephants or anything like that, it wasn't the alcohol withdrawal, it was not being able to smoke which was my biggest problem. There was no swearing either. And when I came out and heard someone swear I was quite surprised. It's funny how you get used to things.'

This meant that smoking cannabis was also outlawed, which was an issue for him because, apart from it being a drug, he smoked it to help ease the aches and pains in his back that were a legacy from his crash in 1978. Attitudes toward the medicinal properties of cannabis have been more positive in recent years, with strains allowed to be used legally for certain conditions like multiple sclerosis – although this law varies from country to country. However, nicotine found in cigarettes is particularly addictive and makes smoking notoriously hard to give up. Combined with having to deal with the shakes, the hot and cold sweats and other symptoms associated with alcohol withdrawal, it's not surprising he absconded on a couple of occasions. The important thing was that he went back.

'When you returned you lost all your privileges and there weren't many privileges anyway!' he laughed. 'There were up to six men in a room and three double-bunk beds – it was pretty basic. There was only myself and two other guys while I was there. We were given three minutes in the shower before your time was up. Well after a day working outside in the hot weather that we get in California, I would jump into the shower to cool off. But because our water supply comes from the Colorado River it would take a while for the really cold water to come through the shower – and then just when you were getting the benefit of it I would hear someone say, "Okay Kelly, time's up!"

'During the day we would do community work. For example, we would hand out leaflets about the Church or help clean up or something. Sometimes, someone would want a back garden cleared that hasn't been touched for five years or something like that and I would do that. They would pay you in cheque only, not cash, because if you had cash you might be tempted to spend it on things you shouldn't.'

It would be accurate to say that Kelly was a Christian, although his profession and his lifestyle meant that perhaps you wouldn't describe him as a practising Christian. Nonetheless, given the aims of the organisation where he was located, he was afforded an opportunity to delve into the contents of the Bible like he never had previously. And, like many, he found it instructive.

'I found the teachings of the Bible very interesting,' he said. 'I never realised how interesting it was. I haven't read it all but I carry a copy around with me. So there was a lot for me to learn. I think Psalms is my favourite so far, I find that very interesting.'

Perhaps he found the following passage from Psalms 18 particularly applicable: 'He sent from above, took me, he drew me out of many waters. He delivered me from my strong enemy.'

Of course, he wasn't the first, or the last, person to find strength from the Lord in order to deal with his personal demons and get his life back on track. Nevertheless, he was eager to distance himself from that group describing themselves as 'born again Christians', who often repeatedly preach from the scriptures and cast plenty of aspersions on those who don't subscribe to their views.

'I'm not a Bible basher or a finger-pointer, or anything like that. If people want to talk to me about it, then that's fine – I'm happy to do that. But if they don't then that's cool too, you know.'

It has been said that he was a bit shy about his faith but, as Scott Autrey observed, he certainly studied it in some depth during his remaining years. 'They had a certain set time for Bible study and Kelly probably knew more about the Bible when he passed away than I will in the rest of my life.'

'It was the best thing I ever did for myself,' Kelly believed. 'What the home did was to teach you to focus through the power of prayer and the Bible. It was a religious house but as long as you were of a Christian religion it didn't matter whether you were a Catholic, Methodist or whatever, you were allowed in. I met a lot of different people; people I didn't think would be Christians and they were all very nice and generous. Most of the guys in there were of Hispanic origin and they all liked the very polite, little white guy – which was nice. None of them had heard of speedway racing and that was good for me because it helped me to focus.'

After six months, he emerged clean and sober into an uncertain world. He was then faced with a dilemma that a lot of addicts are faced with – where to go and what to do next? To maintain his sobriety he had to avoid temptation where he could, which meant not frequenting the same places and spending time with the same old faces. He needed a new start and a new direction. Luckily, Ron Preston had a solution.

His friend, Rick Bradford, had agreed to give him a place to stay and a job on his farm. Compared to what he had been used to in his career and the property he was staying in at Rick Kelly's, it wasn't the best but it was a start.

'I picked him up from that rehab, he'd made it through and I was taking him to stay, not at Rick Bradford's, but he had another farm out there and we borrowed a motorhome for him to stay in and I was taking him there,' Preston recalled. 'I took him to the store to get him some survival gear and we got to the checkout and there's a bottle of brandy there! What am I going to say? "I can't be out there with nothing to drink," he said. "You're s******g me man, you just been through that whole thing and now you're going to go out there and get drunk!?' And he sure did.'

'I put him to work,' said Bradford. 'I had a greenhouse operation in Calipatria. So we got him a motorhome, or trailer, a broken-down motorhome, and put him to work … for a while. He was okay, he never worked a day in his life, so work and Kelly was almost an allergic reaction. But he was really personable so he got on with it. We had an Israeli manager and they all loved Kelly. But the local Hispanics started bringing him alcohol and it went all downhill from there. I was partners in the deal so I couldn't entirely protect him, so eventually they said he had to go. That lasted about six to eight months.'

Whether he was daunted by the prospect of his new start or whether he just went through those six months so as not to let his friend down, we'll never know.

But what we do know is that, faced with a new situation, he turned to his 'escape'. Perhaps he thought he didn't really have a problem after all, or maybe he was being stubborn about it. It was his life, and he was going to live it the way he chose. Preston recalled a blunt reaction he received when he challenged him about his lifestyle after what he'd achieved in Victory Outreach.

'He told me, after all those rehabs and all that stuff, he liked drinking and he wished everyone would leave him the f**k alone. That's a quote from Kelly. He said, "I wish everyone would leave me the f**k alone!" Man, that was brutal, a brutal realisation.'

Being in self-denial is a situation that can lead to total oblivion. In an interview he gave to the author in 2006 one can detect that, despite all the help and advice and criticism, denial was still evident when he said: 'Was I an alcoholic? I guess you'd have to say I was.'

Having burned a few bridges over the years and with no job, his options were limited. So he returned to Rick's house. 'I was praying it would work out for him,' said Rick. 'He was pretty good at first, but he fell off the handle a little bit. I have a big property, have parties and stuff, and he couldn't resist. So it probably wasn't the best place for him but he had nowhere else to go.'

Going through the rehab wasn't a total waste, though. He realised that he had to change if he wanted to take control of his life and see more of his family. Sadly he couldn't kick the drinking habit completely. For one thing, after thirty-plus years of abusing his body with booze, his system cried out for it so in his mind he compromised and told himself that he could have a beer but would avoid the spirits – with the company he kept and his reputation, that wasn't easy.

'Sure the Jelly Man still parties, but I don't touch the hard liquor although I'll have a beer now and again,' he said when he came out. 'I see some people I used to know and they say, "Hey Jelly Man, have a drink." When I refuse they stand there laughing at me and try to tempt me, but I just look at them. Then I'd see their smiles disappear from their faces and then they know that the Jelly Man isn't joking and he was being serious.'

He also realised that he needed to earn some dollars. Once again, his options were limited. He'd been a racer as soon as he could, so he had little experience of work outside the racetrack, apart from helping Rick in his business. There was only one thing for it; after ten years out of the saddle, he decided to make a comeback.

# 22

# IT ENDS IN DUST AND DISARRAY

'Sometimes, when you've fallen on hard times, the one thing you can go back to is what you had a lot of talent for.'

Jason Bonsignore, New York promoter

'I just want to get out there and make people happy and have a good time. Just trying it, win or lose, is what I really need to do. I want to entertain people,' Kelly Moran told Scott Rousseau of his comeback plans in *Cycle News*. But picking himself up after a crash wasn't in his plan. Promoter Jason Bonsignore was watching from the pit wall and ran over to assist him, fortunately, all he'd hurt was his pride.

He recalled: 'I just said to him, "Kelly, don't worry, it's okay, it's been a long time," and he got back up and did one lap which was really rough, he was all over the place, so I waved him in. I said to him, "Do me a favour, walk away and sit down and relax. Let me just make a few changes to the bike."'

It was Saturday, 3 May 2003, and Kelly took his seat in Champion Speedway, Owego, New York. In speedway terms it wasn't Belle Vue nor was it the famous 'Bullring' at Costa Mesa, but it was a fresh challenge and even though he'd raced around the world, he'd never competed in New York before. Over the years riders like Rick Miller and Bobby Schwartz had ventured from southern California to compete in their annual US Open Championship and returned with first place. Largely though, the standard in New York wasn't on a par with California and certainly nowhere near the level they compete at in Europe. The scene in New York operated in its own little world. The sport's big names, past and present, were little more than lines or pictures in occasional copies of the sport's publications that were around at the time. Therefore, the Moran name didn't carry quite the same amount of expectation with it as it would have in California, or indeed in England. None of this mattered to him, though. Right now he was worried about looking foolish.

'I was a bit nervous and I didn't want to look like an idiot,' he said.

Since retiring at the end of 1992 he'd only been on a bike twice, once in a disastrous Legends Night at Costa Mesa when he wasn't fit to ride and crashed heavily and was lucky to escape serious injury; and another time at El Mirage on one of Billy Hamill's modern lay-down bikes, which also ended with him eating dirt.

'Billy said you have got to grab more throttle but why should I have to change what I have always been used to for the bike to do what you want? Why should I work for the bike, the bike should work for me,' he complained. Later, though, when he announced his intention to make a track return, he admitted that he wasn't in a fit enough state to ride that day. In fact he rolled his eyes at Rousseau when he related his experience to him and disclosed that he'd been drinking Jim Beam whisky.

After that unfortunate experience on Hamill's GM, he took a dislike to the modern machines and told Bonsignore that he wanted an 'old school' upright, the old-fashioned telescopic forks, solid right footrest and instructed that they put on a gearing that Jason knew wouldn't be suitable.

'There was no way that he was going to get around the track with that gearing on,' Jason recalled. 'He was so good in his heyday that he probably did run such a tall gear that nobody else could run. He's Kelly Moran, so what was I going to tell him? No? We did put on some ridiculous gear that I knew he was going to struggle with. I think he was thinking it was going to be really easy. He lined up at the start-line, pinned the thing and went into the first corner and went over backwards. He got up half-stunned and probably thought, oh wow, I'm Kelly Moran, I should have been able to do this real easy.

'So I changed the gearing right away to a really low gear and he went back out there and started to do some pretty decent laps. A few guys were watching, some of whom didn't know who he was and some of whom did. He came back in again and I said, "Hey Kelly, do the same thing, walk away for a few minutes." We put a leading-link front end on the bike and he went back out there and afterwards he said, "Wow, now this is starting to feel pretty good. These front ends are nice." Then he was getting some confidence in me and what I was telling him. He came in again and I said, "Next time out we'll try a lay-down." "Do you really think so?" And I'm like, "Yeah trust me." So he walked away and we set up a lay-down and he went out there and he was starting to look like he could make a main event with a little bit of luck.

'He came in with a big smile on his face and he'd talk in the third person sometimes and he said, "Yeah, Jelly Man really likes these lay-downs." He was laughing and from that point on he sort of stayed on that same bike. We stayed down there for a week or so and he practised three or four days in a row. He was starting to look like the old Kelly; he was looking good and flying. I had a pair of his old STP leathers and he didn't have a suit anymore, but we stuffed him into his old leathers and that was really cool to see him wearing his old suit again. Of course he was never heavy, but he gained some weight for Kelly and he couldn't zip it up. So we duct-taped the top closed.'

Kelly got so accustomed to the lay-down that, like most of the ex-riders who had a career on upright engines, once he found his feet, he felt they were easier to ride. 'How I wish I had that when I was racing in England, it's such a smooth ride and it's a lot different to the equipment I was using.'

Given his reputation, there were plenty who doubted that Moran's comeback would last or even get started. Some even sniggered harshly at the news and said, 'Oh sure, he's been planning his comeback for years, as soon as he crawls out of the bottle.'

Even Ron Preston warned Bonsignore not to do it, but Jason was a fan and believed that it could work. 'Honestly, everybody told me not to do it and that he was too far gone. But I had a hunch that he could do it again. It was a struggle for sure and we had to keep on him twenty-four hours a day to keep him in riding condition. He told me that he had been going to AA meetings and the Men's Christian home and everything. I had several talks with Ron, who was closest to him at that point and he just told me that I would probably have my hands full and it wouldn't work out so well. I'm hard-headed about that stuff and I really wanted to try it.

'I knew I would have to provide equipment for him because he didn't have anything. I thought it would be a good thing to try and get things going better for him. I knew he wasn't going to go back to being a professional speedway rider again at that point in his life. His skills probably hadn't eroded too much and by racing again it would give him some pride, and give him something to focus on, so from that standpoint I think it was pretty successful.'

It would be unkind to describe the scene in New York as a backwater but the fact that it was off the beaten track was to Kelly's advantage. He was away from the glare of publicity that his comeback would have attracted in California. Therefore, without the weight of expectation on his shoulders, he could slip back into the groove with the knowledge that, in general, people weren't expecting him to tear up the track. Perhaps more importantly he was away from his usual party crew. Sadly, reputations travel very fast.

Bonsignore did wonder about the wisdom of his determination when he picked him up from the airport, though. 'He was a mess because he'd been drinking on the flight. He could hardly pick his head up off the bench and I thought, oh my God, what did I get myself into? It actually took a few days to get him going again and it was nice to meet the real Kelly at that point and know what a genuine person he was.'

There was no doubt about it, it was a disappointing start; yet underneath he did really appreciate the fresh start he was given. 'For someone to be positive about me with all the negativity surrounding my name, for him to give me this opportunity, you can't measure how much I appreciate it,' he said. 'When I'm working in the workshop the time just flies by and I find that I'm not even thinking about having a drink.'

He stayed at Bonsignore's home in Rochester to begin with. The back of his house led onto Lake Ontario and he said the breeze coming off the lake reminded him of the wind blowing off the fields and into the pits at Swindon. Characteristically, he settled in pretty well in the area and it worked out well for him to begin with.

'He had it pretty good,' said Bonsignore. 'We had a decent house on the lake and everything; and when he wasn't drinking he was a pleasure to have around. He was a great person, very helpful and wanted to do things. When he was drinking he could be an absolute nightmare. He was one of those people that would go in the opposite direction when he was drinking. He'd get angry, agitated and confrontational. Had he been a happy-go-lucky drinker, people may have had more time for him but it had the opposite effect. He would get nasty, angry and confrontational – it was a shame to see him go in that direction.'

Turned out in chequered leathers and a blue Arai helmet that was reminiscent of his classic STP suits, he made his track return at Champion Speedway, Owego, on 25 May 2003. Although he didn't transfer to the main event, he put in an impressive performance considering he hadn't competed for eleven years. Two months later, at Action Park, Greene, he won all his qualifying races to make his first Main but missed the start and finished fifth. The following night he finished third in both the Scratch and Handicap finals and he was closer still with a runner-up place at the Square Deal Riders' Raceway on a surface that he found hard going – it seemed only a matter of time before he'd win his first Main event. Unluckily he then had an untimely reminder that speedway, at any level, has a nasty bite.

'I was chasing Cam Rafferty when I pulled a big power wheelie going into the turn. I had to make a split second decision whether to try and save it, or bail out. Well I thought, this isn't the World Final, so I decided to let it go but I landed on the handlebar clamps with my chest in the fall and I was winded. Boy was it sore!'

However, keeping the Jelly Man from over-indulging was hard work for all involved. 'That was the biggest problem and that's why speedway was a double-edged sword,' Jason observed. 'It was great for him to do the one thing in his life that he had so much talent for, have some pride in and have something constructive going for him. But on the opposite side of the fence, it was the worst thing in the world because it was one of the few places where all they want to do is drink and party after the races. There were a few Polish people there who knew Kelly from the old days and came to the track to see him. The first thing they did was buy him a drink, or give him a drink or have a shot with him. That was the worst thing in the world for him. He'd done so well all week and I'd get upset, not only for Kelly but for myself. I'd been hard on him all week to not drink at all, he was doing so good and then after the races people walked up to him and handed him beers. That was pretty difficult.

'For a little while he got interested in a girl and he wanted to stay down at the track more often instead of coming home with me to Rochester. It was hard to tell him no because he was a grown-up. He was doing really well at the start of the season, but it just went completely down the drain because he wanted to hang around the track and stay down there during the week and party. He was hanging out at Warren Diem's house. We used to race at Action Park, Greene on Saturdays and Owego on Sundays. We had a rain-off on Sunday at Owego. The riders all got dressed and were ready to go, but it started raining and Kelly's leathers got soaked while it was raining and he put them in his bag. It was funny because I thought to myself: he'll never open that bag, not do anything this week because he'll be so preoccupied with having fun.

'So the next week we got to the track and I watched him go and get changed. He opened that bag and his leathers were green, green as a clover! Completely covered in mould and it reeked too, the bag smelt so bad. I said, "Gee, I guess you shouldn't have partied so much this week, Kelly," and he just shook his head. So he had to go and wash his leathers and he hung them up on the fence for a little bit. But he'd showed up late too because, again, he was in the partying mode and not thinking about things. So he only had a few minutes to hose the leathers off and wash the mould from them and I think he wore them wet that night. They were completely green. While he wasn't on my watch he was falling apart.'

However, having finished fourth in the East Coast points that year, word got out that one of the sport's most entertaining riders was back and he was invited to compete in the indoor Bonanza meeting in Brighton on 14 December. He was particularly excited about doing that event because he'd also get the opportunity to see Chelsea and spend some time in England afterwards. Moreover he was also included in the field for the country's biggest meeting of the season at Costa Mesa, the US National Championship. Alas, neither was particularly successful.

Jason was keen for him to show them what he'd done on his tracks. Before the National, Kelly called him but it wasn't good news. 'I think he rode one regular night and he did a lap and pulled up each time and he was really uncomfortable. He called me and I asked him what happened and he said, "I don't know, I just felt really uncomfortable. The bike didn't feel right." So I called Brad Oxley and said, "Is there any chance you can give him a couple of practice laps because, trust me, he can still ride?" So Brad went to a bunch of trouble to pick him up, take him to a track and spend time with him, get a bike put together for him and he said that he went out that day, practised, and was all excited that he could still do it. He called me during the week and thanked me. But then the same thing, he went right back out, hardly made a lap around the track and it was embarrassing. I felt bad for him. I knew he could still do it, we all saw it back here, but he was real nervous too.'

Much was made of Kelly's appearance in Costa Mesa, after all he was a former double US National Champion, but it was an anti-climax. He didn't complete any of his three rides and then pulled out of the rest of the event. Apart from being nervous and uncomfortable, the truth was that he wasn't feeling very well. He asked a friend to stick around while he signed autographs. Clearly something was amiss because he wasn't his normal self; he wasn't engaging with the public like he normally would and he was nervously checking the whereabouts of people he knew. All done, he left to return to Rick Kelly's limo and his buddies, but he hadn't progressed more than ten yards when he returned to his seat and said that he felt unwell. In the time it took for someone to look away and back again, he was in a full seizure.

He was taken to hospital where he was told that he had an epileptic seizure. He was advised to have a brain scan, but because he had no medical insurance he couldn't afford to do that, nor could he stick around for medical supervision, so he left. This wouldn't be the last time he would endure a seizure. Rick Kelly came home from work one day and found him on the floor and had to call an ambulance.

Moran preferred not to talk about them, describing them as 'f*****g things'. Someone doesn't need to be an epileptic to experience seizures when they're binge drinking. The brain has a limit to the amount of alcohol it can tolerate, which varies from person to person, and if one continues to exceed that threshold, one of the ways in which the brain reacts to it is by inducing a seizure. As he's no longer here, it's difficult to determine which type of seizure he experienced and being a complex issue it's one we shouldn't speculate about.

However, with the Brighton event on the horizon, those closest to him tried to prevent his appearance. It wasn't that they didn't want him to go to England, it was that they didn't want him to ride. Kelly himself was also worried, but he desperately wanted to travel to see his daughter – so he covered it up.

My heart sank when Kelly Moran answered the phone. He hadn't fallen off the wagon, he'd crash-landed. It was all he could manage to string a sentence together.

'I'm just calling to let you know that I'll be picking you up from the airport,' I informed him. 'That's white of you,' he replied.

I intended to keep it short, because I could tell that he was in a place where he could be argumentative and belligerent. 'Okay, well, I'll see you Saturday.'

'Oh, see ya, see ya!' he responded, although it was more like 'shee-a.' Luckily it was a Wednesday night and he wasn't flying in until the end of the week, but even so it was too late to pull out now. I had been told by various people that it wasn't a good idea that he was doing it, but he had made an arrangement with Jon Cook and his motivation was to see his daughter and some other friends.

When Billy Hamill learned that I would be collecting him, he told me. 'He doesn't want to do it, he's worried about it, dude!' In fact, just before leaving I received a message from Hamill asking me to look after his 'brother' Kelly.

Having not seen him since his last night at Swindon in 1992, when I picked him up from the airport he'd walked by me before I recognised him. To say he had aged beyond his then forty-three years was an understatement. It was clear that years of alcohol abuse had taken their toll on him in a big way – it was quite shocking.

As we travelled to Brighton, armed with the knowledge of his seizure and his reluctance, I said to him that if he didn't feel comfortable and preferred not to do it then I'd tell Jon Cook when we arrived. 'No, the Jelly Man is ready,' he said. 'Are you sure?' I prompted. 'Yeah.' He was in good spirits, was making jokes and waving at the pretty girls as we passed traffic.

On arrival at our hotel I was concerned when he walked straight up to the bar and ordered a drink. 'I don't think that's a good idea,' I commented. 'A beer's okay,' he replied.

Within minutes of our arrival a succession of visitors arrived to see him, including Jon Cook, Tony Millard, Bobby Schwartz and Shawn McConnell – who were competing – and many others. With Bobby we all went out for a pizza and, with the exception of a sandwich that he didn't finish, to my knowledge that was the only thing Kelly ate all weekend. He refused breakfast and just had a cup of tea and even at the venue all he drank was water and turned down further offers from the promotion to arrange a meal.

Soon it became a major operation to moderate the amount of drink he was consuming and keep people away who wanted to take him out on the town and get him plastered. One now ex-rider in particular tried very hard to tempt him with the bright lights and the promise of a good time in his old stomping ground. I was grateful for the support from Glyn Taylor and his partner, who managed to back me up while also come to a compromise in order for him to have some social interaction and to appease this determined rider while maintaining some sort of controlled environment. So we ended up at this guy's house where Kelly became intrigued by a tall fridge/freezer. Luckily he remained on the beer. Of obvious concern was the fact that he was still on US time, the jet lag was going to kick in and he was supposed to compete the next day.

The Indoor Bonanza had established itself as an annual one-off event that was staged during the close season. Held in the Brighton Centre on the seafront, the venue is the largest conference and exhibition centre in southern England and is normally used for concerts and other forms of entertainment – it was the scene of Bing Crosby's last performance before his death in 1977. With a capacity of 4,500, a tiny 131-yard (120-metre) track was installed overnight. Two meetings were held, a best pairs event at 3 p.m. and then a break followed by an individual tournament in the evening.

Race day dawned and it was a particularly mild day for December. We left for the track, which was only about five minutes away, around 12.15 p.m. and when we arrived we were greeted with the news that they had found and arrested Saddam Hussain – who had gone into hiding since the invasion of Iraq earlier that year by a coalition force from mainly America and Britain that was sent to disarm the country of weapons of mass destruction.

Kelly was pleased and showed quite a bit of interest in the news. After obtaining our passes and meeting the Dugards, Bob and son Martin – who would be his partner in the pairs event – he took a nap while I was dispatched to see to his machinery. 'I want a solid foot peg,' I was instructed.

I met his old mechanic, Craig Cummings, who I also knew through my association with Hamill, and he informed me that he needed to come down and adjust the machine to his liking. Oddly he complimented me on my achievement of getting him there.

On returning, Kelly informed me he'd been sick. 'I didn't bring anything up though,' he said. 'That's because you haven't eaten anything,' I replied. 'You're nervous about this, aren't you?'

He reluctantly admitted that he was. 'I think we'd better call it off,' I suggested. But he made it quite clear that he didn't want to do that and he had no intention of letting anyone down and added, 'The Jelly Man will be okay.' After a while, he grabbed his gear and we went down to the pit area. The journey was punctuated by several greetings and pumping handshakes. Unusually, he didn't get changed where everyone else did. After acquiring a roll neck and other bits and pieces from Max Richards of Pegasus Speed Needs, he proceeded to get changed in the van – all the while cracking jokes and discussing the news of Hussain's capture. I can only imagine he chose to do this because he was embarrassed by how thin he was – there really was very little to him. Judging by his suit, it looked as though he'd lost weight since it had been made for him earlier in the year.

His mechanic for this event was Richard Ainslee, who was normally Chris Neath's spanner man. 'I was there for Chris and I ended up looking out for Kelly Moran. I remember seeing him race at Swindon and I knew he was a good rider in his time, but didn't know him. All he said was, "Whatever Chris is using, just make it so that I can ride it." That was it. He was pretty laid back. He was really polite and thankful. He just used what Chris had and was really laid back about the whole thing. That was a bit different because I've worked with some demanding riders, but you just get on with it.'

When Kelly was handed his race jacket and turned it over to reveal the number 13, he was clearly concerned. 'Number 31 backwards,' Cummings assured him. Bobby Schwartz, who had won the Pairs with McConnell three times, came by and offered him some advice on how to ride the track. In actual fact, Boogaloo had been as attentive toward him as he could since we arrived. I could see that Kelly clearly appreciated it.

If there were any doubts about the hype surrounding his return to the UK, they were soon dispelled when Moran was held back from the rest of the riders during the parade. An impressive looking Harley Davidson had been brought up the ramp. The doors were closed, the engine thrummed and in the half-light instructions were given that he was to ride pillion on the back. Except, due to his lack of stature he couldn't lift his leg over the seat, so Craig picked him up like a father would a child and plopped him on the back. He was handed an American flag, the doors opened and he made his entrance like the superstar he'd always been. Cummings turned to me and said, 'I've never known him to be so nervous.' Considering some of the big meetings that he and Kelly had attended during his career, that was some statement. As he waved to an appreciative audience I remember thinking, bloody hell, I hope he's going to be all right because this really wasn't the Kelly Moran vintage from the 1980s.

His first race was heat 4. To me, the bike looked too big for him; the seat in particular looked as though it needed lowering, but he said that it was okay. The tapes went up, all four riders bunched together and he slipped off on the first corner. He got up, had the engine still running and moved to the infield. I could see something wasn't right and as soon as the race had ended, he rode across the track, straight into the pits, around the back, pulled up, ripped off his helmet and was ill. Richard looked at me astonished and for a minute he didn't know what to do.

'The last thing I expected was that. I was shocked,' Ainslee recalled. 'I didn't know what to say. All I could do really was do what I usually did and prepare the bike for the next race. He wasn't the rider that he used to be.'

As soon as he was able I took him away from the pits, down the ramp for some air. 'It's nerves,' he said, 'I'll be okay.'

Luckily his races were evenly spaced but it was a long afternoon. He failed to complete one of his five rides. After a tumble in his second race, he then retired from each one. He looked awkward and uncomfortable. It was painful to watch. You'd be hard-pressed to convince someone that he once found racing against the world's best easy. Cummings, Dugard and Schwartz all came over to offer words of advice and help. Even though it was surprisingly warm, I found myself rubbing his hands because he was freezing, but he still refused to eat anything, only sipping from a bottle of water.

Schwartz and McConnell won the Pairs for the fourth time. As the crowd disappeared it was arranged for him to have a practice in private. A few more adjustments were made and Martin Dugard gave him some advice and he began putting a few laps together. He came in looking and sounding happier and more comfortable. However, it was decided that it was best to pull him out of the evening meeting. Although he was obviously pleased with that news, he was still somewhat reluctant to let people down. He was required to stay around though, which he was more than happy to do.

It was disappointing for all involved. While it seems unlikely that people expected him to carve through the opposition like he used to in the old days, they were at least expecting to see the form that prompted one New York journalist to write: '[It's] quite apparent to all who watched that he is back in a big way.' Given the circumstances, though, it could have been a lot worse.

'It was a shame because there was a bit of hype around him, but he wasn't well enough to continue, was he? A great bloke, though. It just didn't work out for him that day,' Ainslee commented.

After the meeting Moran said: 'I feel I let a few people down and I want to say sorry for that. I only arrived in the UK the day before and didn't have enough time to get myself ready for a meeting like this. My jet lag got the better of me. I just wasn't up to it on the day and I hope I can come back better prepared.'

A second attempt was never on the cards. As Jon Cook handed me his appearance money in an envelope to give him, he glumly said, 'I won't be doing that again.' On reflection, flying him in the day before perhaps wasn't the best idea, but the other side to that is if he'd had too long to wait he could have found some mischief to get into.

When Kelly first told me that he would be racing in the Bonanza and a deal had been struck with Cook – 'Eastbourne Cook 'em up' he dubbed him – I suggested we sell some of *The Moran Brothers* book, get him to sign them and he'd have some extra money for his trip home to visit his family in Sheffield. Therefore, he sort of saw me as his guardian and, honestly speaking, he really wasn't any problem – it was the people around him. For example, when we were packing up and walking back through the bar to the pit area, two guys virtually ran up to us and said, 'I want to buy Kelly Moran a drink.' He looked at me like a child asking for permission. He'd kept his end of the bargain, so I said, 'It's up to you, you've done your part.' And off he went. I didn't expect to see him again, but to my pleasant surprise no sooner had I finished loading the car than he was stood next to me. It turned out he didn't know them at all.

You could only call them fans in the loosest possible way. Some of them were like vultures that would emerge out of the surroundings and prey on his weakness for their own selfish entertainment. Martin Morley, who noted that he'd cut down on his drinking, had a similar experience when he took him to a show the following year and overheard their plans.

'They were saying, "Let's get Kelly pissed, we'll have a right laugh then." I was going absolutely crackers and I said to him and his missus, "If I were you two, I'd f**k off and get out of here now!" I told them off because he was having a few steady pints, but they were taking the piss. It wasn't right.'

We were supposed to have gone for a meal. Bob Dugard said he would arrange it but Kelly still wouldn't go. Rick Kelly recalled that he didn't eat properly in San Diego either: 'He used to lie to me. He would never eat, just drink. I'd get home from work and I'd say, "Kelly, what did you have to eat?" And he'd say, "Oh I had this or that," and I'd go to the dishwasher and there was no dishes and then he'd say he did the dishes.' Therefore, he preferred to stay in the vicinity of where he could meet so many old faces. After we watched some of the racing, all of a sudden he'd vanished.

If there was ever an illustration of his addiction, it occurred at the end of the meeting. The place was virtually empty and they were preparing to take out the track. It was arranged that Kelly would head north to see his family with Glyn Taylor and his partner. All his stuff had been transferred to his vehicle. Even though he was already way past the happy stage, he was tempted to continue the good times with some friends. I told him to go with Glyn; Glyn, rather annoyingly, said, 'It's up to you, Kelly.' You could almost see the quandary he was in, as he stepped from one foot to the other, turning to the path that would lead to his daughter and then in the opposite direction to where the lure of a good time waited. The demon drink that governed his life had put him in a dilemma that just wouldn't be understandable to most people. The anguish on his face was obvious and in his heart he wanted to do the right thing and go with Glyn, but the little devil inside was just showing him too much temptation. He unsteadily departed into the night with a group of people.

That was the last time I would see Kelly. The next day I remember my mother asking me how he was. I found myself replying with a rare example foretelling, 'He's not going to make old bones.'

He spent the rest of the winter in England. Eventually he made it to see Chelsea via Billy Janniro's home in Leicester. Martin Morley, AKA Enzville, received a call and had to sort out somewhere for him to stay.

'All the boys dumped him in a really posh hotel and rang me. It was Darren Boocock who called me and said, "Can you sort Kelly out because none of us can do owt for him. We've dropped him off at this hotel, can you go and pick him up?" I replied, "Oh mate what's going on?" So me, my wife, children and Marvyn Cox went to this hotel near Sheffield and I got him somewhere to stay with a good friend of mine for nearly three months. He'd cut down on his drinking. I used to take him out three times a week for a meal and he'd have three pints and that was it. He was sound, no problem; the rest of the time he'd stay in. He'd clean up and do all sorts, the housework, etc., and he was as good as gold. So I don't want people saying and thinking that he was a bad lad.'

Sadly, the welcome mat wasn't put out for him at any speedway meeting. His former promoter, Ian Thomas, ran the Telford Indoor Ice Spectacular and that year, February 2004, he lured Bruce Penhall out of retirement to make an appearance. In what Thomas described as a 'very sad incident', he related: 'We arranged an evening with Bruce Penhall the night before, which was a question and answer show hosted by journalist, Richard Bott. Bruce was very worried that, knowing he was there, Kelly might come in and spoil the night. I told him I'd keep an eye on the situation and keep Kelly out if he arrived the worse for wear. He did turn up and, unfortunately, he did justify Bruce's fears. I had to leave him outside and while it was the right thing to do for the benefit of the people who had come to listen to Bruce, it made me very, very sad indeed. I hadn't the heart to keep him out for the autograph session which followed.'

Through his travel company, James Easter would arrange speedway tours to Grands Prix and other events. When he arranged one for southern California he met Kelly at one of the tracks, where again he was being refused entry, and was stunned by his appearance.

'The last time I saw Kelly was at the pit gate at Industry Hills around 2006; he was begging to be let in. He looked shocking. I gave him $40 or $50 and

I said to him, "Don't piss it all away Kelly," but it was gone by the end of the night.' Enzville was a mechanic for one of the Oxford riders at the start of the 2004 campaign, but the club's promoter, Nigel Wagstaff, refused to let him bring Moran – much to Enzville's annoyance.

'He wouldn't let him come because, as he said, he didn't want the riders to be distracted by Kelly Moran and his alcoholic ways. Well, you behave yourself mate, because you don't know what you're talking about in that respect. It wasn't very nice. I was trying to look after Kelly and I had all these different riders to look after for Wagstaff and it would have been a lot easier, a lot better, and we could have had a couple of better riders with Kelly around to help because he was good at helping young riders.'

Given the chance, he could be particularly good with advising youngsters on competing in the sport. In his heart he was disappointed that speedway hadn't given him an opportunity to remain involved in one form or another – he once joked that he'd like to be the team manager of the Polish national team! However, with the help of Darren Boocock, a training school was arranged in which he could pass on some advice and tips at Buxton's High-Edge Raceway on 22 February 2004. Later in the year, in New York, a young Canadian rider called Kyle Legault crossed the border to compete in America. He was ambitious and wanted to try his luck in Britain. Sheffield, whom Kelly had raced for in the British League, was interested in him and he approached the former World No. 4 for advice.

'I was riding in New York state quite a bit then, so I was seeing Kelly on a weekly basis. He told me stuff about the track, what to expect, who was who and stuff like that. We rode quite a bit together. He taught me a lot of things that helped me in my career and riding against him, because he was a world-class rider, helped me a lot.'

It was sometimes hard for Kelly to take that the sport had mostly turned its back on him. Happily, though, Jason Bonsignore had not. After a few reservations, he invited the Jelly Man back to New York for a second term.

'I wasn't sure I could put myself through that again, it was weighing on my mind. I felt bad for him because he called me a few times and I could tell that he really wanted to come back and ride. He really enjoyed being with my family and he missed everybody, so I gave in and I was happy that I did because he rode really well in the second year and he wasn't getting out of my sight so much either.'

The highlight was his Scratch Main victory at Owego on 29 August. He defeated Jeremy Parsons, Kyle Legault, George Lazor and Tom Sephton. 'You could see his sense of pride when he won that Scratch Main. You could tell that riding again and having people respect his talent was making him happy at least,' said Jason.

'When he did buy into the system, not drink, he was starting to look healthier and was able to walk straight. When the guys from California came here at the end of the season they were astonished. I tried to have heart-to-hearts with him because I was concerned about how hard the road ahead was going to be for him if he didn't change. Sometimes he was very stubborn about it; but especially during the second year it was starting to sink in a little bit. He realised that maybe he wasn't heading down the right road.'

A week later was the US Open Championship, a prestigious title, so it would have been a nice crown to add to his two National triumphs. In spite of his main victory, Kelly probably wasn't one of the fancied contenders, but he was expected to be among the front runners. Unfortunately, his season and career came to a painful conclusion.

'I was coming out of turn two when the bike lifted and came down on my leg. The frame, which I later found out had been re-welded, snapped again and the weight of the bike broke my ankle. You should never give a rider a re-welded frame to use,' he said.

'It's a shame it ended the way it did,' Bonsignore reflected. 'He was really getting his feet back under him a little bit in the second year. He won three races in a row and was actually leading Chris Manchester, who was one of the top riders in the country still, when he hooked up, got some drive, the bike launched and he may have tried to hang on to it a little too long and he came down on his ankle – that was the end of it. I think he really wanted to carry on riding, even after an injury like that. But the problem was that it was right at the end of the season, and my wife and I were expecting our second child and his plane ticket was that week to go back to California for the winter. So it was getting really hard for me to be able to have somebody else in the house with the new baby coming. He went back and he wasn't going to get fit for a long while and I couldn't afford to do another season again.

'Everybody loved him. He was so generous and easy to talk to. He was very well liked by the other riders. Put it this way, he wasn't the best rider as far as his performance went when he was here – there was three or four guys that probably were the best riders – but he was able to recapture his skills a little bit. There were a few glimpses of the old days when he would look impressive, and he had a lot of fun, I think, and felt pretty good about himself again. It brought a bit of notoriety to New York Speedway because people were talking about Kelly Moran racing here. But it was a real struggle to keep him straight for those two summers.'

He returned to San Diego to Rick's place and cut the cast off himself when he felt it was ready. However, with no job and plenty of time on his hands, it wasn't the best of times for him and his body was beginning to break down from years of abuse. It was around this time that he began to develop what some called his 'Donald Duck thing', when he'd make a sound resembling that character in order to clear his throat when he spoke. It was probably a sign that his respiratory system was beginning to struggle from the effects of smoking since he was a young lad.

Rick and Moran sparked off each other and sometimes that energy created a very volatile inferno. One day in early 2006, things came to a head when they had a big fall-out and Kelly was homeless. 'I said to him that I had enough and he had to go. I had just started a new company by myself, my dad had just passed, I had too much stress and Kelly used to stress me even more and I couldn't cope with it no longer, so I said he had to go.'

He bounced around a few places, including his mother and brother's, friends and a few occasions at Billy Hamill's, until one night he met a guy at the races who said that he could stay in his converted garage. All was seemingly going well until one day a SWAT team surrounded the house and a helicopter was circling overhead. Kelly grabbed the phone, hid himself and called Ron Preston.

'He called me and said, "Hey Ronnie, I got a problem, man. I'm hiding in the corner with helicopters flying over the house. This guy I'm living with fixed somebody's car; he didn't do a very good job, and he wanted his money back. Then this guy threatened to kill him! So he called the police and the police called the guy, and he told them that if they come he's going to kill them." Everybody was there and Kelly's hiding in the corner of the backroom as the cops swarm the house. They arrested this dude. So now Kelly was the man of the house with the kid, he had no money and the ex-wife told him she's going to move back in and he needed to be out of there by tomorrow! I was standing at my house, looking up at God as Kelly is telling me this and I'm going, "God why me? Why would you put me through this?! If I'm supposed to help Kelly then I need some help myself."'

Perhaps miracles do happen, because after a few phone calls and fifteen minutes later he'd found a trailer home for him to live in at Rick Bradford's – and it was twenty minutes away from Bradford's farm at Thermal. First of all, he had to get him out of there and he called Keith Lewis, his old mechanic from his racing days.

'It turned out that Kelly was twenty minutes away from where Keith was, so he went down there to pick him up and took him to his house. It just happened to be the weekend of one of the football finals. So there was a big party at Keith's and I said to him, "Keith, do not give Kelly any alcohol, dude." He understood. I was on the cell phone with him as he's driving up to Kelly, and he goes, "There he is, sitting on the kerb with his helmet bag." He hadn't seen him for years and he goes, "Wow, he looks like shit, man." So he took him back to his house. Unfortunately, Kelly asked him to loan him a few bucks because he needed to get some smokes. So he gave him some money to go to the store. They're partying and these guys are all shit-faced, nobody even noticed that Kelly's nowhere to be found. The next morning, about 6 o'clock, Kelly came walking up and Keith goes, "Where were you?" And he said, "I got lost man, I slept under a tree over there." He had no idea where he was when he woke up in the morning. I'm sure what happened was he'd gone into the store, bought a bottle, had a smoke, drank the whole thing and passed out!'

After picking him up and attending to some business in El Centro, Ron then travelled to get the trailer. Unfortunately it had two flat tyres. He was just about to check the bulletin board for a tow truck when he decided to call his uncle Bill. Luckily, he was in the area and offered to tow it for free. While they waited for him to arrive, Preston set about making the trailer road-worthy for the short trip.

'I worked on the tail-light, fixed the back tyre and where's Kelly? Sitting in my truck smoking weed! From then on the story of life at Rick Bradford's is … I would get a call every day from Rick saying, "The little bastard charged $300 last month at the grocery store down the street," or "I can't get that little bastard to get out of his trailer," or "now the little bastard has adopted the Mexican family and my foreman and his family," or "now the little bastard is watching Mexican soap operas and eating burritos with the Mexican family!" and I was thinking, man this little bastard is in trouble all the time!'

# 23

# *FIDES NON TIMET*

'We will be known forever by the tracks we leave.'

Dakota proverb

## 11 September 2009

It was Friday night; twenty years ago he would have been getting ready to race at either Belle Vue or Costa Mesa. He was lying on the couch in his trailer and was feeling pretty comfortable when his mind drifted back to those unforgettable days. He didn't have a great deal of knowledge about the machinations of a speedway engine, yet he vividly recalled the beat of metal motion that played out a sweet melody in the pages of his memory. The thrill and sensation of racing was so clear that his recollections drowned out the noise from his TV.

Kelly lifted up his right hand and clenched his fist; he could almost feel the power from an imaginary twist of the throttle. He held this memory for a moment and remembered the adrenaline rush of competition, that distinctive aroma of castor-based oil that would fill the air, the appreciative audiences, the camaraderie between the riders, travelling the world, the fun and the girls … yes sir, it had been quite a ride and it had all gone by so fast. As he opened his palm he stared at it for a moment, studying the lines and wondered where the mark was that signified the point where his career had ended; or where his current plight would have been etched. Following all those years racing a motorcycle, he had to wonder how it had come to relying on the generosity of friends and dwelling in a trailer in Thermal, California. It wasn't that he wasn't grateful because he was; but he missed the attention from friends and admirers. In fact, he regretted not taking care of his finances better because he didn't have a dime to his name.

'I was foolish with my money – that's the only thing I regret,' he said in 2001. 'I just thought all I had to do to get some more was go out and race. I always thought it won't stop. When I was younger I thought, okay, I blew £100 that night at the pub. It wasn't just on drink, but I liked to help my mates if they were a bit short. I didn't know I was going to stop riding.'

It wasn't all fun, of course. He remembered the crash at Bradford in 1989 from which Erik Gundersen was lucky to survive; then there was dear Denny Pyeatt's death and the horrific demise of his team-mate at Birmingham, Zdenek Kudrna. His own body was wounded by a succession of injuries. Being in the arid climate in California helped to manage the level of irritation and he realised how difficult it could be when he made a visit to England's damp environment.

On television the news channels were full of coverage marking the anniversary of the 9/11 attacks in New York and, to be truthful, he was bored with it. But his attention was caught by some local news that the oldest person in the world at that time, Gertrude Baines, had died in Los Angeles aged 115. In ten days' time he would be forty-nine years old and at that moment he'd be happy to see fifty, never mind a century or more.

While the aches and pains from speedway crashes were unpleasant, it was nothing compared to what the hospital discovered when he had a chest X-ray – he had emphysema. Emphysema is included in a group of deceases called Chronic Obstructive Pulmonary Disease (COPD). It's a progressive disease that primarily causes a shortness of breath. Although his overall lifestyle certainly hadn't helped his present condition, emphysema had caught up with Moran due to his smoking. Cigarette smoke destroys the lung tissue, which is the reason for the obstruction, and it causes inflammation and irritation of the airways. Smoke directly affects the cells in the airways that are responsible for clearing mucus and other secretions – hence the 'Donald Duck thing' of clearing his throat. Furthermore, continuous smoking damages the tiny hairs called cilia that line the airways and with constant abuse they disappear. Without their constant sweeping action mucus secretions cannot be cleared from the lower respiratory tract. Moreover, the immune cells whose job it is to fight infection cannot fend off bacteria effectively or clear the lungs of other particles such as tar build-up from smoking. He later told *Backtrack* magazine that he had altered his smoking habits by swapping from Marlboro Red to Marlboro Lights and had managed to reduce the number of cigarettes to seven a day.

Sadly it was too late. He couldn't walk the short distance from the edge of the pits at Belle Vue across the dog track to the speedway circuit without having to stop, bend down, place his hands on his knees and pant to catch his breath – it was hard to see a man, a great man, who had been adored for his talent and personality, gasping for air. He also carried an inhaler and the last twelve months weren't living, it was more like existing from day to day. Bradford recalled an example of the trouble the former speedway star was having.

'He couldn't walk twenty yards without getting winded. In fact, I took him to buy a pair of work boots – I don't know why, he never worked! – and he got so winded putting them on that he had to stop. He was really bad, he'd put it on that he wasn't, but he was. Poor guy.'

Preston, who had seen him at his peak running rings around some of the best riders of their era and also knew how stubborn he could be, found it hard to see him having to give in to his illness and to other people – because he needed the help.

'The last years of his life sucked, man,' he said. 'Being as humble as he was forced to be – and he was a pretty humble guy – but when you're dying, you look like shit, everybody is looking at you, you're skin and bones walking around and you can't get your breath. I tried to give him some dignity towards the last few years. I'd bust his balls about some of the things he did and make fun of stuff, and he'd always say, "Oh, thank you very much for that!"

'For some reason, he never had anybody. I just felt that he was a long-time friend and he needed somebody. He probably spent more time in my off-road truck than anybody; he was a great co-pilot. He never complained about how fast I was going or how hard I'd hit the jump. He knew that he would eat – everywhere I'd take him I'd make him eat. Toward the end he didn't eat because he couldn't. He'd have like a handful of food and then the rest was put in a 'to go' box. He didn't have much. Billy Hamill left this really nice Oakley jacket, like a nice wear-out jacket. It was a little bit small for me so I said, "Kelly, here's your new jacket, man," and he was like, "Oh man, I miss getting all that free stuff." I called Billy and said, "Hey, you know that jacket you left in my truck, I gave it to Kelly." And he goes, "You mean that $500 jacket!" "Yeah, that one," "Oh that's cool man, that's my bro."'

In order to get around, Bradford had bought him a $2,000 golf-type buggy so that he could get to the store. It was called a 'workhorse' but Kelly took a razor blade to the lettering and scratched out the SE so that it read: 'Workhor'!

His routine was that he'd get up around 9 or 10 o'clock and leave on his buggy to make the three-quarter mile journey to the store, buy a coffee, a newspaper and a pastry or a muffin. At the weekends he'd get his TV guide and plan his viewing for the week ahead. Rick had arranged a weekly credit at the local store in order for him to be able to purchase some essentials, but when he first arrived things didn't go smoothly, as he recalled.

'When we first started out it was \$50–60 a month for Kelly – that was okay. Then he started buying beer on my charge account, so it went from \$50–60 a month to \$200–300 a month. I talked to him about it, and I went to the store and told them that he can't buy any alcohol. He could buy food, coffee, burritos, toilet articles, but no alcohol … if you gave him an inch he'd take a mile.'

'Rick was at the store by his house and he told Kelly: "I told him [store keeper] not to sell you cigarettes and alcohol anymore." "Oh, thank you very much!" So Kelly made a deal with the locals. He'd sit out front on his golf buggy and he'd go, "What do you need?" "Hi Kelly, oh we need coffee, bread, eggs …' this and that. Kelly'd go in and charge it, they'd give him the money and he'd go back in and get his booze and cigarettes! Classic Kelly, man!' laughed Preston.

For someone who didn't like to spend long on his own, it was pretty hard putting the realities to the back of his mind and fending off the ghosts that can come with being alone. Sometimes, though, he seemed to live in the past. Bradford advised him that he shouldn't spend so long thinking about the old days; he should be putting his energies toward the future. 'You're not a speedway star anymore,' he said. 'You can't walk across the street, how the hell are you going to ride a speedway bike? You need to stop living in the past and figure out what the hell you're going to do in the future.'

Kelly knew he was right and there were times when he felt that he was watching the world go by. Therefore, Preston bought him a kitten from the roadside. His children were horrified that this guy was selling this cute bundle of fur by holding him up by the scruff of the neck with 'Kitten for Sale' written in ink on a piece of old cardboard. Ron's kids implored him to do something, so he bought it for \$10. Not knowing what to do with it he took it to Kelly's. Black and grey striped, he called it Lucky; and it may have been a ten bucks cat, but his heart was pure and he was his best friend.

One Christmas Eve, Bradford realised that Moran was in his trailer with just his satellite TV for entertainment and Lucky for company – a scene that he felt wasn't in keeping with the festive spirit.

'Kelly was all alone out here on this ranch in the middle of nowhere, and I thought that wasn't right. So I put him in my truck and drove him up to where his mom and brother were living, Adelanto. I pulled up at the parking lot where they were living and Kelly and I were the lightest by ten shades there and I said, "Kelly, get your stuff and get out of here, dude." When I got home my wife was mad at me for driving two and a half hours there on Christmas Eve. But he needed to be with his family. So I left him there for three or four days and then went back and picked him up.'

Bradford farmed around 700–800 acres of land at Thermal where he'd grow vegetables, red and green peppers and some watermelons. Given Kelly's interest in gardening, one would have thought he would have been quite drawn to the goings-on there. And he was, to a point.

'He would ask me lots of questions about everything and he'd drive around and notice things. I used to say to him, "If you drive by trash, pick it up for me," and he'd do that. He'd basically cruise around in his little "workhor". The funny thing with the United States, it's a free country, so everyone thinks everything is free. So fruit stealing is a big issue. This one Sunday I said, "Kelly, I need you to work today. Just drive around the watermelons and make sure nobody steals them." "Huh, I don't work on Sunday!"

'He really got on well with my foreman Ricardo and his wife, and they have a son, José, "Hot Cheetos" is what Kelly called him. I'd go to the store and buy all this food and keep it in the freezer, but he'd go over to their mother Chello's to eat and he would order what he wanted. "I want beans and egg burritos." And she'd make whatever he wanted. He had a pretty easy existence.'

It's a testimony to his liberal attitude and his experience of travelling around the world that he had little problems endearing himself to the Conchito family. Mexicans are often confronted by prejudice and racism in the USA, yet Kelly had neither in his soul. He loved everyone and he wanted everyone to love him. The youngest boy could speak a little English and he was able to translate their conversations.

While their English was limited and his knowledge of Spanish was far from good, this proved no barrier to their relationship because they took Moran into their hearts and treated him like one of their family – he'd even watch the Mexican soaps with them. They had no idea that he was once one of the world's best speedway riders, adored by thousands of fans, feared and respected by his rivals and team-mates; in fact, they didn't even know what speedway was. No matter, his charm, good manners and his cheerful personality soon won them over just as it had with so many others during his travels.

'He was a fun guy to have around but he just couldn't stay off the drink,' sighed Bradford. 'I told my foreman, "I'm not his mother, but if he wants two or three beers in the evening or something, I don't have a problem with that, but don't give him hard liquor." For a while we were able to keep him sober … he would get a buzz, but he didn't get wasted. Again, he was a friendly chap and he was friendly with everybody and the next thing you know he's getting people to bring him bottles of tequila. He couldn't stop at a drink or two – he had to drink the whole damned thing.'

While phone calls were kept to a minimum, as soon as he could Kelly would call his family and friends. Telephone calls overseas to Lorna, Chelsea and other people he liked to stay in touch with were important to him, but costly to Mr Bradford!

On the outside looking in – and it's likely that Bradford felt the same way when the bill arrived – he was taking advantage of the situation by making those long distance calls. Of course to some extent that's true, but when someone is so far away from the people he loves and cares about, it's not surprising that he wants to contact them and hear their reassuring voices. The sound of loved ones and close friends provided medicine for an aching heart.

Therefore, while Rick celebrated Christmas Day 2009 in his home in La Quinta, Kelly had access to a phone and called as many family and friends as he could. He knew that time was short.

## 22 January 2010

Bill, who had been evicted from his house, had been a resident on Rick's farm for a few months and parked his trailer next to Kelly's. Like most of the people that the former racer had come in contact with, Bill liked him. However, as he stepped out of his trailer that morning he found his neighbour in a very bad way. He was gasping for air like a fish that had been flung on a riverbank. He couldn't talk, he could barely do much else apart from reach for air and his lips were blue – so he called Rick Bradford.

'I was busy and Bill said, "Well he's blue!" "There's only one thing you can do, I can't get there for a while, so call an ambulance," I told him. They took him to hospital and one of the emergency room nurses lives right across the street from me and she said, "He's not going to make it." That's when I called Ronnie and said, "You've got to get your ass over here and help me. I've been taking care of this little bastard for two years, so you've gotta get over here and help me."'

With sirens wailing, Kelly was rushed the eight-mile journey from Bradford's farm at Thermal to JFK Memorial Hospital in Indio. Dark skies were passing over him and the battle was on to prevent his health from fading to black.

Preston recalled: 'Rick said, "We just took Kelly by ambulance to the hospital we don't expect that he is going to make it through the night." I got in my truck and I was praying going there, I was saying, "Man I don't know what I'm going to tell him, or what you expect, but I need some help with this guy again."'

'What happened, he'd got a bottle of tequila from somebody and got shit-faced drunk,' Bradford revealed. 'When he'd drink like that it would upset his stomach and he'd get diarrhoea. The trailer had a bathroom but he didn't want to use it. So I kept a portaloo right next to the trailer that they'd come and clean every couple of days. That's where he'd go to the bathroom because he didn't want to go in the trailer. Well that particular night he was that drunk he couldn't even make it to the bathroom so he was crapping in a bucket. Just the whole physical activity of being sick like that, basically that's what threw him over the edge. Then Bill found him.'

Ron Preston arrived not long after Moran had been admitted and if he had any doubts about his buddy's grave condition then there was no uncertainty when Bradford handed him a form to sign.

'Rick made me sign the DNR [Do Not Resuscitate] form; I was the power of attorney all of a sudden. I was like, okay, I guess this is God's plan, and signed it. It was pretty heavy duty, especially as he was my buddy. At times like that, you've just got to give in to God and say I am just along for the ride, this is way bigger than I am, show me what needs to be done and we'll do it. So they started pumping him with fluids and steroids.'

'They wanted to ventilate him,' said Rick. 'But we got lucky because another young nurse in there said, "You know, I'm going to hold it off." Once you ventilate them, that's it, they're on life support. So this nurse was able to talk them out of it. I went home but Ronnie stayed.'

Preston slept on a little couch beside his friend. 'I sent a text message to Mike Donaldson to send to the speedway world to pray for Kelly, he's got COPD. A bunch of people started responding and Mike said we should start a Facebook page for him, and I said: "I've not heard of Facebook, but go for it." So he started that and Kelly had 2,500 friends in two weeks. It gave him a little bit of sunlight at the end of the road.'

The Facebook phenomenon was a story in itself. Word spread around the globe and that collective will gave him a boost – the message was that Kelly Moran wasn't leaving this world just yet. When Rick arrived the next day he couldn't believe the transformation.

'I went back at noon the following afternoon and he was sat up in bed talking to Ronald. Eight or nine hours before he was dead; and there he was sitting up in bed talking – he made a marvellous recovery. He wasn't ready yet. He was a tough little bastard!'

Soon everyone that could showed up at the hospital: his brother, mother, Pete Rovazzini, Bruce Penhall, Bobby Schwartz, Dennis Sigalos, Kenny Best, Carol Stock, his step-sisters and many, many more he hadn't seen for years. He enjoyed seeing so many old faces again, but even he had to wonder where some of them had been because there were times when he could really have done with their support. Overall, though, he was grateful that so many had dropped in, called and sent get well messages and that somehow, through the grace of God, he'd pulled through.

'People have been telling me what's been appearing on my Facebook page … yeah, it's humbling. I don't really know how to put it into words but I'm awe-struck by it,' he said.

He wasn't out of the danger zone yet though, and he had to take eighteen tablets every morning. Also, he needed what he called 'roxy', a drug that hung above his bed that helped calm his heart rate when his breathing became difficult. For the first time in years he was also completely free of drink and nicotine – and he had to stay that way.

It's said that, despite the fact that he was still having problems breathing, his eyes lit up when Marice came to visit. It was an opportunity for reconciliation and also re-kindled their past. 'I got this message from Debbie Sigalos that he was in the hospital and they thought that he was going to die. So I went and visited him there. I was nervous about it because I didn't really know what to expect, so I just expected the worst. When I walked in he just sort of looked at me and goes, "Marice" and sat up. He said, "You look so much younger than me!" "I quit partying." We'd talk on the phone every night for a couple of hours, until he couldn't breathe anymore because he tried so hard to keep me on the phone. There were times when he didn't feel good and he didn't want to talk, and he would let me know that. He told me that I was the last person he was going to see before he died.'

He was released from hospital on 5 February and moved to Odyssey House hospice in Palm Desert. It was here that he experienced the biggest surprise yet – the arrival of Lorna and his daughter, Chelsea. Pete Rovazzini had arranged passage for them from England, and Kelly said at first he couldn't believe his eyes, he thought that his medications were playing tricks on him.

'We hadn't seen each other for so long he didn't recognise me at first,' Lorna laughed. 'And then he saw Chelsea, and Chelsea and Kelly were so alike, snappy remarks, the same. Pete Rovazzini said, "Oh God it's like being in a room with two Kelly Morans." It was just funny. At the end, we sat and talked with him. It was really hard for Chelsea. On our way back to the hotel she said, "Do you think he knows he's dying?" "Yeah he does." But you couldn't come out and say that. We were there for him.'

In his heart he realised that he was on borrowed time; all the support from his family, many friends and thousands of fans from around the world had persuaded someone to extend him a line of credit with Joe Black. The only thing was, no one really knew how long that time would be and it would be remuneration of the biggest kind. Therefore, every day was a gift.

For most people, the hospice is their last stop on this earthly journey before stepping off into the next world. Happily, Kelly wasn't at that stage. He was, though, still seriously ill. When the cold reality of his situation was brought home to him with the 'do not resuscitate' band around his wrist, he calmly nodded that he understood its meaning and remarked: 'I don't want to be a vegetable.'

However, one thing was clear: going back to where he called 'home', his trailer in Thermal on Rick's farm, was out of the question. Yet as much as he would have loved to have taken care of Lucky and whizzed back and forth in his buggy to the Conchita family, the truth was that even the short journey from his trailer to the portaloo outside was beyond him. Therefore, a place was found for him at Palm Springs Healthcare, which was also an assisted living accommodation.

Lorna helped settle her former husband into his new accommodation: 'I went with Rick Bradford and Chelsea went with Pete. We got there first and we had to sign in; all the people in the foyer were all senior citizens in wheelchairs and they were circling. And Kelly said, "Oh f★★k, what have you brought me to? I think I'm the youngest one here. Oh f★★k, they're circling like sharks," and they were all doing these exercises in their wheelchairs. We were just trying to hold the laughter in.

'We got into the room, a guy came in, he didn't speak to us, and he was covered from head to toe with tattoos and only spoke Mexican. Rick spoke it, so he said a few words to Rick, nothing too friendly – he was a gang member. It was written on his tattoos. So Kelly said, "Oh f★★k, if I don't get killed by this, he'll f★★★★★g kill me!" It was quite funny. Then the nurse came in and she said, "Oh my God, you're only a baby. What have you done to get in here?" And he said, "Well, I had a really good time getting here and I have no regrets." That's exactly what he said when we were in that room.'

Leaning on his walker for support, Kelly accompanied Lorna and Chelsea as they prepared to say their goodbyes. After the fun and laughter inside, it was a poignant and emotional moment for them. He was stood near the door ready to wave them off. Lorna got into Peter Rovazzini's vehicle and took a long, lingering look at the man she married. 'I remarked: "That's the last time we're going to see him, isn't it?" And he replied: "It might not be," and I said, "It is," and that was it. I spoke to Kelly when I came back. He'd been out with Pete and he got into one of those trollies, the disabled ones, and was speeding up and down the aisles and said it was so much fun that he didn't know why he hadn't done it before!'

Having no finances of his own, Kelly relied on the help and generosity of his friends. He wanted to be at Huntington Beach and with the help of Schwartz in particular, he moved to Huntington Nursing Home in the area.

The calls and visitors didn't stop though and this prevented him from reading a book, *One Good Run: The Legend of Burt Munro* by Tim Hanna. The subject was made into an inspirational movie called *The World's Fastest Indian*, starring Anthony Hopkins.

'He was really happy there, but he was kinda bummed that so many people would come by so often that he didn't even f****n' know!' laughed Bobby. 'He didn't know what to say to them. They were only speedway fans who wanted to be there at the end, but it was good that he had visitors.'

He wasn't left to his own devices. Bobby collected him and took him out practically every day, certainly as regularly as Kelly was able to – he could only go out with a supply of oxygen. Going out was good for his soul but doctors said that it would probably shorten his life ... but what the hell, you only live once, right? And many times they exceeded the time he was supposed to be out. 'He didn't really want to go anywhere but the house most times,' said Bobby. 'One time, though, I remember stopping at a place called Hadley and I got him a big milk shake. He wanted one of those so bad because he had had one before and loved them. It was just cool to have him around and do this kind of stuff for him.'

Even though he was still frail, he maintained his sense of humour right to the end. Danny Becker visited with his partner, Jojo Guerin, and she remembered a characteristic quip that was typical of him. 'My brother and I visited Kelly in Palm Springs a few months before he passed and I helped him to acquire benefits so that he could come to Huntington Beach as my friend. We brought a video camera for kicks and one of his friends said it would be okay. One of the questions that my brother asked was, "Do you have any advice for any young racers?" And he was so deadpan about it, he said, "Yeah I do, wear a cup!" He had the best sense of humour of anyone I have ever known.'

Kelly had good days and bad but overall it was a struggle. Schwartz saw his buddy smiling through as he fought for his breath and together they maintained a positive outlook. 'He couldn't breathe very well one day and the next he would be better. We were always worried about his breathing, that's what it was all about wasn't it? At one point he couldn't get from the sink to the shower in the bathroom, he had to hold on to the side of the sink, pant and struggle – that was hard to watch. I didn't think he was going to die, though. I didn't think about that, he was in my care and we didn't talk about it.'

During the first day that he was rushed into hospital, fearing the worst, Preston arranged for Pastor Pete Kinney from Racers for Christ to attend. RFC's motto is 'Bringing Inspiration to the World of Motorsports'. But a racer's busy lifestyle doesn't always allow time to attend church so RFC go to the events – if there needed to be an illustration that motorsport was a brotherhood then the support for Kelly from his old team-mates/rivals and fans from around the world had proved it.

'He didn't share his faith,' said Kinney. 'When I met him, he wasn't secure in his eternal fate, but we did that, we secured that with prayer. We had many Bible studies together. I remember one time when he was moved to Palm Springs, God gave us three hours – his phone was ringing constantly, people were coming into see him – but we had three hours of alone time, it was amazing. I walked into this room, he saw me, and literally jumped into my arms and gave me a big kiss on the lips! He was just crazy. I couldn't believe it,' he laughed.

On the morning of 2 April he fell out of bed and received a small cut above his eye for his trouble. He didn't have a very good day and was tortured by his breathing. However, it was amazing what a reasonable night's rest could do and the following day he was in good spirits – all things considered. He raised a universal laugh from his friends when he commented about one of the nurse's very fine qualities. Pete Rovazzini and Bobby Schwartz were there and Rovo noticed that perhaps his time was coming to an end.

'I can still feel this; Bobby and I were there late that night and I knew Kelly wanted us to pray with him,' he recalled. 'So I said to Bobby, "Come on, we're going to pray with Kelly." I said to Kelly, "Do you want us to pray with you?" He was so receptive to it, it was unbelievable. You could feel the presence of God in the room with him. And Kelly was a kind of shy person, but he grabbed that hand of mine and I knew the true meaning of death grip. He gripped so hard and he was having a hard time breathing and I said, "Lord, have it upon you, if it's his time, give him some peace and let him rest good." I feel bad sometimes that I left at 11.30 and said goodnight, but I wanted him to get some rest. He was very weak and I promised him that I would be back early that morning. I didn't think it was going to be at 4.30 that morning. He went into a coma.'

Schwartz received a call from the hospital at 5 a.m. and Rovazzini was already there when he arrived. Kelly was comatose as Ron Preston, Bruce Penhall and others gathered around for the Jelly Man's last hours on earth. Sadly, there would be no magic words or sacred verse that could save him this time. Unsurprisingly, the mood was very sombre, yet as time passed their stories and recollections of Kelly lightened the mood. Also present was Peter Kinney.

Preston remembered: 'Bruce had a weird sense. He said, "He looks different, he's going." So we all kept talking and then five minutes later Pastor Pete said, "I've just got this real overwhelming feeling to read this scripture."'

'I was sitting on his left side and I had the Bible on my lap,' added Kinney. 'It was the Holy Spirit of God that spoke to my heart and said, "Read a passage. You need to share scripture." So I said, "Hey everybody, God wants me to read a scripture right now," and everybody was quiet. I just opened my Bible randomly. I didn't try to find anything, I just opened it. It landed on Second Corinthians 5, verses 1–8 and I read …

*For we know that if the earthly house of this tabernacle were dissolved, we have a building of God, a house not made of hands, eternal in the heavens. For in this we groan, earnestly desiring to be clothed upon with our house which is from heaven. If so be that being clothed we shall not be found naked.*

*For we that are in this tabernacle do groan, being burdened: not for that we would be unclothed, but clothed upon that mortality might be swallowed up of life. Now he that hath wrought us for the self-same thing is God, who also hath given unto us the earnest of the Spirit.*

*Therefore we are always confident, knowing that, whilst we are at home in the body, we are absent from the Lord. For we walk by faith, not by sight …*

'When I read that last verse, that's when he took his last breath. I was going to continue on but everybody started crying. It was amazing, because when he took his last breath he went to be with the Lord.'

Rovazzini: 'I remember telling the pastor, "He's gone." I felt his spirit leave the room. So we sat there real peaceful and everyone said their goodbyes. I think Kelly knew that it was his time to go. For me, it was the most fulfilling moment because I knew that my little guy was safe and he wasn't going to have any more pain and suffering.'

'It was horribly sad,' said Preston. 'Without Mike Donaldson he would have died and it would have just been, "Hey dude, Kelly's died." But through Mike's Facebook page he got all these people back in his life and it made his last couple of months really memorable instead of a blip on the radar.'

'If he would have died and I didn't get to see him, I would have been devastated. I always loved him; he was the love of my life – my little Kelly,' said Marice.

Some have simply described his passing as pulling two electric wires apart and breaking the circuit – it was that peaceful. Except of course, the circle is never broken. Bobby had headed off on the 90-minute drive to Adelanto to pick up Shawn and their mother, but he received the news when he was an hour away – it was too late.

Lorna and Chelsea were informed that he had deteriorated and they had the opportunity to go back to California, but it was a bit too much for them.

They wanted to remember him as they last saw and spoke with him. 'When he did get poorly Pete said that he'd pay for us to come back, but it was difficult because I'd got the boys and everything else. Chelsea said that she had seen her dad, she was happy, so we didn't go back; she said that she didn't want to go back and watch him die – she didn't want to do that.'

No matter how prepared you think you are, it's never how you expect it to be. Nonetheless, Lorna remembered a conversation with one of the nurses that predicted the circumstances with almost prophetic accuracy.

'When he was leaving the hospital, I said, "He looks so much better," and the nurse replied: "Don't be fooled, they usually do get better, and then they have the downfall. His liver is very, very damaged, he'll have a fall, it will bleed and that is how he will pass away." And she was spot on. He fell out of bed, went out and had to be brought back and that was it. The Facebook thing put him back in the racing seat again, back on the bike, it gave him a boost. It was like a star had been born again, he loved it and revelled in it – and good for him is all I can say. All these people that sent him good wishes made a huge difference. It was smoking that killed him, well a bit of both because all his vital organs packed in in the end because he was that far gone. Drink takes over your life. And it did. It's a strong, strong thing and not everybody can beat it. When you're in a position where people around you drink and you're in this speedway world where everybody wants to be your friend, it's very, very difficult to give it up. It was hard for him. In the end he stopped didn't he, but that was due to his health. Prior to that he had a bloody good time getting to where he got to.'

The long goodbye was over … Kelly Moran was forty-nine when he passed away at 11.40 a.m. local time on 4 April 2010, Easter Sunday – some allowed themselves a wry smile, like he'd chosen that date to make sure we wouldn't forget.

Before he passed he drew up his last words, which read: 'During the time that I've been at JFK Hospital, a Facebook page was created for me that allowed my fans, family and fellow racers to post comments and pictures and video about me and my racing career. The response has been overwhelming to me and, at times, a burden with all the phone calls.

'The one message that my page has proven and given me is that we CAN put down our guns and swords and get along. When Ivan [Mauger] called me, he said that because of my page he's now talking to people he never gave a second look to in the pits at his races back then. And because of my page, there are riders from all over the world creating their own Facebook names and writing really neat stuff to me and re-connecting with other riders all over the world. I'm humbled this has all happened, it's like the Lord made me sick so this could happen.

'My wish, after I'm gone, is that they will continue to communicate and expand on it. In other words, I want more riders and their families to talk to each other. I don't care whether it's on my page or not. But if Ivan can talk to people he used to dislike, then don't you think we should follow his lead?

'In the words of that guy during the LA riots … "can't we just get along?" I'm especially appreciative that my boys from the US team have all gotten back together.

'Thank you for all the great messages, I love all of you! See ya, see ya, see ya! (Oh yeah, one more thing … don't smoke and don't drink!)'

Tributes poured in from around the world. *Speedway Star* said of him, 'Kelly was the ultimate headliner, a rebel and someone who lived practically every single day of his life in the fast lane.' *Backtrack* added: 'Incredibly talented and thrilling speedway racer, born showman and irrepressible party animal all rolled into one.' The *Orange County Register* described him as 'talented', and went on: 'someone who had a gift for making others feel special'.

On 10 April, a public memorial service was held at Costa Mesa and the Spring Classic race in the evening was dedicated to his memory. Some of his ashes were spread on the Costa Mesa track, and some in a private, family ceremony in the high desert where he learned to slide a motorcycle. The touring USA Dream Team carried No. 31 in his memory while they were competing in Britain.

However, four hours after Kelly had passed away, an earthquake ripped through the southern border area of California that measured 6.9 on the Richter scale, shaking San Diego and Los Angeles – anything above 6.2 can cause structural damage over a 100-mile radius. After the shuddering and shaking had finally subsided, someone remarked, 'Sounds as though Kelly's got the party started already!'

# CAREER RECORD

International Honours:

*World Championship*

1979 – Katowice, Poland, 11 points, 4th

1982 – Los Angeles, USA, 11 points, 4th

1984 – Gothenburg, Sweden, 11 points, 4th

*World Team Championship*

1982 – White City, England, 10 points, 1st

1983 – Vojens, Denmark, 6 points, 3rd

1984 – Leszno, Poland, 5 points, 3rd

1987 – Held over three rounds, 3rd (Coventry, England, 4 points, 1st; Prague, former Czechoslovakia, 10 points, 3rd), missed first round due to injury

1988 – Long Beach, USA, 5 points, 2nd

1989 – Bradford, England, 6 points, 4th

1990 – Pardubice, former Czechoslovakia, 12 points, 1st

*World Pairs Championship*

1979 – Qualified with Bruce Penhall but was unable to compete due to injury

1986 – Pocking, Germany, 46 points, 2nd (Kelly 23 and Sam Ermolenko 23)

1987 – Pardubice, former Czechoslovakia, 36 points, 3rd (Kelly 18, Sam Ermolenko 18)

1990 – Landshut, Germany, 28 points, 6th (Ronnie Correy 15 and Kelly 13)

## Other major honours:

US National Champion 1983 and 1984
US Best Pairs Champion (with Mike Faria) 1984
England v. USA Test series winner 1982 and 1992
Sweden v. USA Test series winner 1982
American Final runner-up 1984 and 1987, 3rd 1979, 1981 1982
3rd Overseas Final 1987
3rd British Open 1982
runner-up 1990 British League Riders' Championship
3rd 1987 British League Riders' Championship
Runner-up British Open Pairs Championship 1988 (with Shawn Moran)
Peter Craven Memorial Champion 1988 and 1990
Diamond Jubilee Champion 1988
Challenge Cup Champion 1986 (Sheffield)
Fair Derby Champion 1983
Ventura Track Champion 1984
Bruce Penhall Classic Champion 1985
Spring Classic Champion 1986

## British League club record:

Hull 1978–9
Birmingham 1980
Eastbourne 1981–2
Sheffield 1986–8
Belle Vue 1989–1992
Swindon 1992

# BIBLIOGRAPHY


*The Moran Brothers* by Brian Burford (Tempus Publishing, 2002)
*Back from the Brink* by Michael Lee with Tony McDonald (Retro Publishing, 2010)
*Chris Morton: Until the Can Ran Out* by Chris Morton and Brian Burford (Tempus Publishing, 2005)
*The Daily Mirror Speedway Yearbooks*, 1979, 1980, 1981, 1982, edited by Peter Oakes (Souvenir Press)
*Speedway Yearbook*, 1990, 1991, 1993, edited by Peter Oakes (Front Page Books)
*Loaders International Speedway Annual*, 1990, 1991, 1992, edited by Tony Loader (Loader Publications)
*One Man And His Speedway* by Barrie Palmer (privately published)
*Wayne Rainey: His Own Story* by Michael Scott (Haynes, 1997)
*Simmo: The Whole Truth* by Malcolm Simmons with Tony McDonald (Retro Speedway Publishing, 2006)
*Wheels and Deals* by Ian Thomas (Pinegen Limited, 2006)

'Shale Trail' (*Speedway Mail*, 1985 and 1986)
'The Inside Line' (*Speedway Mail*, 1986)

## *Periodicals:*

*Speedway Star*, 1977–2007, 2010
*Speedway Mail*, 1978–92
*Speedway Magazine* (USA) 1983–7
*Backtrack* magazine, No. 11, 37, 38 and 43
*The Vintage Speedway Magazine*, Volume 10 No. 4 and Volume 11 No. 3
*Cycle News* (USA), 1970–90, 2003
*Track Action*, May 1986

# INDEX